Falling in Love

Second Edition

PRAISE FOR THE FIRST EDITION

Ayala Pines teaches us about the love in our lives with a clinical tour de force and a rich practical guide. *Falling in Love* is a remarkable achievement that will shape our understanding of love.
—Prof. Dale Larson, author of *The Helper's Journey*

With the scholarship, wisdom and insight we have come to expect from her, Ayala Pines sheds new light on perhaps the most exciting and important of human endeavors. Falling in Love is an important book and a good read.
—Prof. Elliot Aronson, author of *The Social Animal*

… addresses every conceivable aspect of the psychology of mate selection and the material is intellectually stimulating.
—*Publisher's Weekly*

A couples therapist's clinical look at how and why we fall in love removes some of the mystery from that most magical of human experiences. Pines (*Romantic Jealousy*, 1992; *Keeping the Spark Alive*, 1988), a social psychologist and researcher who is also a clinical psychologist specializing in relationship issues, tackles her subject from both perspectives. As a social psychologist and researcher she analyzes how we fall in love; her clinical experience and psychodynamic theories come into play in the exploration of why we choose a particular person. As to why we fall in love with a particular person, Pines looks at various psychological theories and concludes that an internal romantic image plays a key role in whom we choose and that childhood experiences of love shape this image. Not a how-to guide for the lovelorn but a serious, research-oriented work of special interest to those involved in couple therapy.
—*Kirkus Review*

What I like about her approach is it reminds us to "shine the flashlight" more on ourselves than point fingers at partners when relationships fail. Knowing yourself and why you have certain attractions can prevent you from making the same mistakes, she says. That's a vast simplification of a complex theory outlined in detail in her book, but it does make sense, not to mention interesting reading.

  —*Tennessean*

... she provides a trenchant analysis of this most exciting, most significant experience without once diminishing its "divine madness."

  —*Foreword*

If you expect no definitive answers on either the conscious or unconscious nature of falling in love and making it work, if you are looking for a plausible excuse to examine the intimate relationships of those around you and, perhaps, your own, if you're interested in relationships in the abstract, whether "true" in its conclusions or not, *Falling in Love* is a fascinating book on an ever engrossing topic.

  —Isadora Alman, *San Francisco Bay Guardian*

Falling in love is one of the most important and life-changing of human experiences. Ayala Pines' book displays a sweeping, deep command of the burgeoning scientific literature on the topic, yet her treatment of these ideas is deeply informed by her clinical experience. The concepts and research findings are consistently brought to life with revealing examples and anecdotes. The book is thoroughly scholarly and up to date and also an engaging and exciting read. I would recommend this book to everyone from my social science research colleagues to the commuter train conductor.

  —Arthur Aron, Dept. of Psychology,
  SUNY Stony Brook

...very thorough...includes a remarkable amount of research and analysis.... Her intellect and empathy pour through the pages.

  —Anya Lane, Assistant Clinical Prof. of Psychology,
  University of California, San Francisco

Falling in Love

Second Edition

Why We Choose The Lovers We Choose

Ayala Malach Pines

Routledge
Taylor & Francis Group

NEW YORK AND HOVE

Published in 2005 by
Routledge
Taylor & Francis Group
270 Madison Avenue
New York, NY 10016

Published in Great Britain by
Routledge
Taylor & Francis Group
27 Church Road
Hove, East Sussex BN3 2FA

© 2005 by Taylor & Francis Group, LLC
Routledge is an imprint of Taylor & Francis Group

Printed in the United States of America on acid-free paper
10 9 8 7 6 5 4

International Standard Book Number-10: 0-415-95187-9 (Softcover)
International Standard Book Number-13: 978-0-415-95187-6 (Softcover)
Library of Congress Card Number 2004030816

Library of Congress Cataloging-in-Publication Data

Malach-Pines, Ayala.
   Falling in love : why we choose the lovers we choose / Ayala Malach Pines.-- 2nd ed.
      p. cm.
   Includes bibliographical references and index.
   ISBN 0-415-95187-9
   1. Man-woman relationships. 2. Love. 3. Mate selection. I. Title.

HQ801.M366M34 2005
306.7--dc22   2004030816

Taylor & Francis Group
is the Academic Division of T&F Informa plc.

Visit the Taylor & Francis Web site at
http://www.taylorandfrancis.com

and the Routledge Web site at
http://www.routledge-ny.com

For the people I love most,
My children Itai and Shani
My husband Israel
My parents Judith and Zeev

Contents

Acknowledgments

I am a very fortunate woman to be surrounded by brilliant, loving, and generous colleagues who are also my dear and cherished friends. Each of them are extremely busy professionals who nonetheless found the time to read an early version of this book and improve it immensely with their profound feedback. Dr. Anya Lane, my dear friend for many, many years, has contributed to the book her deep knowledge of psychoanalytic theory. Dr. Lillian Rubin, my dear friend and admired role model, has helped make the book more concise and my voice in it clearer. Dr. Carole Pettiet, my spiritual and clear-thinking soul sister, read every word of the book and gave me priceless feedback that helped improve both its organization and its writing style. Dr. Orenya Yanai helped clarify my thinking about the irrationality of falling in love.

But my deepest gratitude is reserved for the hundreds of people who took part in my research and clinical work, who shared with me their moving, exciting, poetic, better-than-fiction, love stories.

Introduction

ABOUT FALLING IN LOVE
AND ABOUT THIS BOOK

Love to faults is always blind,
always to joy inclin'd,
lawless, wing'd, and unconfin'd,
and breaks all chains from every mind.
 —William Blake, "Poems," *William Blake's Notebook*

Love blinds the eyes from seeing faults.
 —Moshe Ben Ezra, *The Song of Israel*

PSYCHE AND EROS

PSYCHE WAS AS BEAUTIFUL AS A GODDESS. THE BEAUTY OF THE MORTAL WOMAN became so famous that people came from far and wide to see and admire her. This aroused the envy of Aphrodite (Venus), the goddess of love and beauty. Aphrodite approached her son, Eros, for help. Eros was a beautiful winged youth whose love arrows no one on earth or in heaven could escape. Her wicked plan was to have Eros make Psyche fall in love with an ugly monster. But, when the god of love laid his eyes on the perfectly beautiful Psyche, he fell madly in love with her, as if one of his own arrows had struck his heart. He abducted her, carrying her blindfolded (see Figure 1) to his enchanted castle, where he made her his wife. There was only one condition she had to obey: She was never to see him. Psyche could not stand the temptation, and one night she lit a candle and peeked at her husband in his sleep. Dazzled by Eros' beauty, her hand shook. A drop from the burning candle woke Eros up, and realizing what she did, he disappeared. Psyche, now desperately

---

* The quotations throughout the book have been modified to protect the anonymity of the people interviewed.

** Most of the cases described in the book apply to the case of homosexual couples as much as they apply to the case of heterosexual couples.

FIGURE 1. Eros, the god of love in Greek mythology, carries Psyche, the human personification of the soul, in his arms, her eyes closed.
When we fall in love, our psyches are carried
blindfolded on the wings of Eros.

in love with her husband and determined to gain him back, appealed to
the gods, among them Aphrodite.
Only after many trials and troubles,
with the help of Zeus (Jupiter), the
head of all the gods, who found that
even he could not refuse the god of
love, Psyche became immortal, and
her marriage to Eros was sanctioned
by the gods.

And so romantic love (Eros)
and the human soul (Psyche) remain
united forever.

*From the first time I met him,
there was something that attracted
me to him. I was actually going
out with someone else, but there
was something about the way he
conducted himself that attracted me
... . With the couple of men I really,
really liked, it's been the same thing.
Right off I knew. But it wasn't
lust. There are definitely better
looking people out there. There
was something about him, or a
combination of things ... . the look
in his eyes, the way he held himself
... . this kind of animal thing.*

*This is really funny. When I first
saw her, I got the wrong impression.
She was the good-looking blond
chick that lived next to my friend*
Bob. *I had the impression that she was the party type. This turned out to be totally
wrong when I got to know her better. Since I spent a great deal of time with Bob,
I saw a lot of her, too. I helped her with her Italian. Later it turned out that her
Italian is far better than mine.*

*A friend of mine wanted me to meet him because she was madly in love
with him. When I first met him, I didn't understand what she saw in him.
The next time I met him, we had a chance to talk, and then I found what was
so wonderful about him. He was interesting, and it was really pleasant to talk
with him. He made me laugh, and I fell in love with him. I thought he was
adorable, funny, warm ... . I had a boyfriend at that time, but I lost interest
in him real quick. I did everything I could to see more of him. I changed my*

bike route so I would go past his house. But he didn't seem to notice. Later I discovered that he is very shy. He thought I was dating the other guy and didn't want to make waves. So, it took him a very long time to get it. Finally, after about 6 months, we started dating. I think I said something like: "that guy is history," and he said, "So, let's go out." From then on, our relationship took off. Now it's really hot. We are together all the time.

She was a student in a class I taught. She was very interested in the class and spent a lot of time with me. With time, we became good friends. At first, I wasn't attracted to her. Now, it's so obvious ... . I feel sorry for people who don't have this kind of relationship. She makes me feel complete. The best thing is the actual living together ... the simple things. We love each other, and we love the relationship. She once said to me on the phone, "I'm in love with being in love with you."

THE MAGIC OF LOVE

What sparks love? Why does one person ignite it, and another person, who seems much more appropriate, does not? Throughout history, people have tried to understand and control the mysteries of love with magic potions, spells, prayers, and the powers of witches and sorcerers. This is not surprising given the fact that for most people falling in love constitutes one of the most emotionally intense, exhilarating, exciting, and significant of life's experiences. Alan Watts described falling in love as a "divine madness" that is akin to a mystical vision.[1]

> Falling in love is a thing that strikes like lightning and is, therefore, extremely analogous to the mystical vision ... . We do not really know how people obtain [these experiences], and there is not as yet a very clear rationale as to why it happens. If you should be so fortunate as to encounter either of these experiences, it seems to me to be a total denial of life to refuse it. (p. 23)

Even after many years, couples can describe in great detail how they fell in love with each other. Occasionally, but it is rare, the love is at first sight.[2] More frequently, it springs from a long friendship. At times, it is the beloved's look that sparks the romantic attraction; at other times, it is a wonderful and endearing quality or a deeply moving, shared experience. The infatuation may evolve into a rewarding, committed love or end in a destructive and painful relationship. And, it may just fizzle out. These last cases make us wonder. Because there was obviously nothing there to love, "What was it that made me fall in love with this unworthy person?" The inevitable conclusion is, "I was blinded by love." Like the Romans, who believed that Cupid, the naughty angel, arbitrarily shot his love arrows at his unsuspecting victims, so, too, do many of us believe in the arbitrariness of love. (See Cupid in Figure 2.)

We *fall* into love, it seems, both literally and figuratively. It is as if we were walking down the street, minding our own business, when all of a sudden we fell

FIGURE 2. Cupid. In Roman mythology, Cupid is the god of love and passion; in Latin, *cupido* means passion. He is the son of Venus, the goddess of love and beauty. Naughty Cupid has no respect for age or social rank. He flies here and there, shooting his arrows arbitrarily at his victims—gods and mortals alike. Instantly, they fall in love and burn with boundless passion. (Cupid is identified with the Greek god Eros.)

into love, struck by Cupid's arrow. Indeed, infatuation commonly determines our final romantic choice from a broad field of potential candidates, and some researchers claim that infatuation is "inherently random."[3]

Thus, many people, both lay and professional, do not believe that falling in love is a good enough reason for getting married. After all, love is blind, irrational, and temporary, whereas choosing a marriage partner is serious business. Because it is expected to last forever, marriage is, and should be, given careful thought and consideration. But, is love really blind?

IS LOVE BLIND?

A large body of theory and research and my own research and many years of clinical work have convinced me that the answer to the question of whether love is blind is a firm "No!" In this book, I try to show that we fall in love neither by chance nor by accident. Rather, we choose those with whom we fall in love carefully in both conscious and unconscious ways. I try to show how and why we choose the lovers we choose. From the discussion of these questions, it becomes apparent why it is that we so often make what seem to us to be "errors in judgment." But, insight and understanding are not enough. This is why the last part of the book suggests steps for turning such errors into opportunities for individual and couple growth. For people who are looking for love, each chapter of the book offers concrete tips.

TWO HATS

This book represents the two hats I wear as a psychologist. One is the hat of a social psychologist and researcher who, for many years, has studied various aspects of couple relationships.[4] The other is the hat of a clinical psychologist who has worked with hundreds of individuals and couples on relationship issues. Although I am comfortable wearing both of these hats, my colleagues in these two branches of psychology tend to be rather dismissive of each other. Social psychologists like to conduct controlled studies involving large numbers of subjects. They regard clinical psychologists' data, which are based on clinical work with a small number of subjects who are often patients, as nonscientific at best. Clinical psychologists find social psychologists' obsession with complicated statistical procedures boring and their findings often insignificant and trivial.

I find the contributions of both approaches valuable and complementary.[5] In addition to using different research methodologies (quantitative as opposed to qualitative), they ask different questions about falling in love. Social psychology focuses on the question of how people fall in love. What are the conditions that increase the likelihood that romantic love will ignite? Clinical psychology focuses on the question of why we fall in love with a particular person. Using social psychological research, it is possible to arrive at specific and concrete recommendations that tell people what they can do to increase the likelihood of falling in love and what criteria they should use to ensure that the romantic relationships they enter will be satisfying. Using theories in clinical psychology, people can figure out why they fall in love with particular persons or a particular category of people.

Although researchers find clinicians' preoccupation with such questions unscientific and their conclusions unfounded, clinicians often find researchers' conclusions simplistic and insignificant; I value and use both approaches in my work. I believe that we need both to decipher the romantic attraction code. Therefore, I do not hesitate to present in this book (a) concrete suggestions on how to increase the likelihood of falling in love and to find a romantic partner and (b) guidelines for deciphering the romantic attraction code that defines for each of us with whom to fall in love (or why, in some cases, it is safer to avoid love). The first part of the book presents the social psychological perspective; the second part presents the clinical perspective; and the third part presents my perspective as both a social and a clinical psychologist who specializes in work with couples. Researchers, students, and readers interested in the details of a particular study or theory can find them in the "Notes" section at the end of the book.

In addition to an extensive review of the research done by others, this book is based on studies in which I took part. In particular, three qualitative studies are mentioned prominently throughout the book. The first study involved about 100 young men and women who were interviewed about their most significant romantic relationships.[6] The second was a cross-cultural study that compared American and Israeli accounts of falling in love.[7] The third study, using 100 couples, compared the reasons each partner gave for why he or she had fallen in love with the reason behind the greatest stress that each later experienced in the relationship.[8]

If you had been a subject in one of these studies, you would have been asked the following questions (it is a good idea to think about these questions, even write down your answers, before reading the book):

THINKING ABOUT YOUR MOST SIGNIFICANT ROMANTIC RELATIONSHIP

Are you in a romantic relationship? If your answer is no, think about the most important relationship you have ever been in.
What was happening in your life at the time the two of you met?
How did the two of you meet?
What was your first impression?
What attracted you most?
At what point, if any, did you fall in love?
How did the relationship evolve?
What was, or is, the relationship like?
What was or is most stressful for you about the relationship?
If the relationship ended, what caused it to end?

In analyzing the transcribed interviews, I examined different aspects of falling in love that previous studies and theories pointed out as critical. Do situational variables such as proximity and arousal really have an effect? Are traits of the beloved such as beauty and personality what make us fall in love? What about the effect of such things as similarity, our needs being satisfied, or feeling desired?[9]

Although the majority of these studies focused on one particular aspect of falling in love, the romantic attraction interviews, in which interviewees spoke freely about any aspect of falling in love that was relevant for them personally, enabled me to examine simultaneously all the aspects of this fascinating process.

WHAT THE BOOK IS ABOUT

The first part of the book answers, in seven chapters, the question: What enhances the likelihood of falling in love? Each chapter presents one of the answers to this question and the most fascinating, well-known, or important studies that support it. The first two chapters discuss variables that have nothing to do with the beloved. These are *situational variables* that encourage falling in love.

The first chapter presents studies documenting the power of *proximity* as a hidden matchmaker. Repeated encounters between people who live, work, or play together, it turns out, increase liking and attraction.

The second chapter focuses on the role played by *arousal* in falling in love. Fascinating studies show that adrenaline is the elixir of love. People who are aroused, because of a painful loss or a thrilling success, are sitting ducks for Cupid's arrows. A woman who met her partner just when he was expected to leave for a long trip abroad describes the effect of the expected separation on the development of their romantic relationship:

> *Our first date was unbelievable. We came home at 2 a.m., talked the whole night, and then collapsed. There was magic in the fact that we got along so well. He had to leave for Europe in 2 months. During these 2 months, we spent every moment together. Everything went so well that we were a bit suspicious. In the past, we both had short-term relationships, after which we were happy to be alone. All of a sudden, we discovered each other. He was supposed to be away for 6 months and was thinking about canceling the whole trip. In those 2 months, we got out of the relationship what you get out of a 3-year relationship. When he was away, he wrote and called. A phone bill of close to a $1,000 waited for him when he returned.*

Suppose I asked, "What made *you* fall in love?" Chances are that at least part of your answer would mention some endearing personality traits that captured your heart. In another part of your answer, you would most likely mention some attractive feature in your beloved's look. *Beauty and character* and the role they play in falling in love are the subjects of the third chapter.

A woman says: "He was open and friendly and looked cute." A man says: "She looked very good, attractive, with her feet on the ground, and she was easy to talk to." She mentions his cute looks last; he mentions her good looks first. A coincidence? No, say evolutionary psychologists, whose theory is presented in chapter 7.

In addition to situational variables and beloved variables, there are *relationship variables* that influence the likelihood of falling in love. One such variable—*similarity*—is the matchmaker's rule of thumb. Chapter 4 analyzes the role of similarity in romantic attraction, including similarity in interests, values, background, attractiveness, intelligence, and even in genetic makeup and psychological health. Hundreds of studies from all over the world suggest that we love our reflection in the other. A young woman described it as follows:

> *We have many things in common. For example, we are both first-born children in our families, and as a result we had similar childhood experiences, and we play similar roles in our families. We have similar insecurities about things.*

The other relationship variables, which are discussed in chapter 5, are *reciprocity* (the knowledge that the other is attracted to us) and *need satisfaction* (the fact that the other satisfies an important need). The man who laughingly said, "*The thing that I found most attractive about her was the fact that she was attracted to me*" is an example of reciprocity. The man who said, "*She needed me, she needed someone who will respect her*" describes need satisfaction.

After presenting the seven variables that influence when and how people fall in love, chapter 6 describes the different roles these variables play at different stages of the falling-in-love *process*. During the getting-acquainted stage, physical appearance is a most important selection criterion; a person whose appearance repulses us in most cases is rejected outright, even if otherwise wonderful. In later stages, personality traits become more important, and even later than that similarities in attitudes, values, and interests. Only a person who has successfully passed the selection criteria of stage 1 can proceed to stage 2, in which other selection criteria need to be passed to proceed to stage 3. A man described the first stage of this process:

> *What attracted me most was her looks, at first. Later, that she's great. She's nice. There was something about her, she would put my mind at ease.*

The subject of chapter 7 is *gender differences* in love. Is it true that different selection criteria direct the romantic choices of men and women? Do women really prefer men who are rich and successful, whereas men prefer women who are young and beautiful? Evolutionary psychologists present a large body of evidence that suggests that the answer to this question is yes. They explain the gender differences in romantic choices in the different evolutionary developments of men and women. (It may be worth noting that these explanations have been sharply criticized, especially by social construction theorists.)

A woman described the attraction of an older, well-to-do man: "*He was older than me. There was a difference between him and the boys my age … . He could go out and spend money … the maturity … I don't know.*" A man described the appeal of beauty: "*She totally dazzled me … . She is very beautiful, a natural beauty, and quiet. There was something mysterious about her that charmed me.*"

The first part of the book deals with variables that are observable and thus the subject of a huge number of studies. Social psychologists are primarily interested in how the environment, both physical and social, affects the individual. Consequently, this part focuses on external variables that enhance the likelihood of falling in love. The second and third parts of the book are based primarily on clinical experience— others' and mine—and on the psychoanalytic theory that emphasizes the internal environment. The internal environment includes such things as internal images and unconscious forces that determine the person with whom we are likely to fall in love.

Chapter 8 asks why some people seek and find intimate relationships easily and are happy in them, and others avoid love (because they are not interested or because they are "too busy"); yet others cling to love so desperately that they scare off potential partners. Chapter 9 discusses Freud's well-known dictum that a woman falls in love with a man who reminds her of her father and a man falls in love with a woman who reminds him of his mother. Chapter 10 focuses on the internal *romantic image* that determines with whom we fall in love. Chapter 11 demonstrates the operation of the romantic image in four stories told by a man and a woman who describe intimate and satisfying relationships and a man and a woman who, at the same age, have never been in intimate relationships.

The third and last part of the book answers the question why people so often believe that they have made mistakes in their romantic choices and how such seeming errors can be turned into opportunities for growth. This part is based almost entirely on my experience as a couple therapist and on the writings of other couple therapists. It represents my conviction that the best place for us to grow as individuals is in the context of an intimate relationship. It is far more challenging, and thus more beneficial, than individual therapy, which takes place only one or a few hours a week in the security and comfort of a therapist's office.

Chapter 12 is based on an analysis of the relationships of 100 couples. A number of these couples, who came for couple therapy, are described in detail. In each case, the problem that brought the couple for treatment is presented, followed by key points in the personal history of the partners and their history as a couple from their first encounter through falling in love and deciding to form a committed relationship to their problems becoming serious enough to seek help. In each case, it is clear that the traits and behaviors that made the couple fall in love with each other continue to play a significant role in their later relationship. This connection has practical implications that are translated into step-by-step instructions for couples on how to turn their relationship problems into opportunities for growth.

Chapter 13 offers a provocative proposition of a relationship between the unconscious reasons for our choice of a particular romantic partner and for a choice of a particular career and the implications of this relationship for couples.[10]

A caveat. The last parts of the book discuss falling in love from a psychodynamic perspective that has been criticized for putting too much emphasis on childhood experiences and unconscious forces and not enough emphasis on conscious goals, hopes, aspirations, and spiritual quests. This is an important point to address because romantic love exists within a particular cultural context,[11] and people today, more so than in other periods of history, have high hopes when they fall in love. Some even try to derive a sense of meaning for their lives from their love relationships.[12] Thus, it is extremely important to acknowledge people's ideals, hopes, and goals as much as their past.

The book includes three appendixes. The first appendix presents step-by-step instructions for conducting a workshop, based on the material presented throughout the book, aimed at helping people decipher their romantic attraction code. The second appendix presents the categories used to analyze the relationships described in the romantic attraction interviews. It enables interested readers to analyze their own relationships using the same categories. The third appendix presents research data based on these categories. It enables the readers who graded their own relationships to compare them to these research data. Researchers and students can find in this appendix the type of "hard" data that they need but most readers can happily do without.

All in all, the book addresses the following fascinating questions about falling in love:

QUESTIONS ABOUT FALLING IN LOVE ADDRESSED IN THE BOOK

- What situations increase the likelihood of falling in love?
- What traits and behaviors make some people easier to love?
- What is it about certain relationships that enhances romantic love?
- What selection process underlies falling in love?
- What is the role of beauty in falling in love?
- Are the things that make men and women fall in love similar or different?
- Is it true that men fall in love with a woman who reminds them of their mothers and women fall in love with a man who reminds them of their fathers?
- Why do some people fall in love easily and are happy in their relationships, some want desperately to be in a relationship but are unable to, and some avoid love altogether?
- How do we choose with whom to fall in love?
- Is it true that love is blind?
- Is it true that we fall in love with our worst nightmare?
- Why do some people fall in love repeatedly with people who are bad for them?
- What is the dynamic of obsessive love?
- Where in the brain does falling in love happen?
- What brain chemistry is responsible for the elation of falling in love?
- Why is it that we can fall in love with only one person at a time?
- What is it about certain men and women that causes many people to fall madly in love with them?
- Is it true that the falling in love stage is short-lived and has no impact on long-term relationships?
- Is it possible to break a romantic attraction code?

I now need to address some of the many fascinating and important things that have been written about love that the book does not address.

WHAT THE BOOK IS NOT ABOUT: ON THE STYLES, COMPONENTS, AND FORMS OF LOVE

> Love is such a tissue of paradoxes, and exists in such an endless
> variety of forms and shades, that you may say almost anything
> about it that you please and it is likely to be correct.
> —Finck, *Romantic Love and Personal Beauty*, 1891

A huge number of books and articles describe the different styles, components, faces, and forms of love. Greek philosophers distinguished among six *styles of love*: the love between best friends, unselfish love, possessive love, practical love, playful love, and romantic love (called *eros*). Contemporary scientists, in large-scale studies, found confirming evidence for the existence of these very styles of love.[13]

Although love styles point to the consistent differences in the way people experience and express romantic love, this book assumes that each and every experience of falling in love is unique because it is determined by both conscious and unconscious elements in *both* partners. The same person, whether passionate, game-playing, logical, or selfless, will be somewhat different in each romantic relationship because the lover is different and brings unique elements to the interaction between them.

Another well-known model of love is Robert Sternberg's triangular model. Sternberg is convinced that he discovered the three *basic components of love*: intimacy, passion, and commitment. The presence or absence of any of these components explains the different faces of love. A relationship with only intimacy is liking. A relationship with only passion is infatuation. A relationship with only commitment is empty love. According to this model, romantic love has passion and intimacy but not commitment, whereas the love that includes intimacy, commitment, and passion is consummate love.[14] This book examines the relationships between what Sternberg calls infatuation, romantic love, and consummate love with the assumption that the three are much more interrelated than Sternberg believes, and that there are many more than three components involved.

Love can take different forms not only because of the different components that comprise it, but also because of the different people or objects to which it is directed. Among the different *forms of love* are love between parent and child, brotherly love, motherly love, erotic love, self-love, and love of God.[15]

The use of the same word to describe so many different forms of love caused psychoanalyst Theodore Reik to complain that,

> Love is one of the most overworked words in our vocabulary. There
> is hardly a field of human activity in which the word is not worked to
> death. It is not restricted to expressing an emotion between the sexes, but
> also expresses the emotion between members of a family. It signifies the
> feelings for your neighbor, for your friend, and even for your foe, for the
> whole of mankind, for the home, social or racial group, nation, for all that

is beautiful and good, and for God Himself. It is almost incredible that it can be equal to its many tasks.[16]

From all these wonderful forms of love, this book focuses only on romantic love—the hunting grounds of Eros. Psychoanalyst Rollo May explained:

Eros is the drive toward union with what we belong to—union with our own possibilities, union with significant other persons in our world in relation to whom we discover our own self fulfillment. Eros is the yearning in man which leads him to dedicate himself to seek *arate*, the noble and good life ... . The ancients made Eros a god, or more specifically a daimon. This is a symbolic way of communicating a basic truth of human experience, that eros always drives us to transcend ourselves.[17]

Rollo May makes a distinction between romantic love—eros—and sex. "Sex is a need," he writes "but eros is a desire." Eros is a mode of relating to others; in eros, we do not seek the release of sex but seek rather "to cultivate, procreate, and form the world." For most of us, however, sex is an important feature of romantic love. Studies show that its presence or absence in a dating relationship is believed to have implications for the emotional tenor and interpersonal dynamics of that relationship.[18]

Besides psychologists, whose interest in love is not always appreciated—Senator Proxmire once awarded the Golden Fleece Award, for stupid and insignificant research that wasted taxpayers' money, to social psychologists who attempted to measure and study love—there are many others who write about romantic love. Poets and writers have written wonderful poems, stories, and books about romantic love. Philosophers, historians, sociologists, anthropologists, and more recently biologists and biochemists who describe the chemistry of love have studied romantic love. Despite the richness and beauty of the poets' descriptions and despite the depth and sophistication of the scholars' analyses, this book focuses on the contribution of just one field of scientific endeavor—psychology.

In addition to this limited, and by definition limiting, point of view, the book does not address any other stage in the life of a love relationship besides falling in love, the stage that was described by Italian sociologist Francesco Alberoni as the flower, the "nascent state," from which can evolve a fruit that is marriage.[19]

Not only is falling in love a unique stage in a love relationship—a stage that is far more intense than other stages—but also some psychotherapists view it as a rather insignificant stage. Scott Peck, for example, defined love as an "effortful act of will." It is "the will to extend one's self for the purpose of nurturing one's own and another's spiritual growth." According to this definition, Peck rightfully concluded that falling in love is not real love because it is not an act of will: It is effortless (and I might add that denying it often requires a great deal of effort). Peck suggested that the clearest proof lies in the annoying observation that "lazy and undisciplined individuals are as likely to fall in love as energetic and dedicated ones." Furthermore, falling in love cannot be true love because it is "specifically a sex-linked erotic experience." And, the final proof is that "the experience of falling in love is invariably temporary."[20]

I believe that falling in love is one of the most wonderful, exciting, moving, and significant experiences in life, most definitely so in my life. Furthermore, I believe that falling in love is one of the most important stages in the life of a love relationship. As I attempt to show in the third part of this book, falling in love explains not only the most wonderful and rewarding aspects of a love relationship, but also its most challenging problems[21] and the path to healing these problems.

The last boundaries of the book that I want to acknowledge are the time in history for which it is appropriate and the Western audience for which it is intended. Despite the feeling of people in love that their love is timeless and boundless, romantic love exists within a particular historical and cultural context.[22]

Love is a social construct. Societies differ in their understanding of the nature of love, and cultures in different time periods define love differently. In some time periods, for example, we see a belief that romantic love includes a sexual component, whereas in other eras, it is described as a lofty, asexual experience.[23] Although romantic love has reigned supreme among other forms of love since time immemorial, only in recent years has it been promoted as the basis for marriage, and there is a universal wish to believe that it can provide a strong enough foundation and last through the life of the marriage.

ROMANTIC LOVE AND THE SEARCH FOR EXISTENTIAL SIGNIFICANCE

According to Greek mythology Eros is a god (see Bouguereau's *Eros* in Figure 3). Romantic love has been described as divine by contemporary psychologists as well. The Pulitzer Prize winner psychologist Ernest Becker described romantic love as one of the ways we satisfy our need to feel "heroic," to know that our life matters in the larger "cosmic" scheme of things, to "merge with something higher" than ourselves, something "totally absorbing." The "urge to cosmic heroism" is fixed on the beloved who becomes the "divine ideal" within which life can be fulfilled, the one person in whom all spiritual needs become focused.[24]

I am well aware that one of the reasons why so many today are attributing such great importance to romantic love is that we are living at the beginning of the 21st century in a Western, secular society. In such a society, as Otto Rank noted, people are looking for romantic love to serve the function that religion served for their predecessors—to give life a sense of meaning and purpose.[25]

Romantic love is an interpersonal experience through which we make a connection with something larger than ourselves. For people who are not religious and have no other ideology or calling in which they strongly believe, romantic love can be the only such "divine" experience. The unparalleled importance given to romantic love in modern Western society was noted by Denis de Rougemont, who wrote: "No other civilization, in the 7,000 years that one civilization has been succeeding another, has bestowed on love known as romance anything like the same amount of daily publicity."[26]

In summary, this book deals with the falling-in-love stage (only) of romantic love relationships (only) from a psychological perspective (only) as it applies to people living in Western secular society at the start of the 21st century.

ON A PERSONAL NOTE

I started this introduction by saying that throughout history people have tried to understand the mysteries of love and control it with magic potions and spells. Psychologists have joined this quest with their tools of trade—research and clinical work. I remember myself as a young girl wishing I would decipher the secret that makes people fall in love. When I grew up, instead of learning how to brew magic potions or cast spells, I developed the skills of a researcher and a couple therapist. But, even today, I find people's stories about how they fell in love the most enchanting and fascinating of all. In every workshop that is even remotely related to couple issues, I

FIGURE 3. Eros, the god of love according to Greek mythology (Cupid in Roman mythology) is the son of the goddess of love and beauty, Aphrodite (the Roman Venus), and is portrayed as a winged naked youth. Gods represent the totality of experiences that humans experience in moderation. Only when they are struck by Eros' arrow can mortals experience the totality of falling in love.

ask participants to describe how they met their partners and what made them fall in love. I ask these questions of every person I see in individual therapy for relationship issues and of every couple in couple therapy. I find that this is a good way to start, even when (or especially when) people come to talk about relationship problems.

This is my tenth book and the book I have enjoyed writing the most. As I write these words, I can hear my close friends saying, "Yes, yes, we know, this is what you say about every book you write." These are the same friends who have heard me say about every period in the lives of my children, "Forget everything I said before, *this* is the most wonderful age." So forget everything I said before because deciphering the romantic attraction code and figuring out why we choose the loves we choose are the most exciting topics I have ever explored. I hope that after reading this book you will agree.

DIAGNOSE YOUR LOVE LIFE: HOW TRUE FOR YOU IS EACH OF THE FOLLOWING STATEMENTS?

Please answer each question using the appropriate 10-point scale. Note that the first scale starts with 1, and all other scales start with 10.

How is your love life? (from 1 = terrible to 10 = wonderful, perfect) _____

How often do you feel that your most important needs are not met in your love relationship(s)? (from 10 = never to 1 = always) _____

How often do you feel that your love relationship is a compromise? (from 10 = never to 1 = always) _____

How often did you fall in love with the wrong person? (from 10 = never to 1 = repeatedly) _____

How often do you fantasize about a true and perfect love? (from 10 = never to 1 = repeatedly) _____

How often did a romantic relationship end when you wanted it to continue? (from 10 = never to 1 = repeatedly) _____

How often do you feel that all the right people for you are already taken? (from 10 = never to 1 = all the time) _____

How often do you feel that you have not yet met the right person? (from 10 = never to 1 = all the time) _____

How often do you feel like a failure in the game of love? (from 10 = never to 1 = all the time) _____

Do you have difficulty meeting people who could be right for you? (from 10 = not at all to 1 = definitely yes) _____

To calculate your score and figure out its meaning, add the numbers you have written next to each question and divide the result by 10.

If your score is 9–10, you are doing exceptionally well. If your score is 7–8, you are doing fine. If your score is 5–6, things are not too good and need serious attention. If your score is 1–4, things are really bad, and you may want to consider getting professional help.

Part One

CONSCIOUS ROMANTIC CHOICES

Increasing the Likelihood of Falling in Love

*T*HIS PART OF THE BOOK DEALS WITH THOSE ASPECTS OF FALLING IN LOVE that are familiar to matchmakers and serve as their major criteria for identifying potential marriage partners. As the following story suggests, matchmakers are not the only ones who are in on these secrets.

Some years ago, in a workshop I led in enchanting Big Sur, California, a man in his early forties described how he had found his "true love." After a long series of stormy, unsatisfying, and destructive relationships, he decided to let go of the dictates of his heart and choose a partner according to strictly logical considerations. He spent many long weeks preparing a list of traits he was looking for in a mate, his previous relationships having helped him define what he could not accept. The result was a list of 68 traits!

Lest we conclude that whoever makes such a list must be a demanding and unreasonable person, I hasten to add that most of the items on his list were rather reasonable. For example, he wanted his partner to be close to him in age and in height, preferably a little shorter. It was important to him that she not be too fat or too skinny, and that she be reasonably attractive. He wanted her to be an independent woman who could support herself, enjoyed her work, had her own interests, but was also open to exploring new things. And, he thought it important that she be able and willing to discuss problems as they arose. The best proof that these were not unreasonable demands is the fact that not long after making the list, he found, through a group at his church, a woman who answered every single one of his criteria. It is true, he admitted, that their relationship lacks some of the incredibly intense, verging on the insane, highs that characterized his previous relationships, but it did not have the horrible devastating lows either. The relationship was good, warm, and close, and with time, love grew in it, too. Orthodox Jewish couples who marry through a matchmaker also report that love frequently grows in the marriage that took place between people who hardly knew each other. Although this type of love relationship seems different from "love at first sight"—a love that is closer to our prototype of romantic love—the people in these relationships, and the studies about them, indicate that they tend to be warm, stable, and satisfying.

This part of the book deals with the type of reasonable variables the man had on his list. This is not to say that these variables are always obvious. As we will see, some of them are not obvious at all. What they are, however, is observable and thus can be the subject of research. As a result, the evidence for the roles they play in romantic attraction is documented in a huge number of studies. The more interesting and significant of these studies are presented in the next seven chapters. Based on this research, each chapter ends with suggestions on how to increase the likelihood of falling in love.

Chapter 1

PROXIMITY:
THE HIDDEN MATCHMAKER

When I'm not near the one I love, I love the one I'm near.
—E. Y. Harburg, *Finian's Rainbow*

Advice for good love: Don't love
those from far away. Take yourself one
from nearby.
The way a sensible house will take
local stones for its building,
stones which have suffered in the same cold
and were scorched by the same sun.
—Yehuda Amichai, "Advice for Good Love,"
Love Poems

WHEN MIMI FIRST MET AARON, SHE HARDLY NOTICED HIM. BUT, BECAUSE they both worked for the same large computer company and happened to take their coffee break at the same time, she kept running into him. Once Aaron made a funny remark about the coffee, and Mimi laughed. This broke the ice, and they started exchanging comments when they met. Then, one day Aaron introduced himself; Mimi responded by telling him her name, and they talked briefly about their work. The conversation was so pleasant that they decided it would be nice to continue talking over lunch. During lunch, they discovered that in addition to a similar interest in computers, they also had a similar situation in their private lives. Mimi was getting out of the most significant relationship in her life, and Aaron was debating making a similar step. The ability to talk to a kindred spirit about what was troubling them was so wonderful that they started meeting for lunch regularly, both convinced that what they had was a close friendship, but no hint of a romance. Because neither was involved with anyone else, it seemed only natural to go to the company's New Year's Eve party together. Seeing Aaron dressed up, Mimi was surprised that she had not noticed before what an attractive man he was. Aaron, for his part, had noticed how good looking Mimi was from the first time he saw her but never intended to do anything about it. After all, she was his buddy, wasn't she? But, the deep affection they felt for each other and the new physical attraction that was sparked between them, with the help of the great music, the special evening, and the alcohol (Mimi's feeble excuse for letting go of her defenses), all combined. The kiss they gave each other at midnight lingered, and when Aaron took Mimi home, he stayed. That was the first night of many. The relationship that evolved between them was as deep as the friendship that preceded it.

> *We were friends as soon as we met at school. I was actually going out with his roommate, so I spent a lot of time in their house, and we became really close friends. And then, we started falling in love.*
>
> *We both used to work in the same coffee shop. We just started hanging around together after work. I don't know, we just got to be good friends. He is my best friend.*
>
> *I started working at his office. Actually, he was my boss's boss, so we would see each other often, and we would always make fun of each other. Then, we started flirting with each other. First, it was only with words. Things would get really hot between us just talking. Then, he asked me out."*
>
> *She was in class with me. One evening, we did our homework together, then we continued talking the whole night. Then, we did it again and again. I never spent so much time with anyone except my parents and my closest friends, and I loved every moment.*

These quotations are from interviews with young men and women who talked about their most significant romantic relationships. An analysis of the interviews suggests that, in over half of the cases, the romance started between two people who had known each other previously.[1] More often than not, the initial acquaintance was through work ("we worked at the same coffee shop"), through school ("we sat next to each other in class"), or through the place of residence ("we lived on the same floor"). Obviously, to fall in love, people first have to meet. Although love relationships can and do start in other ways (for example, correspondence), Internet romances are becoming increasingly popular; usually, the relationships either take off or die out after the couples have met face-to-face. As will be seen shortly, however, there are other, perhaps less-obvious, reasons for the power that physical proximity exerts over romance.

THE EFFECT OF PROXIMITY ON ATTRACTION

A number of classical studies demonstrated that as the geographic distance separating potential couples decreases, the probability of their marrying each other increases. In one of these studies, conducted in Philadelphia in the 1930s, some 5,000 marriage licenses were examined. Results showed that 12% of the potential couples lived in the same building, as evidenced by the same address, when they applied for a marriage license. An additional 33% lived a distance of five or fewer blocks from each other. The percentage of marriages decreased significantly as the geographic distance between the potential couples increased.[2]

In another study, conducted in Columbus, Ohio, in the 1950s, 431 couples who applied for marriage licenses were interviewed. It turned out that 54% of the couples were separated by a distance of 16 blocks or fewer when they first went out together, and 37% were separated by a distance of 5 blocks or fewer. The number of marriages decreased as the distance increased between the couples' places of residence.[3]

The two most famous studies documenting the relationship between proximity and attraction were conducted in college dormitories. Because most of the students who live in dormitories have not known each other previously, a dormitory provides a good setting to study how close relationships develop.

Renowned social psychologist Leon Festinger conducted a study of the residents of married student housing on the Massachusetts Institute of Technology campus in Cambridge. These dormitories were built in a U-shape around a central court covered with grass. The exterior sides of the buildings faced the street; the central section faced the inner courtyard. Festinger's famous conclusion was that the architect had inadvertently determined the patterns of relationships among the dwellers of these buildings.

Two factors appeared to exercise the greatest influence on personal relationships: the location of the apartments and the distances between them. The most important factor in determining who would be emotionally close to whom was the distance between their apartments. The closer people lived to each other, the more likely they were to become friends. Next-door neighbors were far more likely to become friends with each other than with people who lived in adjacent buildings. As a matter of fact, it was difficult to find close friendships between people who lived more than five apartments away from each other. In more than two-thirds of the cases, close friendships were between next-door neighbors.

In addition, the location of some of the apartments created more opportunities for their residents. Those residents who lived near staircases or mailboxes met more of their fellow residents and met them more often. The frequent encounters increased the chances that these well-located people would talk to others, get to know them, form friendships, and increase their own popularity. On the other hand, people who lived in apartments that faced the street had no next-door neighbors. As a result, these residents made half the number of friends made by those who lived facing the inner court.[4]

The second study was conducted in a student dormitory at the University of Michigan in Ann Arbor. Again, the results showed that what most influenced the formation of close personal ties between the students was not their compatibility, but their physical proximity. Roommates were far more likely to become close friends than people were who lived several doors down from each other.[5]

And, when a group of new recruits to a police academy were asked about their best friend, most described a person whose last name started with the same letter as

theirs. The reason? Assignments to rooms and classroom chairs were made according to last names. This meant that the recruit's roommate and neighbor in class was
someone whose last name started with the same letter. This constant physical proximity was found to better predict the development of close ties than did similarity
in age, religion, marital status, ethnic background, level of education, membership
in organizations, and even leisure time activities.[6]

Seventy years of research on attraction between neighbors, roommates, classmates, coworkers, and members of organizations testifies to the effect of physical
proximity on attraction. Students tend to develop closer friendships with other
students who take the same courses, sit next to them in class, live with them, or
live next to them in dorm rooms. Sales people in department stores form closer
friendships with people who work right next to them than with people who work
just several yards away. Most important, the likelihood of individuals marrying increases as the physical distance between them decreases.[7]

Is it simply laziness that attracts us to people who are close to us? Among young
people in California, GUD is the acronym for Geographically Undesirable, which is to
say living too far away to be considered seriously as a candidate for dating. Or, is there
some other explanation for the strong positive effect of proximity? One of the most interesting explanations was offered by the noted researcher Robert Zajonc, who viewed
the positive effect of physical proximity as the result of "repeated exposure."[8] Repeated
exposure, it turns out, increases our liking for practically everything, from the routine
features of our lives to decorating materials, exotic foods, music, or people.

REPEATED EXPOSURE

During his military service, a friend of mine who grew up in a home where classical
music was the only type of music he heard, was assigned to a unit whose heroine
happened to be the Egyptian singer Omm Kolthum. At first, her seemingly endless, wailing songs were a torture. He would shut his ears and cover his head with a
pillow to escape the never-ending torment. But with time, the torment decreased,
and he got used to the songs. One day, he discovered that he was nuts about Omm
Kolthum. Then, he started torturing his family and friends in an effort to get them
to appreciate the wonders of her incredible voice.

Robert Zajonc showed that repeated exposure to almost everything we encounter, from Chinese characters all the way to the faces of unfamiliar people, increases our
tendency to like these things. In one of his studies, subjects were shown 12 pictures of
people. Each picture was shown for 35 seconds, but some pictures were shown only
once, and others were shown 2, 5, 10, or even 25 times. Results of the study showed
that the subjects' positive feelings toward the individuals pictured increased with the
frequency that their pictures were shown.[8] In other words, even when the exposure
is brief and does not involve direct communication, the more times we see a person's
face, the more positively we are likely to feel toward that person.

Another proof of the effect of repeated exposure with special relevance for students was obtained in a large lecture hall on a university campus. Four young women

pretended to be students in the class. Avoiding contact with the other students in the class, the first woman attended 1 lecture, the second attended 10 lectures, and the third attended 15. The fourth woman did not attend any of the lectures. At the end of the course, students were shown slides of the four women and asked about their feelings and attitudes toward them. Despite the fact that the students had no personal contact with the women, the liking they reported toward them was inversely related to the number of times that they had seen them in class. The woman who did not attend any lectures was liked the least, and the woman who attended all the lectures was liked the most. In addition, the more lectures a woman attended, the more likely she was to be perceived by the students as attractive, intelligent, interesting, and similar to themselves.[9]

How can exposure be used to increase romantic attraction? Men and women who did not know each other were asked to look in each other's eyes for 2 minutes, a long time when you look into the eyes of someone you do not know. The result was that both the men and the women reported an increase in their romantic attraction to the person with whom they locked eyes.[10]

The positive effect of repeated exposure seems to arise from an inborn discomfort that we feel around strange and unfamiliar things, an inner programming that warns us that the strange can be dangerous and should be avoided. As children, we are taught not to talk to strangers, and even as adults we are not likely to respond positively to a stranger who, approaching us on the street and introducing himself, says that he would like to get acquainted. Most of us are likely to assume that the stranger is crazy, drunk, trying to sell us something, convince us of something, or even hurt us. If, however, we have seen the same stranger every day in the supermarket, on the bus, or in the elevator, we are likely to respond differently. After a number of such casual encounters, if the person were to ask our opinion on the weather or the political situation, chances are that we would respond positively and willingly continue the conversation, possibly the acquaintance. Repeated exposure tells us that the person, or thing, is not dangerous, so we can relax and enjoy the encounter.

Repeated exposure makes us respond positively to strangers who just happen to look familiar to us.[11] The mere fact that a person looks like our uncle Harry, our old friend Mary, or the cashier at our neighborhood grocery store is enough to make him or her seem familiar and thus less threatening. This occurs even when we are not consciously aware that we were exposed to a particular face. In a study that demonstrated this, subjects were asked to talk about some neutral topic with two people who were confederates of the experimenter. Before the conversation, a photograph of one of the confederates was flashed on a screen so quickly that the subjects were unaware of it. Despite their lack of awareness of this subliminal exposure, the subjects still responded more favorably toward the familiar person than they did toward the person whose photograph was not flashed.[12]

The attraction to the familiar may have a greater effect on romantic attraction than a certain look. This provocative conclusion is based on the results of a study in which men and women were asked to choose from groups of photographs the person they could possibly marry. Next, some of the photographs were projected on a screen several times. At the end, the subjects were asked to note their romantic preferences a second time. In many of the cases, both men and women changed their original preferences and chose someone whose photograph they had seen several times.[13]

The effect of repeated exposure can help explain the high frequency of romantic relationships that start between people who work together.[14]

> We both used to work in the same coffee shop ... . I don't know, we just got to be good friends.
> I started working at his office ... . Then, we started flirting with each other. We worked at the same place, and that made things go faster.

We may not be aware of our preference for familiar faces, but this preference seems to play an important role in our attraction to certain faces. Actually, our preference for familiar faces includes even certain aspects of our own faces. This was elegantly demonstrated in a study on the effect of repeated exposure on the way we view ourselves. In the study, female subjects were asked to arrive with a close friend. The researchers took two pictures of each subject. One was a regular picture, the other a mirror picture that showed how the woman looked when she saw herself in the mirror. The women and their friends were asked which picture they liked more and which one they thought flattered them more. Results showed that the women preferred the mirror pictures, and their friends preferred the regular pictures. The reason is obvious: Because the women most often saw themselves in the mirror, this is the view of themselves that they liked. Their friends, who more often saw them straight on rather than left-side-right as is the case in a mirror picture preferred the regular pictures.[15]

The preference for familiar faces can explain people's tendency to fall in love with, and marry, people who look like them and like members of their family. Because we often see our own face in the mirror and see the faces of our family members around us, people with similar features seem familiar to us and hence pleasant and attractive.

Contrary to the poet's view, familiarity breeds content. We prefer the faces of people we see often on television, the music we hear often on the radio, and the foods to which we grow accustomed. Advertisers know that the more contact we have with a certain brand name or a new product, the more we are likely to prefer them. Similarly, repeated exposure to a person who lives, works, studies, or spends leisure time near us is likely to increase our comfort with, our liking for, and, at times, our romantic attraction to that person.

Could this process also work in reverse? Could we develop liking, attraction, and comfort because we know we are going to spend time with a certain person? If we know that we are going to meet a certain person often—because he is going to work next to us, study in the same class, or live next door—do we not have a vested interest in seeing him as warm, pleasant, and friendly? After all, who wants daily contact with someone who is cold, nasty, and uncooperative? Once we convince ourselves that a person is warm, friendly, and pleasant, we treat him as such, which makes him respond in a way that confirms our expectations.

This provocative notion received support in the following manner. Female students were told that as part of a psychology department survey of sexual habits among college students, they would have to meet other students, whom they did not know, and discuss their sexual habits. Every subject received two similar descriptions: One was of the student she was going to meet; the other was of a student another subject would meet. The results showed a clear tendency for each subject to like more, and attribute more positive traits to, the student she was going to meet.[16] Clearly, the students preferred to talk about an issue as intimate and private as their sexual habits with someone they considered pleasant and likable.

There are two final points that need to be made about the effects of proximity and repeated exposure. One point addresses an ongoing argument about the effect of separation on romantic attraction. That is, does geographic distance enhance or diminish love? The other point concerns the negative effects of proximity and repeated arousal. That is, does proximity increase hostility and dislike as well as attraction?

DOES TEMPORARY SEPARATION INCREASE OR DECREASE ROMANTIC LOVE?

According to one view, separation causes longing that enhances romantic love. From afar, people can see clearly, and appreciate, the wonderful qualities of a partner, qualities that daily proximity may prevent them from seeing. Indeed, my studies of marriage burnout suggest that a temporary separation, especially one that involves some danger and worry, such as a husband's army reserve duty, increases the romantic spark in the marriage.[17]

According to the other view, "what is far from the eye is far from the heart." Just as physical proximity enhances emotional closeness, physical distance reduces it. Indeed, it was shown that married couples who do not live together are significantly more likely to divorce than couples living together.[18] The problem with reaching a conclusion based on these findings is that couples who do not live together may have problems in their relationship. It is possible that these problems—and not the physical distance in and of itself—are what eventually cause the divorce.

What then can we conclude about the effect of separation between lovers? Although there are wonderfully romantic stories of mythological loves, such as the one between Odysseus and Penelope, that remained deep and intense despite long years of separation, for most mortal couples a long separation may prove too big a challenge. When the relationship is close and loving, however, a separation—especially when short—may help intensify the romantic spark. But, when the relationship is not good and the separation is long, it is easy to get used to life without the partner and come to prefer it.

REPEATED EXPOSURE INTENSIFIES ALL
FEELINGS, POSITIVE AND NEGATIVE

When someone annoys us, repeated exposure, rather than making us like that person more, will intensify our negative feelings. This is why police records show that most acts of violence do not happen between strangers but between people who are close, such as husband and wife, family members, friends, and neighbors. In other words, repeated exposure intensifies the dominant emotion in the relationship. When the dominant emotion is anger, repeated exposure enhances the anger. When the dominant emotion is attraction, repeated exposure enhances the attraction.

This conclusion is indirectly supported by the findings of a study in which subjects were shown 20 different pictures and were asked how much they liked each of them. Some of the pictures were shown 1 more time, and other pictures 5 or 10 times. It turns out that those pictures that were either liked or felt neutral toward at first were rated more positively after subjects were exposed to them several times. On the other hand, repeated exposure to those pictures that subjects disliked served only to increase the dislike.[19]

SUGGESTIONS FOR PEOPLE SEEKING LOVE

An opportunity to meet and get acquainted is almost a prerequisite for the development of a romantic relationship. Although platonic love relationships do develop by means of letters, telephone, and more recently electronic mail and can be extremely exciting and rewarding as such, most people need to meet in person before they allow themselves to fall in love. And, when people live, work, or play in close proximity, their likelihood of meeting (and of a romantic spark getting ignited) increases.

But, meeting once is not enough. The results of my analysis of the romantic attachment interviews suggest that *in only 11% of the cases was the love* described in the interview *at first sight.* Repeated exposure is yet another requirement for a romantic spark to turn into the steady flame of a love relationship.

Meeting repeatedly, however, does not guarantee love. If the first impression is negative, it is best to cut contact, let the first impression dissipate, and then give the relationship another chance. In such a case, repeated exposure will not change the initial dislike or disdain into love but will most likely increase them.

The conclusion for people who are seeking romantic love is obvious. Try to arrange your life in such a way that you have many varied opportunities to meet regularly people through your work, place of residence, or recreational activities who are likely candidates for a romantic relationship. It is important that your repeated exposure be to the type of people you want to engage in a relationship, whether a friendship or a romantic attachment. Being involved in activities you love or could love is important not only because such activities are the most likely meeting grounds for people who are kindred spirits (and what group offers a better pool of candidates for a romantic relationship?) but also especially because such activities guarantee living more genuinely and therefore more happily.

When seeking candidates for a romantic relationship, the encounters should offer not one-shot opportunities, the type that take place on a busy street or in a crowded bar, but instead opportunities for meeting repeatedly and spending time together. The meetings should either take a while—such as a spiritual retreat, a ski vacation, or mountain hiking trip—or recur regularly as daily encounters at the cafeteria at work, next to the elevator or the mailboxes at the apartment, during a year-long class, or a regularly scheduled athletic activity, so long as they offer repeated encounters and deepening acquaintance.

Chapter 2

AROUSAL: THE ELIXIR OF LOVE

To start love like this: with a cannon shot
… That's a religion! Or with the blowing of a ram's horn,
… That's a religion! That's a love!
—Yehuda Amichai, "Ideal Love," *Love Poems*

I sleep, but my heart waketh; Hark! my beloved knocketh:
—*The Song of Songs by Solomon, 5:2*

WHEN DAN MET SUSAN, HE WAS GOING THROUGH ONE OF MOST DIFFICULT periods in his life. He was burned out in his job and knew he had to leave it if he wanted to save his sanity. But as the family's breadwinner, he was reluctant to take a step that might put his family in jeopardy. His wife, Annie, was no help. She was out most evenings and was cold and distant when he tried to talk to her. Annie had been cold and distant for a long time, and he kept wondering why she insisted on staying married to him when it was so clear that she had neither love nor respect for him. Yet, when an extramarital affair she had was discovered a year before and he suggested a divorce, she insisted that she loved him and did not want to break the family. She promised to stop seeing the other man and kept her promise, for a while at least. Now, her frequent absences made Dan wonder if she was seeing that man again, so he hired a detective to follow her when she went out. After a week, the detective informed him that Annie was indeed meeting the other man—playing tennis. He was not able to discern what they were doing after tennis but promised to find out later that week.

Dan was shaken but not really surprised; somehow, he knew this was going to be the answer. He waited anxiously for the detective's next report, deciding that if he had proof of a sexual liaison, he would demand a divorce. But, the detective called him sounding sick and said that he was hit with the flu, was running a high fever, and could not possibly spy on the couple that night. Dan could not imagine continuing the torment another week, so he made up his mind to do the spying himself. Because the tennis club was located in the city where the other man lived and he knew his name and because he was desperate, Dan decided on a desperate move. That night, after Annie left, he called the other man's house. When Susan, the man's wife, answered, he introduced himself. To his great astonishment, she said "I've been expecting your call for a long time now." "Do you know where your husband and my wife are?" asked Dan. "Of course," answered Susan. "Do you want to come over and see them for yourself?" "As a matter of fact, I do," answered Dan. So, Susan gave him instructions where to meet her. When they met, Dan was struck by Susan's good looks and lively personality. As they sat in the dark, spying on their spouses, the attraction between them grew. She was so sexy, so warm, so open, and he was so emotionally stirred up, so open to love … the rest was inevitable.

> *To both of us everything seemed too much. All the people around, the madness, and the whole college experience. Both of us wanted at least one good friend. I came into the class and she was the first person I noticed. She looked at me that very moment, and both of us said "waawoo… ."*
>
> *Our relationship started in such a romantic way that neither of us wanted to accept the fact that we had nothing in common. We were at a party out of town. I was drunk, and the guy who drove the car was drunk. He hit the side of the road, and it was a miracle that we didn't get killed. She was in a car right behind us, and they stopped when they saw the accident. She got out of the car, and I got out of the car. We ran toward each other and hugged. That's how the relationship started.*
>
> *I met him a couple of months after my divorce. I initiated the divorce, but it struck me harder afterward. He was there for me after the divorce, and it just went on from there.*
>
> *We met when my mother died and my whole world fell apart. I was new, and he was the caring and considerate person who couldn't hurt another person's feelings. I needed stability, and he is very different from those guys who can leave someone for another. I was very depressed about my mother … . We took care of each other.*

In one-fifth of the romantic attraction interviews, the relationships described started during stormy periods in the lives of the men and women interviewed.[1] Sometimes, the heightened emotional sensitivity followed an experience of loss, such as the death of a parent or a painful breakup. At other times, the heightened emotions followed an exciting adventure, such as a trip abroad, leaving home for college, or a particularly dramatic event, such as miraculously surviving an accident.

THE TWO-FACTOR THEORY OF LOVE

A terrified person is potentially a person in love, as is an angry person, a jealous person, a rejected person, and a happy person. Actually, every person who experiences the physiological arousal that accompanies strong emotions is potentially a person in love. This is the basic proposition of the two-factor theory of love first articulated by Elaine Walster and Ellen Berscheid.[2]

A woman who meets a man after the excitement of winning a great promotion in her work is more likely to fall in love with him than she would be on a routine day. Likewise, a man is more likely to fall in love with a woman when mourning a terrible loss. The reason, in both cases, has to do with the two components of love: *arousal* and a *label*.

The two-factor theory of love is a derivation of a more general theory of emotions.[3] According to this theory, like a car that in order to arrive at its destiny needs for us to start the engine and then determine its direction, to define a certain emotion we also need two things: One (which is analogous to starting the engine) is a general state of arousal; it is similar for all strong emotions and includes such physiological responses as a rapid heart beat and fast breathing. The second (which is analogous to steering the car in a certain direction) is an emotional label that explains the arousal—love, anger, fear, jealousy. We learn the appropriate labels for different states of arousal (which is what we are supposed to feel in different situations) from our parents, teachers, friends, the media, and personal experience. We know, for example, that we are supposed to feel delighted when a dear friend comes for a visit, but anxious when followed on a dark street even when the physiological arousal involved is the same. And, what we are expected to feel has a major influence on what we actually feel.

Walster and Berscheid explained the combined effect of physiological arousal and a romantic label on the experience of romantic love:

> To love passionately, a person must first be physically aroused, a condition manifested by palpitations of the heart, nervous tremor, flushing, and accelerated breathing. Once he is so aroused, all that remains is for him to identify this complex of feelings as passionate love, and he will have experienced authentic love. Even if the initial physical arousal is the result of an irrelevant experience ... once he has met the person, been drawn to the person, and identified the experience as love, it is love (p. 47).

We all know the phenomenon of love on the rebound, when someone who has just come out of a long or significant relationship jumps immediately into another one. Feeling vulnerable and lonesome, the person has a difficult time being alone and is desperate to be coupled again. Folk wisdom warns against love on the rebound because it is seen as fragile and temporary.

The threat of death precipitates the phenomenon of war love. In Israel during the Gulf War, this phenomenon affected couples who had just met, couples of long-standing whose relationships were cemented by the war, and divorced or separated couples who reunited after spending long hours in shelters.

Stories of hostages who fall in love with their captors never fail to amaze us, and stories about hot romances that started during exciting vacations and unusual adventures delight us. Cruise love even received the recognition of a comedy show on television. Every week, viewers of *The Love Boat* tuned in to watch the exciting affairs of the cruise travelers, affairs that, in the main, were far more exciting than they would have been on land.

Many people are personally acquainted with the phenomenon of spring fever. This wonderful love ailment strikes during the early days of spring, arriving with the sun, the blossoms, and the fresh air after the long gloom of winter. But, as the personal experiences that opened this chapter suggest, every major life change causes arousal. From the exciting yet anxiety-provoking change of starting school or a new job, to a change in residence, to the painful loss of a significant person, major life changes increase the likelihood of falling in love.

Cindy, a professional woman in her early forties, had decided that she was no longer interested in a committed relationship with a man. "Men are too much trouble," she explained. "You get much more from investing your energy in your career." Yet, when her sister, the sole surviving member of her family, died of cancer, Cindy fell in love. She fell in love with a man different from the type of men she usually dated and to whom she always looked up. He was a simple, unsophisticated man from an Italian background. He was warm and affectionate, supportive during the last stages of her sister's illness and after her sister's death. The relationship lasted about a year, the customary period of mourning in Judaism, and was Cindy's most significant romantic relationship as an adult.

THE EFFECT OF AROUSAL ON ROMANTIC ATTRACTION

In the last 30 years, a number of fascinating studies have documented the impact of arousal on romantic attraction. A significant number of these studies were conducted by Arthur Aron.[4] Art became interested in the topic of romantic attraction when he fell in love with Elaine, then his girlfriend, now his wife. After an extensive literature search, Art concluded that people are more likely to be attracted to those they meet during an unusual and exciting experience, an experience that involves the use of force, mystery, loneliness, or powerful emotions. The question he wrestled with was how to create such an experience in the laboratory. The solution he chose was role-playing.

In his study, the male students who served as subjects assumed the role of a soldier who was captured behind enemy lines. The soldier was tortured by an interrogator, played by an attractive female research assistant, who was trying to force him to reveal army secrets. The interrogator "tortured" the soldier by dropping "acid" (actually water) into his eye. Each subject was instructed to imagine that the acid caused him unbearable pain, that it burned his eye, that if the torture continued, it would burn his brain and eventually result in a horrible death. The subject was encouraged to scream every time the "acid" touched his eye. The students really got into the role. They shook and sweated, later reporting that they had felt terrible fear. Even the female assistant had to be comforted and calmed after going through the difficult experience of "torturing" six soldiers every day. A control group, also playing captured soldiers, had water dropped into their eyes but were told that the water represented the first, easy stage of interrogation.

What were the results? The young men who went through the hair-raising experience of being "tortured" were far more attracted to their interrogator. They expressed a greater desire to kiss her and be close to her. In addition, there were more erotic and romantic themes in the stories they wrote afterward.[4]

Another study, one of my all-time favorites, used two bridges over the Capilano River in Vancouver, British Columbia.[5] The experimental bridge was the Capilano Canyon suspension bridge. (A photograph of the bridge is presented in Figure 4.) The bridge is 5 feet wide and 450 feet long and is constructed of wooden boards attached to wire cables that run from one side to the other of the Capilano Canyon. It has many arousal-inducing features: a tendency to tilt, sway, and wobble, creating the impression that one is about to fall over the side; low handrails of wire cable, which contribute to this impression; and a 230-foot drop to rocks and shallow rapids below. The control bridge was a solid wooden bridge further upriver. It is only 10 feet above a small, shallow rivulet, has high handrails, and does not tilt or sway.

When potential male subjects had crossed one of the bridges, an attractive young woman intercepted them. The woman was a research assistant and unaware of the study's hypothesis. The woman explained that she was doing a project for her psychology class on the effects of attractive scenery on creative expression. She then asked if the subject would fill out a short questionnaire, one part of which asked the subject to write a brief dramatic story based on a picture of a woman (Figure 5).

This photograph is part of a projective test called the Thematic Apperception Test (TAT). The assumption, as with all projective tests, is that every person sees the picture differently, according to his or her psychological screens, and projects onto the figure his or her perception of self in relation to others.[6] For example, one person may see the woman as sexual. "She is blinded by the bright sun because she just got out of bed after spending a whole night making love." In another person's description, the woman's sexuality may not be mentioned: "She just woke up from a

FIGURE 4. The Capilano Canyon suspension bridge.

FIGURE 5. A picture inspired by the Thematic Apperception Test (TAT) card. What is the story in this picture?

terrible nightmare and is trying to shake it off" or "She has just come home after working hard all day and has a terrible headache."

After the subject had completed the questionnaire, the research assistant thanked him and offered to explain the experiment in more detail when she had more time. She tore off a corner of a sheet of paper, wrote down her name and phone number, and invited the subject to call if he wanted to talk further. To classify the callers more easily, men who had crossed the suspension bridge were told that the interviewer's name was Gloria; control subjects who had crossed the safer, wooden bridge were told that her name was Donna.

Results showed that the stories written by the men who went through the heart-and-leg-shaking experience of crossing the suspension bridge had significantly more sexual and romantic themes than did the stories of the men who crossed on the safer wood bridge. The aroused men were also more likely to be romantically attracted to, and show an interest in, the young woman who interviewed them on the wobbly bridge. This was evident in the fact that many more—eight times more!—of the men called Gloria "to find out more about the study." How do we know that it was she they were interested in and not the study? We know, because in a control study done on the same two bridges with a male experimenter, almost none of the male subjects called the experimenter.

Another of Art's studies was done in a room full of electrical equipment. Volunteers for a study on learning, all men, were surprised to discover that they are about to receive an electric shock as part of the study. Some were told that the shock would be "quite painful"; others were told that it would be "a mere tingle" that "some people even describe as enjoyable." In both cases, there was a second "subject" in the laboratory, an attractive young woman who was in fact the researchers' confederate. Comparison of the responses of the men in the severe shock group to those of the men in the mild shock group showed that here, too, the arousal caused the men in the severe shock group to be significantly more attracted to the young woman. They expressed greater desire to ask her on a date and kiss her, and their TAT stories had far more romantic and sexual themes.[5]

The arousal that causes romantic attraction does not have to be fear or anxiety. Sexual arousal can work just as well. Here is an example. Male students volunteered to take part in a study on university dating. While waiting for their assigned dates, they were given a story to read. Half read an erotic story; the other half read a boring story about the life of seagulls. Both groups were then given the same description and picture of the woman each man was about to date. The woman was described as active, smart, easy-going, and liberal; her picture showed an attractive blond. After they read their stories, the men were asked for their opinions of their prospective dates. Analysis of their responses showed that the men who were sexually aroused described the woman as more attractive and sexier than did the men who were not sexually aroused. Furthermore, and I really like this next finding, the men who were sexually aroused described themselves as more attracted to their own girlfriends.[7]

Many of us get regular infusions of arousal by going to the movies; some of us translate that arousal into attraction. In an original field study, expressions of love and affection, in words and physical gestures, were recorded between couples on their way in and out of movie theaters. Some of the couples watched an action movie; others watched a movie that was less arousing. It turns out that the couples who watched the arousing action movie expressed more affection toward each other after the movie than they did before seeing it. The nonaction movie had no effect on the amount of affection expressed by the couples who watched it.[8]

Anger is yet another strong emotion that can be translated to sexual arousal. This was demonstrated in a comparison between two college classes. In one class, students were angered by a professor who berated them viciously for having done poorly on a recent test. The second class served as a control. The angered group, as evidenced by the explicit sexual content of stories they wrote in response to a projective test, was significantly more sexually aroused than the control group.[9]

Even when we mistakenly believe that we find someone sexually arousing, the person seems more attractive to us. Here is an elegant demonstration of this surprising finding. Male subjects were told that their heartbeats would be amplified and recorded while they looked at 10 slides of half-nude Playboy Bunnies. In fact, the subject heard not his own heartbeat, but prerecorded heartbeats arranged to beat faster when various, randomly chosen, photographs were projected. In other words, the men believed that their hearts were beating faster in response to certain photographs when in fact they were not. Then, they were asked to rate the attractiveness of the 10 Playboy Bunnies. Results showed that the men rated those women who supposedly made their hearts beat faster as significantly more attractive and chose their pictures when offered a poster of a Bunny as a token of appreciation for taking part in the study. Even a month later, in a totally unrelated situation, when asked to rate the same 10 pictures, they again rated the same women as more attractive.[10]

AROUSAL IS NOT ENOUGH

Obviously, arousal is not enough to make us fall in love. After being aroused, we still
need to meet the "right person." The woman whose father had died a short time before
she met her boyfriend described the many reasons that made her fall in love with him:

> *He looked very nice* [attraction to good looks] *and after talking to him I
> discovered that he is a good thinker as well* [attraction to intelligence]. *When
> I went to his place for dinner, I really liked his room and his apartment*
> [attraction to similar tastes]. *I was so comfortable with him that it seemed
> weird. He is a very good listener. He really understood me. He understood
> right away what I meant and this was new to me. I think I am a complicated
> person, but he understood me. His comments were always right on target.
> And he was very supportive and understanding about my father and always
> interested in me and in being with me. He was always interested in what was
> best for me* [attraction to someone who fills important needs, especially
> during the emotionally intense period after her father's death]. *From the
> very first moment, I was myself with him because I didn't have the energy to
> be something else. Our relationship was based on honesty, and this was new
> for me.* [The vulnerability caused by the father's death created a greater
> openness to intimacy.] *We're different, but we complement each other.
> Whatever is lacking in me, he has* [attraction to the complementary].

Arousal enhances romantic attraction when a potential candidate is attractive.
When the potential candidate is not attractive, the result can be different. To create
either high or low arousal, men were asked to run in place for either 2 minutes, creating high arousal, or 15 seconds, creating low arousal. After running, they watched a
short video in which they saw a young woman they were going to meet later. By using
professional makeup, the woman was made to look either attractive or unattractive.
Results showed that both the woman's attractiveness and the arousal had an effect.
When the woman looked attractive, the arousal caused an increase in the men's attraction to her. But, when she looked unattractive, the arousal actually caused a decrease in
their attraction to her.[11] It is noteworthy that the woman was the same in both cases,
and that the difference in the men's response to her was caused by makeup.

It is interesting that the nature of an emotional arousal (a terrible loss or a great
victory) has no impact on romantic attraction, but the physical attraction of the potential partner does. In a study that examined the effect of different types of arousal,
subjects listened to one of three tapes: a tape that described the brutal murder of a
missionary in front of his family (negative arousal), a tape with one of Steve Martin's funniest comedy routines (positive arousal), and a tape of a boring lecture on
the physiology of the frog (no arousal). Each subject then watched a video clip that
showed either an attractive or an unattractive woman (the same woman with different makeup) he was going to meet. Again, results showed that both the arousal and
the woman's attractiveness had an effect. The men who were aroused (by either the

funny tape or the horrible tape) found the attractive woman more attractive than did the men who were not aroused (who listened to the boring tape). The aroused men found the unattractive woman even less attractive than did the men who were not aroused.[11] In other words, arousal (either positive or negative) intensifies our reactions (attraction or repulsion) to potential dating partners.

WHY DOES AROUSAL INFLUENCE ROMANTIC ATTRACTION?

What causes the aphrodisiac effects of arousal? One explanation is known as *misattribution*: The arousal is attributed, incorrectly, to sexual arousal when in fact something else causes it, such as fear, as was the case for the young men who crossed the Capilano Bridge.[12] Alternatively, *excitation transfer* is operating when: The arousal caused by one thing, such as an expected electric shock, is added to the arousal caused by another, an attractive woman. A third explanation is known as *response facilitation*: The state of arousal resulting from running in place, for example, enhances every other reaction we have, whether attraction or repulsion.

When we are aroused, the origin of the arousal does not matter, and it does not matter whether we are aware of the reason. Arousal automatically reinforces our natural response, including attraction to a potential partner.[13]

This helps explain the phenomenon of folk dancing love affairs, well-known among people who are hooked on this type of leisure activity, which has reached epidemic proportion in Israel. Some such addicts dance 4 and 5 days a week. The physical arousal, caused by the dancing, and the emotional arousal, inspired by the music or the words of the song, reinforce the dancer's natural response of attraction to the partner. When couples are in the midst of the ecstasy of performing a dance they love, to the sound of a song they love, do they say to themselves that the strong excitement they feel toward each other is the result of misattribution or excitation transfer? Probably not. Neither in all probability do they dismiss the excitement they feel as merely resulting from the arousal of the dance rather than the irresistible charm of their partner. Instead, they become excited, attracted, sexually turned on, and, at times, fall madly in love.

People do not always fall in love when aroused, however. They also need to feel that their partner is an appropriate mate in terms of such requirements as appearance, age, education, and social class. If these prerequisites are satisfied *and* they are aroused, then they are far more likely to misattribute their arousal and think they are in love.[14]

OBSTACLES ENHANCE LOVE

Some obstacle is necessary to swell the tide of libido to its height; and at all periods of history whenever natural barriers in the way of satisfaction have not sufficed, mankind has erected conventional ones in order to enjoy love.
—Sigmund Freud, "The Most Prevalent Form of Degradation in Erotic Life"

The less my hope, the hotter my love.
              —Terence, *Eunuchus*, I, 160 B.C.

The story of love is always in the search for it.
              —Lynn Freed, *The Mirror*

I'm too close for him to dream about me.
              —Wislawa Szymborska, *I am too close for him ...*

Strephon kissed me in the spring,
Robin in the fall,
But Colin only looked at me
And never kissed at all.
Stephon's kiss was lost in jest,
Robin's lost in play,
But the kiss in Colin's eyes
Haunts me night and day.
              —Sara Teasdale

Why are some people attracted to those who are not interested in them? Could it be the challenge that intrigues them? The thrill of the chase? Clearly, not having is more arousing for such people than having.

Folk songs are one of the best sources of folk wisdom about strong emotions such as longing and romantic love. "The jukebox, a particularly American institution, has long been a rich source of social psychological truths" wrote James Pennebaker and his colleagues.[15]

According to Mickey Gilley's country western song, "all the girls get prettier at closing time." Is it true that when the time for closing the bar draws near, and with it the painful thought of going home alone, the standards go down, and the attractions of the available people in the vicinity go up? To test this hypothesis, Pennebaker and six of his colleagues conducted a study that sounds like it was a lot of fun for them. They approached men and women in one of three "drinking establishments within walking distance of a respectable Southern University." Subjects were selected randomly, with the restriction that they not be in conversation with a member of the opposite sex. They were approached by a same sex experimenter and asked to rate the attractiveness of members of the opposite sex present that night. This was repeated three times: 9:00 p.m., 10:30 p.m., and midnight, a half-hour before the bars closed. Findings showed a linear increase in attractiveness rating of both men and women. As the hour grew later, the opposite sex in the bar appeared more attractive. A later study showed that this effect was not the result of alcohol consumption. It is noteworthy that men rated women as more attractive than women rated men.

Why do girls get prettier at closing time? One explanation is offered by *reactance theory*: When our freedom to act, think, or feel is threatened, we are motivated to try to get it back. This is why people want more the things they have lost and why, in the case of romantic love, they desire those who are not interested in them and those they could not or did not have. This is also why the kiss that did not happen continues to haunt us.

Reactance theory also explains why obstacles enhance love.[16] To enhance love, says reactance theory, the obstacles need to be outside the relationship, for example, an enforced separation or parental objection. The most famous case of such obstacles to love is, no doubt, the tragic story of Romeo and Juliet, a story that pulls on our heart strings hundreds of years after it was written.

Does parental interference really enhance love? Researchers who investigated the "Romeo and Juliet effect" found that, for both married and unmarried couples, there was indeed a positive correlation between romantic love and parental interference. The greater the interference was, the greater was the love.[17] The implications of this finding for parents who disapprove of the romantic choice of their offspring should be obvious.

Obstacles increase attraction. We tend to love more the people for whom we had to work or suffer, which explains the psychological significance of initiation rites. In a well-known study on this subject, young women had to go through an embarrassing initiation, which included reading aloud explicit pornographic material, to be accepted to join a certain discussion group. These women liked and appreciated the group significantly more than did women who did not have to make such a big effort to join the group.[18]

Is it true, then, that people win who play hard to get in the game of love? Playing hard to get means creating challenges, putting up obstacles against being easily won. Despite the wide acceptance of this assumption, five different studies failed to find any evidence for the "hard-to-get effect." It turns out that people like choosy partners, but only those who are choosy toward others, not toward them.[19]

This conclusion was criticized on the grounds that there is a big difference between choosiness and rejection. A person who is choosy about the people with whom he or she will go out is different from a person who will not go out with us, which is to say a person who rejects us personally. In a study that proved this point, subjects, all single, received information about members of the opposite sex that differed in their levels of choosiness. The "very choosy" were described as ready to go out only with people of "exceptional" quality. The "choosy," selective about their friends, were not willing to go out with just anyone. The "not choosy" were willing to go out with practically anyone. Findings showed that subjects were most attracted to the people who were described as choosy and were not attracted to the very choosy people, who were perceived as snobs. Women were even more likely than men to respond negatively to very choosy potential dates.[20] These results, only partially confirming folk wisdom, suggest that women, but not men, should play hard to get.

MOOD AND LOVE

When we are in a good mood, we feel good about ourselves, and we feel good about people around us. When we feel happy, satisfied, excited, interested, or curious, we show greater interest in people and are friendlier and more open than when we are sad, depressed, or despairing.[21] Our mood also influences our romantic attraction.[22]

Music is one of the things known to influence mood. It was shown that with pleasant music in the background, women looking at photographs of men they did not know rated the men's attractiveness higher than women who rated the photographs with no music in the background. The former women liked the men more and found them more physically attractive.[23]

Hearing good or bad news also has an effect on our moods and consequently on our feelings toward others. People who hear good news that lifts their spirits respond to strangers more than those who hear news that depresses them.[24] The same effect on attraction can be seen when people watch happy or sad movies. Again, a good mood enhances attraction.[25] When people are depressed or nervous, regardless of the reason for these feelings, they like the people they meet less and evaluate them more negatively.[26] They are also less likely to respond to attractive new people. Men who received a "good-mood treatment" (watching a funny movie and receiving a positive evaluation of themselves) or a "bad-mood treatment" (watching a depressing movie and receiving a negative evaluation) responded differently to a young and attractive woman who started talking to them. The men in the good mood group responded to her much more positively; they were friendlier, more open, and more ready to talk to her.[27]

What is the reason for the influence of mood on attraction? At the most basic, most simplistic level, we love everyone and everything that makes us feel good, and we dislike everyone and everything that makes us feel bad. Our attraction and repulsion are based on the feelings, either good or bad, that are generated in us.

At a more complex level, we not only respond to the person, object, or event that is directly responsible for our emotional reaction, but also to every unknown person or neutral object that was present when our strong emotions were aroused. The stranger or the object becomes connected in our minds with the good or bad feeling. This connection is called *conditioning*. After conditioning has occurred, the person or the object continues to generate the same emotion in us.[28] This is why we like a stranger who just happens to be around when we heard good news. The person is not responsible for our good mood, the good news is. Nevertheless, we make a connection between the person and the good feeling we have while hearing the news, and our feelings toward the person change accordingly. The conditioning effect is so powerful that even a washed-and-pressed shirt worn by a despised person is ranked as far less desirable than a washed-and-pressed shirt that was worn by a person who is loved and admired. In other words, a contact between a neutral object and a person who generates in us either good or bad feelings is enough for the feeling to be transferred to an object as neutral as even a clean shirt.[29]

THE AROUSAL CAUSED BY EXPECTING ROMANTIC LOVE

We live in a culture that builds in us great expectations for and from romantic love. Expressions such as "love at first sight," "a match made in heaven," and "made for each other" are familiar to all of us and generate high expectations of romantic love and for falling in love. Romantic movies, books, and mythologies about great loves help build these expectations. A poll showed that over 56% of the people polled believed in love at first sight;[30] analysis of the romantic attraction interviews showed that only 11% actually experienced it.

Most people growing up in a Western culture know what romantic love is and have experienced it at some point in their lives. For many, romantic love is one of the most powerful positive emotions ever felt. Some believe that love can answer the question of human existence, celebrate the freedom of choice and pursuit of happiness, and provide the best basis for marriage.[31]

In the beginning of this chapter, I presented the two-factor theory of love. Let me end the chapter with a three-factor theory of love. The third factor is *social expectations*. The three requirements for falling in love are (a) a social-cultural background that builds the expectation to fall in love; (b) an appropriate candidate (in terms of such things as appearance, personality, background and values); and (c) arousal that obtains the label "romantic love."[32]

Because we live in a culture that builds high expectations of romantic love, we clearly fulfill the first condition. After reading this chapter, the importance of arousal is known, and there is some idea how to create such a state or else make use of an existing one. All that is left is the small matter of finding the right person. According to the three-factor theory of love, two of the most important features identifying a potential partner as appropriate are his or her appearance and personality. These are the subjects of the next chapter.

SUGGESTIONS FOR PEOPLE SEEKING LOVE

We can safely assume that every effective elixir of love has to have adrenaline or a similar substance. This means that it is important to take advantage of times in which our body is naturally flooded by adrenaline because these are times in which we tend to be more open to love. Situations of high physical and emotional arousal include folk dancing, playing tennis, hiking, aerobics, jogging, trips abroad, stimulating classes, action movies, exciting concerts, and spiritual journeys. It is always best to choose activities that we really enjoy and find exciting. For people who are looking for a romantic relationship, there is an additional qualification: Make sure the activities you choose are favored by people of the sex and age disposition for which you are looking, and that these individuals are open and free to have an intimate relationship and are likely to be appropriate as your romantic partners.

Before entering a situation in which you are likely to meet candidates for a romantic relationship, try to put yourself in a good mood. If needed, do not hesitate to put yourself in a good mood artificially by listening to music with a beat, listening to a funny tape, reading an entertaining book, or watching an uplifting movie. A good mood—even if temporary and artificially induced—will make the candidates for your affection seem more attractive and is likely to make you look more attractive, too. And remember that external obstacles enhance romantic attraction.

Chapter 3

BEAUTY AND CHARACTER

The most poetic love depends not on moral qualities but …
on the way of doing up the hair, the complexion, the cut of
the gown.
—Leo Tolstoy, *The Kreutzer Sonata*

All the beauty of the world. 'Tis but skin deep.
—Ralph Venning, *Orthodox Paradoxes*, 1650

Even virtue is fairer in a fair body.
—Virgil, *Aneid*

BARRY SAT LISTENING TO THE LECTURE. IT WAS A FORUM HE ENJOYED attending, interesting topics and, for the most part, good speakers. But, his mind must have wandered because he noticed her the minute she entered the room. Flushed from hurrying not to be too late, she glowed. The sun came through the window behind her, and her golden hair looked like a halo; the sweet expression on her beautiful face made her look like an angel. Barry was transfixed. Who is this heavenly creature? he wondered. He hardly heard the lecture as he focused his complete attention on every expression on her face, every gesture. She was without a doubt the most beautiful, most enchanting woman he had ever seen. She sat listening attentively. At one point, she asked a question that made it abundantly clear that she was knowledgeable, articulate, and bright. When a coffee break was announced, Barry maneuvered his way to be close enough to hear her. She was joking and laughing with a group of people who gathered around her. She had a laugh that rang like silver bells. It was obvious that people were drawn to her. When one of the people in the group moved away to get a cup of coffee, Barry approached him. He had never approached a total stranger before, but he just had to know. "Who is she?" he asked. The man did not ask who Barry meant. It was obvious. "Isn't she charming?" he said. "Everyone loves her. She is as beautiful inside as she is on the outside. Let me introduce you to her." When they were introduced and she focused her beautiful brown eyes and her radiant smile on him, Barry knew he was in love.

She was very attractive, very beautiful. Appearance is more important to me than to most people … . She is attractive, quiet, knows she is attractive. She has a presence, and she's aware of it. She is sure of herself and very aware. Not a woman for a flirt only, but a person with awareness, a serious person.

He is an all-around nice person, really nice, friendly, warm. He had a friendly presence, a warm presence, and was full of life, with a good sense of humor. And I thought he was cute, not stunning. With two feet on the ground.

I thought she was very beautiful, very striking, long dark hair. The first night we met, we talked the whole night—we had a lot in common.

What attracted me most at first was his personality. I also thought he was very sexy. He carried himself well, and dressed nicely. He's a very real and honest person. He comes off as being very confident, almost cocky. That's what attracted me to him.

My first impression was that she is beautiful and quiet and insecure. When I started talking to her I discovered that she is very sweet, wonderful. What attracted me most was that I could talk to her about everything. She is very understanding.

He's sort of handsome, and he's very nice, very laid back. He made me feel good.

She's a knockout, long hair, blue eyes. She seemed very nice, really sweet.

From the beginning he was really cute, really nice, real sensitive.

Which attracts us more, personality or appearance? Analysis of the romantic attraction interviews revealed that more than 90% of the men and women interviewed mentioned some aspect of a partner's character when they tried to explain why they fell in love.[1] About two-thirds of the interviewees, this time more men than women, mentioned the partner's appearance.[2] In other words, personality traits play a greater role in falling in love than physical appearance, at least if we are to trust what people say.

If I were to ask you what it was that made you fall in love, chances are that at the top of your list you also would have mentioned the charming, pleasant, or interesting traits that captured your heart. It is also likely that you would have mentioned your beloved's physical appearance, but as secondary in importance (especially if you are a woman). But, is physical appearance *really* less important than character? And, are women *really* less influenced by it? Or do people (especially women) tend to underreport the impact of physical appearance on their dating preferences? In a study that attempted to find out, women were shown profiles containing photographs and information about the personalities of potential dating partners. When the women thought they were connected to a lie detector, they admitted being more influenced by the physical attractiveness of the men and described physically attractive men as more desirable. When they were not connected to the apparatus, women tended to underreport the impact of the men's physical attractiveness on their preferences.[3] Apparently, a social norm tends to inhibit, especially women, from admitting the importance of physical attraction.

Research showed that we can look at a face for 150 milliseconds and rate its attractiveness, giving a similar rating to the one we would give after prolonged examination. This evaluation, either positive or negative, is made before we are consciously aware of it.[4] In romantic attraction, the decision whether the person in front of us is attractive is also made within a split second.

Because it serves as a selection screen, appearance plays a crucial role at the beginning of a romantic relationship. If someone's appearance is repulsive, the chances for a romantic involvement are slim. But, as the lovely story "Beauty and the Beast" suggests, on those rare occasions when we are forced to spend time with an unattractive person and get to know that person well, we may discover that under the repulsive appearance lies a hidden treasure of endearing traits. In such a case, it is possible to fall in love despite the initial disdain. The following example is a case in point.

An attractive widow in her early forties wanted to build a new, and significant, intimate relationship. She had met many men, but did not like any of them, especially when she compared them to her late husband and recalled the depth of the emotional bond she had with him. Then, her close friends arranged a blind date with a "charming man" whose company they were convinced she would enjoy. When he rang the doorbell and she first saw him, she could not believe that her friends, who knew how sensitive she was to people's appearances, could have introduced her to such a funny-looking man. Her late husband had been a handsome man, and the men she had dated after his death were also attractive. But, this man was short, possibly even shorter than she, chubby, balding, and wore glasses. She saw no chance of a romantic involvement with so unbecoming a man. Within the first seconds of meeting him, she made up her mind that, at the end of the evening, she would gently dismiss him and never agree to another date. But, because she was stuck with "chubby" for the night and they had a reservation to a wonderful restaurant that was one of her favorites, she decided to go ahead with the original plan and spend the evening with him. While driving to the restaurant in his elegant car, she discovered that he was a pleasant and entertaining man. At the restaurant, she learned that he was a connoisseur of wines and enjoyed good food as much as she did. She also discovered that he was a successful lawyer who loved his work. Moreover, he was a fascinating conversationalist with a great sense of humor, and when she talked, he listened attentively and seemed a sensitive and caring man. Among the last to leave the restaurant, she realized that hours had gone by without her noticing, and that she had enjoyed every minute. Furthermore, it had been years since she had enjoyed herself so much. So, despite her earlier decision, she responded happily when the misnamed chubby invited her out again.

Unfortunately, most of us reject outright those whose appearances we do not like, and we do not give unattractive people a chance to reveal their personalities. A woman who escaped a blind date told me, "When I saw him at the café and saw how he looked, I decided not to go in. Why bother? There was no way I was going to go out with a man who looked like that." Beauty may be skin deep, but the role it plays as an initial screen gives it enormous power in romantic relationships. Through this attractiveness screen, many a person who might have made a wonderful lover and an ideal spouse is discarded. The reason for our prejudice against unattractive people is, at least in part, the result of a connection we make, whether consciously or unconsciously, between beauty and love.

BEAUTY AND LOVE

> She walks in beauty.
> —Lord Byron

> Beauty is a better recommendation than any letter of recommendation.
> —Aristotle

In Roman mythology, Venus is the goddess of both beauty *and* love (see Figure 6). And, in modern times, a large number of studies have demonstrated the

FIGURE 6. *Venus Awaits the Return of Mars,* by Lamert Sustris, ca. 1560. Venus, the Roman goddess of love and beauty (the Greek Aphrodite), reclines with her winged son Cupid (Eros). Venus, the magnificent golden goddess, carried beauty around her. Flowers sprang up wherever her feet touched the earth. Her single divine duty was to make love and inspire others to make love as well. She was desired by all. Gods and mortals alike lost their heads when they heard her voice. There was neither happiness nor beauty without her. (Reprinted by permission of Cameraphoto/Art Resource, New York.)

connection between beauty and love.[5] When we meet new people, we tend to be far more attracted to beautiful people than we are to the less attractive. Of course, what is considered beautiful is different for different people, in different periods of history, and in different cultures.[6] Nevertheless, studies repeatedly showed a significant relationship between finding people attractive and evaluating them positively. We want to meet and get to know attractive people, and we want them as friends and as romantic partners.

One of the earliest studies to document the power of beauty on romantic attraction was done at a university dance. As the students entered the dance hall, a team of judges, themselves students, scored each participant for attractiveness. In addition, the researchers had a lot of information about the participants' personality traits, attitudes toward a variety of topics, and intelligence scores. With the help of a computer, they paired the students according to these characteristics. During a break, the students were asked how satisfied they were with their dates and if they were interested in meeting them again. Results showed that the level of satisfaction with the blind date, the desire to meet again, and the probability of meeting again were all a function of only one thing—the physical attractiveness rating. Personality traits, intelligence, and similar attitudes had little effect.[7]

We assume that what is beautiful is good, that attractive people possess positive traits,[8] and that attractive men are more masculine and beautiful women are more feminine.[9] We see them as more desirable partners for sex, romance, and marriage. We see them as exciting, sexy, interesting, secure, calm, warm, intelligent, strong, generous, open, giving, pleasant, polite, modest, sensitive, friendly, stable, and poised.[10] We expect them to be famous and successful socially and professionally, their marriages to be happy, and their lives to be full and exciting.[8] When things do not work out that way, we are surprised and disappointed.

This positive bias toward beauty can even be found in people's attitudes toward beautiful babies[11] and children. Beautiful children are not only more popular among their peers, but also tend to be treated more kindly and blamed and punished less by their kindergarten teachers.[8]

The prejudice toward beauty was found in people over sixty as well as young children.[12] It was found in men as well as in women, even though the gender difference may be larger when men and women talk about what attracts them than when one examines what really attracts them.[13] And, it was found to be more important in romantic relationships than other qualities, including, for example, quality of communication.[14]

Beautiful people have a strong influence, both negative and positive, on us. This fact was nicely demonstrated in a classic study that involved young men and a beautiful woman confederate, because men are supposed to be more influenced by physical appearance. In half of the cases, the woman was made to look extremely unattractive. She wore ill-fitting and unattractive clothes, a badly cut blond wig that did not suit her skin color, and makeup that made her skin look oily and unappealing. The woman pretended that she was a doctoral student interviewing psychology students for her dissertation research. At the end of the interview, she gave each subject her personal clinical evaluation of him. Half of the men received a positive evaluation, the other half a negative evaluation.

Results of the study showed that when the woman looked ugly, it did not matter to the men whether her evaluation of them was positive or negative. In both cases, they did not like her. When the woman looked beautiful, they liked her very much—but only when she gave them a positive evaluation. When she gave them a negative evaluation, they disliked her even more than when she looked ugly. Yet, the men who received negative evaluations from the beautiful woman were anxious to be given another chance to interact with her in other studies. It seems that her evaluation of them was so important that they desperately wanted a chance to try to change her opinion of them.[15]

WHAT IS BEAUTIFUL?

Although beauty may be "in the eye of the beholder," to a large extent social norms and fashions determine what is considered beautiful.[16] The athletic look that characterized attractive women at the end of the 20th century is different from the voluptuous look that characterized beautiful women in previous eras.[17] Despite the general agreement among people in a particular culture about what is attractive, most of us find it difficult to describe exactly what makes certain people attractive to us.

When pictures of women from college yearbooks and beauty pageants were presented to men who were asked to rate their beauty, it was found that the men ranked two types of faces as most attractive: the baby face (a childish face with big eyes, a little nose, and a little chin) and the sexy woman (high cheekbones, high brows, wide pupils, and a big smile). The same features were ranked as attractive for white, black, and oriental women.[18] Another large cross-cultural study showed that 17- to 60-year-old men and women in five different cultures were attracted to large eyes, small noses, and full lips.[19] It is interesting that people around the world show remarkable agreement about the features of an ideal male face and an ideal female face no matter which ethnic group they are judging.[20]

Harvard brain researcher Nancy Etcoff claimed that our attraction to beauty and definition of beauty are deeply embedded in our genes and are not culture dependent. Beauty is not in the eye of the beholder: We all find women with delicate features, big eyes, and a small chin attractive because this type of face reminds us of a baby's face and therefore triggers in men a desire to protect. This desire has an evolutionary function, and this is why it evolved in us during human evolution.[21] Etcoff cited many studies that showed that we are attracted to the average, not an average beauty, but average features. Scientists who mixed, with the help of the computer, hundreds of digital photos showed that the faces created using this digital mix are more attractive than the individual faces that comprised it. As the number of the photos in the mix increases, the attractiveness of the artificially created face increases. It is possible that we are attracted to the average because the average in a population represents the ideal depiction of that particular feature. This can also explain the surprising finding that strikingly attractive faces are perfectly symmetrical.[22]

Besides a beautiful face, a beautiful body is obviously important for the general attractiveness of men and women. Actually, a woman with a pretty face and an unattractive body gets a lower attractiveness score than a woman with a attractive body and an unattractive face.[23] The most attractive body type for women is of normal weight, rather than skinny or fat.[24] An important contributor to the attractiveness of a woman's body is her bust size. The most attractive bust—despite the stereotype of the sexy woman with the large breasts —is medium size, not too big and not too small.[25]

An interesting physical feature is the waist-to-hip ratio. Men, from young adults to 85-year-olds, find women whose waists are 30% narrower than their hips more attractive.[26] Narrow waists and wide hips are an impossible physical ideal that cause women to do unhealthy things, from wearing corsets to cosmetic surgery to their bodies. An examination of the winners over the last 30 to 60 years of the Miss America contest and *Playboy's* Bunny of the Month shows few changes in the waist-to-hip ratio of these declared beauties. Narrow waist and wide hips are important contributors to a woman's sex appeal. Madonna is a legendary example. (See her perfect waist-to-hip ratio in Figure 7.)

When judging men as potential marriage partners, women also prefer a waist-to-hip ratio that suggests an athletic build.[27] The most important contributors to the attractiveness of a man's body are a muscularity, a well-developed chest, wide shoulders, narrow legs and hips, and small buttocks.[28] (Interestingly, men who are involved in body building have shoulders that are almost twice as wide as their hips.) Height is another contributor to a men's attractiveness. Eight different studies documented "the male-taller norm" in romantic attraction.[29] Responses to lonely hearts advertisements showed that men who mentioned the fact that they are tall received more letters from interested women than men who do not mention their height.[30] When students were asked about their height preference in an ideal partner and whether they were currently in relationships, it turned out that tall men enjoyed a noticeable dating advantage. The height advantage seemed to diminish for men taller than 6 feet, and height had no dating consequence for women.[31] In yet another study, 95% of the women questioned

FIGURE 8. Madonna, the mythical image of feminine sex appeal.

preferred to date a man taller than they were, whereas 80% of men interviewed preferred to date a woman shorter than they were. Shorter women had more dates; men described them as more attractive and preferred to go out with them.[32]

Another physical feature that both men and women find attractive is body symmetry. Nancy Etcoff summarized a large number of studies, all showing that men whose hands, feet, elbows, heels, and ears were symmetrical seemed more attractive and sexy to women than men with a body that was less symmetrical. Interestingly, men with a symmetrical body tend also to have a symmetrical face and a more muscular body, and they tend to be taller and more solidly built. They start having sex 3 or 4 years earlier than other men; they have sex earlier in the courting process, exchange two or three times more sexual partners, are more exciting to their sexual partners, and experience more orgasms with them. Women with a symmetrical body are also preferred. They have more sexual partners than women with a less-symmetrical body, and they tend to be more fertile.[21]

WHY ARE WE PREJUDICED TOWARD BEAUTY?

Different explanations were offered for our attraction to beauty:

- We enjoy the company of attractive people because their appearances give us aesthetic pleasure, just as we enjoy beautiful art objects.
- We assume that whatever looks good on the outside is also good inside. This assumption can influence attraction in one of two ways. First, if what is beautiful is also good, then we not only double our reward from an attractive person, but also a person who can give us greater rewards seems more attractive to us. Second, it is possible that our belief creates reality. If we believe that beauty implies goodness and we behave accordingly, our actions can encourage attractive people to develop the positive traits we expect from them.
- Attractive people may have more social skills. Because they have long histories of rewarding interactions with people around them, they develop social skills that, in themselves, attract people. Studies showed that attractive people indeed have better communication skills.[33]
- What attracts us to beautiful people may be the social benefit we get from associating with them, the reflected glory that shines on us. A person of average attractiveness is perceived as more attractive when in the company of a highly attractive person of the same sex. The same person looks less attractive when in the company of a highly unattractive person.[34]
- Another explanation has to do with our need to believe in a "just world," a world in which people get what they deserve and deserve what they get. In a just world, good things happen to good people, and bad things happen to bad people. We want to believe that people of unusual good looks deserve them because of their wonderful traits. Indeed, it was found that the more people believe in a just world, the more they attribute positive

personality traits to beautiful people and assume that they are going to be successful in their lives.[35]

- The last explanation was offered by evolutionary psychologists, who believe that stereotypes of beauty are the result of evolutionary processes and are based on requirements for breeding and survival.[36] During human evolution, attractive men and women had a higher probability of finding a mate, reproducing, and raising their offspring to maturity. In this way, they ensured that their genes—including the genes responsible for their good looks—were passed on to future generations. Why is a low waist-to-hip ratio considered attractive in a woman? Because this shape is associated with fertility. Why are height and an athletic body attractive in a man? Because, in the long-ago past a tall muscular hunk was more likely than a short and scrawny fellow to function well as a hunter, protector, and provider. Offspring of men who were good hunters had a higher probability of survival and thus passed on the genes responsible for their height and athletic build.

Are attractive people really better? The answer, overall, is no. Attractive people do not seem to have more positive traits, skills, or abilities,[5] but they have several important advantages that are probably related to our positive bias toward them. They have better social skills and are correspondingly more popular.[13] They have more friends and pursuers (especially women), they communicate better with members of the opposite sex,[37] and they have more active sex lives.[38] It may even be that, because of the greater social acceptance that they enjoy, they are less at risk for emotional disturbances.[39] Attractive people tend to work in better jobs, make more money, and in general report more satisfaction from their lives than unattractive people.[40] Analysis of yearbook pictures of business school graduates showed that the more attractive the graduate was, the higher his future earnings.[41]

THE COST OF BEAUTY

Despite the importance of beauty in romantic attraction and despite the positive stereotypes we associate with beautiful people, beauty does not guarantee happiness and does not ensure success in love. It may even be the case that the positive effects of our prejudice toward beauty and the negative effects associated with it—such as unwelcome sexual advances as well as envy and resentment from members of one's own sex—cancel each other. Unusually beautiful women tend to be viewed as snobs, insolent, materialistic, and unfaithful.[42] I have often heard such women complain that their beauty scares men away. At parties, men the beautiful woman would like to have gotten to know do not dare approach her. In addition, attractiveness can cause envy, distrust, and hostility in members of one's own sex and constant harassment by members of the other sex. And, because beauty tends to fade with time, its loss can be devastating. A woman who was exceptionally beautiful in her youth grew up to be a merely beautiful woman. When people see her, they often gasp and say, "You were soooo beautiful." It does not comfort her when they explain, "Now you are a 10, but then you were a 12!"

Although good looks may be good for future earnings, they are not always good for self-esteem. Actually, the opposite may be true. Even though attractive people may feel more comfortable in their interactions with the opposite sex, they are not more self-confident. The reason is their concern that they are liked and sought after because of their looks and not because of who they "really" are.[43] A beautiful young woman I saw in therapy is an example. Her problem was a severe lack of confidence because all her life people only saw her pretty face, long flowing blond hair, and big blue eyes and did not see her obvious intelligence. "And what will happen to me when I am old and no longer beautiful?" she asks with pain and anxiety.

SIMILARITY IN ATTRACTIVENESS

There is extensive evidence that the lovers we choose share with us a similar level of attractiveness. Although we may have preferred to get involved with the most attractive person we knew, most of us eventually have to compromise and accept someone who is neither more attractive nor less attractive than we are.

It is possible that this similarity results not from an active selection process, but rather from a screening process that operates in the following manner. The first to be snapped are the most attractive people, leaving in the pool the people who are second in their level of attractiveness. Once these people are picked, those below them in attractiveness are taken. The process continues until only the most unattractive people remain in the pool, and those are forced to choose from whoever is left.[44]

Those dreaming of a romantic relationship with a movie star or a famous beauty and unwilling to get involved with the less-attractive mortals they meet in their everyday lives should be aware of the advantages of choosing a lover who is similar to oneself in attractiveness—greater satisfaction in a relationship and greater success for the relationship. Furthermore, a relationship with a person of unusual beauty, unless one is also exceptionally attractive, can generate enormous romantic jealousy.[45] The unattractive partner feels threatened, and with good reason, by the admirers who flock around the beautiful partner like bees around honey, admiring, desiring, flirting, and coveting either overtly or covertly.

BEAUTY IS IN THE EYE OF THE BEHOLDER

> Some are prettier,
> But none as beautiful.
>   —Natan Alterman, *Love Poems*

> Here we are, naked lovers,
> Beautiful to each other—and that's enough—
>   —Wislawa Szymborska, *Openess*

Even though some men's and women's beauty is uncontested, they can look more beautiful to some people than to others. As we go down the scale to the average levels of attractiveness, the levels of most of us, the role played by subjective perception increases. The following story demonstrates just how subjective the perception of attractiveness can be. A young man met a woman while traveling in the Far East and fell madly in love with her, sure that in addition to all her other virtues, his beloved was a stunning beauty. He could not wait to introduce her to his friends. But, when he returned home, he was shocked to discover that his friends not only did not see her as beautiful, but actually considered her rather homely.

A woman, convinced that her best friend is extremely beautiful, can similarly discover, to her great dismay, that men find her friend totally lacking in any type of appeal. On the other hand, she can watch with amazement as the same men flock to a woman who she finds totally unappealing. Not only can someone who appears attractive to us appear unattractive to others, but our perceptions can change in reaction to things that have nothing to do with physical appearance. People we learn to love look more attractive to us than they did initially, whereas people we learn to despise can come to look ugly.

For unattractive people, disheartened by the unfairness of the bias toward beauty, there is the comforting evidence that beauty does not guarantee finding the best marriage partner or succeeding in romantic relationships. Indeed, one of the most unattractive girls who went to elementary school with me was the first one to get married and is still happily married today. On the other hand, the most beautiful girl in high school married late and is twice divorced.

When people calculate their own overall levels of attractiveness and the levels of attractiveness of their partners or potential partners, physical appearance is just one of the components in the formula—and its importance is different for different people. Many other traits, including intelligence, sense of humor, social and economic status, interests, and, of course, character can enhance or diminish our and others' overall attractiveness.

CHARACTER
Traits of the People We Love

About 40 years ago when social psychologists asked people what are the traits of the people they like most, it was discovered that at the top of the list of traits that made people likeable were honesty, competence, ability, intelligence, and energy.[46] Thirty years later, the desired traits were sociability, high activity, and low emotionality.[47] Honesty went down in importance, sociability went up, and level of energy/activity remained. The problem with studies of this type is that it is not clear whether the people we like really have these traits, or whether we convince ourselves that they have the traits because we like them. Probably both are true to some extent.

A Formula to Calculate an Overall Attractiveness Score

A mathematical model attempted to put the different ingredients of attraction into a formula and calculate an overall attractiveness score. According to this model, attraction is in direct proportion to the value given to a person's traits. The model assumes that every trait can be given a numerical value, and that this value can be different for different people. The more positive the overall value of a person's traits, the greater the attraction to that person. If, for example, you really value intelligence in people, you will rate "intelligent" very positively (+4), whereas a trait such as "hesitant" you may rate as somewhat negatively (–1). The overall attraction score is a summary calculated after all the values of all the traits are entered into the formula.[48] If you want to figure out why a certain person attracts you and a second does not, the best way to do it according to this model is to analyze the traits of both people, enter the value of each of their traits, and calculate their overall attraction scores.

It would be easy to assume that the more able, talented, and competent a person is, the more attractive he or she will be to us. Noted social psychologist Elliot Aronson, who studied this issue during the presidency of John F. Kennedy, demonstrated that the relationship between abilities and attraction is not so simple. Aronson was intrigued by the finding that Kennedy's popularity went up after the Bay of Pigs fiasco. The explanation he offered was that Kennedy had been simply too perfect. He was young, handsome, bright, witty, charming, athletic, a voracious reader, and a war hero who had endured great pain. In addition, he had a beautiful and talented wife who spoke several foreign languages; two lovely children, a boy and a girl; and a rich, close-knit family. The testimony to a human weakness that was offered by being responsible for a humiliating national blunder could have made him appear more human and hence more likable.[49]

To test this explanation, Aronson and his colleagues told subjects that they were going to evaluate the attractiveness of four candidates who were being interviewed for a famous quiz show. They listened to one of four tapes. In the first tape the interviewee was nearly perfect; in the second, he was nearly perfect but committed a blunder; in the third, he was mediocre; and in the fourth, he was mediocre and committed a blunder. The questions included in the interview were difficult, of the type often used on quiz shows. The almost-perfect candidate exhibited during the interview a great deal of knowledge and skill. He answered 92% of the questions correctly and admitted modestly that he had been an honors student in high school, the editor of the yearbook, and a member of the track team. The mediocre interviewee answered only 30% of the questions correctly and admitted during the interview that he had received average grades in high school, had been a proofreader on the yearbook, and had failed to make the track team. The blunder involved spilling coffee. Toward the end of the interview, sounds of commotion and clatter were heard as was the scraping of a chair and an anguished voice saying, "Oh my goodness, I've spilled coffee all over my new suit."

Results showed that the nearly perfect interviewee who committed the blunder was rated most attractive; the average interviewee who committed the same blunder was rated least attractive. "Clearly, there was nothing inherently attractive about the simple act of spilling a cup of coffee," wrote Aronson, "although it did serve to add an endearing dimension to the perfect person, making him more attractive. The same action served to make the mediocre person appear that much more mediocre and, hence, less attractive."[49]

In other words, although high ability and competence increase a candidate's attractiveness, a certain evidence of human weakness increased this attractiveness even more. Later studies showed that Aronson's conclusion applies more to men, who tend to compete with the perfect candidate, and therefore like him more when he blunders. Women, on the other hand, prefer capable men and women who do not blunder.

Are Ability and Competence Important for Romantic Attraction?

Let us examine some of the traits that men and women mentioned when they talked about the reasons that made them fell in love.

The first thing that attracted me was the smile on his face. He looked so happy. He was just smiling at me. And he had the nicest smile. He's like that all the time. It's nice to be around someone who is like this. You can just forget everything that bothers you. And I tend to carry that kind of stuff with me. He's a lot different from anyone else. He's real. He's really calm, and he's funny. He's really outdoorsy. He does what he wants. He's also independent, which is the way I am, which makes me happy.

She is smart and dynamic and sensitive and nice. It's easy to trust her. People like her. She gets along well with people. She's easy to like.

He is very funny and witty. I don't know what attracted me, but I know I immediately felt comfortable, just his conversation, and he is so outgoing. He is one of those people that you immediately feel comfortable with. He is interesting, funny; witty, it's fun. He's outgoing and not shy, sort of opposite than me.

She is very attractive, smart, and artistic. And she had an innocent side that I liked. I hung around with a lot of people who weren't like this, with her I could simply relax.

In none of these examples or in any of the quotations at the beginning of the chapter are abilities or competence mentioned directly. Of the traits mentioned several times, intelligence—and its close relative wit—come closest to competence.

What, Then, Are the Traits That Attract Us to a Romantic Partner?

The personality traits that attract us to a romantic partner that were mentioned most often by both men and women were nice, friendly, and a sense of humor. The traits that were mentioned several times by the men were easy to talk to, understanding, warm, sweet, smart, energetic, funny, self-confident, and quiet. The traits that were mentioned several times by women were easy-going, sensitive, and intelligent.

The picture that emerges is one of attraction to people who make us feel good, people who are warm, sensitive, and funny. In studies that examined what men and women look for in a marriage partner, a similar list of traits emerged. At the top of the list—for both men and women—are warmth and consideration.[50] An analysis of personal ads also showed that at the top of the list of desirable traits in a romantic partner, both men and women put understanding and a sense of humor.[51]

The importance of warmth and sensitivity can explain the surprising findings of a study in which young college women read various descriptions of men and were found to prefer feminine men over masculine men, both as friends and as romantic partners. When rating the attractiveness of the men described, the women gave greater weight to personality factors than they did to success factors. They found the feminine men to be most attractive and the masculine men most repulsive. A man's belief in gender equality had the greatest influence on both the women's platonic and romantic attraction to him.[52]

Some of the desirable traits in a mate that people mention today are similar to the traits mentioned by their parents and grandparents, and some—such as the attraction of college women to men who believe in the equality between the sexes—characterize young modern people.

A comparison of traits that were considered attractive in a candidate for a romantic relationship at the end of the 1930s and the early 1980s (50 years later) shows that, although emotional stability and trustworthiness remained important, mutual attraction became more important, and sexual purity decreased in importance.[53]

Warmth, sensitivity, and sense of humor are not the first traits that leap to mind when we imagine a wild love affair. Why, then, do they come up again and again in people's descriptions of the type of person to whom they are attracted and would like to have as a romantic partner? One obvious explanation is that these traits are more closely related to intimate relationships than they are to wild sexual affairs. Even if the popular portrayal of falling in love is of blind physical passion, the people to whom most of us are attracted are people with whom we can be intimate, people who make us feel understood and loved. Warmth and sensitivity are also important because most of us prefer to feel good about ourselves, and people who like themselves prefer the company of those who like them and make them feel good. Warm, sensitive, considerate people make those around them feel good. And, as we now know, when people feel good they are more open to love.

BEAUTY AND CHARACTER

> Grace is deceitful and beauty is vain.
> —Proverbs, 31, 30

When you think about your most significant romantic relationship, what was it that most attracted you? Arthur Aron and his colleagues asked men and women who had fallen in love within the previous 8 months to think about the experience for a few minutes and then describe it in detail. Analysis of their stories revealed that the variable mentioned most often was either physical attractiveness or personality traits; they did not differentiate between the two.[54]

Beauty and character influence each other, and both influence us. A warm, sensitive person with a good sense of humor tends to look more attractive, and a highly attractive person tends to look warmer, nicer, wiser, and more exciting. The *halo effect* refers to our tendency to perceive people consistently. If we see a person as attractive, we will attribute to that person other positive traits that are associated in our minds with attractiveness—whether these traits are there or not. The best example of the halo effect is falling in love, which makes us see our beloved with starry eyes blinded by love, passion, and admiration.

All of us are also influenced by the norms and values related to attractiveness in our culture. In dating games and personal ads of the 1990s, many more men described themselves as "sensitive" than did men in the 1970s or the 1980s. Admiring the personality traits of the beloved is part of the romantic ideal on which we were raised, which may be the reason why people today are likely to mention it.

SELF-FULFILLING PROPHECIES

When we perceive people as attractive—because of their appearances or personalities—we expect them to behave in ways that characterize attractive people. These expectations in turn encourage behaviors that make our expectations come true. A lovely example of this process was provided in a book written almost 70 years ago by Edwin Ray Guthrie.[55]

The classmates of a shy and reserved young woman decided to conduct an experiment. (In another version of this story, the idea was suggested by their psychology instructor.) Their goal was to make their shy classmate feel attractive and desirable. The students made sure that one of them always sat next to her in class, in the cafeteria, or in any other social place on the campus; one of them invited her to every social event and asked her to dance at parties. At first, the shy woman responded with shock and confusion. But with time, she started enjoying their advances and developed a feminine self-confidence that was expressed in the way she dressed, did her hair, talked, and acted.

The critical question was whether the positive change would transfer to other social situations. To find out, her classmates visited her other classes. They discovered that their shy and homely classmate continued to act like an attractive and self-confident woman who was sure of her desirability. But, what was even more surprising, and exciting in its implications, was the fact that the men in those classes—unaware of the experiment under way and its progress—treated her as an attractive woman. With no external encouragement, they showed genuine interest in her and pursued her.

The behavior of the men reinforced the shy woman's self-confidence and perception of herself as an attractive and desirable woman, which in turn caused her to behave accordingly. The more self-assured her behavior was, the more open she was with men; the more attention she gave to her appearance, the more responses she received from the men around her.

With time, the experiment started affecting the men who initiated it. They no longer had to pretend to be attracted to their classmate. They came to see her as attractive and started competing earnestly for her attention. The students' attention helped turn the ugly duckling into a beautiful swan.

The story of the shy young woman who blossomed into a woman sure of her attractiveness because of her classmates' attentions is reminiscent of the moving story in Greek mythology of Pygmalion's passionate love for Galatea (see Box and Figure 8).

THE STORY OF PYGMALION AND GALATEA

Pygmalion was a young and gifted sculptor who lived on the isle of Cyprus. Pygmalion hated women and vowed never to marry. Nevertheless (or possibly because of this), he invested all of his artistic genius in a sculpture of a woman, a beautiful woman. There was no living woman that could compare to it in beauty. The sculpture transcended its static nature; it appeared to be a real woman standing motionless just for a moment. So the legend goes, Pygmalion fell in love with his beautiful sculpture. His love was passionate and boundless. No man in love ever suffered so much pain. He kissed her seductive lips, but she did not return his kisses. He held her in his arms, but she remained cold. His strange love drew the attention of Venus, goddess of love, and she decided to help the young man. She made the sculpture come alive. Pygmalion named his beloved Galatea and married her.

Our behavior influences the people around us. A woman who treats a man like the most kind and generous man on earth is going to help bring out more of his generosity; a man who treats a woman like a strong able person is going to help bring out more of her competence. An elegant proof of the power of self-fulfilling prophecies was provided in a study by Mark Snyder.[56]

Young men and women were invited to take part in a study that supposedly examined the process of getting acquainted. Arriving alone into different rooms, they were asked to talk on the phone and try to get acquainted. Before the telephone conversation, the experimenter entered the room in which the man sat and took a photograph of him with a Polaroid camera. The experimenter explained that, to help the conversation flow, each subject receives a photograph of his or her telephone partner. In truth, only the men received a photograph of their supposed partner to the conversation, and it was a photograph of a woman randomly selected from a group who had been prejudged as either very attractive or very unattractive. The women who took part in the study did not receive photographs and knew nothing about the photographs that were given to the men. Every couple spoke on the phone for about 10 minutes on any subject they chose. Their voices were recorded on separate tapes. Judges were then asked to listen to the tape recordings of

FIGURE 8. *Pygmalion and Galatea*, Etienne Falconet, 18th century.

the women's voices only and to rate them on such characteristics as liveliness, warmth, intimacy, sexiness, and sociability. Results of the study showed that the women who spoke to men who thought they were talking to a beautiful woman were friendlier, more open, more flirtatious than the women who spoke to men who thought they were talking to unattractive women. In other words, the fact that the men *thought* that the women were beautiful made the women act in ways that fulfilled the men's expectations.[56]

The conclusion is obvious—beauty and character are, at least to some extent, the result of an interaction. The way we perceive a person's appearance and personality influences that person's self-perception, which in turn influences the person's behavior, which reinforces our perceptions. This is the power of self-fulfilling prophecies. We can choose to use this power or not use it.

A movie I saw some years ago portrayed a young man who believed he was Don Juan. He treated every woman he encountered, even the most unattractive, as if she was the most sexy and desirable woman in the world. As a result, the women around him started behaving in a sexy and attractive way, especially toward him.

Self-fulfilling prophecies and positive illusions have positive effects on romantic relationships. Satisfying romantic relationships reflect, at least in part, the ability of people to see their imperfect partners through adoring eyes. A study that examined the benefits (or costs) of positive illusions demonstrated that. It involved 100 couples who were asked three times during the course of a year about their levels of "partner idealization" and satisfaction from their relationships. The results revealed that partner idealization worked as a self-fulfilling prophecy. The more the partners idealized each other, the higher was the probability that they would stay together—even when the couple had conflicts and reservations. Those couples in which the partners tended to idealize each other more at the beginning of the relationship reported an increase in satisfaction and a lower level of conflict during the year. And, a result that I find especially exciting, among the couples who adored each other, each partner tended with time to accept the other's perceptions of him or herself—seeing oneself more positively as a result of the partner's positive view. Contrary to the popular belief that love is blind, partners who adore each other are prophets. With time, they shape their love relationships according to their own visions.[57]

Freud explained the idealization of the beloved as the "projection" of an "ideal self." The individual projects onto the beloved traits and values that the individual views as supreme, perceiving them as being in the beloved. Freud believed that, in the progression from the immature stage of falling in love to the mature stage of love, the idealization of the beloved needs to be abandoned and replaced by a mature view of the beloved as he or she really is.[58] The findings of the positive effect of partner idealization suggest that this is not necessarily so. Positive illusions continue to have the power of a self-fulfilling prophecy even after falling in love has turned to love.

THE LOVER'S PERSONALITY

So far, the discussion has centered on the personality of the beloved. What about the lover's personality? What makes some of us more open to love and more comfortable in intimate relationships? Eric Erikson believed that we need to develop a strong sense of ourselves and know who we are before we can develop truly intimate relationships.[59] A study that compared the levels of people's self-identity to the levels of intimacy in their relationships showed that Erikson was right.[60] The stronger people's sense of self, the higher their ability to be intimate.

People without a well-developed sense of identity are afraid of intimacy because they are terrified of being engulfed and losing themselves in relationships. When people with a low sense of identity fall in love, their feelings are unusually intense, overwhelm them, and cause obsessive, tumultuous loves.[61]

A fascinating example of such obsessive love is *de Clerambault syndrome*, named after the French psychiatrist who first described it in 1942. People who suffer from this syndrome (most of them women) have a powerful delusion that a certain person, most often a person of a much higher social rank than theirs, is in love with them. They have limited contact, or no contact at all, with the object of their delusion. The fact that he is married is perceived as irrelevant. Declarations of lack of romantic interest in them, or even of repulsion and rejection, are received with equanimity and understanding as a paradoxical expression of love. The woman who suffers from de Clerambault syndrome is convinced that the object of her love is "truly" in love with her, that he fell in love with her first, and that he has declared his love by secret messages. She is also sure he will never find another love as true as hers, and that the bond between them is widely known and accepted with respect and understanding; she is willing to go to great efforts to try to protect their love. De Clerambault described as an example the case of a 53-year-old French woman who was convinced that the British King George the Fifth was in love with her. She pursued him relentlessly for years and even arrived in London several times, where she waited for him outside of Buckingham Palace. When she once saw a curtain move in one of the palace windows, she explained it as a sign from the King and was sure that all the people in London knew of his love for her.

Sense of identity and self-confidence influences our ability to give and receive love. People who have a high frequency of love experiences tend to have high self-confidence and low defensiveness.[62] To be able to love, we first have to love ourselves and feel secure in our own lovability.

Another personality dimension that is related to the ability to love is *self-actualization*. Self-actualization refers to a person's constant effort to grow, to develop his or her inherent talents and capabilities. Abraham Maslow described the need for self-actualization as the highest in the human hierarchy of needs. He believed that being self-actualized is the foundation of the ability to give and receive love.[63] An early study that supported Maslow's theory showed that people who had been in romantic relationships within 3 years preceding the study were more self-actualized than people who had not been in intimate relationships during that time.[64] Later studies showed a more complex relationship between self-actualization and the ability to love. On the one hand, being self-actualized was related to a richer and more satisfying love experience; on the other, a high level of self-actualization correlated with a lower need for romantic relationships.[65] This suggests that self-actualized people enjoy love relationships more but need them less than people who are not actualized.

Self-confidence and self-actualization influence people's style of love.[66] Insecure people who do not have a coherent sense of self and who are not self-actualized tend toward a game-playing style of love and have relationships with low levels of intimacy and high levels of conflict. People who have a coherent sense of self are self-confident and self-actualized and tend toward unselfish and romantic styles of love, and their relationships tend to be highly intimate.[67]

SUGGESTIONS FOR PEOPLE SEEKING LOVE
Beauty

Look for a lover who is as physically attractive as you are. Despite the importance of physical beauty in the selection of fashion models and movie stars, when you are selecting a lover, the rule of thumb is not to choose the most attractive person. Rather, select the most attractive person among those similar to you in attractiveness. People who follow this guideline are likely to have more harmonious and satisfying romantic relationships.

Although beauty can be subjective and skin deep, it still plays an important role as one of the first screens in romantic relationships. This implies what most people know well: You should do everything possible to look your best when meeting someone in whom you are interested. If you are rejected because of an appearance that could have been enhanced with some effort, your potential partner will never have a chance to discover the wonderful treasures buried deep inside your unkempt appearance.

Character

It ought to be encouraging that you need not have exceptional skills or abilities to find love. Neither should you look for a lover who has unusual skills or abilities. The emotional state that should guide the search for love is a feeling of pleasure, joy, and comfort. According to this criterion, despite its obvious subjectivity, people who are warm, sensitive, considerate, and preferably have a good sense of humor are the best candidates.

Finding Love

Use the power of self-fulfilling prophecies. Treat your potential partners as if they were exactly what you want them to be—sexy, exciting, attractive. Your behavior will help bring out those traits in them.

Work toward improving your self-confidence and toward enhancing the attractive parts of your appearance and personality. Clearly, these suggestions require an enormous effort, can take a long time, and may require professional help. Yet, as Ovid, the first century poet, wrote in *The Art of Love*, "To be loved, be loveable."

Chapter 4

BIRDS OF A FEATHER OR OPPOSITES ATTRACT?

Birds of a feather flock together.
—A proverb

The starling went to the raven, because it is of its kind.
—Baba Kama, *The Mishna*

THE STORY OF NARCISSUS

NARCISSUS WAS A BEAUTIFUL YOUTH. SO GREAT WAS HIS BEAUTY THAT ALL the young women, and all the nymphs, were in love with him, but he did not desire any of them. Rejected and despairing, many an admirer took her own life. But Narcissus was proud, stubborn, and heartless. Then, one day, a rejected admirer called out to the gods for vengeance, and Nemesis, the goddess of righteous anger, punished Narcissus. As he bent over a pristine pool of water to get a drink, Narcissus saw his own reflection and fell in love with himself. Now, it was he who suffered the terrible pain of unrequited love, the despair of knowing that he would never consummate his love or possess his beloved. His gaze fixed on his reflection in the water, Narcissus died of grief and longing. When the nymphs went to bury his body, they could not find it. In the place where it had lain now grew a beautiful new flower that was given his name.

Like Narcissus (see Figure 9) many of us are attracted to our own reflections, that is, other people who share our characteristics.

> *We had a lot in common. We both come from these highly intellectual neurotic families, have an interest in the environment, not too much in a hurry to get into graduate school.*
>
> *We were both in an orchestra. I felt that we were similar … . We tended to think alike in many ways.*

FIGURE 9. *Narcissus*, Caravaggio ca. 1594–1596.

> *We have a lot in common. We're both really affectionate, we both like to travel, and she plays tennis and I play. Everything we do together is fun.*
> *She was overweight, just like me. I felt comfortable with her. I'm attracted to people who are sensitive and quiet because that's the way I am.*
> *She is a Native American like me and looks like me, same color tone.*

Analysis of the romantic attraction interviews suggests that, in one-third of the cases, similarity played a role in the initial attraction.[1] Given the great importance attributed to similarity (especially in background) by matchmakers and the huge number of studies that have addressed it, it is surprising that so few are aware of the role it plays in their romantic attraction.

The similarity that interviewees mentioned was in many different areas:

- family background
- personality traits
- appearance
- ways of thinking
- goals and interests
- leisure activities

In all of these cases, the similarity was mentioned as a positive factor that enhanced the initial attraction and helped facilitate the development of the relationship. Studies on who falls in love with whom show a huge range of variables in which intimate partners are similar. These variables include age, personality traits, appearance, height, weight, eye color, and other physical characteristics, including physical defects, behavior patterns, professional success, attitudes, opinions, intelligence, cognitive complexity, verbal ability, education, social and economic class, family background, number and sex of siblings, feelings toward the family of origin, the quality of the parents' marriage, race and ethnic background, religious background, social and political affiliations, acceptance of sex role stereotypes, physical and emotional health, emotional maturity, level of neuroticism, level of differentiation from the family of origin, moodiness, depressive tendencies, tendency to be a "lone wolf" or a "social animal," tendency to lie and be inconsistent, as well as drinking and smoking habits.[2]

The earliest statistical study that documented similarity between couples is the study done by the British Victorian psychologist Sir Francis Galton toward the end of the 19th century. Galton, who developed the method of statistical correlation, found a significant correlation between husbands and wives not only in such obvious variables as age, race, religion, education, and social status, but also in physical and psychological traits such as height, eye color, and intelligence.[3]

More than 100 years after Galton, studies have reached similar conclusions. People are likely to choose as lovers and marriage partners those with similar characteristics.[4] Furthermore, the more similar couples are in personality and background, the more comfortable they are with each other, the more compatible they feel, and the greater their satisfaction from the relationship.[5] Consequently, couples who are similar in attitudes, temperament, and behavior are more likely to stay together over time.[6]

WHY DOES SIMILARITY ENHANCE ATTRACTION?

One explanation suggests itself: Similarities are generally rewarding, whereas dissimilarities can be unpleasant. Even people who organize their thoughts and perceptions in similar ways are more attracted to each other and find more enjoyment in each other's company.[7] In addition, people are attracted to romantic partners who are similar to them in height, size, and weight. Short men, it turns out, tend to marry short women, and tall women tend to marry tall men. Fat men tend to marry fat women, and skinny women prefer skinny men.[8]

Another fascinating topic is the similarity found in couples' mental health and mental illness. It was shown, for example, that husbands of schizophrenic women also tended to show symptoms of mental disturbance.[9] And, a study of people who suffered from depression showed that in 41% of the cases, both parents suffered from a mental problem.[10] Some evidence also exists that moody people with depressive tendencies tend to be attracted to people who are similar to them in unhappiness. There is much stronger evidence, however, that happy people are attracted to happy people. In all of these cases, it is clear that similarity in emotional makeup increases a couple's attraction to each other.[11]

When we consider the long and impressive list of variables in which couples are similar, a question suggests itself. Are some similarities more important than others? Evolutionary psychologist David Buss looked at this question and said the answer is "Yes." Similarity in the more important variables is reflected in couples' compatibility. Age, education, race, religion, and ethnic background are the most important, as evidenced by the fact that they account for the highest correlations between partners and have the greatest effect on relationships. Next in importance are similarities in attitudes, opinions, mental ability, social and economic status, height, weight, eye color, behavior, personality, siblings, and physical features.[12]

It seems that when looking for marriage partners, we eliminate first those we perceive to be inappropriate in the most important ways. They are too old or too young: *"He is madly in love with me, and I think he is adorable, but I could never have a real relationship with a 25-year-old kid"* said a woman approaching her forties. They have too much or too little education: *"I can't discuss things that are important to me with a woman who didn't finish high school and never reads, even if she is attractive and sexy."*

Their ethnic or religious backgrounds are too different from our own: *"I could never get seriously involved with a non-Jew."* After passing this initial screening, we turn to look at the other dimensions of potential mates. Here, too, the greater the similarity, the greater the chance that the person will pass the test successfully. In the second screening, we assess the candidate's basic values; it would be difficult for a liberal democrat to continue dating a white supremacist even if attractive and otherwise appropriate. The candidate's social and economic status is also important (it is best if it is similar to our own or a little higher), as are similarity in temperament and behavior.

It is possible that underneath all these similarities exists a more basic, more fundamental similarity in genetic makeup. Indeed, a number of studies showed that people are able to identify, and prefer as romantic partners people who are similar to them genetically.[13]

Clearly, people tend to fall in love with, and choose as marriage partners, individuals who are similar to them. Fairy tales about great loves between Cinderella and the prince or between the beautiful call girl and the millionaire are rare. This is probably why we enjoy hearing about them and seeing them in movies. In the original version of the movie *Pretty Woman*, the couple parted in the end. But, at an early screening, viewers objected. They saw the story as a fairy tale and demanded an appropriate ending, which they got. When such miracle romances do occur, they usually do not lead to marriage. On the rare occasions that they do, the marriages are characterized by a high frequency of conflicts.

People who come from similar cultural and social backgrounds have similar expectations and assumptions. This makes communication between them easier and prevents conflicts. They do not need to discuss who does what and how; these things are mutually understood and accepted. Similarities in attitudes, interests, and personality also make communication easier; consequently, married couples who share them report greater happiness and satisfaction from their marriages.[14]

From the long list of similarity variables shared by couples, I have chosen five to discuss in detail because they play a special role in romantic attraction: similarity in physical appearance, attitudes, personality, psychological maturity, and genetic makeup.

SIMILARITY IN PHYSICAL APPEARANCE

"Are you two related?" the woman asked, smiling. She seemed amazed by their resemblance, and she was not the only one. Since they arrived, there were several other people who had asked if they were brother and sister. And, these were people who knew them both. How did they not notice before how similar they looked? They both were slightly built, had a head full of blond hair streaked by silver gray, bright blue eyes and a pink complexion. But, what was even more striking was the similarity in their facial expression. Both were quick to smile, a youthful happy smile, and both had a cheerful disposition. They, of course, knew about each other. They had heard each other's names mentioned often enough by their many mutual friends and colleagues. What was most surprising was that they had never met before, but now that they had, they were both intrigued. They liked each other's look and felt an instant attraction. When they started talking, they felt an immediate comfort, as if they had known each other all their lives. It was magical.

One of the most important aspects of similarity in appearance, at least at the beginning of a romantic relationship, is similarity in level of attractiveness. A study at a matchmaking agency demonstrated this. The agency gave its customers background information and a 5-minute video clip of each potential partner answering a series of standard questions. If the customer expressed an interest in meeting one of the potential partners, the agency approached the person and asked for permission to release his or her name and phone number. The agency used a grading system to evaluate how a romantic relationship was developing. When one party was interested but the other party refused to release the name, the relationship received the lowest grade. After a couple had two or more dates, the relationship received the highest grade. In addition, the agency graded each party's attractiveness based on their videotapes. Results showed that the greater the similarity in attractiveness between a customer and a potential partner, the more likely it was that a romantic relationship would develop between them.[15]

Another study examined the progress of courtship by following couples for 9 months. The more similar the partners were to each other in attractiveness, the greater interest they showed in continuing the relationship, the less likely they were to break up, and, with time, the more likely they were to express love toward each other.[16] Other studies showed that the similarity in attractiveness between dating couples is smaller than that of couples living together, and their similarity is smaller than that of couples planning to marry or already married[17] (see Figure 10).

On those rare occasions when a significant difference exists between the attractiveness of romantic partners, it is explained by the exceptional qualities possessed by the less-attractive member, as in the romantic story of Beauty and the Beast. It is noteworthy, however, that the happy ending happens when it turns out that the ugly beast is in fact a handsome prince who Beauty's love released from an evil spell, which means that they are actually similar in attractiveness.

With time, the role of physical attractiveness may diminish in importance; yet, when a partner's attractiveness changes drastically, it

FIGURE 10. Similarity in appearance of a couple getting married.

can have a major effect even after many years of marriage. A study of couples with sexual problems showed that husbands who reported the highest number of sexual difficulties believed that they had remained as attractive as they were at the beginning of the marriage, while their wives had become significantly less attractive than they used to be.[18]

Why Are Couples Similar in Appearance?

- According to *equity theory*, when choosing a partner, it is important for us to feel we are getting someone we deserve. The more similar partners' attractiveness, the more the relationship is perceived—by the couple and by onlookers—as equitable. The more attractive you are, the more attractive the dates you choose. The more unattractive you are, the more unattractive the dates you have to accept.[19]
- The second explanation is based on the positive effect of *repeated exposure*. From the time we are born, we are surrounded by family members, especially parents and siblings, who tend to look like us. This repeated exposure causes us to develop a preference and attraction for those who look like them and like us. Thus, there is far greater similarity between the photographs of married or engaged couples than there is between photographs of randomly selected couples.[20]
- A third explanation is that, with time, couples tend to grow increasingly similar to each other. They eat the same foods, share the same leisure activities, and pay more or less attention to their appearances. When students were given yearbook pictures of couples who had graduated from high

school 25 years earlier, they could not guess who was married to whom. When they were given current pictures of the same couples, they were able to identify easily who was married to whom. In other words, after 25 years of living together, the couples came to look alike.[21]

Which explanation is correct? Probably all three. We tend to be attracted to people who resemble us, have to accept partners who are similar to us in attractiveness, and after many years together grow to look like our partners.

SIMILARITY IN ATTITUDES

After people have noticed and assessed the physical appearance of a potential partner and have found it sufficiently attractive, they go on to examine the person's attitudes toward issues they care about. It is on this topic of attitude similarity that most of the studies were done on the effect of similarity on attraction. The conclusion, over and over again, is the same—the greater the attitude similarity, the greater the attraction and the greater the satisfaction in the relationship.

In 35 years of attraction research, Don Byrne and his colleagues showed that people are more attracted to others they perceive as sharing similar attitudes.[22] In an early study, he began by identifying the true attitudes of students who were going to be subjects in the study and asking judges to rate the physical appearance of each subject. Byrne then separated the subjects into couples who were either similar or dissimilar in their attitudes and sent them on a date. He found that after their dates, the couples who had similar attitudes were more attracted to each other than were the couples who had dissimilar attitudes. The attraction was greatest when the date was physically attractive *and* had similar attitudes. In a repeat check at the end of the semester, those students who had gone out with an attractive person with similar attitudes were most likely to remember the date's name and express a desire for another date.[23]

The effect of attitude similarity on attraction has been known for a long time. When Charles Darwin listed the causes for people's attraction to each other, similarity in attitudes and interests was at the top.[24]

Dale Carnegie, who gave millions of readers prescriptions on "how to win friends and influence people," recommended using the positive effect of similarity in attitudes and interests. "The royal road to a person's heart is to talk about the things he or she treasures most."[25] Even if a real similarity in attitudes does not exist, Carnegie recommends pretending that it does. I am not sure people who are seeking a significant romantic relationship should follow Carnegie's advice because, even if they succeed in making the other attracted to them as a result of pretending to be interested in the same things, they will have to go on living with that person, something that is much harder to do if your interests and views are different.

Why Are We Attracted to People Who Share Our Attitudes?

- A person who shares our attitudes validates our opinions and gives us the pleasant feeling that we are right.[26] Because we like feeling that our view of the world is reasonable and correct, such social validation is rewarding and hence an element in attraction.[27]
- If a person perceives the world as we do, we feel fairly confident that it would be rewarding to spend time with that person,[27] but if he or she expresses attitudes that are different from our own, it may suggest a type of person we have found in the past to be unpleasant, immoral, dangerous, or just plain stupid.[26]
- If we love ourselves, it only makes sense that we will love people who are similar to us.[27]
- When we learn that others are similar to us, we assume they will like us; thus, we like them in return. When we perceive people as different, we tend to avoid them and thus reduce the chance that they will pass through our other attraction screens.[27]
- People who are similar to us seem familiar. And, as we know, the familiar is more comfortable and pleasant to us than the unfamiliar.
- We are more likely to meet and get to know others who are similar to us in familiar surroundings. They are more likely to live in our neighborhoods, belong to the same clubs, and attend the same schools and leisure activities.

Despite this logical reasoning, it should be noted that attraction is not always the result of a true similarity in attitudes. When we like a person, we assume that he or she shares our attitudes. If I like you, I just naturally assume that you hold attitudes similar to mine, and that our tastes and preferences are similar. The attraction develops an illusion of similarity, and the assumed similarity enhances the attraction.[28]

The effect of assumed similarity on attraction can be explained by *balance theory*: People strive to organize their likes and dislikes in a symmetrical arrangement that results in balance. When two people like each other and agree about something, they create a state of balance. When they like each other and disagree, there is imbalance, an unpleasant state that motivates them to do something, such as develop an illusion of similarity, to restore balance.[29] It is interesting to note that our attraction to the similar is greater than our repulsion of the dissimilar.[30]

One would assume that once we get to know people well, we would discover whether they indeed share our attitudes. Yet, several studies have found that husbands and wives tend to assume that they are far more similar than they actually are.[31] In one of these studies, couples were asked their opinions on various political issues and then asked to guess how his or her spouse would respond. Results showed that the discrepancy between the real opinions of the husbands and wives was far greater than the discrepancy between their assumed opinions. It was also found that the more couples assumed that they shared attitudes and opinions, the more satisfaction they drew from the marriage.[32] This suggests that a couple's attitudes do not really have to be similar as long as the couple assumes, correctly or incorrectly, that they are similar. It is possible, too, that in the interest of harmony, husbands and wives tend to emphasize their similarities and conceal or avoid areas of disagreement.

One variable that plays a particularly important role as a predictor of marital satisfaction is similarity in sex role ideology.[33] Sex role ideology can be traditional in assigning different and complementary roles to husband (the breadwinner) and wife (the homemaker), and it can be egalitarian in assigning equal roles and shared tasks. When both husband and wife share the same sex role ideology, whether traditional or egalitarian, they are happier in their marriage than couples who do not (e.g., when the wife wants an egalitarian relationship and the husband wants a traditional one). The reason is obvious. When a couple agrees on the roles of men and women in a marriage, they significantly reduce the probability of conflicts.

Similarity in sexual attitudes also bears directly on romantic attraction and marital satisfaction.[34] Discrepancy in a couple's sexual attitudes predicts sexual dissatisfaction in both partners. Interestingly, the woman's sexual attitudes are a better predictor of sexual satisfaction in both the wife and the husband. A couple's ability to talk about sex, and their communication and social skills in general, are also related to their marital satisfaction.[35]

In summary, we are attracted to people who possess attitudes, interests, and social skills similar to our own, and we perceive ourselves to be more similar to people we like and to whom we are attracted.

SIMILARITY IN PERSONALITY

The proverb "birds of a feather flock together" refers to an attraction between people of similar personalities. A couple of the quotations at the beginning of the chapter refer to this attraction—"*We're both really affectionate*" or "*sensitive and quiet*"—and a number of studies documented it.[36] However, the evidence for an attraction between people with similar personalities is far weaker than the evidence for an attraction between people with similar attitudes. It appears that although similarity in attitudes serves as an important screening variable in the early stages of a love relationship, similarity in personality becomes important at a later stage, as the relationship develops. Indeed, a number of studies indicated that couples with similar personalities report greater happiness and satisfaction from their marriages than couples who have different personalities.[37]

Why Are We Attracted to People with a Similar Personality?

- For the same reasons that attract us to people with similar appearance and attitudes: Similarity in personality validates and reinforces our self-perceptions.
- We surround ourselves with people similar to ourselves in an effort to keep our personalities stable in the face of the many situations, changes, and transitions that characterize our lives.[38] In other words, we choose to love and marry people who are similar to us because they help us maintain the stability of our own personality.
- According to what has been called a *theory of narcissism,* as with Narcissus, we love in other people what we see and love in ourselves.[39]

In one of the studies that tested the theory of narcissism, a personality test was given to young women at the beginning of their first year of college. Six months later, they were asked to name the three classmates they liked most and the three they liked least. Results showed that the personality of each young woman was similar to the personalities of her friends, but dissimilar from the personalities of the classmates she disliked.[40]

It is possible that our attraction to people with a similar personality is based on a similarity we sense intuitively but of which we are not completely conscious, that is, a similarity in emotional maturity.

SIMILARITY IN EMOTIONAL MATURITY AND MENTAL HEALTH

Family therapist Murray Bowen believed that our ability to separate from our birth families and develop as independent individuals defined our level of emotional maturity and mental health (he was criticized by feminist psychologists who believe that our ability to be intimate is as important for mental health as differentiation).

Bowen ranked people according to their levels of "differentiation" from their families of origin. At the bottom were people who were totally "undifferentiated"—unable to separate from their families of origin and still totally enmeshed in them. At the top were people who were totally "differentiated"—individuals who succeeded in separating from their families and had mature, independent, healthy self-identities. Bowen's important contribution to the subject of attraction to the similar is his notion that people choose as intimate partners others who are at the same level of differentiation.[41] Even when one of the partners, usually the husband, seemed significantly more differentiated, Bowen assumed that both partners actually functioned at a similar level of differentiation. My clinical experience concurs. When a crisis occurs in such a couple, the partner who has appeared to be less differentiated often functions at a much higher level as the functioning of the supposed healthier partner deteriorates.

Harville Hendrix, a marriage therapist and pastoral counselor, popularized Bowen's ideas. According to Hendrix, we all suffer from psychological injuries that happened during different stages of our development. We remain stuck in the stage in which the injury was the most serious. We are attracted to people who are stuck in a similar developmental stage and suffered a similar psychological injury.[42]

GENETIC SIMILARITY

One fascinating discovery has been the role that genetic similarity plays in romantic attraction. Evolutionary psychologists believe that an innate biological mechanism influences our sexual attraction, because it is not possible that such an important thing as mate selection will not have been influenced by evolution. This innate biological mechanism directs us to be attracted to potential mates with optimal genetic similarity. We are not attracted to people who are very different from us genetically (people of a different race), and we are not attracted to people who are very similar to us genetically (members of our family).

The existence of this mechanism was documented by evolutionary psychologist Philip Rushton,[43] who examined approximately 1,000 paternity claims brought by women against men with whom they allegedly had borne a child. Because such a claim is resolved by a genetic test, Rushton was able to look at 10 different genetic markers in both partners. He discovered that partners who were involved in a legal battle around a paternity claim—which is to say they had sexual intercourse at least once and had some type of an emotional connection—were closer genetically than were couples, from the same subject pool, who were randomly matched by a computer. Furthermore, in all cases in which the paternity of the man was proven, there was a greater genetic similarity between him and the mother than there was in the cases in which the paternity was disproved. Clearly, genetic similarity is somehow detected and is romantically attractive.

Evolutionary psychologist Ada Lumpert cited a series of studies that testified not only to the existence but also to the advantages of romantic attraction between genetically similar couples. The greater the genetic similarity between couples, the greater their fertility rates, the smaller their rates of natural abortions, and the healthier the children born to them. In addition, there is greater marital harmony, stability, mutual support, and satisfaction from their lives together.[44]

OPPOSITES ATTRACT

> I wanted you
> that day on the beach
> because you were different
> and because you smiled
> and because I knew your world
> was different.
> —Rod McKuen, *Stanyan Street and Other Sorrows*

Although research and folk wisdom tell us that "birds of a feather flock together," folk wisdom also provides us with an opposing rule of human behavior, namely, that "opposites attract." While reading this chapter, the question of attraction to the opposite probably crossed many a reader's mind. After all, we all know that just as the opposite ends of a magnet attract each other, opposite personalities do as well. Let us examine the relevant evidence.

> *We look like total opposites. He's tall and dignified, and I'm short and hysterical. We are opposites in terms of the way we look and the way we act, but because we get along so well we balance each other out. Or maybe we get along so well because we are opposites.*
>
> *When people first see us they think that we kind of look weird because I'm 5 foot 3, and he's 6 foot 5. "You guys don't look like the perfect couple." Then, after they get to know us and see how I know what he's thinking and how he does the same with me, they say "You guys kind of click." It just works really well between the two of us, and a lot of people have been commenting on it.*
>
> *He's very laid back. He could sit through my temper tantrums and not blink an eye.*
>
> *We tend to argue about politics, and we tend to have different outlooks. He's in a different world—not in science. I learned a lot about banking and economics. It's fun.*
>
> *It's interesting. We come from totally different backgrounds.*

In all these quotations, the interviewees were attracted to an aspect that was different in their romantic partner

- in personality ("*He's dignified, and I'm hysterical*")
- in appearance ("*He's tall, and I'm short*")
- in attitudes ("*We argue about politics … we tend to have different outlooks*")
- in areas of interest ("*I'm in science, he's in banking*")
- in background ("*We come from totally different backgrounds*")

In all cases, the difference is viewed as a positive aspect that enhances the relationship ("*It's fun." "It's interesting.*") There is clinical and anecdotal evidence that opposites attract. Highly cerebral men are often attracted to highly emotional women, and placating women are attracted to aggressive men. And, research shows that people in complementary relationships, specifically submissive people with dominant partners, report more satisfaction than do people with similar partners.[45]

Differences can be more exciting than similarities. One of the early studies on this topic showed that although it is nice to discover that we are liked by a person who holds views similar to ours, it is much more exciting to discover that we are liked by a person whose views are different.[46] The reason is that when we are liked by a person who holds opinions different from ours, we assume that the person likes us because of who we are and not merely because of our views.

There are other rewards that differences can provide. When we interact with someone who holds different views, we are more likely to learn something new and valuable.[47] We are also more likely to feel special and unique instead of being just like everyone else.[48]

ATTRACTION TO THE SIMILAR VERSUS ATTRACTION TO THE OPPOSITE

Are we more attracted to people to whom we are similar or to people from whom we are different? Despite the evidence for the rewards obtained from people from whom we are different, the lion's share of the research on attraction indicates that similarity has far greater influence. Here are some examples. Similarity was found to exert the major influence on the definition of the ideal mate.[49] Similarity in attitudes was found to account for 81% of interpersonal attraction.[50] Similar partners were found to be enjoyable and exciting, dissimilar partners repulsive.[51]

Some couple therapists not only point to insufficient research support for the attraction of opposites, but view people's belief in this attraction as a dangerous myth. It is one of those unrealistic beliefs, which also include a "match made in heaven" and the "perfect relationship," that creates unrealistic expectations that are bound to be disappointed. It has even been suggested that such unrealistic myths should be addressed in premarital counseling.[52]

If there is such limited support for the notion that opposites attract, why do people continue to believe in it? A clue to the answer can be found in the words of the woman who said, "*We are complete opposites … but we complement each other.*" In other words, it is not the difference per se, but the compatibility that enhances the attraction.[53] It seems that we are attracted to partners to whom we are similar in general—in background, values, interests, and intelligence—but who complement us in a particular, significant personality dimension.[54]

Family therapist Murray Bowen believes that the general similarity that attracts potential partners to each other is psychological maturity, and the complementary personality dimension is contrasting "defense mechanism."[41] For example, a man who copes by suppressing his feelings will be attracted to women who dramatize their emotions. It may also be that the crucial factor that divides people who are attracted to partners similar to themselves from those who are attracted to partners different from themselves is self-acceptance. Zehava Solomon analyzed the effects of similarity and compatibility on the romantic choices of couples. She discovered that people with high levels of self-acceptance chose partners they perceived as similar to themselves, whereas people with low levels of self-acceptance chose partners they viewed as different from them. Self-acceptance also influenced the degree to which one viewed the partner as different from the "ideal mate" and was willing to live with the compromise.[55]

Returning to the question of what affects romantic attraction more, similarities or differences, the answer is that it depends on the similarities and differences in question and on such things as the couples' levels of self-acceptance and styles of coping. But, the general rule is still the attraction of the similar. Furthermore, people who enjoy their partners perceive the partners as similar to themselves. In other words, perceived similarity can act as an indicator of satisfaction in a relationship that, at times, can be satisfactory because it is complementary.[45]

SUGGESTIONS FOR PEOPLE SEEKING LOVE

Do not look for Prince Charming to come riding on a white horse from a faraway land or for an exotic and mysterious princess to arrive from a unknown kingdom. The person who is similar to you in background, appearance, intelligence, attitudes, interests, and emotional maturity is the person with whom you are most likely to live happily ever after. Furthermore, you are likely to find this most appropriate romantic partner in your nearest and most familiar surroundings. It is, perhaps metaphorically, the boy or girl next door with whom you are most likely to live in harmony and marital bliss. Once you have found someone who is similar to you in all the important dimensions, look for someone whose personality complements yours in a way you find exciting and rewarding. This, according to the evidence presented throughout the chapter, is your "match made in heaven."

Chapter 5

SATISFYING NEEDS
AND RECIPROCATING LOVE:
WE LOVE THOSE WHO LOVE US

Love at best is giving what you need to get.
— Rod McKuen, *Stanyan Street and Other Sorrows*

There are many people who would never
have been in love if they had never heard
love spoken of.
— La Rochefoucauld, *Maximes*, 1665

Love begets love.
— Theodore Roethke, *The Motion*

IT WAS FRIDAY NIGHT. THE GROUP WAS NESTLED INTO LARGE PILLOWS scattered over the thick carpet. The murmur of the ocean down below could be heard through the large glass windows. It was the first evening of a weekend workshop, "Deciphering the Code of Romantic Attraction," in enchanting Big Sur, California. I talked for few minutes about the topics that would be covered in the workshop, mentioning as an example the unconscious attraction between "wounded birds" and "rescuing heroes" and then invited the participants to introduce themselves. Each participant spoke about the pattern in his or her intimate relationships in a way that made it clear that, for several, deciphering the romantic code and some change was urgently needed. The fourth to talk was a lovely and sad-looking petite young woman, who had the round face of a girl. She told the group that she had just gotten out of an intense relationship and was heartbroken because the man, who promised he would always be there for her and always take care of her, had disappointed her bitterly. She was wounded to the core. "I feel like a bird with a broken wing thrown out of her nest," she told the group, teary eyed, "I need desperately to feel loved and cared for." A few more people spoke and then came the turn of a large masculine man. "I just got out of an intense relationship with a woman who reminds me very much of you," he said looking directly at the tiny sad woman. "I had with her the highest highs and the lowest lows. There was nothing I wouldn't do for her, but with time I felt that nothing I did was enough. It was devastating. I need to feel that what I give is important, that I make a difference in the life of the woman I love. The honest truth is that I need to feel like I am her hero." The woman looked at him, her wet eyes glowing with admiration, and he was visibly moved. They continued looking at each other as the rest of the participants spoke, their mutual attraction so obvious you could see the sparks flying. When the group broke up, he went and sat next to her. "I cannot believe what is going on between us," he started. "I think you are the man I have always been looking for," she said. "I have waited all my life to hear a woman say this," he answered.

Studies that investigated who falls in love with whom have identified the important roles played by the needs the beloved satisfies and the amorous effect of knowing that someone is attracted to us. When men and women were asked to describe in detail a time when they felt especially loving or were falling in love, the two most frequent causes for feeling loving or falling in love were (a) the fact that the beloved provided something that the person wanted, needed, or loved; and (b) the fact that the beloved expressed love, need, or appreciation of the person.[1]

THE BELOVED SATISFIES IMPORTANT NEEDS

He is caring and considerate. When he's with me, I know it's the most important thing.

She was so easy to talk to. I could talk to her about anything. She was very understanding.

He's a very good listener. He really understood me. He got everything I said right off the bat. That was new. I'm a bit complicated but he would get things. His comments were always right on the ball, and he was supportive, friendly, understanding. And he was always interested in me and in being with me. He's always interested in what's best for me.

I loved her because of all the things she was willing to do for me.

In all these quotations and in more than half of the romantic attraction interviews, the interviewees attributed their attraction to the fact that the beloved satisfied an important need or provided something of value.[2]

Psychoanalyst Theodore Reik believed that people fall in love with each other for selfish reasons. They sense something lacking in themselves and seek the missing quality in a romantic partner. Thus, each partner provides a portion of the components required for a complete personality.[3]

The selfishness in this type of romantic selection is not consciously articulated. The rational man who is disconnected from his feelings is not saying to himself, "Here is someone who will complete me." What he is thinking, as indeed I was told by such a man, is, "She was cute and lively and seemed like a warm and sensitive person. She approached me and introduced herself. I tend to be rather uptight with new people, but with her it was easy. I felt very comfortable in her company." Likewise, the emotional woman who is uncomfortable expressing her intellectual abilities is not saying, "Here is a rational man who will complete me." Rather, as the man's wife told me, she is thinking, "He seemed very different from other men. He looked like a very smart man, a thinking man, a true intellectual. I was very attracted to him."

A similar idea about the utility of our romantic attractions was proposed by Bernard Murstein, who explained who marries whom from the perspective of *social exchange theory*.[4] According to this economic model of human behavior, people's romantic choices, just like their market behavior, are motivated by a desire to maximize their earnings and minimize their losses. The more rewards (such as love, support, or sex) that a relationship provides and the lower the cost (for example, doing what one does not want to do), the more satisfying the relationship is and the longer it will last.

Murstein believes that attraction depends on the "fairest exchange value" of personal assets and liabilities that each partner brings to the relationship. He views people as rational beings who choose to marry a person who provides them with the best all-around package. According to Murstein, love is the feeling of mutual satisfaction that two partners derive from knowing that they got the best "exchange value" possible. In other words, they made the best possible deal.

This rather unromantic view of our romantic choices is shared by other psychologists and sociologists convinced that we are attracted to people who provide us with the most rewards for the lowest price.[5] If people behave like rational, calculating, businesspeople in other social relationships with colleagues, neighbors, and friends, would they not be much more likely to do so when choosing a mate? Accordingly, it has been argued that the ideology of the marketplace invaded and altered love and sex by transforming intimacies into commodities;[6] people pursue the important goal of making a good deal in marriage by evaluating, rationally, the alternatives available in the market. Here, for example, is the way renowned sociologist Erving Goffman described such a romantic choice:

> A marriage proposal in our society tends to be a way in which a man sums up his social attributes and suggests to a woman that hers are not so much better as to preclude a merger or a partnership.[7]

Undeniably, young urban professionals were said to consider each other's assets, including country house, income potential, schooling, and family, before deciding on suitable partners.

Does this steely-eyed materialism give a true picture of falling in love? A man in the romantic attraction study who felt that he and his wife had made a good deal in getting together described their "exchange" in far more romantic terms:

> *We are very good for each other. She needed me, she needed someone who would respect her, and I needed her too … . I feel sorry for people who don't have this kind of relationship. She makes me feel complete. What hurts most about being away from her are the simple things—going to the store, making lunch. The best thing is the actual living. We love each other, and we love our relationship.*

This man described love as the main asset that he and his future wife brought to their life together. Of course, love is only one of the assets couples bring to relationships. According to *resource theory*, people use six categories of resource: love (warmth, affection, care, and comfort); status (which can either increase one's sense of self-worth or decrease it); information (advice or knowledge); property (money); goods (things); and services (such as cooking or car repair).[8]

In most interactions, we tend to exchange resources of the same type; we return love when we receive love and offer help or service when we receive help or service. When students were given descriptions of something they received from a friend—a hug, a compliment, or lecture notes—and were asked how they were likely to reciprocate, the data showed clearly that they tended to reciprocate in kind—love for love and service for service.[9] A notable exception to the reciprocity rule of giving what we have received and receiving what we have given was found in personal advertisements, in which women and men tend to offer different things and ask for different things when looking for romantic partners.[10]

Dale Carnegie, in his advice in *How to Win Friends and Influence People*, turned the link between satisfying needs and attraction into a recommendation. If you want someone to love you, make sure you satisfy for that person an important need we all share, the need for appreciation. Express genuine interest in the person, writes Carnegie, be pleasant, smile, remember that a person's name is to him or her the sweetest and most important sound. Be a good listener, encourage the person to talk about him- or herself, make him or her feel important, and give honest and sincere appreciation.[11] A number of studies supported Carnegie's recommendations; we tend to like people who appreciate us and compliment us.[12]

Well aware that compliments are not always genuine, it is important to us that appreciation does not disguise an ingratiation that is aimed at getting us to do or give something. It was shown that, although people liked most an evaluator who gave them a positive evaluation, as compared to a neutral or negative evaluation, the liking dropped sharply when they suspected the evaluator's motives.[13] This finding helps us understand why highly attractive people do not take seriously the compliments they receive for their performance. They assume, for good reason, that their attractiveness has influenced compliments that, in fact, are not genuine.

Although we may like positive, pleasant people who compliment us and express appreciation for our views, we respect more the people who are critical, especially when their criticism is directed at someone else. We tend to view such people as more intelligent, even if unpleasant. In a study that showed this, students read two book reviews, similar in style and quality, that had appeared in the *New York Times Review of Books*. One review was positive; the other negative. Results showed that the students saw the negative reviewer as more intelligent, competent, and expert and saw the positive reviewer as a nicer and more pleasant person.[14]

Criticism is always difficult to hear, hence Dale Carnegie's Rule 1: Do not criticize, condemn, or complain. It is especially difficult when the criticism comes from someone we respect. It is doubly hard for people with low self-esteem, for whom approval and acceptance provide significant rewards and criticism and rejection constitute powerful punishments. People with low self-esteem were shown to be more attracted to members of their group after receiving from them positive evaluations and to be more repelled by group members who gave them negative evaluations.[15] Thus, it is important for people with low self-esteem to ask themselves if they prefer a romantic partner to be pleasant, kind, and sensitive; to compliment them; to be good company; and to express genuine interest in them and the things that are important to them or whether they prefer someone of superior intelligence, knowledge, and education from whom they can learn. Feeling judged and criticized can be part of the package when a person with low self-esteem chooses a brilliant and superior person for a romantic partner.

Of course, everyone wants a partner who is pleasant, kind, and sensitive as well as intelligent and knowledgeable. And obviously, a pleasant personality and a brilliant mind are not mutually exclusive. The point I am trying to make has to do with the effect of self-esteem on our romantic choices. When a person with low self-esteem chooses a person to admire, the result is an asymmetry in which one partner is the admirer and the other the admired. This type of asymmetry is bound to create later problems in the relationship. But, when both partners admire each other, the result is a positive loop of mutual admiration that can last indefinitely.

Most of us prefer romantic partners who most appropriately gratify important psychological, emotional, intellectual, sexual, spiritual, and social needs. The best candidate for gratifying those needs is someone whose needs are complementary.

LOVERS' COMPLEMENTARY NEEDS

Plato, the fifth century B.C. philosopher, had an interesting theory about the origin of love. In *The Symposium*, he expounded on this theory as he told "the myth of Aristophanes."

THE MYTH OF ARISTOPHANES

In primeval time, humans were round with four hands and four feet, back and sides forming a circle. They had one head with two faces looking in opposite directions. These humans were insolent, and the gods would not suffer such arrogance. So Zeus punished them by cutting them in two, thereby condemning each half to look for the other. When one half finds the other, "the pair are lost in an amazement of love and friendship and intimacy ... . This meeting and melting in one another's arms, this becoming one instead of two is the very expression of "the ancient need" ... . The reason is that human nature was originally one and we were whole, and the desire and pursuit of that whole is called love.

Plato described primeval humanity as divided into three types of people: men, women, and the androgynous, who were a union of the two. Men had a pair of masculine sex organs, women had a pair of feminine sex organs, and the androgynous had both a masculine and a feminine sex organ. After humans were cut in two, a man's separate halves that longed to be reunited became homosexuals; the woman's separate halves became lesbians. The separate halves of an androgynous individual became heterosexuals attracted to members of the opposite sex.

According to this Greek myth, people long to find in romantic love that which is missing in themselves. Here, we come back to complementarity as a cause of attraction, not in the simplistic formulation of "opposites attract," but in the deeper meaning of mutually satisfying important needs.

Most people, like the split androgynous, fall in love with a person of the opposite sex, a person who has different and compatible sex organs. These biological sex differences are often associated with different gender roles.[16] In traditional marriages, men and women are expected to exhibit different assets and skills and perform different tasks. Breadwinning has been "men's core role" and motherhood "women's core role."[17] Even among the growing number of egalitarian couples,[18] the attraction of complementary roles remains. A woman who hates cooking will find appealing a man whose hobby is gourmet cooking, and a man who lacks any mechanical sense is likely to find a woman mechanic especially fascinating.

Robert Winch believes that love is the experience of two people jointly deriving maximum gratification for important psychological needs. We are attracted to and tend to marry people whose psychological needs complement our own. Psychological needs can be complementary in content, as in rational twined with emotional, or in degree, as in an alliance between strong and weak control needs. In a well-known study done over 40 years ago, Winch conducted in-depth interviews with 25 married couples about their early childhoods experiences and about their current lives. The couples also responded to a battery of personality tests. On the basis of the interviews and personality tests, the psychological needs of the couples were assessed by five experienced psychoanalysts. Their well-known conclusion was that people tend to choose marriage partners whose psychological needs complement their own needs—more than they choose partners whose needs are similar to their own.[19]

Romantic partners can also complement each other's sexual, intellectual, and spiritual needs—one partner enjoys being active sexually, and the other prefers being passive; one enjoys teaching, and the other prefers being taught. The more complementary the needs, the easier and more satisfying their gratification.

RECIPROCATING LOVE: WE LOVE TO FEEL LOVED

For some people, the most attractive thing about a romantic partner is the fact that he or she first found them attractive.

> *What attracted me most was her choosing me.*
> *He went through three different people to get my phone number.*
> *What attracted me to her at first was the fact that she liked me.*
> *I'm very shy. I tend to like men who find me attractive.*

Analysis of the romantic attraction interviews showed that, in almost half the cases, an indication of attraction and romantic interest played an important role in the initial attraction.[20] Feeling desired is clearly attractive.

Elliot Aronson best summarized the influence of reciprocal attraction: "The single most powerful determinant of whether one person will like another is whether the other likes that person. What's more, merely believing someone likes you can initiate a spiraling series of events that promote increasingly positive feelings between you and the other person."[21] Let us imagine, for example, that a man and woman are introduced at a party by a mutual friend and engage in a brief conversation. A few days later, the woman runs into the friend on the street, and the friend tells her that after the party the man had some complimentary things to say about her, including that he was attracted to her. How is this woman likely to act next time she and the man meet? Chances are, the woman's knowledge that the man finds her attractive will lead her to like him; and she will behave in a way that lets the man know that she likes him, too. She will probably smile more, disclose more about herself, and generally behave in a more likable manner than if she had not learned that the man liked her. Faced with her warm and likable manner, the man's attraction and fondness for her will undoubtedly grow. The man, in turn, will convey his attraction in ways that make him even more attractive to the woman ... and so on.

The rule of reciprocity in attraction works even when we assume erroneously that another person finds us attractive and likable. In a study that demonstrated this, people were led to believe that another person either liked or disliked them. In subsequent interaction with that person, the people who thought they were liked behaved in more likable ways. They were warmer, more pleasant, disclosed more about themselves, and agreed more with the other person than did the people who thought they were disliked. What is more significant for our discussion is that the people who erroneously believed that they were liked were in fact liked more after the interaction. In other words, the behavior of the people who thought they were liked led the others to reciprocate in kind.[22]

This finding demonstrated again the power of romantic attraction as a self-fulfilling prophecy. The master in the use of this power was Don Juan, who seduced endless numbers of women by giving each the feeling that she was the most attractive, most desirable woman in the world.

Pretense of romantic attraction influences not only the person on the receiving end, but also the actor. This important fact was even known in ancient Rome. Ovid, the Roman poet, in his counsel to lovers seeking romantic success, said: "Often the pretender begins to love truly and ends by becoming what he feigned to be" (*Ars Amatoria*).

Love generates love. A children's song describes the circle of love with charming simplicity:

> Love is something if you give it away,
> you end up having more.
> It's just like a magic penny
> hold it tight, you wouldn't have any.
> Lend it, spend it, you'll have so many
> they'll roll all over the floor.

A word of caution. It should be obvious that, in an ongoing romantic relationship, being loved more than one loves is not necessarily a positive experience—definitely not as positive as it was to discover that someone was attracted to you. It can evoke guilt, which can lead to anger, which can lead to some negative feelings about the person who loves us too much or more than we want to be loved. People who tend to find themselves in relationships in which they love too much know well that it is impossible to force someone to love you. It is also inadvisable to cheat, bribe, seduce, demand, or threaten to get love. Forcing love on someone who is clearly uninterested will not make that someone's negative feelings turn into love. The only thing we can influence, to some extent, is our own feelings. If we want to live a life of love, we have to be open to love, and we have to choose romantic partners who are open to loving us.

SATISFYING NEEDS VERSUS RECIPROCATING LOVE: WHICH PLAYS A GREATER ROLE IN LOVE?

In romantic attraction, how does the role of feeling loved compare to the role of gratifying needs and the other variables we have discussed so far? An extensive survey of stories people told about the partners they chose for love and marriage revealed 11 factors that influence this choice.[23] Some of these variables have been discussed, and some are discussed in other chapters:

Variables That Influence Falling in Love

1. Similarity in attitudes, background, personality traits
2. Geographic proximity
3. Desirable characteristics of personality and appearance
4. Reciprocal affection, the fact that the other likes us
5. Satisfying needs
6. Physical and emotional arousal
7. Social influences, norms, and the approval of people in our circle
8. Specific cues in the beloved's voice, eyes, posture, way of moving
9. Readiness for a romantic relationship
10. Opportunities to be alone together
11. Mystery, in the situation or the person

When you consider your most memorable experience of falling in love, which of these variables played the greatest role? Which did not play a role at all?

To examine the relative influence of the 11 variables, Arthur Aron and his colleagues examined three types of falling-in-love accounts. The first was a detailed account obtained from people who had fallen in love during the previous 8 months. Analysis of the stories, which averaged three pages, revealed that reciprocal liking and attraction were mentioned in practically all the stories. Satisfying needs appeared in fewer than a quarter of the stories. The second type of account was obtained from people who were asked to "just tell the story" of either "falling in love" or of "falling in friendship" on 11 × 14 cm index cards, detailing how it happened, what they felt, and what resulted. Analysis revealed that two thirds of these stories mentioned reciprocal liking. Satisfying needs was mentioned in only one tenth of the stories. The third type of account was obtained using a questionnaire. Respondents were asked to recall their most recent experiences of falling in love, especially the moment when they had felt a strong attraction, and then to rank their feelings on different scales, for example, the extent to which the person you fell in love with "filled your needs." In the analysis of their responses, again reciprocal affection appeared most frequently as the reason for falling in love. Filling needs was mentioned in one third of the cases.[23]

Why was filling needs mentioned so infrequently in all three types of accounts of falling in love? One explanation is that satisfying needs is something people are uncomfortable admitting, even to themselves. We all prefer to believe that falling in love is pure of selfish motives. In the questionnaire, people were asked directly whether their beloved filled an important need for them. It is possible that respondents reported the socially desirable answer rather than the full extent to which filling needs truly affected their romantic choices.

The descriptions of the most significant romantic relationships in the romantic attraction study suggested how often filling significant needs played a role in the initial attraction. When a young woman says, *"He is very loving and makes every effort so I will enjoy myself. Like he knows that I like champagne, so he always buys champagne when I arrive,"* it is obvious that what the man does for her plays a role in her attraction toward him. And, when a man says, *"What attracted me at first was that she used to buy things for me,"* it is clear that his attraction to her is associated with her actions. Indeed, as noted, over half the romantic attraction interviews, as compared to fewer than a third in Aron's studies, mentioned the partner's satisfying a need as part of the initial attraction.

In summary, even if there may be a question about the degree of influence of need satisfaction on romantic attraction, there is no question about the fact that it plays a role. As for reciprocity in love, there is no question about its central role.

The best way to end this chapter is with the finding I cite most often to couples with whom I work. Over time, the love and rewards that couples give to each other in an intimate relationship become related to the love and rewards that they receive from that relationship.[24] When we express love and show consideration, we increase the level of love and rewards in the relationship and with them the probability that we will receive more love and rewards in it.

SUGGESTIONS FOR PEOPLE SEEKING LOVE

It is wise to use both the power of reciprocity of love and the power of need satisfaction in the search for a partner in love.

Starting with need satisfaction, it is important to address both your needs and the needs of your candidate for love. In other words, what do you want, and what are you willing to give? If you want to have your needs met in a romantic relationship, you should first figure out what your most important needs are. Do you need to be taken care of and protected? To be looked up to and admired? To be listened to and validated? To be challenged and stimulated? Once you define what it is that you are looking for, you increase the likelihood of finding it. You should be careful to look for a potential partner who is willing and able to provide it. If not, it is better to look elsewhere. Because you know that people are attracted to partners who have either similar or opposite needs, your search can be more focused, preferably leading you to someone whose needs complement your own.

The best strategy with a promising candidate is to be attentive, open, warm, and pleasant. Show interest and be a good listener; give honest and sincere appreciation. Most important, be sensitive to your partner's needs and respect his or her right to feel, think, and do things differently—even if you are convinced that your way of expressing care is the right way. Insensitive and excessive giving is as destructive to romantic relationships as are withholding and distancing.

The information about the reciprocity of love leads to a more general recommendation. Do not hold back love, waiting for the perfect partner who will come carrying the magic key to your heart. Giving love freely and generously to the less-than-perfect mortals who happen to cross your path can assure you of receiving many coins of love from those around you. Among them, you just might find your true love. If you want to live a life of love, you need to start the cycle of love. Then, often, the love you send "over the water" will come back to you in surprising, wonderful ways.

Sounds simple, doesn't it? Why is it then that so many people do not do this and sentence themselves to loveless lives? Why are some people attracted to those who torment them, cause them pain, and reject them? Why are so many attracted to those who do not reciprocate their love? These types of questions are addressed in the second part of the book.

Chapter 6

THE COURSE OF ROMANTIC LOVE: FALLING IN LOVE AS A PROCESS

The course of true love.
— Shakespeare, *A Midsummer Night's Dream*

This bud of love, by summer's ripening breath,
May prove a beauteous flower when next we meet.
— Shakespeare, *Romeo and Juliet*

EVEN WHEN SHE FIRST SAW HIM, SHE FELT A POWERFUL ATTRACTION. THERE was something about his tall lean frame, the head full of curls, the humorous twinkle in his eyes. He exuded masculine energy that made her heart beat faster. When they were introduced, he gave her a long look that made it clear that the attraction was mutual. The disappointment she felt when she discovered that he was leaving the country the next day made no sense given the fact that they had only spoken for a few minutes. It was several years before they met again, and at first she did not remember meeting him before. But her heart recognized him right away and responded with the same intense attraction and strange longing. Again, a mutual friend introduced them at a party, and again she found herself drawn to him, to the twinkle in his eyes and his powerful masculine energy. When he invited her to dance, she felt that energy engulfing her, pulling her toward him. She did not resist. Being with him seemed so natural, as if she had known him all her life. Because the party was noisy, they went out to the garden to talk. She found herself laughing, charmed by his wit and sense of humor. When they met again a few days later, he invited her for a walk on the beach. Somehow, it did not surprise her. It seemed only natural that her favorite place would be the place he would choose for their first date. The more they talked and the more she discovered about him, the more amazed she was about the similarities between them. Like her, he traveled extensively and was now ready to settle down. They came from a similar background, had a similar childhood, and were the first born in similar close-knit families. They both went to graduate school and had similar professional aspirations. But, what was most amazing was that they wanted the same, seemingly impossible, thing from an intimate relationship: total intimacy and total freedom. Their love was the most

71

passionate affair she had ever had, and it continued to grow deeper and stronger with the years of their marriage.

> *I didn't feel physically attracted to him until we went out a couple of times. So it was a kind of gradual thing. It took a year before we were really close. We knew each other because we went to the same school. He was a kind of all-around nice guy, friendly, warm. He had a friendly presence, a warm presence. And he was a kind of lively, good-humored sort. And I thought he was cute, nothing stunning. Down to earth.*
>
> *I thought she was gorgeous. From the first time I saw her I was really attracted to her. And then I got to know her. We were in a couple of classes together, and we would do homework together and just joke around. And so sooner or later we just started going out. She was a really neat person, fun to talk to, fun to get to know, fun to hang out with, fun to goof around with or be intimate with.*
>
> *I didn't like him at first. I didn't like him at all. He didn't like me either. We would kind of butt heads when we first met. We had the same job, but in different branches. We were in class together, and there was only one seat available, and I sat next to him. I didn't like him. I don't know … . He started talking to me, so we ended up being friends. And he was there for me after the divorce. He was there for me, and I guess it just went on from there. It was different than any other sort of attraction. It was the way he treated me, his ideas, his attitude, his overall values and views about life.*
>
> *We sat next to each other in class, and we sort of became good friends. I can't remember who wanted to become intimate, her or me, but it progressed … .*
>
> *I met him when I was a freshman and he was a senior. We lived in the same dorm, and he was always a nice guy, but you know, I really wasn't interested in him because he was so much older. I mean, 3 years can seem like a lot. Here I was taking Freshman English, and he was finishing his major. I mean, he was big-time. He was friendly and asked me out a couple of times, but nothing more than that at first. My heart didn't beat real fast. It wasn't love at first sight. We were just buddies. I never even thought about it for a year and a half. After that period we started getting closer. We were talking on the phone a lot, we started doing things together. We liked a lot of the same things … . There was some tension at first because I still thought of him as a friend, but he didn't necessarily think of me that way. I felt great actually.*

Analysis of the romantic attraction interviews showed that, in one-third of the cases, falling in love was described as a gradual process. Only in about one-tenth of the cases was love at first sight.[1]

When people fall in love, different variables play roles in different stages. The backdrop of the entire process is cultural. From birth, we are inculcated with certain expectations about falling in love. In Western society, the romantic ideal calls for a man and a woman, rather than a same-sex couple, to meet, fall in love, marry, and live happily ever after. When a man and a woman meet, they share these expectations of the way things ought to progress between them. In the getting-acquainted stage—more likely when a couple lives or works at the same location, and, preferably, when in a state of arousal—appearance is important, especially to men. But, in order for a romance to spark, the couple needs to feel attracted to each other's personality. For the spark to ignite, it is best if they are similar in background, personal assets, views, and emotional maturity. For a romance to evolve into a relationship, the love must be reciprocated and gratify their most important psychological needs.

A romantic relationship starts in different ways. It may be love at first sight— "*From the first time I met him, there was something that attracted me to him,*" or it may develop after years of friendship: "*We knew each other 5 years, no, 4 years, as friends … . When I returned from a trip abroad, none of my old friends was around, so I called him, and then it started getting more serious.*" A romantic relationship may start at a significant encounter ("*It was a setup. We talked the whole night*") or evolve into a deep connection over time ("*At first, I wasn't attracted to her, but since we were involved in the same project, we talked a lot. We became closer and closer. Then I became more attracted to her.*"). In all these cases, a state of acquaintance, such as friendship or mere physical attraction, develops into a state of passionate, romantic love—a development that has been documented in many studies.[2]

In secular Western society at the start of the 21st century, romantic love is an important element in the choice of a mate. Even in the arranged marriages of some traditional societies, romantic love is an important background criterion.[3]

Despite the different starting points and different rates of development among romantic relationships, there is usually a certain point at which both partners say, "This is love!" This turning point starts a series of physiological changes.[4] It is often preceded and marked by a special mutual gaze. Victor Hugo described the power of this gaze in *Les Miserables* (1862):

> Few people dare now to say that two beings have fallen in love because they have looked at each other. Yet it is in this way that love begins, and in this way only. The rest is only the rest, and comes afterwards. Nothing is more real than these great shocks which two souls give each other in exchanging this spark.

THE STAGES OF FALLING IN LOVE

How do people fall in love? Several theories rest on an assumption that romantic relationships go through certain steps that occur in a certain order; thus, the falling-in-love process is described as a series of stages that are qualitatively different. In some theories, falling in love happens in two stages; in others, it happens in three or even four stages. But, all stage theories assume that there is a qualitative difference among the different stages.

According to a *two-stage theory* of love, falling in love involves a two-step screening process. People screen first for those they consider unsuitable. They do not notice these people when they meet, and they forget them right away. A typical example is screening for age. Many young people do not even notice older people because they do not perceive them as potential romantic partners. When someone does not fit our selection criteria, we simply do not notice them. Thus, the unsuitable becomes invisible. In the second stage, people select the most appropriate partners among those who are judged suitable.[5]

The initial automatic screening of unsuitables is influenced by social norms that dictate for us the category of people that contains suitable marriage partners. Robert Winch coined the term *candidates field of eligible spouse* to describe the range of people with whom we are permitted to fall in love and marry.[6] In other words, the society or specific subculture in which we live determines the first stage of screening and happens even before we start operating our own love filters.

Most societies use similarities in background and social assets as their main selection criteria. Societal norms tend to prefer that marriage partners be from the same race, social and economic class, religion, and age group. A person who does not conform to these social dictates, such as an old man who marries a young woman, is often criticized and ridiculed and can become the object of jokes and gossip. Reactions of this sort teach both the person to whom they are directed, as well as the people watching from the sidelines, who is appropriate and who is inappropriate as a marriage partner.

Societies influence the screening process of romantic partners in two major ways. Most prominently, social norms reward people who follow the norm and punish those who deviate, as, for example, when friends and relatives shun or express outright criticism of an unsuitable, potential partner. Second, meetings are arranged between people who are judged to be suitable romantic partners, such as parties in schools, workplaces, and clubs or social events arranged for singles of a certain age group and a certain social or economic status.[7] Societal agents such as parents, teachers, friends, and the media teach the social norms. They reward and encourage suitable romantic connections and discourage unsuitable ones.

Only after people pass through this social screening and choose a suitable partner can falling in love take place. And, according to another stage theory of love, it also happens in two stages. In the first stage, shared values are most important; in the second stage, compatibility of needs is most important.[8]

In the first stage of a romantic relationship, similarity in views, values, and interests is especially important. Disagreement about a value that even one of the partners considers significant limits the possibility of a romantic relationship. Consider, for example, a devoutly religious woman who finds herself attracted to a man who is a committed atheist. If she cannot see herself building a life with this man, she will no doubt try to quench her attraction to him. Or, consider a cowboy who loves open space and makes his living raising cattle who is attracted to an urban woman who loves theater and opera and is an editor. Because it is unlikely that two such people will be able to make a living and be happy in the same place, it is unlikely that a relationship between them will go beyond the stage of romance.

It is important to note, however, that when people are strongly attracted to each other they are capable of ignoring such glaring differences; they assume that they can overcome incredible odds with the sheer power of their love.

Only growing intimacy can provide couples with the foundation of trust that enables them to reveal their deeper psychological needs to each other. Most people have to feel a certain degree of security in the relationship before they can remove their defenses and admit their more infantile, immature, and, some say, neurotic needs. This is why complementary emotional needs become central in the later stage of the relationship.

The most famous *three-stage theory* of love was proposed some 25 years ago by Bernard Murstein. According to this theory, in the first stage of a love relationship, the *stimulus* stage, external features such as appearance have the greatest impact. In the second, the *value* stage, the attraction is based primarily on similarity in values and interests. In the third and last stage, the *role* stage, the couple examines whether they function well in the roles related to their identity as a couple: friend, lover, roommate, and husband and wife.[9]

In the stimulus stage, people know only what they can learn from minimal interaction. Attraction is a function of the other's physical, mental, and social attributes. Potential partners assess and arrive at an overall evaluation of the other, which each compares to his or her own overall attractiveness. Only if both partners perceive each other's attractiveness as roughly equal to their own can the relationship progress to the value stage. When a man and a woman begin dating, they talk about their views about things. If they discover that their attitudes are similar, their attraction grows, and they can move to the role stage, in which they become concerned about their ability to function as a unit. How is each of them expected to act in certain situations or roles? How are holidays and birthdays going to be celebrated? Should a wife develop an independent career? Should a husband cook? And so on. When both partners discover that the other behaves in a way that fits his or her expectations and that their needs are complementary, the relationship can become highly satisfying.

Other stage theories talk about four stages of falling in love. One of these theories focuses on rewards, roles, and norms (rather than compatibility in deep psychological needs). A romantic relationship develops in the following stages: In the first stage, the *exploration* stage, the rewards and cost of the relationship are weighed. In the second, the *negotiation* stage, the relationship is defined, and the behaviors that bring the most rewards to both partners are learned. In the third stage, *commitment*, mutual dependence develops between the partners as a result of their deepening involvement with each other. In the final stage of *formalizing*, both the couple and the people in the couple's social circle view the relationship as sanctioned by society.[10] Not a word about love!

According to another multiple-stage theory of love, all romantic relationships start with the attraction based on similarity, which causes feelings of comfort and closeness: *"You also love staying at home next to the fireplace and reading on stormy nights?! That's incredible!!"* When couples feel close and comfortable with each other, they start opening up about their deeper issues and needs. Only if they feel and express empathic understanding for each other in the self-disclosure stage can the relationship move on to the next stages. The final stages of a love relationship demand compatibility in the roles involved in being a couple, making a commitment to the relationship and the development of an identity as a couple.[11]

One of the most complex and comprehensive stage theories of love was proposed by Israeli psychologist Avner Ziv. The theory is based on interviews with men and women, young and old, married and single, who were asked to describe an experience in which they fell in love. Analysis of the interviews suggested that falling in love involves emotional, behavioral, mental, and social components. Ziv combined all these components into a four-stage model of falling in love.[12]

The first stage of *attraction* is influenced by past experiences and the partners' physical attributes, physical beauty being the most prominent among them. In the second stage of *examination*, the partners examine their social compatibility (social and economic background), their intellectual compatibility (education and areas of interest), and their emotional compatibility (feeling of comfort with each other). Because both partners know at this stage that they are on trial, they try to present as positive a picture of themselves as possible. In the third stage of *self-revealing*, intimacy is created when deeper thoughts and feelings, including negative ones, are revealed to the partner. In the fourth and last stage of *mutual expectations*, each partner learns about the expectations of the other and makes a conscious effort to respond to these expectations in all areas (including economic, emotional, social, and sexual).

When a couple first meets, if there is an attraction between them, the romantic relationship will start. If there is no attraction, it will not. As the relationship progresses and they examine each other, if there is no social, intellectual, or emotional compatibility, the relationship will end. If compatibility exists, the relationship will continue evolving. With intimacy growing between them, the couple starts revealing vulnerabilities and negative sides to each other. If either partner does not understand or fears what is revealed, the relationship ends. If they understand and are empathic to each other's vulnerabilities, the relationship continues to the stage of mutual expectations. If partners do not satisfy each other's needs and expectations, the relationship is terminated. If the needs and expectations of both partners are filled, the result is love—mutual dependence respectful of each partner's independence.[12]

Which one of these stage theories of love is the correct one? Or, better still, is any of the theories correct? One critical question in the evaluation of any stage theory is the question of the order of the stages. In Murstein's theory (stimulus, value, role), for example, does the value stage always precede the role stage? Or, are couples able to deal with role issues—"Will she be able to be a professor's wife?" "Can I invite him to the New Year's Eve party at the office?"—before they have examined their similarity in values? A number of studies have shown weak evidence for the existence of fixed stages in the development of intimate relationships. One of these studies referred specifically to Murstein's stage theory.[13] Another study asked newly-wed couples to describe how their relationship had evolved. Analysis of their stories revealed different patterns of development from the first meeting until the marriage.[14] The romantic attraction interviews I analyzed also showed that couples go through different stages at different times and at different paces in the development of their love relationships.

Even if we accept the premise that romantic relationships change and evolve with time, it does not mean that we have to accept the existence of definite stages in which different variables play key roles. Indeed, there are several theories that describe the evolution of an intimate relationship without describing distinct stages. Here is the evolution of a romantic relationship according to one such theory.

The couple starts meeting more frequently and for longer periods of time. They feel comfortable when together and make efforts to meet again and again. They become more open with each other, are less reserved, and are ready to express negative feelings. They develop a unique style of communication. They develop an ability to predict each other's expectations, feelings, and views. They adjust to each other's behaviors and goals. Their investment in the relationship and its importance for them grow. They consider each other in their goals. They feel growing affection, trust, and love. They view the relationship as unique and irreplaceable. They see each other as partners.[15]

In another example, the development of a romantic relationship is described in terms of the growing influence and interdependence of the partnership. As the partners' influence on each other grows and as their mutual dependence grows, the relationship becomes closer and more intimate. Because this is a gradual development that takes time, only long-term relationships can achieve true closeness, intimacy, and love.[16]

And, did you know that couples first choose each other according to physical traits but only stay together and marry if they are also similar psychologically? The proof is that although married couples and dating couples have a similar number of shared physical traits, married couples have significantly more (11 to 1) shared psychological traits.[17]

FALLING IN LOVE AS A FUNNEL-SHAPED SCREENING PROCESS

All this brings me to propose that falling in love is the result of a funnel-shaped screening process. There are no distinct stages in this process but "love screens" at different points of the funnel.[18] The first five chapters described these love screens. Now, we can see how they operate in the process of falling in love.

To enter the funnel of love, people need to grow up in a society that acknowledges and values romantic love; they need to be socialized to expect falling in love (the subject of the introduction). Geographic proximity (the subject of the first chapter) determines to a large extent the pool of potential candidates for first encounters. A state of emotional arousal (the subject of the second chapter) increases the probability that a pleasant encounter will be defined as romantic. Only after they are ready to fall in love, which is to say they have met and are aroused, are potential partners likely to notice each other's exciting appearance and pleasant personality (the subject of the third chapter). Having noticed each other and concluded that they deserve each other's romantic attention, they start heart-to-heart talks that help them discover whether they have similar values and interests (the subject of the fourth chapter). The greater the similarity, the greater the feelings of comfort and validation and the greater the desire for closeness. The greater the discrepancies, the more misunderstandings and conflicts that can break up the relationship. A notable exception to the rule of attraction to the similar is the attraction to the complementary. With growing involvement and intimacy, a couple's deep psychological needs are revealed and with them their ability and willingness to satisfy those needs (the subject of the fifth chapter). The higher a couple's willingness and ability to satisfy each other's needs are, the higher their mutual attraction and love.

Even this long summary does not do justice to the complexity of the process of falling in love. Perhaps it is better this way because the result is the subjective feeling of every couple that their experience of falling in love was unique only to them and could have happened to no one else in the whole world. Han Suin said it most poignantly in the preface to *A Many Splendoured Thing* (1952):

> Do you really think, then, that other people get as much pleasure and happiness out of their bodies as we do?

> Dear Love, even the paunchy, ugly people of this world believe they love as much as we do and forever. It is the illusion of all lovers to think themselves unique and their words immortal.

I cannot end the discussion of stage theories of love without mentioning my favorite stage theory, a two-stage theory proposed by one of Italy's great sociologists, Francesco Alberoni, in his book *Falling in Love*.[19]

According to Alberoni, the significant stages of a romantic relationship are simply "falling in love" and "love." If falling in love is like taking off or flying, then love is like landing. Falling in love is being high above the clouds; love is standing firmly on the ground. Falling in love is like a flower; love is like a fruit. The fruit comes from the flower, but they are two different things. "And there is really no point in asking if the flower is better than the fruit or vice versa. By the same token, there is no point in asking whether the nascent state is better than the institution. One does not exist without the other. Life is made of both."

Falling in love is a positive, energizing process that causes both physiological and psychological changes. Arthur Aron demonstrated the positive influence of passionate love on people's self-concept. Over a 10-week period, he followed students who were in love and students who were not in love. Results of the comparison revealed that the students who were in love expressed greater self-confidence and higher self-concept. In addition, they expanded the scope and range of their self-definitions, probably as a result of their partner's admiration of certain aspects in their personalities that they had ignored or underappreciated.[20] In other words, falling in love helps develop self-confidence and enhances self-concept; it makes us expand emotionally and develop more expansive personalities.[21] Clearly, falling in love is a positive and highly recommended experience.

GENDER DIFFERENCES IN THE PROCESS OF FALLING IN LOVE

In the romantic attraction study, a similar percentage of men and women described falling in love as a process.[22] However, there was a significant difference in their description of the process. Men were more often initially attracted to the physical appearance of the woman, followed by a discovery of her charming personality. Women, on the other hand, frequently felt no initial physical attraction. The attraction followed the development of friendship and emotional intimacy. To put it more bluntly, for many men the physical attraction caused the relationship; for many women, the relationship caused the physical attraction.

Here are examples of the way women described the development of their romantic relationships.

> *"The relationship started as a friendship. I was actually going out with his roommate, so I spent a lot of time in their house, and we became close friends. We got to know each other really well. We got to be close friends before we became involved. As soon as the other relationship was over, he and I became romantically involved. I felt very attracted to him because I loved him so much. He had been attracted to me ever since we met. He initially told me that he loved me. I wasn't interested in him. Then I started to fall in love with him.*
>
> *I wasn't attracted to him at the beginning, but he was there during the difficult time. He's not a macho type. I didn't have to put on an act. He was always nice to me, really understanding when I was upset. Now we have a friendship behind the relationship. He's my best friend.*
>
> *I didn't find him particularly sexy. We were just buddies, and we started getting closer. On our first date, I didn't really know what to expect, I wasn't really thinking about him in a romantic way. I guess he had a different idea than I had, so there was some tension at first because I still thought of him as a friend.*

The following are examples of how men described the development of their romantic relationships:

> *I liked her. She would tell you it was for the wrong reasons because I was always looking at her. She's slightly top heavy, and my eyes were always wandering. And she knew it too ... . Before we really got into the relationship, we talked about a lot of things.*

I thought she was gorgeous. From the first time I saw her, I was really attracted to her. And then I got to know her. She was a really neat person.

It started initially as a sexual thing. I met her in the students' office. She was a secretary in the office. We started talking. There were interesting things about her physically, also her personality. She's one of the nicest people I've met.

These quotations suggest that for many men the initial sexual attraction is dominant. It makes them listen to the woman to whom they are attracted, to be attentive and supportive. For many women, the attention, the listening, and the support are the most attractive and are what make them fall in love. Men should remember this when they want to conquer a woman's heart.

What is the reason for this gender difference? One explanation has to do with gender stereotypes and gender roles that define the correct courtship behavior for men and women.[23] During the getting-acquainted stage, men are supposed to take the initiative. Women can hint their interest by flirting but not initiate directly. One study discovered 52 nonverbal courtship patterns of women flirting with men to attract their attention.[24] Despite the sexual revolution and the openness and tolerance that characterize romantic relationships today, women who take the initiative with men are often still perceived negatively.[25]

According to young singles' scripts for a first date, men are expected to be more influenced by the physical appearance of their dates, and women are expected to be more influenced by the emotional closeness and intimacy. For both men and women, sexual attraction is expected to be important. All these expectations are part of a well-defined social script. The script is so familiar that when young men and women are asked to describe the order of events on a first date, the similarity in their descriptions is amazing.[26]

The feminine script of courtship emphasizes attractive appearance, ability to carry on a conversation, and control of sex, usually by refusal. The masculine script covers planning the date, paying for it, and taking the initiative in sex. Women who break the script by, for example, taking the initiative sexually, are perceived as aggressive and masculine. Men who break the script by, for example, demanding that the woman pay her share of the meal are perceived as cheap and unmanly. These scripts structure and exacerbate the differences between men and women. The penalties for breaking their scripts force men and women to comply with them.

Gender differences exist in courtship and in the move from courtship to committed relationship. Although women tend to be more cautious during the courtship stage, men tend to fall in love faster and stronger.[27] In the move from courtship to marriage, women tend to move faster, and men tend to be more cautious.

Women's cautiousness, especially about sex, can function not only as part of a script, but also as part of a social norm. In a survey conducted among American female students, for example, it was discovered that 30% of these young and educated women sometimes said no to sex when they actually meant to say yes. Women's token resistance to sex is culturally prescribed and is part of the mating game.[28] It is comforting to note that after the initial stages of courtship in which both sexes behave according to the socially prescribed scripts, men and women tend to fall in love at a similar pace and with similar intensity.

Another explanation for the gender differences in the process of falling in love arises from the difference in men's and women's innate programming for mate selection. This difference is a major topic of evolutionary theory, which is discussed extensively in the next chapter. As we will see, according to this theory, different evolutionary developments have dictated different courting strategies for men and women.[29] Indeed, the difference between men and women in the way they view sex and love is one of the most significant gender differences found based on studies involving thousands of subjects.[30] The conclusion, which should be taken with the appropriate caution, is that men are more likely to use love to get sex, whereas women are more likely to use sex to get love.[23]

Evolutionary theorists assume that because these, and other, gender differences result from evolutionary dictates, they are universal. This assumption has received a great deal of criticism arguing against a universal, biological explanation and in favor of a cultural explanation. The findings of an anthropological study that examined the courtship patterns in several North American countries supported this criticism. These findings showed that courtship is a well-defined process of specific meaning and prescribed verbal and nonverbal content. The subjective experience of this process is the development of strong mutual feelings of attraction and sexual arousal. None of this is new, of course, but the findings are augmented by comparing the parts of the falling-in-love process that were shared by different cultures to the parts that were not shared. Because the latter were unique to each culture, it was possible to conclude that the gender differences in courtship are not universal.[31]

This suggests that the evolutionary theories that present themselves as universal may be nothing more than ethnographic theories that describe how men and women in certain cultures view the process of mate selection, a description that includes some narrow assumptions about the roles of men and women. In other words, even if there are certain differences between men and women in falling in love and choosing a mate, there are also some powerful social and cultural influences that can account for these differences.

Furthermore, as most people know from personal experience, there is a personal and private aspect to falling in love. This is the aspect that lies behind the choice of a particular man or woman from all the eligible, appropriate, and attractive potential partners that people meet. It is this choice of one particular person from all the appropriate people in the world that gives love its magical quality. In the words of the 15th century poem, *The Nut-Brown Maid*:

> For in my mind, of all mankind
> I love but you alone.

SUGGESTIONS FOR PEOPLE SEEKING LOVE

Be aware of your love funnel. Think about the two most intense, most significant falling-in-love experiences you have ever had. Did you fall in love at first sight, or was the falling in love preceded by a long process of getting acquainted and becoming friends? Do you like the way you fall in love (either fast or slow), or would you like to change it? Identifying your preferences in love is the first step. Doing something about it should come soon after. The previous chapters offer a number of practical suggestions on how you can increase your likelihood of falling in love.

Once you have identified your love funnel as a whole, you can focus on specific love screens. Think about the two people with whom you were most in love. What did they have in common: something about their looks, their personalities, their intelligence, their social standing, their sex appeal, the way they treated you, or the fact that they loved you? The quality, or qualities, they had in common says more about you than about them. The commonalities point to the screens you use for choosing a romantic partner.

Once you have identified your love screens, try to evaluate the extent to which these screens are truly yours. Are they part of a social script you adopted that does not really suit you—or does not suit you any longer? The more honest you are with yourself, and with potential partners, about your true love screens, the more likely you will be to find a partner who will pass through them successfully.

It is also important to recognize the mating script in your own social group. But, be ready to abandon, as fast as possible, the gender-related part of the script in order to assure yourself of a genuine and authentic love relationship.

Chapter 7

ON MEN, WOMEN, AND LOVE:
THE ROLE OF STATUS AND BEAUTY

Behold, thou art fair, my love; behold, thou art fair; thou hast
dove's eyes behind thy veil; thy hair is like a flock of goats, that
cascade down from mount Gil'ad … . Thy lips are like a thread
of scarlet, and thy mouth is comely; thy cheek is like a piece of
pomegranate within thy locks … . Thy two breasts are like two
fawns, twins of a gazelle, which feed among the lilies

… . Thou are all fair, my love; there is no blemish in thee.
What is thy beloved more than another beloved, O thou
fairest among women? What is thy beloved more than another
beloved, that thou dost so charge us?
My beloved is white and ruddy, distinguished among ten
thousand. His head is as the most fine gold, his locks are wavy,
as black as a raven … .
—Old Testament, *The Song of Songs*

WHEN TERRY MET TOM, SHE WAS NOT LOOKING FOR LOVE. WHAT SHE WAS
looking for was a television set because she and her roommate did not
have one. She noticed that the guys who lived in the apartment across the hall had
a set; her urge to see the evening news became irresistible, and she could hear when
the news was on in their apartment. She decided to brave it. She knocked on the
door. A large guy opened it and smiled a big smile when he saw her. When Terry
explained what she wanted, he invited her in with a big wave of his hand. There
were three other guys sprawled on the couch and armchairs around the room,
and the place looked cheerful and friendly. After watching the news, Terry hated
the thought of going back to her own gloomy apartment. Tom, the one who had
opened the door, seemed like such a nice guy, and she loved the way he and his
friends teased and joked with each other. She started visiting them every evening
when the news was on and then at other times as well. With time, her friendship
with Tom and her feelings for him grew deeper. He was always there for her, always ready to listen and empathize. He did not talk much himself, but whenever
he commented about something she said, it was always wise and helpful. She also

loved the fact that he was studying medicine. It seemed like such a caring profession, with status and good prospects.

When Tom saw Terry that first time, he was stunned by her beauty and grace. She was tall and slim, with legs from here to eternity. Her green eyes and long wavy auburn hair seemed to him the most beautiful he had ever seen. A shy and quiet man, he never had a girlfriend before. Terry made things easy for him because she talked so freely. He loved looking into those gorgeous green eyes and listening to her, his heart pounding.

WOMEN TALK ABOUT THE REASONS THAT MADE THEM FALL IN LOVE

I was attracted to his personality. I also thought he was very sexy. He carried himself well and dressed nicely. He is a very real and honest person. He comes off as being very confident, almost cocky. That's what attracted me to him. He is also a very loving person. There's nothing he wouldn't do for me.

When I saw him for the first time, it was totally dark, and he started talking about the stars. He knew all about astronomy and astrology and seemed very knowledgeable. He was also very funny and had an odd sense of humor. We started as just friends. I felt comfortable talking to him. I felt we were compatible in many ways.

We met at a party. I was with someone else. He asked around, discovered where I worked, and came after me. It was very passionate. I thought he was handsome. He was very reserved and that attracted me. He keeps things close, and it feels like he's special. He's busy all the time. He has three businesses and works all the time.

He noticed me before I noticed him. He looked too old for me, but he was always there to listen. He is very reliable. If he says he'll do something, I know he'll do it. He takes care of me, and he is very loving. He spoils me.

MEN TALK ABOUT THE REASONS THAT MADE THEM FALL IN LOVE

She's a very pretty woman. What attracted me first was her looks. Later, that she's very much like me. She's giving toward me. She cares a lot.

I remember thinking that she was pretty. What attracted me most was her looks, at first. Later, that she's great. She's nice. There was something about her, she would put my mind at ease.

She's very attractive, very pretty. Good looks rank higher for me than it does to the average person. She knows she's attractive, has presence, is very aware, a serious person.

I thought she was really striking. I was really attracted to her. I don't like picking up women, but I was so attracted to her that I came over and started small talk. A week later we started going out.

She's very pretty. I was attracted to her. I talked to her, and we have a lot in common. She was very responsive and fun, intelligent.

GENDER DIFFERENCES IN ROMANTIC ATTRACTION

Do these quotations suggest a gender difference in the romantic choices of men and women? Most of the attraction variables presented in the first chapters did not. Men and women seem to be equally influenced by proximity, arousal, pleasant personality, similarity, satisfying needs, and reciprocity in love.[1] Only the importance of appearance is significantly different between men and women. Most of the men, as compared to less than half of the women, mentioned appearance as triggering their initial attraction. Furthermore, men described appearance as playing a far greater role in their romantic attraction.[2] Other studies have also documented a gender difference in the effect of appearance on romantic attraction.

Particularly persuasive evidence was provided by Alan Feingold, who reviewed different types of studies (questionnaires, personal ads, and so forth). The conclusion in all types of studies was the same: Physical appeal, even if important to women, is far more important for men.[3] It is noteworthy that the difference found in men's and women's responses to questionnaires was larger than the difference found in their actual behavior. In other words, men are less influenced by women's appearance than they say, and women are more influenced by men's appearance than they say. What they say may reflect social expectations more than personal preferences.

A LIST OF ATTRIBUTES PEOPLE CONSIDER WHEN DECIDING WHOM TO MARRY

The following is a list of attributes that some people consider seriously in their decisions to marry. Please rate on a 7-point scale (where 1 = not at all, and 7 = very much) to what extent you would be interested in marrying someone who

____is younger by 5 years or more

____was married in the past

____has children

____is not likely to hold a steady job

____belongs to a different religion

____is of a different race

____will earn far less money than you will

____will earn far more money than you will

____is not physically attractive

____has more education than you have

____has less education than you have

____is older by 5 years or more

This list was presented to an unusually large and representative sample that included over 13,000 men and women, aged 19 to 35, all single, from different social classes. The results showed that beauty and youth are more important to men, and earning ability is more important to women. Women were more willing than men to marry someone unattractive or someone older by 5 years or more if that someone earned more and had more education than they did. Men, on the other hand, were more willing than women to marry someone younger by 5 years or more, who was not likely to hold a steady job, who was likely to earn far less, and who was less educated than they were.[4]

Another study used photographs of models and models in bathing suits. Results showed again that for men a "visual scan" of a potential partner's "physical attributes" was enough to establish a "pool of coitally acceptable partners." For women, "nonphysical attributes," such as ambition, status, and dominance, were needed to establish a pool of potentially acceptable partners for sexual liaisons and "higher investment relationships," which is to say, marriage.[5]

While men emphasize physical attractiveness, women more often look for social and economic status, ambition, strong character, and intelligence. Indications that men are more romantically attracted to beauty and women to status and ambition were found in a large number of studies totaling hundreds of subjects in different cultures. No gender difference was found in the attraction to a pleasant personality and a sense of humor; men and women value these qualities equally.[3]

Is it a personal economic shortage that leads women to put an emphasis on financial resources? Not necessarily. A study showed that the higher the income young women expected to earn, the more important to them was the income of their potential partners and the higher the income they wanted a potential partner to earn.[6]

WHAT ARE WOMEN AND MEN ASKING FOR AND WHAT ARE THEY OFFERING?

An analysis of 1,000 classified "lonely hearts" ads showed that men seek "cues to reproductive value" (physical appearance and youth), whereas women seek "cues revealing an ability to acquire resources" (maturity and actual or potential financial security). Women also seek to ascertain a man's willingness to provide resources in the form of time, emotions, money, and status. Both men and women offer those traits sought by the opposite sex.[7] (See examples of "lonely hearts" ads in Figure 11.)

Sex appeal, as a specific element in physical attraction, was also found to be far more important in the romantic interest of men,[8] whereas quality of communication was more important to women.[9] When young men and women were asked about the physical appearance and professional level of an acceptable partner at various degrees of intimacy and commitment, women were more likely to prefer, or insist, that sexual relationships occur in the context of intimate emotional involvement with the possibility of marriage.[10]

WRITER SEEKS 65+ educated, moral, articulate, poised, person empathetic to feminist. Liberal democrat. Send background in own handwriting between fifty to hundred words.

HONEST, CARING, CHRISTIAN, SWF, Full figured, humorous and fun to be with. Enjoys most sports, talking and cuddling. ISO SDWM 27-42 No drugs, or drinkers. Serious replies only.

NATURE LOVER 53 y.o. blue eyed professional female, lives in the mountains, is looking for fun loving professional male 50-65 to share canoeing, hiking and romantic dinners by the fire.

WANTED WHITE MALE Intellectual snob, must be 5'4" tall or taller. Sense of humor is a plus. I'm in my 40's and I'm a very attractive white female, brunette/brown eyes, 5'2" 125lbs.

SUN AND BEACHES SWF, 51, enjoys the beach, boating, dining out, movies, travel, dancing. ISO gentleman with similar interests, affectionate, financially/emotionally secure.

SWF, 21 ISO SWM, 19-26. Love is the answer, but while you are waiting for the answer, romance raises some pretty good questions.

ACTIVE, HAPPY SWPF available for LTR. 41, 5'3, "weighty", brown hair, hazel eyes, ISO intelligent, openminded, kind-hearted, tolerant, spiritual, mellow fellow of wit and character. Mail Box 700

LIFE MATE WANTED: DWM seeks slender to medium N/S, WF under 64, sensuous, passionate, affectionate, loving, classy dresser to jeans, who loves holding hands, country and popular music, slow dancing, movies, video's, cooking, dining out, some sports, cards, good conversations, quiet times, gardening, home life, for a life time of happiness. Mail Box 705

SEEKING SPECIAL LADY: SWM, 35, 5'10", DDF, muscular build, handsome, respectful, loyal, compassionate, protective, charming, personable. ISO SF, must enjoy cuddling, romance, dining, walks on beach. If interested call Voice box #8634.

SWPF, 34, N/S stunning brunette. ISO tall, strong, dynamic, blue-eyed Irishman (S/DPM 32-40) for committed relationship. Passion for golf, baseball, fun, romance, laughter, communication, kids.

ATTRACTIVE 39, DPCBF, ISO DPCBM 41-50, intelligent, honest and loving, easy going gentleman that appreciates friendship first. ND/NS, financially secure and caring that enjoys sports, movies, dining out, music etc. DDF, photo appreciated.

GIRL EINSTEIN with artistic touch ISO witty male 30-36 with similar fondness for dark humor and propensity for creativity

LOOKING FOR THAT CERTAIN SOMEONE: are you looking for me? Intelligent, articulate, creative, caring, silly, wise, thoughtful, quiet, communicative SWF50, ISO S/DWPM with brains n' spark 45+.

5'2" BUNDLE OF ENERGY Slim, NSSWF likes dancing, swing music, movies, travel, biking, walking, gardening. ISO fun loving energetic, NSSWM 55/65. To share in life's good times.

ARE YOU MY RHETT BUTLER? S/DNSPM 45-55 needed to tame this Scarlet. Must be dashing, daring and an incurable romantic. Love of golf and/or dancing a bonus.

FIGURE 11. The Personals. What are women and men asking for, and what are they offering?

Another indication of the greater interest of men in sex is the finding that men are more likely to pursue someone else while in a dating relationship.[11]

The *age preference* of men and women in a romantic partner is also different. An examination of personal ads in the United States, the Philippines, Europe, and India showed that young men prefer women their own age, but as they grow older, their preferences change to younger women. The age preference of women does not change as they age but remains steady for men older than themselves.[12] An examination of marriage licenses granted during a 50-year period also showed that in 75% of the cases, the husband was older than the wife.[13]

As we have seen, men and women also differ in their *height preferences* in a spouse. While the majority of women prefer a man who is taller than they are,[14] most men prefer women who are shorter than they are. As a matter of fact, shortness is more of a liability for a man than tallness is an asset.[15]

Women prefer not only to look up to their husbands, but also tend to marry up; men tend to marry down. This leaves many unmarried women at the top of the worlds of politics, science, and business and many unmarried men in prison, at the bottom of the social ladder.

Men and women are attracted to different personality traits. One such trait is *dominance*. Expressions of dominance in men were found in four studies to increase their sexual appeal for women. Dominant behavior did nothing to enhance women's attractiveness to men. Interestingly, although dominant behavior increased the sexual appeal of men, it did not increase the degree to which they were liked.[16] To appeal to women, dominant men have to demonstrate other traits as well, such as a willingness to help, empathic ability, and a willingness to cooperate.[17] Women find men who are cooperative and helpful much more attractive physically and sexually and more socially desirable as potential mates. In other words, dominant men are more appealing than submissive men, but only when they are helpful and cooperative. Men who are dominant and egotistical do not appeal to women.[18]

WHAT CAUSES THE GENDER DIFFERENCES IN ROMANTIC ATTRACTION?

In their different answers to the question of what causes the gender differences in romantic attraction, two theories—one evolutionary, the other psychoanalytic— rest on an assumption that the gender differences in romantic attraction are real. Conversely, the different answers of two social theories rest on an assumption that these gender differences are *not* real. One social theory explains the differences in the operation of sex role stereotypes; the other argues that individual differences in romantic attraction are more significant than gender differences. If you are not interested in any of these explanations, you can skip to the recommendations at the end of the chapter for people seeking love. For those who are interested, I discuss the explanation offered by each theory in some detail.

GENDER DIFFERENCES IN ROMANTIC ATTRACTION: EVOLUTIONARY THEORY

According to evolutionary theory, gender differences in romantic attraction are the result of different requirements for genetic survival that dictate different criteria for mate selection in the two sexes. In men, evolution dictates preferences for qualities that indicate a woman's ability to procreate, namely, youth and beauty. In women, evolution dictates preferences for qualities that indicate a man's ability to obtain resources, namely, earning potential and status. Because only women give birth, their investment in their offspring through gestation, birth, and nursing is far greater than the men's, and they can produce far fewer offspring over a limited duration, whereas men can produce offspring from puberty until they die, men and women are attracted to different qualities in potential mates. A woman looks for a man who is willing to commit to her and her offspring and who is able to provide for them; a man looks for a woman who can bear children.

She Loves His Success, He Loves Her Youth and Beauty

The evolution of sex differences is one of the central themes in Darwin's theory. Charles Darwin believed that evolution occurs in a continuing process of change through which different traits are selected because of their greater adaptability to environmental demands. This process of "natural selection" favors those individuals who adapt better to their environments. The evidence for "good adaptation" is simple: more offspring in the next generations.[19] To these basic Darwinian concepts, modern evolutionists added the term *parental investment,* meaning the energy invested by parents in giving birth and raising an offspring.[20] The larger the difference between the sexes in their parental investment, the larger the differences between their criteria for romantic attraction.

In humans, the differences between the sexes start with the difference between the sperm and the egg. The slow-moving egg is 50,000 times larger than the fast-moving sperm. Women release one egg per month compared to hundreds of millions of sperm produced by men every day. This is why, says evolutionary psychologist Ada Lumpert, a woman is cautious about her egg, but a man readily spreads his sperm around. Sperm is cheap, and the man has nothing to lose. The further and faster he wanders, the greater his chances of success. A woman carries the baby in her womb for 9 months; she nurses and cares for the baby after birth. A man invests 10 pleasant minutes in passing his sperm into the womb of his partner; even if we add the time involved in rushing her to the hospital, the difference in time invested is still large. Because her parental investment is so much greater than his, the optimal way for her to ensure having as many healthy offspring as possible is characterized by caution, his way by speed. Because she is going to invest so much time and energy in her offspring, she has to be sure before she starts that they will survive.[21]

The difference between her caution and his speed puts them in the stereotypical situation in which he pushes her to agree to have sex, and she resists, saying, "Wait." So he waits, and she assesses his loyalty. Will he stay with her after they make love? Will he help her raise their offspring? He promises he will. So they make love, and she is exposed to the danger that despite his promise he will get up and leave. Dishonesty is a common strategy, and everyone can promise eternal love. The greatest danger a woman must guard against is a man's abandonment. So, the woman guards with extra caution, her instincts tuned to detecting liars. She searches for a man who is loyal, who does not abandon but stays and lends a hand.[21]

An examination of the romantic attraction interviews indicated that loyalty is indeed an attractive male trait for women:

> *He is very reliable. If he says he'll do something, I know he'll do it.*
> *He is honest, he is moral, he is smart, he is responsible, he is everything you can want.*
> *He goes out of his way to help people, and you can rely on him. He doesn't play the kind of games that some men play with women.*
> *I can trust him. He's responsible.*
> *With him I know that if he says he'll be somewhere, he's really going to be there.*

Sociobiologist David Buss also emphasized the role of evolutionary processes in creating different mating strategies for men and women. Because women can have fewer children and need to care for them, they look for men of means who can provide for them; they measure men according to their earning potentials, as evidenced by their status, money, ambition, and diligence; and they are attracted to expressions of love, such as expensive restaurants and gifts, that demonstrate men's economic resources. Alternatively, because men can produce children from adolescence through old age, they measure women according to their youth, health, and beauty and are attracted to shows of affection that symbolize a woman's fertility.[22] Buss organized a huge cross-cultural study that involved over 50 researchers and close to 10,000 people in 33 countries, 6 continents, and 5 islands and showed a consistent gender difference in the importance of earning potential versus physical attractiveness. Women gave the greatest weight to signs of men's earning potential (ambition and hard work), whereas men gave the greatest weight to signs of women's fertility (youth and beauty).[23]

Many other studies have examined a particular culture or a certain aspect of mate selection. A study of mate preferences among the Kipsigis women in Kenya, for example, found that the women prefer men who offer "high-quality breeding" as evidenced by their numbers of inhabitable acres of land. Furthermore, Kipsigis women prefer single men, followed by monogamous men, and finally polygamous men. The reason for this is that when several women are married to one man, even a rich man, it reduces the quality of care they can provide for their offspring.[24]

A study done in India showed that although physical appearance is important to *both* men and women, caste and economic security exercise different gender appeal. Indian men will ignore the economic security of a potential partner if she is from a similar caste; women will ignore the caste of the man if he is sure to provide economic security.[25]

Men and Women, Love and Sex

Evolutionary psychologists believe that although parental investment influences mate selection in birds as well as humans, romantic attraction intervenes in humans as the "active ingredient" in mate seeking, courtship, and flirting.[26] Romantic love was co-opted by evolutionary forces to maintain the human pair bond. How then can we explain promiscuity in humans, especially human males?[27] According to evolutionary theory, human males have evolved two different "reproductive strategies": the "cad" for short-term mating and spreading their seeds and the "dad" for long-term mating and raising of offspring.[27] In short-term mating, men are looking for sexually accessible women. In long-term mating, they are looking for fidelity. Short-term sexual partners require different attraction tactics than long-term romantic partners. Indeed, when the effectiveness of different mate attraction tactics was evaluated, "a show of resource potential" was judged most effective for men seeking a long-term mate (aspiring to be dads), whereas "furnishing immediate resources" was most effective for men seeking short-term partners (cads).[28]

Similar findings emerged when men and women, aged 17 to 43, were asked about the tactics they used to attract potential marriage partners. Women who expected an investing partner said that they tried to attract him by behaving modestly and emphasizing their sexual fidelity. Women who expected a noninvesting partner flaunted their sexuality to get "preparental investment" from as many men as possible. Men who believed that one should invest in children were more likely than other men to emphasize this willingness and ability to invest as a way to attract women. They were also likely to emphasize their sexual fidelity. Men who did not believe in the importance of investing in children demonstrated their sexuality and their attraction to women as a way to attract them.[29]

Emphasizing those traits in yourself that are likely to attract the opposite sex may seem a legitimate and acceptable tactic, but it can also be considered deception. Not surprisingly, there are also gender differences in "patterns of deception" in "mating strategies." When men talk to other men, they tend to exaggerate their success in general and their sexual conquests in particular. On the other hand, when they talk to women, men exaggerate their commitment, their honesty, and their ability to generate resources. Women try to enhance their physical appearance in the company of men as part of a strategy for attracting a mate.[30]

One of the biggest differences between men and women has to do with their approaches to sex without love.[31] In the most famous study on this subject, young men and women specified their minimum criteria for 24 different traits for (a) a date, (b) a sexual partner, (c) an exclusive dating partner, (d) a marriage partner, and (e) a one-night sexual liaison. Findings showed that the gender differences were greatest for casual sexual liaisons, with men's criteria consistently and significantly lower than women's. Men's criteria were as high as women's criteria for marriage partners.[32]

Similar findings are reported in a study that compared men's and women's minimum standards for short-term and long-term relationships. Again, it was found that both men and women expressed higher minimum standards for long-term relationships, and that women were far more selective than men when considering potential short-term partners.[33] In an amusing study that was conducted on a large university campus, an attractive young man and woman approached students of the opposite sex and offered to go to bed with them. The offer was accepted by 75% of the male students approached by the young woman and 0% of the female students approached by the man.[34]

What about women who are as sexually active as men? Interviews with highly sexual men and women showed that in women (only) the large number of sexual partners was related to emotional vulnerability and anxiety about the partner's willingness to invest in the relationship. This may reflect women's greater difficulty in dissociating sexual pleasure from a partner's emotional involvement.[35]

All the studies mentioned in this section support evolutionary theorists' dictum: She loves his success, and he loves her beauty, as can be seen in the famous example in Figure 12.

Criticism of Evolutionary Theory

With the growing popularity of evolutionary theory grew the number of its critics. One of those critics, a biologist, noted the great leap that evolutionary theorists make "from the seemingly innocent asymmetries between egg and sperm" to such "major

FIGURE 12. The apotheosis of the successful man and the beautiful woman, newlyweds Donald Trump and Melania Knauss enjoying an evening in New York.

consequences" as female fidelity, male promiscuity, women's disproportional contribution to the care of children, and the unequal distribution of labor by gender.[36] Another critic, this time a primatologist, argued that evolutionary theorists' notion of "the coy female" persists "despite the accumulation of abundant and openly available evidence contradicting it." Why, then, does such a notion persist? The reason is a cultural congruence. Because the evolutionary explanations for the competitiveness and promiscuity of men and the choosiness, sexual inhibition, and flirtatiousness of women fit many elements in popular culture, coyness became one of the most commonly mentioned attributes of women in the evolutionary literature.[37]

Regarding gender differences in romantic attraction, evolutionary theory uses the same concepts to explain contradictory behaviors—not only why women are coy, but also why they flaunt their sexuality; not only why men are promiscuous, but also why they emphasize their sexual fidelity. Despite this theoretical flexibility, there are numerous findings that do not fit evolutionary theory. In addition, there are other convincing explanations for the gender differences in romantic attraction and mate selection strategies.

Most of the theories that oppose evolutionary theory offer a social explanation for the gender differences in romantic attraction. While evolutionary theory views romantic love as a cultural means to a biological end,[38] the social theories emphasize the role played by social forces such as norms and sex role stereotypes.

GENDER DIFFERENCES IN ROMANTIC ATTRACTION: SOCIAL THEORIES

The evolutionary explanation of the gender differences in romantic attraction, as well as the psychoanalytic explanation discussed later, are based on the assumption that gender differences in romantic attraction are real. They are both challenged by social explanations that are based on the assumption that these gender differences are *not* real. According to one explanation, gender differences in romantic attraction result from the operation of social forces such as social norms, gender stereotypes, social roles, and differences in social power. Socialization toward different gender roles and scripts and different social norms for men and women dictate different preferences in a potential mate.[39] According to another social explanation, based on social construction theory, reality is socially constructed. The similarity between men and women in most things, including romantic attraction, is far greater than the differences. Individual differences and cultural differences in romantic attraction should be noted and emphasized more than gender differences.

Gender Stereotypes and Their Influence on Romantic Attraction

A review of many studies of gender differences in attraction led the six researchers who conducted it to conclude that these differences result from "a common, perhaps representative, stereotype."[40] *Gender stereotypes* are those rigidly held, oversimplified beliefs that males and females possess distinct psychological traits and characteristics solely by virtue of their sex. Such overgeneralizations tend to be widely shared in a given culture.[41] Even though the division by sex is one of the most basic classifications of every known human society, the division of labor and the behaviors and traits of males and females differ in different societies. Consequently, the associations people have for the words *masculine* and *feminine* are characteristic of the society and specific subculture in which they live.

What Function, If Any, Do Stereotypes Serve?

The answer to the question of what function, if any, do stereotypes serve seems clear: They help us process social information faster. Because we cannot possibly process the endless amount of information we absorb through our senses, we organize that information into cognitive categories or *schemas*.[42] We categorize people, including ourselves, according to different social schemas, such as race, religion, nationality, profession, and, of course, gender.

To all apparent purposes, there is nothing wrong with stereotypes. After all, they are nothing more than cognitive schemas that help us make sense of the ocean of information threatening to drown us every moment. The problem is that while organizing and processing all this information, we make mistakes, and these mistakes tend to be consistent. One notable example is that we tend to see groups to which we do not belong as more homogeneous than groups to which we do belong. Thus, women tend to assume that men are closer to the masculine stereotype than men really are, and men tend to assume that women are closer to the feminine stereotype than women really are. In a study that demonstrated this, men and women examined sentences that described masculine and feminine stereotypes, such as, "Losing a competition is depressing" or "Taking care is a way of showing love." Findings showed that both men and women assumed

that a higher percentage of members of the opposite sex agreed with these stereotypical sentences than the members of the opposite sex actually did.[43]

By their nature, stereotypes perpetuate themselves and acquire the power of
self-fulfilling prophecies. Here is an example. Men and women, out of sight of each
other, were asked to use a signaling board to negotiate with a coworker about the division of labor on different tasks. Some of the tasks were stereotypically masculine,
for example, repairing an electrical outlet; some were stereotypically feminine, such
as decorating a birthday cake; and some were neutral, such as painting a chair. One
third of the men were told that they were negotiating with a man, one third were
told they were negotiating with a woman, and one third were told nothing. Findings showed that women who were thought by their partners in the negotiation to
be men chose more masculine tasks, whereas the women who were thought by their
partners to be women chose more feminine tasks. The reason was that the women
behaved according to the men's expectations. When the men thought they were
negotiating with a woman, they chose masculine tasks for themselves and tended
to compromise less when a conflict arose. These behaviors caused the women to
behave in ways that confirmed the men's expectations. In other words, the men's
expectations, based on gender stereotypes, produced behaviors that confirmed these
stereotypes.[44] The different behaviors of the women thought to be men and the
women thought to be women suggest that these are not innate sex differences that
evolved during thousands of years of human evolution. Rather, these are differences
that result from gender role stereotypes and self-fulfilling prophecies.

Gender Stereotypes Define Normative Behavior

Behavior according to stereotypes ensures social acceptance. Because it is important
to most of us to be accepted and popular, we feel pressured to behave according to
gender stereotypes. At the getting-acquainted stage of a romantic relationship, it is
important to make a good impression. This forces us to behave according to gender
stereotypes more than we might otherwise.

We are especially likely to behave according to gender stereotypes when we
expect to meet an unusually attractive potential mate. A classic study that demonstrated this involved four groups of women: One group was told that they were
going to meet an attractive and brilliant Ivy League student who held conservative
views. The second group was told that they were going to meet an attractive and
brilliant Ivy League student who held liberal views. The third group was told they
were going to meet an unattractive and mediocre student at a mediocre university
who held conservative views. The fourth group was told they were going to meet
an unattractive and liberal mediocre student at a mediocre university. The women
were asked to describe themselves and were told that their descriptions would be
given to the man. These same women had also participated in a previous, uncon-
nected study in which they had given detailed descriptions of themselves.

Results showed that the women who thought they were going to meet an
attractive, conservative man described themselves as more feminine and less intelligent. The women who thought they were going to meet an attractive, liberal

man described themselves as less feminine and more intelligent. The women who thought they were going to meet an unattractive man did not alter their descriptions of themselves. The changes in self-presentation of the first two groups of women were not related to the women's real views, either conservative or liberal.[45]

Here is the paradox. Both men and women play their prescribed gender roles and then complain about the results. Couples are first attracted to each other because each fits the stereotype. She is attracted to him because he is strong, silent, masculine, assertive, and skilled. He is attracted to her because she is warm, sensitive, open, and verbal. Later, she will complain that he does not talk, and he will complain that she is a nag.[46]

Why are people attracted to potential mates who are stereotypically masculine or feminine in light of the evidence that relationships of men and women with traditional gender roles are far from optimal and are generally worse than those of nonstereotyped men and women? One answer that was offered is that the attraction to stereotypes reflects a conflict between what old imprints and past values dispose people to do and what modern cultural values prescribe, such as more egalitarian intimate relationships.[47]

Do Gender Stereotypes Have a Basis in Reality?

Carol Martin believes that gender stereotypes do not have a basis in reality. Martin showed that when students were asked about the traits that characterize men and women, they described the familiar stereotypes. When they were asked to describe themselves, the stereotypes disappeared almost entirely.[48] An exercise I do in my classes on the psychology of gender shows the same thing. I ask my students to write down the traits they associate with masculinity and those they associate with femininity. I then summarize their individual lists on the board. The traits that are mentioned by the largest number of people invariably describe gender stereotypes. When I ask them how many of the traits they wrote down describe themselves, it turns out, to their great surprise, that few do.

Other studies also showed little basis for stereotypes. When men and women were asked what attitudes and qualities they, personally, and members of their sex value, the values of men and women were mostly similar. Both sexes value such traits as honesty, responsibility, and open-mindedness. These are characteristics that are not included in studies of sex role stereotypes. Nevertheless, when they were asked about the values of the other sex, the stereotypes appeared; women exaggerated the importance that men attribute to achievement, and men exaggerated the importance that women attribute to nurturing. The conclusion is that gender differences are far smaller in reality than they appear to be in stereotypes.[49]

In another study, 800 women were given three questionnaires: "self-perception," "the ideal woman," and "the ideal woman as seen by men." Comparison of their responses to the three questionnaires revealed a small discrepancy between their perceptions of themselves and their perceptions of the ideal woman. However, there were large differences between their own views of the ideal woman and their assumptions about the male view of the ideal woman. When men described the ideal woman, their responses were similar to the women's descriptions of the ideal woman, but there were big differences between the men's descriptions of the ideal woman and the women's descriptions of the men's ideal woman. Men's ideal woman was less conservative than the women assumed.[50] Similar findings emerged when men were asked to describe themselves, the ideal man, and the ideal man as seen by women. In similar fashion, there was a big discrepancy between men's perception of women's ideal man and women's true ideal. Men thought that women preferred family men. In fact, there was a great similarity in the descriptions of the ideal man by both men and women.

Gender stereotypes convey a clear message about how men and women are supposed to behave toward each other, to whom they are supposed to be attracted, and how they are supposed to express this attraction. Handsome men are seen as masculine, and beautiful women are seen as feminine.[51] Men are supposed to be attracted to "feminine" women, and women are supposed to be attracted to "masculine" men.[41] But, are they really?

To What Are Men and Women Really Attracted?

In one of the studies that examined the question of what attracts men and women, it turned out that both men and women prefer nonstereotyped—androgynous— partners who combine masculine instrumentality with feminine expressiveness over sex-typed partners.[52]

When the types of men most attractive to women were examined, it was discovered that women are most attracted to "masculinity with a feminine touch." In the study, young educated women either listened to prerecorded responses or read verbatim transcripts of two men answering questions on topics such as car repairs, career opportunities, and romantic interests. One set of answers was constructed to reflect stereotypically masculine activities and interests; the second set reflected stereotypically masculine as well as feminine activities and interests. Findings showed that women rated the nonstereotyped, androgynous, man as more likeable, intelligent, moral, mentally healthy, appropriate, and honest than they rated the "masculine" man.[53]

Another study showed that young women prefer feminine to masculine men as both friends and romantic partners. Income contributed to a man's romantic attraction only when the man had desirable personality traits. This suggests that women consider income only after personality criteria are met. In fact, a man's personality factors relate more consistently to his romantic appeal to women than do his success factors—and a man's belief in gender equality has the greatest influence on his attractiveness to women.[54]

Attraction to stereotypical macho men can be dangerous for women. "Hyperfeminine" women who adhere to a traditional gender role are attracted to macho men, prefer them as husbands and sex partners, and think they resemble past and current boyfriends. These women also report more attraction to, and interest in, nonconsensual sexual dates, as well as less anger and more sexual arousal. These findings point to the risk associated with the attraction to macho, aggressive, and coercive men, namely, sexual aggression.[55]

Attraction to stereotypical feminine women is not dangerous, but it may suggest a low self-evaluation. A study showed that men with a low self-concept are more attracted to traditionally feminine women, whereas men with high self-concept are more attracted to modern, nontraditional, liberal women. This is because liberal women are perceived as more assertive, self-confident, and independent than traditional women and therefore may present a threat to the sense of independence and control of men with a low self-concept. In an attempt to enhance their egos when they feel threatened, these men need to reject nontraditional women. A man who is sure of himself is not threatened by women and therefore does not have a need to criticize assertive and independent women.[56]

Social theorists are convinced that gender differences in romantic attraction are explained by social forces. They are not a result of genetic programming, but of living in a different social reality.[57] Social norms, stereotypes, and differences in social power dictate what is attractive in a potential mate.[58] Women choose men who are older, taller, wiser, and more educated because these men have more social power. Similarly, men choose women who are younger, shorter, less intelligent, and less educated because they can more easily maintain their social power over them. Neither the men nor the women are necessarily aware of the fact that their romantic choices are influenced by power considerations. Their sex role socialization and the acceptable social norms make it easy for them to be.[59]

There are different sexual scripts for men and women.[60] According to the masculine sexual script, a man who has casual sexual relationships is a playboy or a Don Juan. According to the feminine sexual script, a woman who has casual sex is a slut. Because the label playboy is rather positive and the label slut is negative, the labels, or more accurately the norms behind them, dictate different behaviors for men and women. These different sexual scripts can explain the difference between men and woman when offered casual sex.[61] Even if there is a significant gender difference in their approach to casual sex, it does not mean that there is a difference between men and women in either level of sexuality or romantic attraction. The stereotype that women have little interest in their sexual functioning or are unable to function sexually at a level similar to that of men is just that, a stereotype with little base in reality.[62] Clear norms influence men and women's sexual expectations of a dating relationship. Men generally expect sexual intercourse after approximately 9 to 11 dates, fewer than women's expectation of approximately 15 to 18 dates,[63] and expect more sexual activity in encounters with women in general.[64]

Gender stereotypes influence what we look for in a potential mate and what we offer.[65] Sadly, young men and women whose personalities were shaped by gender stereotypes in their late teens continue to be influenced by and shaped by their romantic relationships according to these stereotypes.[66] The good news is that stereotypes have greater influence during the early stages of young people's romantic relationships than they do on more established long-term relationships.[67]

GENDER DIFFERENCES IN ROMANTIC ATTRACTION: PSYCHOANALYTIC THEORY

We turn now to the third fascinating theory that attempts to explain gender differences in romantic attraction. Several well-known feminist psychoanalysts agreed with evolutionary theorists about the existence of gender differences in romantic attraction, but they explained them in different childhood experiences and different developmental tasks that boys and girls face growing up in a patriarchal society such as ours.[68]

Their explanation for gender differences in love starts with a fact so obvious that most of us do not even acknowledge it. As poet Adrian Rich stated, we are all "of woman born."[69] All of us, men and women alike, are born to a woman. This simple biological fact carries an enormous psychological significance. Because a woman gives birth and nurses, the woman in most human societies, even if she is not the biological mother, is almost always the baby's primary caregiver. "No fact of our early life has greater consequences for how girls and boys develop into women and men, [and] therefore for how we relate to each other in our adult years," writes Lillian Rubin.[70]

Because a woman, most often the mother, takes care of them in the first months of their life, a woman is the first "love object" for both baby boys and baby girls. It is she with whom they form their first attachment and first symbiotic bond, the bond they will later try to recreate in their adult romantic love relationships. During these first stages of development, their love for her is both emotional and erotic. When they develop the ability to differentiate self from other, mother is for both of them the first object of identification.

To develop a mature personality, both boys and girls have to accomplish two tasks: develop a sense of self that is separate and autonomous and develop the ability to relate to others.[71] The accomplishment of these two tasks is related to the development of gender identity, which is different for boys and girls.

Boys, in order to develop a masculine gender identity, need to suppress their emotional attachment to mother and shift their identification to father. Because their penis defines them at this stage ("I have a penis like my father, that's why I'm a man like him"), it becomes the center of the man's masculine identity. The infantile identification with mother is repressed, and defenses are erected against the needs and emotions of infancy. As a result of the early separation from mother, the basic masculine self is separate and autonomous. It is easy for most men to be independent and maintain firm ego boundaries, but they have a hard time being intimate. In other words, men accomplish easily the developmental task of self-definition but have a harder time accomplishing the task of relatedness. When men fall in love, they find again the emotional bond with a woman. The boyhood conflict between longing for the symbiosis with mother and anxiety about losing himself in this symbiosis is repeated in intimate relationships. Men long for closeness and intimacy with a woman but are also terrified by it.[70]

Girls do not need to separate from the mother to develop a feminine gender identity. As a result, for most women it is easy to develop a feminine gender identity, to be like the mother, and easy to be intimate, but difficult to develop an independent self and establish firm ego boundaries. In other words, women easily accomplish the developmental task of relatedness but have a more difficult time accomplishing the task of self-definition.

As a result of these developmental processes, the basic masculine self, one of independence and separation, derives satisfaction in competition and achievements,[72] whereas the basic feminine self, one of relatedness, derives satisfaction from being in an intimate relationship.[73] For boys, although the emotional attachment to the mother is suppressed, the bodily bonding of infancy, which is to say the erotic or sexual aspect of the attachment to her, is left undisturbed and is later transferred to other women. For girls, the erotic attachment to the mother must be denied, shifted to the father, and later in life transferred to another man, but the emotional involvement and identification with the mother remains intact.

Because women had to repress their sexual attraction to the mother but not the emotional connection, the emotional connection is dominant in their love experiences. For them, there is no satisfying sexual relationship without an emotional connection. On the other hand, because men had to repress their emotional connection to their mother but not the sexual attraction, the sexual connection is dominant in their romantic relationships. This is why "for men, the erotic aspect of any relationship remains forever the most compelling, while for women the emotional component will always be the most salient."[70]

Psychological development also affects the different roles of words and sex for men and women. Because the repression of the attachment to the mother happens at such an early age for boys, men do not connect feelings with words the way women do. For men, physical connection is at the center of intimacy; for women, words are the center of intimacy.[70]

As a result of these different childhood experiences, women, more so than men, look for commitment, intimacy, and security in their intimate relationships, whereas men look for attractive physical appearance and sexual appeal in potential mates. Indeed, in the romantic attachment interviews, women described romantic relationships with higher levels of intimacy, commitment, and security than the relationships men described. And, as noted, men described the physical appearances of their lovers as playing a more important role in their romantic attractions.[74]

One result of these processes is a dance of intimacy in which one partner, most often the woman, is the pursuer and the other partner, most often the man, is the distancer. This dance of intimacy occurs in different versions in different couples and in different stages of intimate relationships.

An extreme example of the dance, which is especially frustrating for women, is the *commitment-phobic man*. Often, this is a man that a woman does not even notice at first, but he pursues her with such enthusiasm and determination that she cannot possibly ignore him. His most impressive trait is his ability to express love. Contrary to most men, this type of man can talk for hours about feelings, show vulnerability, bond, and appear truly intimate. The woman, who is dazzled by this outpouring of verbal sensitivity, starts to think that she has found her true love. But, when she finally surrenders and reciprocates his love, sure that now they will live happily ever after, he disappears. At first, she is convinced that something terrible has happened to him. After all, he never failed to arrive for a date or call when he promised he would. She starts searching for him, only to realize that she does not know where he lives. He always came to her house when they went on a date, something she viewed as yet another testimony of his love for her. She does not know where he works; he was kind of vague about it and seemed much more interested in what she was doing, which was also wonderfully flattering. She does not know his family or any of his friends because they always spent time with her friends and family. Gradually, it dawns on her that Prince Charming is really gone. Men like him are capable of expressing their need for a symbiosis only as long as the woman is not interested in them. The minute she reciprocates their love, their anxiety about being engulfed surfaces, and they run away. After the woman has overcome the trauma of his disappearance and has given up on him, he can reappear in her life as enthusiastic as ever, with some feeble explanation for his disappearance. She learns quickly that the only sure way to hold a man like this is by refusing him.

There Are No Significant Gender Differences in Romantic Attraction: Social Construction Theory

Throughout this chapter, I mentioned repeatedly the observation (noted and explained by evolutionary theory, social theory, and psychoanalytic theory) that physical appearance plays a more significant role in the romantic attraction of men than of women. As luck may have it, just as I was writing this chapter, two of my closest female friends were looking for an intimate partner. (One of them attended high school with me, the other one was with me in basic training and officers' course during our compulsory service in the Israeli army, which all Israeli men and women start when they are 18.) Both were married in the past and had recently come out of long intimate relationships. Contrary to all three of these theories, both of them were *very* interested in the physical appearance of potential partners. One told me that she decided not to date a man who seemed otherwise appropriate and extremely nice because he had a huge belly. She met him at a restaurant and enjoyed the encounter very much, but she could not see herself in an intimate relationship with a man with such an enormous belly. The other one told me that she stopped her contact with a man she met through the Internet and who was right in terms of his age and position (both of them attended the same high-prestige high school and college, and both worked as managers in high-tech companies), a man who seemed interesting and friendly, after she saw his picture. She could not imagine having an intimate relationship with a man who looked so unattractive. I must also admit that all the men I have been passionately in love with were good looking. What does that say about us as women?

According to social construction theory, individual differences are more significant than gender differences in romantic attraction. Each of us, man or woman, has a unique pattern of attraction that influences our romantic choices. Indeed, I was never attracted to my closest friends' husbands and boyfriends, even when I could see why they found them attractive. And, similarities in romantic attraction between men and women are more significant than the differences between them.[75]

Social construction theory rests on the belief that reality is socially constructed.[76] There is no, one, particular "reality" that is simultaneously experienced by all people. Different cultures have their unique understandings of the world. Yet, people are not passive recipients of these societal scripts. They actively construct their perceptions of the world and use the culture as a guide. Social construction ideas have been applied to many areas, among them intimate relationships[77] and romantic love.[78] Romantic love is viewed as a social construct. Societies differ in their understanding of the nature of romantic love, and even within the same society, love has been viewed differently in different times and periods in history. Within as complex a society as the United States, there are different subcultures and ethnic groups that have different conceptions of romantic love.[79] The cultural influences far outweigh innate biological and evolutionary influences.

Social constructionists cite studies showing that men and women look for similar things in a mate. Indeed, when the traits *most desired* in a mate are examined, no gender differences are found.[80] Even according to evolutionary theory research, the important traits in a potential mate, for both men and women, are kindness and consideration.[81] Studies done at a university and a dating club concurred. Both men and women put at the top of their lists of desirable traits in a partner kindness, consideration, honesty, and a sense of humor.[82] An analysis of personal ads also showed that the most desirable traits of a potential mate are understanding and a sense of humor.[83] After the relationship has been established, the partner's sensitivity and ability to be empathic and intimate influence the satisfaction from the relationship of both men and women. A study found no evidence for women's allegedly greater concern with having a secure, committed, sexually exclusive relationship. Most of the men and women who participated in the study valued equally these features of intimacy.[84]

A review of studies of differences in the genders' approaches to sex showed that women have a strong interest in sex and are able to function sexually at a level similar to that of men. Furthermore, in many societies, especially Western societies, women have sex outside marriage regularly with no concern for punishment or criticism. On the whole, women are expressing their sexuality far more freely than it was common to think.[85] Sexuality as an aspect of courtship varies with the libido of the couple involved and their ages. Not only because of life experience and comfort with one's body, but also because of when sexual libido peaks for men and women. Women tend to peak in sexual functioning in their thirties and forties—a later age than the sexual peak for men.[86]

Instead of a view of sexuality that emphasizes the differences between men and women, social constructionists emphasize the subjective experience of every individual. The ideal relationship between two sexual partners, either heterosexual or homosexual, is "intersubjective"—that is, two individuals who treat each other as subjects rather than objects and delight in each other's uniqueness.[87] An intersubjective relationship is the exact antithesis of a sex role stereotyped relationship that rigidly defines the different roles of men and women. Jessica Benjamin described an intersubjective sexual relationship using a joke she heard from a friend who grew up in Long Island.

> One full-moon night in midsummer, the horseshoe crabs all come out from the water onto the bay shore, where they mate amid clattering of shells. Then they all light up and say to each other, "It was good for me. How was it for you?"

"Obviously, the joke lies in the attribution of human intersubjectivity to crabs: concern with each other's pleasure, respect for the inevitable difference between my experience and yours."[88]

If our individual differences are so large and the focus on them so beneficial to our intimate relationships, why then are so many people and so many researchers and theoreticians convinced that men and women are attracted to different things in a potential mate? Carol Tavris believes that "human beings love to divide the world and its inhabitants into pairs of opposites," we/them, good guys/bad guys, and, of course, men/women.[89] Western ways of thinking emphasize dualisms and opposites and pose many questions of human life in fruitless either/or terms.[90] Are we uniquely human or basically mammalian? Are we shaped by nature or by nurture? After we divide things, the same tendency makes us emphasize the differences between them. When parents who have two children are asked to describe them, they tend to describe them as opposites; if one is an angel, almost always the other one is a devil. The oversimplification hides the fact that the similarity is much greater than the difference.

GENDER DIFFERENCES IN ROMANTIC ATTRACTION: SOCIAL CONSTRUCTION THEORY VERSUS EVOLUTIONARY THEORY

Social construction theory views gender differences in romantic attraction as minor and as the results of primarily cultural forces; evolutionary theory views them as large and as the result of innate, biologically based differences. The greatest differences are assumed to be in men's attraction to physical appearance and in women's attractions to status. A question typical of the Western way of thinking is, Which theory is correct? To answer this question, I looked at the romantic attraction interviews and compared the responses of the Israeli and American young men and women.[91]

Results of this gender-by-culture comparison provide partial support for both the evolutionary and social construction theories. As predicted by evolutionary theory, more men than women mentioned the physical appearance of their partner.

But, there was no difference in the frequency with which they mentioned status. On the other hand, culture did have an effect on the importance of status as a cause of attraction. Significantly more Americans than Israelis were attracted to the status of their partner. In addition, gender differences were found that evolutionary theory had not predicted would be found: Women were significantly more likely than men to attribute arousal to romantic attraction. And, gender differences were not found when they were expected: Men were as likely as women to be attracted to someone who satisfied their needs.[92]

These findings, as well as other findings reported throughout the chapter, suggest a need for an integrated theory of romantic attraction that combines some aspects of evolutionary theory with the contributions of the social theories. Although there have been several attempts to offer such an integrated approach, there are also those who believe that such an integration is impossible. It has been argued, for example, that although research may show an integration of biological and social influences, such different approaches as evolutionary psychology and social construction theory "cannot conjoin."[78]

I believe that an integration of evolutionary theory, psychoanalytic theory, social theory, and social construction theory is not only possible, but necessary. Each of these theories highlights an important aspect of the way men and women experience falling in love. Biological forces, the physical excitation of falling in love, which I describe later in the book (chapter 10, pp. 152–154), affect falling in love and may be triggered differently in men and women. Different childhood experiences influence the romantic choices of women and men, and social norms and stereotypes prescribe the mating game. Nevertheless, falling in love remains for every person in love the most private and unique experience.

SUGGESTIONS FOR THOSE SEEKING LOVE

What should those seeking love conclude from all this? It is possible, of course, simply to conclude that it is important, especially for women and especially on the first date, to try gain maximum benefit from one's physical appearance. It is important for men to appear successful and ready to commit. This is an obvious conclusion that is applied by most people who come in contact with an attractive candidate. But, it is also possible to conclude, as the social constructionists suggest, that both men and women are looking for a partner who is kind, considerate, and fun to be with. Luckily, these are traits that, with some effort, can be adopted and developed. But social constructionists are saying something else too. They are saying that each one of us is a unique individual, and our uniqueness is more important than the similarities we share with our own sex or the differences that divide us from the opposite sex.

As I was writing this, a young man arrived for his therapy session. He is a handsome and bright young man who just finished his law degree and comes from a wealthy and supportive family. Nevertheless, he has never been in an intimate relationship. Wanting very much to have such a relationship and realizing that there must be a problem if he continuously fails to establish one, brought him to therapy. In this session, he talked about his difficulty in bringing out his "true self," that part of him that is "sensitive and vulnerable and easily hurt" when he meets new women. "Women expect a man to be strong and sure of himself," he told me. By not being himself and by behaving according to the masculine stereotype, he kept himself from the true intimacy he longed for.

This young man had two choices: either play the dating game and present a mask of the masculine persona or take the risk and present his true self. He is familiar with the first option, and if he chooses to continue with it, he may only get to know the feminine persona that women will present in response. If he chooses the second, and scarier, option, the woman he likes may well reject him because she perceives him as, in his words, "weak and feminine." Does he really want to be intimate with a woman who rejects him because he revealed to her his true self? What will happen, if he marries such a woman, when she eventually discovers his true self? Even if many women reject him when they discover his true self—an unlikely yet undeniably unpleasant experience—the probability of him finding a woman who is also looking for true intimacy increases enormously. A woman like that is likely to be attracted to him *because* he reveals his true self, rather than a masculine mask, and she is likely to respond by revealing her own true self, thus taking the first step toward true intimacy.

For those among the readers who hope that once the bridge of first acquaintance has been crossed, they can go beyond stereotypes and social norms to a truly intimate relationship, the path chosen ought to be the one most likely to lead to this end.

Part Two

UNCONSCIOUS CHOICES

How We Choose the Loves We Choose

> The heart has its reasons, which reason knows nothing of.
> —Blaise Pascal

> Lovers and men of intellect cannot mix ...
> Lovers who drink the dregs of the wine reel from bliss to bliss:
> The dark-hearted men of reason
> Burn inwardly with denial.
> —Talal al-Din Rumi, *Lovers and Men of Intellect*

EOPLE OFTEN EXPRESS AN AMUSED SURPRISE WHEN THEY HEAR ABOUT THE effects such situational variables as proximity and arousal have on falling in love. But they readily agree that such variables do indeed have an effect and often have examples of their own to prove it. People usually express less surprise, however, when they hear about the influence of similarity in background and attitudes, a pleasant personality, and physical beauty—qualities found in the beloved. These are the types of things "everybody and his grandmother" know about falling in love. Research on reciprocal attraction, the role of gratifying needs in romantic love, the process of falling in love, and gender differences in romantic attraction helps people make sense of information that they already had in one form or another.

But, even after a detailed discussion of the known and conscious determinants of falling in love, people can be left with a strong feeling that something is still missing. Somehow missing from the studies and theories, interesting and amusing as they may be, is the most important, significant, and mysterious element—the magic of love. The studies do not explain why it is that we fall in love with one person and not with another who is more similar in background and attitudes, whose personality is more pleasant and appearance more impressive, and whom we see more often. The theories do not explain why one person makes us "walk on air" and feel we have "come home" and found our "match made in heaven," whom we had known without knowing our entire lives. Why does another person, who is far more appropriate according to all the relevant criteria, leave us cold? These are the types of questions the second part of the book addresses. Here, we focus on the unconscious processes in falling in love. Because they are unconscious, these processes are difficult to observe directly and study empirically. As a result, the second part relies less on empirical research and more on clinical evidence.

Chapter 8

OPENNESS TO LOVE

Benedick: I could find in my heart that I had not a hard heart, for, truly, I love none.

Beatrice: I thank God, and my cold blood … for that I had rather hear my dog bark at a crow than a man swear he loves me.
      —Shakespeare, *Much Ado About Nothing*,
        Act 1, Scene 1

RACHEL WAS EXASPERATED. AGAIN, HER FRIEND SANDY WAS SPREAD OUT on the couch in her living room crying her heart out because of the ending of yet another nonrelationship with a stupid, undeserving man. What was it about Sandy, a smart, successful, attractive woman and a wonderful friend that pushed her to this obsessive search for an intimate relationship with a man? Every few weeks, or so it seemed, she would arrive at Rachel's apartment with a story about a new love she had found, convinced each time that this was the greatest love of her life, a man she was sure she would marry and live with happily ever after. Then, Rachel would not see her for a while as Sandy pursued relentlessly her new love, until the man said he could not take it anymore, and the relationship would end. Rachel herself avoided intimate relationships. She loved her little apartment, nested next to a park. She would sit near the big window overlooking the park and thank God for the peace and quiet in her life. She loved her work and loved coming back to her beautifully decorated and comfortable apartment. The thought of going through the type of heart-wrenching experiences that Sandy seemed to thrive on was intolerable to her. She knew, of course, that there were other relationships people had. She and Sandy had a childhood friend who had been married happily for years, but it still seemed to her to be too much work and too much trouble to find such a relationship. In the meantime, she was perfectly content to live alone.

I'm single, and I don't have a boyfriend. I would say I've never had a boyfriend … . Other people are more excited about just being with someone than being with someone in particular. I had a few good male friends, but as far as a romantic relationship goes, I just was not ready emotionally. I was not used to it. Most people were moving faster than I was, and I just wasn't comfortable. I have no problem being friends with men, but it's sort of a struggle getting into a romantic thing. Something about it just didn't feel right to me ... the whole idea just scared me.

I've been kind of shy. I haven't pursued relationships with women. I'd like to, but I hadn't bothered to. I'd like to get married, have kids, but the bachelor life suits me. I'm in no rush. It'll happen eventually. Once in a while I may think about it when I see a couple on the street. I'm kind of reclusive. I don't like partners.

I don't have a boyfriend. I never had a serious relationship. The main reason is in me. I would become too dependent on the relationship. Now I understand that I am the one who needs to change. Now people are starting to approach me. Before I had a wall around me because I was so needy.

I have never been in a romantic relationship, not really. I have buddies and stuff, but I have a bad problem with the physical aspect of romantic relationships. When you find someone you like, they don't always like you. I don't tell them what I feel. It's tough 'cause I can be guessing wrong ... . It scares me.

Of the men and women interviewed about their significant intimate relationships, a tenth said that, at age 23, they had never been in a romantic relationship.[1] Their romantic encounters had not gone beyond one or two dates. Other interviewees talked about highly intimate and highly satisfying relationships of many years. Some had had only one such significant relationship; some had had two or even three significant relationships. A small number, all of them men, had had four or more significant intimate relationships.

There are people who fall in love easily, intensely, and repeatedly; some even claim that they cannot live without love. And, there are others who have never been in love and are convinced that all the stories about the great intensity of romantic love are either vast exaggerations or straight out lies.[2] One of these, a good-looking man and a highly respected journalist, told me that he is convinced that passionate love is an invention. He himself has lusted after many women and he knows very well what sexual passion is, but he has never fallen in love.

Why is it that some people can find love and a romantic relationship easy and satisfying, and others want desperately to have a truly intimate relationship but fail? Why do still others avoid intimate relationships all together, like the young girl in Bouguereau's painting, they defend themselves against Eros' arrow (see Figure 13)? The answer to this important question is not simple. One major explanation has been provided by *attachment theory*, formulated first by the British child psychoanalyst John Bowlby.[3]

ATTACHMENT THEORY

Bowlby believed that early childhood experiences have the most profound impact on adult love relationships. The key is *attachment*, the first stable love relationship that the baby develops. The ability to attach is innate, but the form it takes depends

FIGURE 13. Young woman defending herself against Eros (Bouguereau, 1880).

on the relationship that the baby has with his "primary caregiver," most often the mother. An infant needs a reliable, ongoing attachment to the primary caregiver and suffers grievously, even irreparably, if that attachment is interrupted or lost. Bowlby was convinced that the inborn human need for attachment is the result of an evolutionary development. Babies are born with a repertoire of behaviors that are aimed at obtaining and preserving closeness to a "strong and wise caregiver." But, the maintenance of the closeness is related not only to the baby's repertoire, but also to the ability, willingness, sensitivity, and accessibility of the caregiver. The experiences the baby has with the caregiver are internalized into mental models of the self and the other. These "internalized working models" determine how the infant's sense of self and sense of others unfold and are later generalized to other relationships. The internal models change with development because, despite being genetically imprinted, they are sensitive to environmental influences. The internal models are responsible for all patterns of adult attachments, including, first and foremost, romantic attachment.

The major premises of Bowlby's attachment theory are as follows:

- Intimate relationships of adults are guided by internal working models constructed from early childhood relationship experiences.
- These models shape individuals' beliefs about whether they are worthy of love and whether others can be trusted to provide love and support.
- These models also influence the types of interactions individuals have with others and their interpretations of these interactions.

When the primary caregiver is consistent, stable, trustworthy, and responsive, the baby develops a sense of security in love and as an adult will feel comfortable and satisfied in love relationships. When the primary caregiver is not consistent, stable, and trustworthy and if the baby is abandoned or rejected, then the baby will develop an adult pattern of anxiety and ambivalence about love or else will attempt to avoid altogether the dangers involved in intimate relationships.

Although John Bowlby is the theoretical father of attachment theory, Mary Slater Ainsworth, his student, is its empirical mother. Mary Ainsworth and her students observed 76 babies and their mothers in their homes. They paid attention to each mother's style of responding to her infant in terms of such things as feeding, crying, cuddling, eye contact, and smiling. Each mother-baby pair was observed for 72 hours spread over 18 observation sessions, each lasting 4 hours.[4]

The most famous and most original part of the research involved watching the 1-year-old babies respond to separation from mother in a procedure termed *strange situation*. Mother and baby were put in a toy-filled room where a friendly research assistant greeted them and invited the baby to play with the toys. The infant was observed as the mother left the room three times for 3-minute intervals. During two intervals, the research assistant was in the room; during another interval, the baby was alone. Ainsworth identified three distinct patterns in the baby's reaction to the room full of toys, to the mother's departure, and to her return.

The *securely attached*, about two-thirds of the babies, were infants who were ready to explore the room on their own but turned once in a while to make sure the mother was there. They protested or cried on separation, but when the mother returned, they greeted her with pleasure, frequently stretching out their arms to be picked up and molding to her body. They were relatively easy to console.

The *anxiously attached* or *ambivalent*, about 10%, seemed anxious and insecure. They tended to cling and were afraid to explore the room on their own. They became terribly anxious and agitated on separation, often crying profusely. They sought contact with the mother when she returned, but simultaneously arched away from her angrily, resisting her efforts to soothe them.

The *avoidant*, about 20 to 25%, gave the impression of independence. They explored the new environment without using their mothers as a secure base, and they did not turn to be certain of the mother's presence. When the mother left, they did not seem affected, but an examination of their heartbeat showed a strong response. When she returned, the infant snubbed or avoided her.

Because Ainsworth and her team had observed the mother-baby pairs in their homes, she was able to make specific associations between the babies' attachment styles and the mothers' styles of parenting. Mothers of securely attached babies were more responsive to the hunger signals and crying of their infants and readily returned the infants' smiles. Mothers of anxiously attached babies were inconsistent and unresponsive to the baby's needs. Mothers of avoidant babies rejected their infants either physically or emotionally.[4] In other words, the three attachment patterns seen in the laboratory were directly related to the ways the babies were mothered. The insecure babies developed strategies that helped them cope with a mother's rejection or inconsistency.

The anxious baby tries desperately to make the mother pay attention and be responsive and loving. The baby senses that when the begging is loud enough or the scene dramatic enough, the mother responds from guilt. This is why the anxious baby clings to the mother and tries to punish her when she does not respond. The baby is addicted to the mother and to the effort to make her respond.

The avoidant baby chooses the opposite strategy. This baby learns to suppress and ignore his or her needs and emotions. The baby is angry at the mother and distances from her even while remaining as attached to her as the anxious baby. Because pleas for attention have been rejected in an insulting and hurtful way, the baby says in effect to the rejecting mother: "Who needs you anyway? I can manage on my own!" At times, grandiose feelings about the self are added to this response ("I'm perfect and I don't need anyone"), suggesting the early development of a narcissistic personality.

Often, the mother's inattention results from the emotional deprivation she herself had suffered in her childhood. Her baby's emotional needs remind her of her own infantile needs that she had succeeded in repressing at great effort. The reminder generates an internal anger, depression, and rejection, which she then expresses toward her child. In this way, the problem is transferred from one generation to the next in a multigenerational pattern.

In succeeding studies, researchers showed that the attachment patterns formed in infancy persist in adulthood. The patterns of intimate relationships that people exhibit as adults are powerfully influenced by the types of relationships they had with their primary caregivers, most often the mother.[5] In the most famous series of studies, Philip Shaver and Cindy Hazan used a measure of adult romantic attachment that was inspired by Ainsworth's work.[6] These studies, as well as hundreds of others, demonstrated the existence of three romantic attachment styles:

Secure. Adults with a secure attachment style are comfortable depending on others and having others depend on them. It is easy for them to become emotionally close to people. They feel themselves valuable and worthy of love and respect. They can trust people; they believe that people have good intentions and can be counted on in an hour of need. They develop intimate relationships easily and do not worry about being alone or about someone getting too close to them. They are not overly concerned about abandonment or dependency, and they tend to score high in sensitivity to others and low in compulsive giving.

Anxious-ambivalent. Adults with an anxious-ambivalent attachment style see others as reluctant to get as close as they would like. They often worry that their partner does not really love them or will not want to stay with them. They are seeking such high levels of closeness and commitment that they scare away potential partners, who often view them as clingy and suffocating. They are insecure and invest too much in relationships. They tend to think that people do not value them as much as they should, and that, in general, people are untrustworthy. They often separate again and again from the same partner and tend to be jealous in relationships. They have low self-concepts and reveal too much about themselves. They worry about being abandoned and their love not being reciprocated, and they worry about being too close and dependent. They tend to score high in compulsive giving and low in sensitivity.

FOUR ATTACHMENT STYLES (BARTHOLOMEW, 1990)

Secure. It is easy for me to become emotionally close to others. I am comfortable depending on others and having others depend on me. I don't worry about being alone or having others not accept me.

Fearful Avoidant. I am somewhat uncomfortable getting close to others. I want emotionally close relationships, but I find it difficult to depend on others or to trust them completely. I sometimes worry that I will be hurt if I allow myself to become emotionally too close to others.

Preoccupied. I want to be completely emotionally intimate with others, but I often find that others are reluctant to get as close as I would like. I am uncomfortable being without close relationships, but I sometimes worry that others don't value me as much as I value them.

Dismissing Avoidant. I am uncomfortable with close relationships. It is very important to me to feel independent and self-sufficient, and I prefer not to depend on others or have them depend on me.

Avoidant. Adults with an avoidant attachment style tend to be isolated. They are uncomfortable being close to others; they find it difficult to allow themselves to depend on others or to trust others completely. They are nervous when anyone gets too close; often, their partners in a relationship want them to be more intimate than they are comfortable being. They have many separations but suffer less from relationship termination. They are loners, uncomfortable in relationships involving intimacy and closeness, and are more likely to be unfaithful.

Attachment styles influence people's sexual styles. *Secure* individuals are willing to experiment sexually but do so in the context of a committed relationship. They enjoy nearly all physical and sexual contact from cuddling to oral sex. They are unlikely to engage in one-night stands or to have sex outside the relationship. *Anxious* individuals like the physical, nurturing, aspects of the relationship but enjoy sex less. *Avoidant* individuals take less enjoyment from almost all physical, except for sexual, contact; are more likely to engage in one-night stands; and are more likely to think that sex without love is pleasurable.

A study of adult attachment styles in a large, nationally representative sample involving thousands of people showed that 59% of the population are securely attached, 25% are avoidant, and 11% are anxious.[7] I think it is fascinating to note that these percentages are very close to Ainsworth's original observations in infants some 20 years earlier.

Kim Bartholomew divided the avoidant category in two, thus creating four adult attachment categories.[8] If you are wondering about your own attachment style, you can rate yourself on the four categories using her measure (see Box).

Childhood adversities such as physical abuse and serious neglect have been shown to have the most consistent association with insecure attachment styles. Psychopathology in a parent has also been shown to have a strong association with insecure attachment. A parent's substance abuse was related to avoidant attachment, whereas financial adversity during childhood was related to insecure attachment. And, adult attachment styles were repeatedly related to people's ability to function in romantic relationships.[9]

Attachment styles can be measured as early as 12 months of age and, in the absence of major environmental change, persist into adulthood.[10] Attachment styles also affect coping with stress, for example, the way couples respond to an anxiety-provoking situation. In a study that demonstrated this, wives were told that they were going to take part in an activity "that produces anxiety in most people"; their husbands were told that they would take part in a neutral activity. The couples were videotaped as they waited together for the activity. Analysis of the videotapes showed that it was possible to predict the couples' behavior in the waiting room from their attachment styles. The secure women sought the closeness of their husbands; the avoidant women kept their distance. The men showed a similar pattern of behavior. The secure men gave their wives support in words and physical contact; the avoidant husbands shunned their wives. The ambivalent men and women did not show a consistent pattern of behavior.[11]

EVALUATION OF ATTACHMENT THEORY AND RESEARCH

Although attachment theory has inspired a large and steadily growing body of research, it has also raised a fair amount of criticism. Some criticized Ainsworth's "strange situation" for being an artificial base for data that could not generalize to real-life situations. Some criticized the overemphasis on the influence of the relationship between the baby and mother. Doesn't the father have an influence? And what about siblings, grandparents, other relatives, teachers, and close friends? Others criticized the tendency to blame the mother for everyone's problems. Doesn't a romantic relationship that ended badly have more of an impact than the mother's handling in the first months of life? Still others criticized the overemphasis on childhood experiences. After all, we continue to evolve and learn from relationships throughout our life.

Ainsworth's response to these criticisms was to say that both she and Bowlby believe that our internal attachment model is sensitive to environmental influences, and that people continue to influence us throughout our lives. In her later work, she extended attachment theory beyond infancy to "affectional bonds" throughout life, including kinship bonds, friendship bonds, and, of course, sexual pair-bonds.[12]

Bowlby has argued, for example, that in successful psychotherapy, the therapist can become an important attachment figure for the individual in therapy. When the psychotherapist is internalized as an attachment model, it helps build in the patient a feeling of safety and trust that can serve as a secure base from which he or she will be able to examine, without fear, the internalized working models of him- or herself and of others. Even if such a therapeutic relationship is not as primary and not as long as the childhood relationship with mother, it can still be valuable in changing people's attachment styles.

SELF-CONFIDENCE AND OPENNESS TO LOVE

How do you feel and act when you are in love? Do you feel secure in yourself and in the love given to you? Do you avoid getting close and intimate? If so, is this why you are not in an intimate relationship, or are there really no appropriate candidates? Are you longing for a relationship but allow your anxiety and ambivalence to scare potential partners away? It seems rather obvious from all the predictions and studies generated by attachment theory that our self-concept and self-confidence influences our ability to give and receive love. An early study that demonstrated this showed that young people with the highest number of falling-in-love experiences had high self-confidence and low defensiveness.[13]

To love others, we first must love and respect ourselves. Attachment studies show that secure individuals are more self-confident, less neurotic, more extroverted, more agreeable, and more open to new experiences than avoidant and anxious individuals.[14]

The conclusion that in order to be able to love others we first must love ourselves is not big news in psychology. Eric Erikson argued over 40 years ago that we have to develop a strong and positive sense of ourselves before we can develop and sustain an intimate relationship.[15] The finding that people with a highly developed sense of identity have relationships with greater intimacy than people with an undeveloped identity showed that Erikson was right.[16] People whose sense of identity is not well developed are afraid of intimacy because they are afraid to be engulfed. And, their anxiety is well founded. When people like that fall in love, their love is especially powerful, often taking complete control of them and becoming the main focus of their lives, resulting in compulsive, destructive, desperate love.[17]

Does self-confidence always imply greater openness to love? Not necessarily. With greater self-confidence come higher expectations and standards for an appropriate romantic partner. In a study that illustrated this, an attractive, well-dressed, young man approached a succession of young women who were waiting to receive the results of a personality test they had taken. As each woman waited, the young man started talking to her, indicated that he liked her, and asked her for a date. At that moment, the experimenter walked in and showed her to another room, where she received the results of the personality test. Half of the women read positive evaluations that were aimed at raising self-confidence. The other half read negative evaluations that were aimed at reducing self-concept and self-confidence. The experimenter then asked each woman how much she liked various people, such as a teacher or a friend, and because "there was space left on the page," how did she evaluate the young man who approached her in the waiting room? Results indicated that the women who received negative evaluations and felt less confident expressed greater liking for the man who showed an interest in them.[18] The greater the insecurity and doubts we have about ourselves, the greater our liking and appreciation for a person who likes us.

Similar findings were reported in a study on how self-esteem influences the search for a romantic partner. In this study, male students who took an intelligence test received false information about their performance; some were told that they had done extremely well, and the others were told that they had failed miserably. Afterward, during a break, the experimenter joined the subject for coffee. A female confederate waited in the coffee shop. When the experimenter and the subject entered, the experimenter "discovered" the confederate, who sat alone, joined her, and introduced the subject. In half of the cases, the confederate, with the help of makeup, hairstyle, and appropriate clothes, looked attractive; in half of the cases, she was made to look unattractive. The experimenter noted whether the subject expressed romantic interest in the young woman. Did he try to make her stay longer? Did he offer to pay for her coffee? Did he express a desire to meet her again? Did he ask for her phone number? Analysis of the observations indicated that the students who felt more sure of themselves, because of their great success in the intelligence test, expressed more romantic interest in the young woman when she looked attractive. On the other hand, the students who felt less self-confident, because they had performed miserably, expressed more interest in the young woman when she looked less attractive.[19]

The less sure of ourselves we are, the more we need love, appreciation, and respect and the more likely we are to be attracted to people who offer us those rewards. The surer of ourselves we are, the less we need approval, acceptance, and love. We are likely to be choosier and less likely to fall in love with just anyone who offers us love. Like a person who just had a large meal can afford to be choosy about the dessert but a hungry person will eat anything, an insecure person is likely to be indiscriminant and choose someone less attractive because that type of person is less likely to reject him or her and more likely to offer love and appreciation.

In women, self-confidence is often related to physical attractiveness. Women who had been rated for attractiveness by objective judges were asked to describe their romantic preferences. It is not surprising that all women preferred to date a high-status man, such as a physician or a lawyer, over a low-status man, such as a janitor or a waiter. Nevertheless, unattractive women were willing to go out with men holding jobs in the middle of the scale, such as an electrician or a clerk, but attractive women were not.[20]

This brings us back to the relationship between self-confidence and various love styles.[21] You may recall that insecure people who are not self-actualized tend toward a game-playing style of love and have relationships with low levels of intimacy and high levels of conflict. People who are self-confident and self-actualized, on the other hand, tend toward unselfish and romantic styles of love, and their relationships are characterized by high levels of intimacy.[22]

PSYCHOLOGICAL BARRIERS TO FALLING IN LOVE

The question of readiness for love is of great interest for clinicians who work with individuals who seem incapable of sustaining intimate relationships. I am currently working with two such individuals, a young man and a young woman. Both are attractive physically, intelligent, and charming. Both want desperately to be in an intimate relationship. Both have a long list of relationships that lasted from one date to several weeks, but none evolved into the type of truly intimate relationship for which they both long.

The man, who is a wonderful dancer, often falls in love with his ballroom dance partners. He dazzles them with his openness, his readiness to talk about feelings, his ability to express love. Each is delighted to receive the love poem he left in her mailbox after their first date and is ready to join him in this larger-than-life love story. Their amazement lasts a week or two, or even three, and then it turns to distress. He is simply too much. Finding a love poem every time you open your mailbox, every time you put your hand in your coat pocket, every time you open a drawer, is not thrilling; it is suffocating. In therapy, when he asked me if I wanted to see his poems and I said yes, he brought 682 poems to the next session. The women try to distance themselves from this flood of love and tell him that they need some space, but he insists on being true to his feelings and expressing his love. When they cannot take it anymore, they break up with him.

The woman is an attractive professional woman who meets many men through her work. Men are dazzled by her beauty, intelligence, and feminine charm. They pursue her, and she responds enthusiastically, falling madly in love, convinced every time that she has found her true love. The mutual enthusiasm lasts a week or two, and then the men start distancing as she overwhelms them with her phone calls, her generous gifts, and her physical presence—she likes to arrive unannounced and surprise them by cleaning or cooking for them. When they hint that they need some space, she insists that she is a genuine person who needs to express her feelings. So, she continues flooding them with her love, and sooner or later, they walk away, assuring her each time that she is a wonderful person; it is they who do not deserve all the love she has to give.

One of the most famous psychoanalysts to address the psychological barriers to falling in love and maintaining an intimate relationship is Otto Kernberg. Kernberg believed that the ability to love reflects the individual's developmental level.[23] To fall in love and maintain a love relationship, one has to reach a certain emotional depth and maturity. "A capacity for relating to one's own self in depth as well as to others seems to be a basic precondition for a deep and lasting relation between two people who love each other."[23]

Kernberg described people's ability to love on the following five-point scale:

Total inability to love. This most extreme end of the scale represents an inability to establish relationships that involve sexual love. It characterizes the extreme examples of a narcissistic, schizophrenic personality structure. [A narcissistic personality is characterized by unrealistic feelings of grandiosity and a ceaseless need for admiration. The total involvement with the self prevents the establishment of intimate relationships. Schizophrenia is a serious mental illness that causes serious disturbances in perception, motivation. and emotion.]

Sexual promiscuity. The second pattern expressed is usually, but not always, heterosexual. It characterizes a less extreme form of narcissistic personality disorder, and people who suffer from it are capable of establishing intimate relationships. But since they tend to treat others as tools for their own gratification, their intimate relationships tend to be immature, incomplete, and often sexually focused.

Primitive idealization of the beloved and childish dependence. The third pattern is clinging and characterizes borderline personality disorder. [People with this disorder tend to have unstable interpersonal relationships and swing between total idealization and total dismissal of the other. They also tend to be emotionally unstable, impulsive, and desperate to prevent a real or imagined abandonment.]

Ability to create stable relationships, without the ability to enjoy full sexual satisfaction. The fourth pattern characterizes less serious personality disorders and neuroses. [Neuroses, according to psychoanalytic theory, are disturbances that originate in an unconscious conflict that creates anxiety. The anxiety pushes the individual to use various defense mechanisms that distort reality.]

Deep intimate relations with a healthy combination of sexuality and sensitivity to the other. This fifth pattern is at the positive end of the scale.

The different levels on the scale represent levels of maturity or "personality organization" that are determined by the stage in which a "developmental failure" occurred.[24] To understand what a developmental failure is, we first need to understand normal development.

Our personality is the result of a developmental process that the noted psychoanalyst Margaret Mahler calls *psychological birth*.[25] Mahler believes that psychological birth is not the same as physical birth. She and her colleagues followed "normal children of average mothers" from birth to age 3. Their observations led them to conclude that psychological birth requires a successful passage through the following stages:

Autistic stage. The first stage in a baby's life, from birth to 2 months, during which the baby responds only to internal needs, and periods of sleep are longer than periods of being awake.

Symbiotic stage. When the baby's sensitivity and response to outside stimuli grow, at 2 to 5 months, the baby moves to the symbiotic stage. Here, there is no differentiation between self and non-self, between baby and mother. This symbiosis, this experience of oneness with the mother, is the building block for the ability to love and all future love relationships. The successful passage of this stage depends on the mother's ability to mother and the baby's ability to accept mothering.

The symbiotic stage explains why when people fall in love their ego boundaries collapse, and they feel at one in body and soul with the beloved and why people who fall in love are emotionally closed to being in love with anyone else. Symbiosis, and thus falling in love, is by definition only between two.

Separating from the mother and developing an independent self. When a baby has what famous children's doctor and psychoanalyst Donald Winnicott called "good enough mothering," the baby can start separating from the mother and develop an independent self-identity. Winnicott did a great favor to concerned mothers by assuring them that in order to raise an emotionally healthy baby you do not need to be a perfect mother, only "a good enough mother."[26] The process of separation from the mother and the development of an independent self happens in four stages:

- *Differentiation*, 6 to 9 months. At this stage, the baby explores the world with eyes, hands, feet, and mouth. The start of differentiation can be seen in a baby who sucks a fist. The expression of wonder and endless fascination on the baby's face indicates a beginning to understanding that both the sensation in the mouth and on the fist are one's own, and that the baby can make them happen. It has been said that the baby's first reality testing is reality tasting. Only when the baby is able to differentiate between self and what is not self can the baby start internalizing objects, that is, people, relationships, and things. The mother is the baby's first love object and therefore also the first object the baby internalizes. As the baby starts separating from the mother, elements of her are internalized. Those internalized elements become a part of the baby's own independent, inner world.

- *Practicing*, 10 to 16 months. After the baby has internalized the mother, or elements of the mother, the baby can tolerate being separated from her. At this stage, the baby starts to practice separating from the mother. The baby has an affair with the world and is full of enthusiasm and growing independence. At the beginning of this stage, the baby crawls; at the end of the stage, the toddler walks. Children at this stage love to play the game of "getting away from Mom." The mother has to be able to tolerate the distancing and encourage the development of an independent self by recognizing her child's needs and preferences. When the mother encourages her child's independence but is there for him, the child learns that separation can be enjoyable and exciting and does not mean a loss of love.

- *Rapprochement*, 17 to 24 months. This stage of refueling is characterized by growing independence. followed by a retreat, separation, and return for love. It is important for the mother to allow her child to get away from her but to be there with a loving hug and nurturing when the newly acquired independence becomes too scary.

- *Consolidation of individuality*, 24 to 36 months. An inner world of internalized love objects enables the child to form stable emotional relationships, postpone gratification, tolerate frustrations, and enjoy the workings of an independent self.

When the child passes these four stages successfully, the result is a "psychological birth," the first step in the development of an autonomous personality with a unique and coherent self-identity capable of facing challenges, forming attachments, accepting others, and withstanding separation and conflict. An individuated person is able to maintain long-term love relationships even after the first drive was satisfied and despite frustration, disappointment, and attacks. Such a person can postpone gratification, suffer frustration, and enjoy the functioning of an independent ego. Such a person can also distinguish self from other and truly enjoy the other person's separate identity.

Throughout this process, the primal conflict between longing for the infantile symbiosis and the need for independence and fear of engulfment expresses itself. This conflict returns in full force in adult romantic relationships as a dance of intimacy between the pull toward intimacy and the push toward independence.[27]

WHEN SOMETHING GOES WRONG

A traumatic experience in one of these developmental stages can cause a fear of separation or a fear of engulfment. Abandonment, even if temporary, causes mortal dread and is imprinted as such. When the child's drive toward independence is suffocated by the parent's anxiety, the child develops a fear of engulfment and a strong need for space, independence, and autonomy. When the child's need for closeness is frustrated by a parent who pushes for independence too early or is not there to defend the child when in need, the child develops a fear of abandonment and an unusually strong need for closeness and merging. These unconscious needs later define the choice of a romantic partner and influence the couple's dynamic.[28]

Failure in the process of separation–individuation results in the absence of a separate, independent self.[29] At times, people with such a fragile self develop a "borrowed identity." They adopt the values of their family of origin or of other people. They cannot separate from their family, and all their emotional energy is invested in it. When the self is fragile, the person needs constant assurances and cannot stand criticism or rejection. The goal in life is to be loved and accepted by others. Such a person will always try to be what the other wants. A mature self, on the other hand, has boundaries; therefore, a person with a mature self is far less influenced by the opinions and demands of others.

This brings us back to Otto Kernberg, who believed that the ability to love reflects the level of emotional depth and maturity. The level of maturity is determined by the stage in which a developmental failure occurred in the process of separation–individuation. The ability to love can be described on a continuum. On the highest end is the ability to achieve a deep and stable relationship with complete sexual satisfaction, a testament to success in the process of separation from the primal symbiosis with the mother and the development of an independent and differentiated self. On the lowest end is total inability to have intimate relationships that involve love and sexuality, which testifies to a serious failure of individuation. The earlier the developmental failure and the more difficult the trauma that caused it, the more likely it is to severely affect the ability to love.[23]

It is important to note that the view of the separated individuated person as a model of mental health has been criticized by feminist writers as being a masculine model—the ideal of mental health is in fact a masculine stereotype.[30] What is described as normal development is characteristic of a patriarchal society in which the mother is the primary caregiver rather than a partner in shared parenting.[31]

SCHIZOID PERSONALITY DISORDER

I cannot end the discussion of the ability, or inability, to love without addressing the personality disorder that is most relevant to the subject, namely, schizoid personality disorder. People with this personality disorder tend to avoid all close relationships, including sexual love relationships, and treat all people with suspicion and distance. They see in intimate relationships a threat of being controlled or of their inner world being invaded. When they are married or in an intimate relationship, they express little interest in their partners and do not share their thoughts or feelings. They lack, almost altogether, an interest in social involvement and basic social skills, such as carrying on a conversation. They show no interest in either praise or criticism from other people. Because their emotional expression is limited, they are often perceived as cold and distant. Their social world is limited. They have few intimate relationships; few friends, if any; and tend to be extremely isolated. When emotional issues arise during social contacts, they feel tremendous discomfort and tend to escape the discussion of emotions by introducing a theoretical or abstract discussion. In comparison to the poverty of their social lives, their inner worlds are rich in fantasies and daydreams.

It is noteworthy that people with a schizoid personality disorder usually do not experience the lack of intimate relationships as a problem and do not want to change.[32] Things are different for people who find themselves, unwillingly, without a intimate relationship. These people experience great distress and want badly to change their situation.

SUGGESTIONS FOR PEOPLE SEEKING LOVE

Although people can do little about the love they did or did not receive as children, adults can choose to be conscious of their attachment styles and how these styles affect their intimate relationships.

Do you feel good or bad about your ability to love and be loved? Have your intimate relationships been close and satisfying? Or, have you looked all your life for a truly intimate relationship without success? Have you avoided getting close and intimate? Have you been desperate for an intimate relationship, but the intensity of your feelings has kept scaring potential partners away? Instead of finding faults in your partners, as witnessed by the many years of fruitless searching that left you unable to find the right mate and instead of using the excuse of "no appropriate candidates," if you are seeking love, you can try to take responsibility for your love life by shifting the beam of awareness to yourself. The way to do this is by trying to figure out why you respond the way you do to people in general and to candidates for a romantic relationship in particular. If you cannot figure this out on your own, you may want to consider getting professional help. Even if awareness does not necessarily imply an immediate life change, it is an important first step in the right direction.

Chapter 9

THE SON FALLS IN LOVE WITH "MOTHER," THE DAUGHTER WITH "FATHER"

The innumerable peculiarities in the erotic life of human beings, as well as the compulsive character of the process of falling in love itself, are quite unintelligible except by reference back to childhood and as being residual effects of childhood.
—Sigmund Freud,
Three Essays on the Theory of Sexuality

Time present and time past
Are both perhaps present in time future
—T. S. Elliot, *Four Quartets*

LEA WAS DETERMINED NEVER TO BECOME INVOLVED WITH AN AIR FORCE man. As the daughter of a legendary Air Force pilot, she knew all too well the price that this type of a career demanded from the wife and the children. She adored her father but suffered too much from his frequent absences. If there was one thing she knew for sure, it was that she would never let herself fall in love with an Air Force man.

Then came the big party at the Air Force base, and her father introduced her to Jim, who was the new shining star in his squadron. Jim looked like an early version of her father. He was tall and lean, his angular face suntanned and his dark eyes sparkling with intelligence and humor. His love and admiration for her father were obvious. She felt a twinge of jealousy as she watched them together. When Jim came and sat next to her and focused his intense eyes on her, her heartbeat quickened, and despite herself she felt herself responding.

Jim could not take his eyes off Lea. What was it about her that was so intriguing? he wondered. She was gorgeous, of course, and she was the daughter of a commander he admired, but there was something else, something that made his heart beat faster and the blood rush in his veins. It was as if he knew her, which was impossible. He had never seen her before, he was sure of that. So, why did he feel like he had known her all his life? There was something about the way she held herself, the way she moved, the way she looked and smiled, that reminded him of something, of someone. Startled, he realized that there was an uncanny resemblance between Lea and his mother. It was amazing. But his response was even more amazing; he had never felt such a strong immediate attraction to a woman. He knew he would do anything to have her. She was the woman he wanted to marry, the one he wanted to be the mother of his children.

WOMEN TALK ABOUT THE MEN THEY LOVE

I think I attract men who are like my father, very carefree and open. For the most part I like men with his characteristics.

I try to make him fatherly toward me. I make him spoil me like my dad did. He's like my dad in being vulnerable and trusting people.

He's like my dad in being very career oriented. He talks about work a lot. He brings his work mind home with him. My dad did that. And he'll make decisions for you if you let him. He can have a short fuse too. That's kind of like my dad.

He's kind of similar to my father in that he has a strong sense of determination. Whatever he does, he'll try to do to the best of his ability. They are both very caring about me.

MEN TALK ABOUT THE WOMEN THEY LOVE

She is similar to my mother in terms of not having a mean bone in her body and in being real easygoing. Then you feel guilty, which you don't when they're being selfish. My mom is like that.

She is very warm and loving, like my mother. And she takes care of me and spoils me like my mother used to spoil me.

She sort of has the same granola look like my mother, not a lot of makeup, dresses casually. And she is laid back like my mother.

She is overly dependent on me, that's a similarity between my mom and her. And she spoils me in a lot of ways, like she buys things for me.

Sometimes my mother doesn't like to be bothered. They are similar like that.

Sigmund Freud, a man of the Victorian age and a brilliant thinker, provided the pioneering psychoanalytic theory about the unconscious roots of adult love relationships. Many theoreticians and researchers have expanded and refined Freud's early concepts in creating their own theories about the roots of romantic love. (One of these is Bowlby's attachment theory, discussed in chapter 8.)

In his book of fewer than 100 pages, *Three Essays on the Theory of Sexuality*, Freud explained romantic love according to his psychoanalytic theory and described the roots of romantic choices, both normal and perverse, in men and in women.[1] The oversimplified translation of the complex process Freud described is the formula familiar to all of us—a man falls in love with a woman who reminds him of his mother; a woman falls in love with a man who reminds her of her father. The reasons for these romantic choices are "unconscious," which is to say the individual is unaware of them.

Is your partner similar to your mother or father? In response to this question, a significantly higher percentage of men than women in the romantic attachment interviews described their partners as similar to their mothers, and a significantly higher percentage of women than men described their partners as similar to their fathers,[2] thus providing tentative support for Freud's dictum.

Freud believed that the attraction to people who remind us of our opposite sex parent is a universal, biologically based phenomenon, related to the developmental processes of early childhood. In his conception, romantic love is a socially accepted expression of the sexual drive that he termed *libido*. Libido is the instinctual sexual energy with which we are born. It is akin to the biological drive of hunger or thirst that pushes for gratification. People are born with different levels of libido; some have high levels, some low, but most people have average levels. The libido guarantees the survival of the human species.

It is interesting to note that the Greeks called the bonding instinct of the baby to the mother *Eros*, a word that has come to be associated with romantic love. In its origin, the word had a wider connotation of the life force. Freud also saw Eros as the life instinct, as opposed to *Thanatos*, the death instinct, the unconscious and destructive wish to die.

Freud was the first to emphasize the decisive role played by the early years of life in laying the foundations of an individual's adult personality. He believed that the personality was formed by the end of the fifth year, and that subsequent development consisted of elaborating on this basic structure. Other psychoanalytic writers have expanded Freud's formulation both backward, to the earliest days of a baby's life, and forward, to later stages of life, including young adulthood, adulthood, middle age, and old age.

THE PSYCHOSEXUAL DEVELOPMENT OF THE CHILD

According to Freud's theory, to achieve mature sexual identity, a child needs to pass successfully through different stages of psychosexual development that occur in response to innate biological drives. Every stage is defined by an *erogenous zone* of the body, a specific area that is the focus for sexuality, pleasurable sensuality, and instinctual drive, and by an *object* that can satisfy the libidinal drive.

At the first stages of life, a baby's libido is directed toward oneself, loving oneself in narcissistic love and enjoying one's body in "autoerotic" enjoyment. Later, if the development is healthy and normal, the baby can start to direct the libido outside and love people outside the self. These people then become the baby's "love objects."

The first stage in the psychosexual development of a child is the *oral* stage, which takes place during the first year of life. The child's sexuality is centered on the mouth. The principal source of pleasure derived from the mouth is eating, or the "incorporation" of food; it involves suckling and sucking and, with the growth of teeth, biting. These two modes of oral activity, eating and biting, are the prototypes for many traits seen in adulthood. Pleasure derived from oral incorporation may be "displaced" to other modes of incorporation, such as acquiring possessions or knowledge. Oral aggression may be displaced to other modes or metaphors of biting, such as criticism and sarcasm.

The baby's love object in the oral stage is the feeding breast. This is why "a child sucking at his mother's breast has become the prototype of every relation of love. The finding of an object is in fact a re-finding of it (p. 88)."[1] "When children fall asleep after being sated at the breast, they show an expression of blissful satisfaction which will be repeated later in life after the experience of sexual orgasm (p. 388)."[3]

Even after sexual activity becomes disconnected from feeding, an important part of this initial sexuality remains and helps prepare for the choice of a mature love object that can bring back the lost happiness of this early stage of life. In this stage of development, the mother is "teaching the child to love (p. 89)."[1] In other words, the mother's love is necessary for adult romantic love. However, both too much and too little love can be harmful. The lack or the loss of love causes anxiety in romantic relationships, so that with intimacy, the anxious person behaves like an abandoned child. On the other hand, too much love makes it difficult for a person to be without love for even a brief period of time or, alternatively, to manage relationships with small amounts of love.

Second is the *anal* stage, which takes place during the second year of life. At this stage, the sexuality of the child is centered on the anus and is expressed in the enjoyment of both holding back and releasing feces. Depending on the toilet training and the parents' feelings concerning defecation, the child will develop certain traits and values. If parents are strict, the child may hold back feces and later in life may become stingy and obstinate. Or, in response to the parents' pressure, the child may respond with rage by defecating at the most inappropriate times. This is the prototype for traits such as messy disorderliness, temper tantrums, cruelty, and wanton destructiveness. However, when the parents praise the child extravagantly after a bowel movement, the child feels that producing feces is extremely important, and as an adult is likely to demonstrate creativity and productivity.

In the oral and anal stages, there is no difference between boys and girls. Children in these early stages are autoerotic, and the love object for both boy and girl is the mother. From the third stage, the phallic stage, the psychosexual development of boys and girls diverges.

The *phallic* stage takes place between ages 3 and 5. During this stage, sexual feelings associated with the functioning of the genitals come into focus. The phallus and vagina fascinate boys and girls. They masturbate and express interest in the sexual organs of others. Childhood sexuality is at its peak at this stage, and it shapes adult sexuality. However, the sexual impulse is different for a boy and a girl. Because of their "natural" attraction to members of the opposite sex, the son is attracted to his mother, and the daughter is attracted to her father. The pleasures of masturbation and the fantasies that accompany it set the stage for the appearance of the Oedipus complex.

According to the Greek tragedy that became famous thanks to Freud (see Box), King Oedipus killed his father and married his mother. Freud believed that, like Oedipus, every boy is in love with his mother and views his father as a hostile competitor, and every girl is in love with her father and views her mother as a competitor. The boy wants to possess his mother and remove his father; the girl wants to possess her father and displace her mother. Because of the forbidden sexual attraction to his mother, the boy imagines that his powerful rival is going to harm him. His fears center on harm to his genitals because they are the source of his lustful feelings. He is afraid that, in a jealous rage, his father will remove the offending organ. This *castration anxiety* induces the boy to identify with his father. The identification with the father assures the boy that he will not harm him, and gives the boy some vicarious gratification of his sexual impulse toward his mother.

THE STORY OF OEDIPUS

When a baby was born to King Laius of Thebes and his wife Jocasta, the oracle of Delphi told the king that he would be killed by his son. To avert this terrible prophecy, Laius bound the baby's feet and ordered him abandoned on a lonely mountain, certain that within a short time the baby would die. But, a servant took pity on the baby and gave him to Polybus, King of Corinth, who named him Oedipus, "wounded feet," and adopted him as his son.

When Oedipus grew up, he left his house in Corinth because of a terrible prophecy from the oracle in Delphi. The oracle prophesied that Oedipus was doomed to kill his father and marry his mother. Oedipus thought he could escape his cruel fate by abandoning his home and going into exile. During his wandering, Oedipus met his real father at a crossroad. Laius, who had four companions with him, tried to push Oedipus off the road and hit him with his staff. In his anger, Oedipus attacked Laius and his companions and killed them. Only one man remained alive to carry the news to Thebes. The man, too embarrassed to tell the truth, told the people of Thebes that their king was killed by a band of robbers. The people, preoccupied with a disaster that had befallen their city, did not try to verify the story. The Sphinx, a monster in the form of a winged lion with a woman's face and breasts, stood at the entrance to the city and asked passersby a riddle. The person who answered the riddle correctly would be allowed to continue; the person who did not would die. No one had been able to answer the riddle, and the monster had devoured them all. The city was under siege and hunger was closing in. Then Oedipus, the wise and the brave, arrived in Thebes and offered to solve the Sphinx's riddle. "What creature walks on four in the morning, on two at noon, and on three at night?" asked the Sphinx. "A man does," answered Oedipus. "As a baby he crawls on four, as an adult he walks on two feet, and in his old age he leans on a cane." This was the correct answer, and on hearing it, the Sphinx killed itself; the people of Thebes were set free. Seeing Oedipus as their savior, they offered him the throne. Oedipus gladly accepted, married the widow of the slain King Laius, and became the king of Thebes.

Years later, when Oedipus and Jocasta's two children had grown up, Thebes was hit by a devastating plague. Oedipus sent a messenger to Delphi with an urgent plea to Apollo to come to their rescue. The messenger came back with the announcement that the plague would be over only after King Laius's assassin was found and punished. Oedipus started searching far and wide for the king's murderer, only to discover to his great horror that he was the man, and that King Laius was his father. When the horrible truth that he had killed his father and married his mother was revealed to Oedipus, he blinded himself and left Thebes for a life of exile with one of his daughters. His mother/wife killed herself. Only after many years of wandering in exile Oedipus came to terms with his cruel fate, understanding that although he was not at fault, he was still responsible for his actions.

"Anatomy is destiny," declared Freud. The anatomical differences between the sexes cause a different process during this stage in girls and a different resolution of the Oedipal conflict. As the boy discovers his phallus, the girl discovers her clitoris and views it, because of the pleasure it provides, as a phallus equivalent. When she discovers the inferiority of her sex organ, a cavity as compared to the boy's glorious protruding sex organ, it is a traumatic experience with far-reaching consequences. The girl holds her mother responsible for her castrated condition and resents her for it. She transfers her love to her father, who has the valued phallus. Her love for her father, and for other men, is mixed with envy because they possess something she lacks. *Penis envy* is the female counterpart of castration anxiety in males. Penis envy expresses the desire of the girl to have a phallus. The girl envies those who have a phallus and, like the boy, interprets its absence as a punishment, that is, castration. She imagines that she has lost something valuable; the boy fears he is going to lose it. Her penis envy and his castration anxiety are called collectively the *castration complex*.

The boy's Oedipal complex is resolved, under the pressure of castration anxiety, by identification with his father. The boy hopes that if he imitates his father, his father will not hurt him, and he can have a wife like his mother when he grows up. The girl's Oedipal complex is resolved, under the pressure of penis envy, by identification with her mother. The girl hopes that if she imitates her mother, she can have a husband like her father.

In his early writings, Freud termed the Oedipus conflict in girls the *Electra complex*. In Greek tragedy, Electra loved her father and convinced her brother to kill their mother, who betrayed him and caused his death. It is important to note, however, that with the intellectual honesty characteristic of him, Freud admitted that he did not understand the psychosexual development of women with the same clarity that he understood the psychosexual development of men. Women psychoanalysts, such as Karen Horney, indeed criticized the Freudian conception of female sexuality and argued that as women experiment with sexuality, they have a positive experience rather than an inferior experience of loss. Horney also argued that women do not envy men's glorious penis, but rather the societal power that having a penis in a patriarchal society represents.[4] We return to this criticism in the section of this chapter that evaluates Freud's theory.

Resolution of the Oedipal conflict is necessary before the boy can develop a masculine gender identity (by identifying with his father) and before the girl can develop her concommitant feminine gender identity (by identifying with her mother). Resolving the Oedipal conflict is also necessary for both boy and girl to be able to detach themselves from their first love object and "displace" it as adults, which is to say, fall in love with people other than their parents.

Freud described two processes that interfere with this normal development, fixation and regression. *Fixation* occurs when development is halted temporarily or permanently. A child who becomes fixated at an early stage of development continues in adulthood to derive the gratification characterized by that early stage. Gratification from smoking or overeating in an adult, for example, may suggest an oral fixation. Fixation can result from too much or too little gratification of a need.

Regression means a retreat to an earlier stage of development. A young married woman who has difficulties with her husband may return to the security of her parents' home. Regression is usually determined by an earlier fixation; that is, a person tends to regress to the stage of previous fixation.

When boys and girls do not pass through the Oedipal stage successfully, they remain fixated at this stage and cannot detach themselves from their infantile love object. When they grow up, such men remain in love with their mothers and are incapable of loving fully other women. Typically, they get married and declare that they "adore" their wives, who invariably are "wonderful mothers." But, for some "inexplicable reason," they are not attracted to their wives sexually. They are, however, attracted sexually to all other women, but they never love any of these women. Their love is reserved for the mother who is their wife. This type of split has been termed the *whore/Madonna complex*.[5] Other men with unresolved Oedipal complexes are attracted to many women and fall in love easily, each time convinced that this time they have found the perfect woman for whom they have been searching. Shortly afterward, they discover that this one also is not *the* one, the one for whom they will continue to search but never find.

Women who fail to resolve their Oedipal conflict remain in love with their father. There are among them those, like Anna Freud, who remain attached to their fathers all their lives and never marry[6] (see a picture of Anna Freud and her father in Figure 14). Others marry men they view as inferior to their father and thus deserving only cold criticism. Women with an Oedipal fixation tend to be nonresponsive sexually. The sexual problems these women have, as well as the sexual problems men with a whore/Madonna complex have, can be explained by the operation of the incest taboo. Because the husband or wife psychologically represents a parent, he or she is forbidden sexually.

FIGURE 14. Sigmund Freud and his daughter Anna (1913). Anna Freud, a well-known psychoanalyst and the author of *The Ego and the Mechanisms of Defense,* continued the work of her admired father but never married.

Even when the Oedipal fixation is less severe, its influence is clearly evident. A well-known example is a young man who falls in love with older women who represent his mother or a young woman who falls in love with older men who represent fatherly love or authority.

The oral, anal, and phallic stages are collectively called the *pregenital* stages. They are narcissistic and autoerotic, meaning that the child obtains gratification of the sexual drive from the stimulation and manipulation of his or her own body.

The fourth stage is a prolonged *latency* period. These are the quiet years between age 5 and adolescence, in which the sexual impulses are held in a state of repression. The boy's love for his mother and the girl's love for her father are forgotten, and the sexual drive is latent, thus this stage's name. The child starts school, and the libido is directed to new interests and new people. Many of the experiences that produced anxiety in earlier stages are repressed. A screen of forgetfulness covers the experiences of early childhood.

During adolescence and the fifth, *genital,* stage, the sexual drive appears in full force. The focus is again on the genitals, but now some of the narcissistic love of the pregenital stages becomes channeled into other love choices. The adolescent begins to love others and is sexually attracted to people outside the family (most often of the opposite sex). Yet, the love objects of the Oedipal stage influence the love choices of adolescence. The old family love objects get renewed *libidinal cathexes,* or libidinal energy, invested with powerful emotional energies. Because they now arouse the incest taboo, they have to remain unconscious. From this age, the adolescent's task is to differentiate from the parents and become a separate and autonomous individual.

For a boy, this means displacing the libidinal cathexes to mother and substituting for her a woman outside the family, who becomes his love object. For a girl, it means displacing the libidinal cathexes to father and substituting for him a man outside the family, who becomes her love object. Finding a love object is in fact *refinding* it. The infantile desire for the parent is displaced by a desire for a sexual partner.

Even after reaching adulthood and sexual maturity, the love of a son for his mother and the love of a daughter for her father have the greatest influence on their choices of a person to love and marry, but it is not the only influence. Despite the importance of parental love, it is not the only type of love a child experiences. Other significant childhood influences enable people to develop more than one sexual preference.

Freud believed that all people are inherently bisexual, with each sex attracted to members of his or her own sex as well as to members of the opposite sex. This is the constitutional basis for homosexuality. In most people, socialization forces keep the homosexual drive latent. Freud saw proof of restraining social forces by pointing out that in those cultures that permit it, homosexuality is chosen by a significant number of people.

Despite the prevalence of homosexual attraction, evidenced by the deep emotional friendships adolescent boys and girls form with members of their own sex, Freud believed that the childhood experiences of both sexes directed them toward heterosexual attraction. For men, childhood memories of a mother's love and nurturing have a powerful effect that directs them to choose women as love objects. In addition, the infantile experience of competing with the father, who prevented them from expressing their sexuality toward the mother, helps divert attraction away from members of their own sex.

The operation of these two forces can be seen in women as well. Because the sexual behavior of young girls is harshly criticized and penalized by their mothers, or at least it was in Freud's time, women develop hostility toward members of their own sex. This attitude helps direct them to the choice of men as love objects. In addition, competition with other women prevents them from being sexually attracted to them.

Nevertheless, Freud saw in the different sexual "deviations" and "perversions" a common and universal phenomenon, which testifies to the many different ways the human sexual drive seeks gratification. What is considered normal sexual response is the result of such restraining and directing forces as shame, disgust, pity, and the moral and legal norms that society enforces. In other words, civilization controls and shapes the development and free expression of human sexuality. The sexual behavior we consider "normal" is nothing but an expression of these restraining societal forces. Freud was convinced that from the study of sexual deviations and perversions it is possible to learn about the origins and development of normal human sexuality.

Let me summarize the key points in Freud's ideas about romantic love and mate selection. All of these key points can be deduced from the preceding discussion.

- Romantic love is a socially accepted expression of the sexual drive, the libido, which includes both physical and emotional components.
- The libido directs the sexual activity of the person in love toward gratification.

- All people are inherently bisexual; each sex is attracted to members of its own sex as well as to members of the opposite sex. In most people, the homosexual drive remains latent as a result of socialization.
- Romantic love and what seems like the nonsexual love children feel toward their parents have the same roots. Adult romantic love is actually the equivalent of infantile love.
- The romantic and sexual experiences of adult men and women are related to early infantile experiences that take place during the Oedipal stage.
- The libido of adult men and women is displaced to people who are similar in some significant ways to their love objects during the Oedipal stage. For a man, this means mother; for a woman, it means father.
- The adult seeks a lover who represents an internal picture of his or her first love object—the male or female parent. This internal, infantile picture can be very different from the way the parent really is.
- Falling in love represents reuniting with the first love object.
- Because the parental relationships of young children so strongly influence their adult intimate relationships, it is understandable that a childhood disruption in the connection with the parent can have serious consequences for their adult love lives.

If we accept Freud's notion that both son and daughter try to find in a romantic partner the love object on whom their libidos fixated in the Oedipal stage, and if we accept that the first object of a child's love and sexuality is a parent, then it is reasonable to ask, why don't adults choose their parents as love objects? The answer, according to Freud, is the incest taboo that is genetically imprinted and defends against sexual attraction to people who are family members. It develops naturally toward people with whom we grow up. This important point explains why adults can be sexually attracted to their children—they did not grow up with them—but children are not attracted sexually to their parents, despite what Freud thought. Beginning with sexual maturity in adolescence, when the Oedipal attraction toward the parent of the opposite sex is first reenacted, the incest taboo dictates a *displacement* of the libido in favor of love objects outside the family.

In addition to displacement, Freud suggested yet another way in which we divert a forbidden love choice into one that is socially accepted: *sublimation*. As an example, he presents Leonardo da Vinci's paintings of the Madonna. These paintings, Freud argued, are a sublimated expression of Leonardo's longing for intimacy with his mother, from whom he had been separated at a young age.[7]

The operation of displacement and sublimation explains why adult love objects always resemble or represent, in some important way, the first infantile love object.

Falling in love also has a physiological component that Freud knew about far less. He wrote, "The popular mind has from time immemorial paid homage" to the hypothesis that falling in love is akin to "intoxication." He admitted freely that "we know nothing" about the "chemistry" of "sexual desire." He could not even decide whether we are to assume the existence of one or "two sexual substances which would then be named male and female (p.482)."[3] Sexual arousal directs the sexual activity of the person in love and pushes for gratification and release of the accumulated sexual tension. The sexual drive is expressed in intense desire that is one of the most notable characteristics of falling in love. The sexual, physical, and instinctual drive receives in romantic love a pure emotional expression that renders it socially acceptable.

IDEALIZATION OF THE BELOVED IN ROMANTIC LOVE

When we are in love, we tend to idealize our beloved. We see wonderful qualities, which may or may not be there, and are blind to faults that may be glaringly obvious to others. Freud called this love blindness *sexual overvaluation*. Freud described the tendency to idealize when in love as evidence of the flow of "libidinal narcissism" from the self to the beloved. The beloved becomes a substitute for an *ego ideal*. Ego ideal is part of the *super ego*, which includes traits and values the parents approved and rewarded. Super ego is the internal representation of values and ideals as interpreted to the child by the parents. The person in love *projects* his or her ego ideal onto the beloved. The traits and values that are present in this part of the super ego, values and traits the individual hopes to acquire and views as supreme, are projected onto the beloved and perceived as existing in the beloved.[8]

Freud distinguished between two forms of romantic love: *narcissistic love*, or self-love, and *anaclitic love*, the love of a person who resembles a parent. In self-love, the person falls in love with a narcissistic love object that can be similar to oneself, similar to someone one would like to be or had been, or someone who was part of oneself. An anaclictic love object can be similar to the woman who fed and nurtured the child, Mother, or to the man who protected the child, Father. In some cases of narcissistic love, the beloved becomes a substitute for an unachievable ego ideal. The admiration of the beloved enables the gratification of a narcissistic need for self-love. In extreme cases, the "perfect" love object completely takes over the "modest and sacrificing" ego. In such cases, the individual surrenders completely to the adored tyrant, the beloved.

Freud believed that falling in love with a person who resembles a parent, the anaclictic love object, is evidence of mature adult love, whereas the choice of someone who resembles oneself, a narcissistic object, is evidence of an infantile and regressive wish that should be overcome. In making the shift from narcissistic love to anaclictic love, the person changes from romantic love as the reflection in the beloved of one's own ego ideal, to loving the other for what the other really is. In mature love, the person is enriched by internalizing the positive traits and ideals of an admired partner. These internalized values and traits become *introjects*, parts of the person's psyche, that help expand and enrich it.[9]

It is interesting to note in this regard the *Michelangelo phenomenon*, the partner as a sculptor of the ideal self.[10] A paragraph from Lynn Sharon Schwartz's book *Rough Strife* explains this name:

She thought often about Michelangelo's statues that they had seen years ago in Florence, in the first excitement of their love, figures hidden in block of stone, uncovered only by the artist's chipping away the excess, the superficial blur, till smooth and spare, the ideal shape was revealed. She and Ivan were hammer and chisel to each other.

The Michelangelo phenomenon is a mutual pattern in which both partners sculpt each other in a way that moves each closer to his or her ego ideal. Four different studies documented the existence of the phenomenon in romantic love relationships. These studies also showed that when partners feel that they bring each other closer to each other's ideal, it is related to feelings of satisfaction and vitality in the relationship.[10]

EVALUATION OF FREUD'S THEORY OF ROMANTIC LOVE

Freud's theory made an important contribution to our understanding of the unconscious processes involved in falling in love. Later psychoanalytic thinkers, building on Freud's concepts, viewed the earliest experiences in a child's life as more important for the choice of a love object than the experiences in the Oedipal stage. Others objected to the great emphasis Freud put on the role of the sexual drive in the development of personality, and saw not only the mother, but also the father, as responsible for the romantic choice of both men and women. In addition, there are those who objected to Freud's assumption that it is possible to learn about the normal and universal development of children from the phenomena and processes seen in adult pathologies. Some researchers went on to demonstrate that castration anxiety and penis envy are rare, not universal experiences that every child undergoes.[11] Other researchers showed that, when asked to determine a person's sex, children at the Oedipal stage pay more attention to hair length and clothes than to genitals.

The most consistent criticism of Freud's theory, however, came from the ranks of women psychoanalysts, including his students and followers, who criticized his ideas on female sexuality as biased by the facts that he was a Victorian man. One of earliest and most prominent of those critics was Karen Horney,[12] who perceived her ideas as falling within the framework of Freud's theory but wished to correct the fallacies in his thinking about female psychology. Horney objected to Freud's notion of penis envy as the determining factor in the psychology of women, believing instead that female psychology is based on lack of confidence and an overemphasis on love relationships and has little to do with the anatomy of female sex organs. Unlike Freud, Horney believed that the transition girls made from the mother to the father as a love object arises from their attraction to the opposite sex, an attraction that has its roots in feminine sexuality.

Based on her observations of children, Horney contended that feminine sexuality is primal, appears at an early age, and leads the girl to a unique sexual identity that is rooted in an awareness of her unique and preferred anatomy. She saw a proof for this in girls' seductive behavior and enjoyment of dressing up. In other words, the attraction of a girl to her father is first and foremost an expression of her early feminine sexuality and not a compensation for disappointment or penis envy. As for envy, Horney agreed that women envy men, not for their phallus, however, but for the many rights and privileges that this organ entitles them to in a patriarchal society. She believed that the penis envy of girls results from the restrictions and prohibitions imposed on their ability to satisfy their sexual drive, such as the strong prohibition against masturbation.

In her psychoanalytic work with men, Horney saw evidence for the existence of "*womb envy*," men's envy of women's ability to give birth. The tendency of men to underestimate women, to devalue them, and to express low opinions and disregard for them was seen by Horney as rooted in their envy of a woman's ability to get pregnant, give birth, and nurse. In men's castration anxiety, she saw a fear of women. In men's strong need to be successful and conquer, she saw evidence of their overcompensation for their unconscious feelings of inferiority.

Postmodern feminist psychoanalysts argue with every idea suggested by Freud, including, most particularly, his "anatomy is destiny" axiom. Here, for example, is the opinion of Virginia Goldner:

> Freud began with the so-called anatomical difference, a social distinction that fixated on the genitals, from which he derived, in what is now a suspect sequence, the normative dominance of heterosexuality and the dichotomous, complementary division of gender into the polarity male/ female ... . In this narrative of development, the genitals determine sexuality, which in turn, determines gender identity ... . Now, every term in that sentence has been disrupted by doubt.[13]

Despite these and other criticisms, there is no doubt that Freudian theory makes an invaluable contribution to our understanding of the unconscious processes involved in falling in love. The most important conclusion we can derive from his theory is that we do not fall in love with a particular person by chance; we fall in love with careful, even if unconscious, consideration. Our romantic choices, even if we are not fully aware of them, are influenced by childhood experiences, and these childhood experiences are different for boys and for girls.

SUGGESTIONS FOR THOSE SEEKING LOVE

Those among the readers who have a disturbing sense that there is something wrong with the type of person with whom they fall in love over and over again may want to consider the possibility that the cause of the problem is primarily in them or more specifically in their unconscious romantic choices. This does not mean that the problems that come up in their intimate relationships are necessarily their fault. After all, the original causes for their romantic choices are encored in early childhood experiences beyond their control. But, for this reason, the problems are also not the fault of their romantic partners.

We are responsible for our romantic choices, even if these choices are unconscious. King Oedipus understood at the end of his life that, although killing his father and marrying his mother were not his fault, still he was responsible for his actions. We, too, need to take responsibility for our romantic choices even if they are not our fault. Taking responsibility is always a recommended strategy because it is far more likely to bring about positive change than is blaming the partner. Once we decipher our romantic attraction code, we can choose to follow the same scripts or to alter them.

Freud's theory suggests one approach. Try to find similarities between your romantic partner and your opposite sex parent. When you make a list of the most notable characteristics—physical, emotional, behavioral, mental, and temperamental—of your parent and compare it to a list of your romantic partner's characteristics, are there similarities between them? What do these similarities say about you?

Chapter 10

THE INTERNAL ROMANTIC IMAGE

We will be happy together, drink deep, and lose ourselves in love.
My lover is mine and I am his.
  —Old Testament, *The Song of Songs*

This is why a man leaves his father and mother and is united
with his wife, and they become one.
  —Genesis

I let him invent me
In the image of the reflection
In his eyes. I dance, I dance
In the abundance of sudden wings.
  —Wislawa Szymborska, "Drinking Wine,"
  Miracle Fair

As I was writing this chapter, one morning I met my friend Chuck for coffee at the French Hotel, our favorite cafe. "What are you writing about now?" asked Chuck, after we covered the recent developments in both our lives. "On our internal romantic code and how to decipher it," I answered. "Really?" said Chuck, "So how about helping your friend right here, before you start helping strangers?" Chuck's love life was indeed worthy of a master code breaker. The son of a college professor father and a housewife mother, both from wealthy New England families, Chuck was always falling in love with oriental women. The most recent ones were an Indian, a Japanese, and a Vietnamese. With each, he fell madly in love, and with each he had a long-term relationship. All three were exotic, beautiful, bright, professionally accomplished women, but none looked or acted like his mother. What internal romantic image could have possibly directed Chuck to fall in love with exotic, ambitious, career women?

After analyzing this question for a couple of hours, it became clear that all the women with whom Chuck has been passionately in love resembled in significant ways both his parents as well as critical elements in their relationship to each other and to him. The women were brilliant and professionally accomplished like his father and unlike Chuck himself. They were beautiful, elegant, poised women, like

his mother. And, like both his parents, they had an aloofness that kept Chuck longing for greater closeness. He never felt he had these women's complete attention
and heart, like he never felt he had completely his parents' attention as a child. The
dynamic of total admiration and awe on Chuck's part and the natural acceptance
of this admiration as their due on the women's part was also a reenactment of the
relationship he saw at home between the world-renowned scientist and his adoring wife. Why were all these elements combined in the exotic package with which
Chuck was so fascinated? The answer, we figured, probably had to do with a nurturing oriental nanny Chuck had as a young child.

> *She is a good combination of both of my parents rolled into one. She can
> be very compassionate, very loving, very tender, very understanding, always
> smothering you with love and just patting you all the time like my mother.
> Then like my dad she's got her really set ideas. You cannot make her change her
> mind on some things.*
>
> *I think he is like my father in the good ways, like he's very hard working,
> he's honest, he's on time, he's trustworthy. But he is also very affectionate, that
> my father is not. He is very affectionate, and my mother is very affectionate.
> He cares a lot about me and supports me like my mother. He's got a lot of my
> Mom's qualities.*
>
> *She's kind of similar to my dad in that she's as stubborn as hell. But she's a
> genuinely nice person, and in that she's like my mom.*
>
> *I need to feel special and feel that the person I'm with is dedicated to me.
> Actions speak louder than words proving that someone is dedicated to me. With
> my dad, he always told me he loved me, but he surely didn't act it. With [my
> boyfriend] it's similar in that he tells it to me but things don't add up to prove
> it to me. I question it because of the way he acts. With both of them I hear it
> but it doesn't add up. Also it's easy for me to get into the position of "you've hurt
> me," or "I'm being hurt." It's almost as if I'm looking for it. With my parents
> I didn't talk about how I felt. I was afraid of conflict. I still have a hard time
> defining my feelings and expressing them. I didn't have practice in saying what
> I feel and I can still see myself doing that.*

Is your romantic relationship similar to the relationship you had with your parents when you were growing up? The majority of women and men who were asked
this question responded affirmatively.[1] In some cases, they described a similarity in
the quality of the relationship. "The similarity between my relationship with him
and with my parents is in the suffocating love." "[I have] the same sense of not quite
living up to someone's expectations." In other cases, the similarity was in appearance,
personality, or behavior. "He is similar to my father in the way he's built, tall and
skinny." "My mother is passive, and he is passive." "She can be nice like my mother,
and when she gets angry she gives me 'the look' that my mother used to give me."

It is not surprising that people who described an adult relationship as similar
to a childhood relationship with their parents were also likely to note a similarity

between a partner and a parent. What is surprising is that noting this similarity has a positive impact on intimate relationships. The more similarity people saw between a childhood relationship with their parents and their adult romantic relationship, the more likely they were to describe themselves as feeling secure in the relationship, to be themselves in the relationship, to have fewer conflicts, and to handle well the conflicts that arose.[2]

Clinical experience, mine as well as others', suggests that the childhood relationships with parents have a much a greater influence on people's adult romantic relationships than even these data, based on people's subjective perceptions, might suggest. One of the important revelations for couples in therapy is just how powerful and profound the connection is between their childhood relationships with their parents and their romantic relationship with each other. The discovery of this type of a connection is helpful in getting people to understand qualities they may have had difficulty comprehending and accepting about each other. Examples are presented in the next chapter (11), in which four people describe their childhood and their adult romantic relationships. What becomes abundantly clear when reading those stories is the lack of people's awareness of the obvious effect their childhood experiences have on their romantic relationships.

Falling in love is a powerful emotional experience. The dominant component in it is the feeling of togetherness, of bonding, of being like one. "My lover is mine and I am his" says the woman in the biblical *Song of Songs*, and her words are echoed in love songs throughout the ages. Lovers feel as if their ego boundaries have melted away as they blend into one entity. In many respects, it is possible to see in this melting-into-one a return to the primal symbiotic bond with mother. Both partners feel that all their emotional needs are totally satisfied, the way they were in their infantile Garden of Eden.[3] Even the Bible tells us that this is as it should be. "This is why a man leaves his father and mother and is united with his wife, and they become one" (Genesis, 2:22). Man needs to leave his mother and father and become an independent individual before he can be united with, and have a truly intimate relationship with, his wife. We choose carefully the person with whom we fall in love. Our main guide in making this choice is an internal, largely unconscious, *romantic image*. We develop our internal romantic images early in life. As we saw in the previous two chapters (8 and 9), the romantic image is based on powerful emotional experiences children have in their first years of life. The mother and the father, and anyone else who played a significant role during the childhood years, influence the development of the internal romantic image in two primary ways:

- By the way they expressed, or did not express, love toward the child. *"My dad, he always told me he loved me but he surely didn't act it. With* [my boyfriend] *it's similar in that he tells it to me, but things don't add up."*
- By the way they expressed, or did not express, love toward each other. *"Something in my relationship with him reminded me of the way my mother treated my father: a lot of patience, a lot of listening."*

Although Freud emphasized the role that the parent of the opposite sex plays in falling in love, in fact the internal romantic image appears to be quite broad. It encompasses a reenactment of the positive and negative elements of both parents, their relationship, and the relationship each of them had with the child. Even though the sex of the parent has an effect, unresolved issues seem to have far greater impact.

There are several theories that explain how this reenactment happens. Among them are object relations theory, which emphasizes the role of internal "objects"; Jungian theory, which emphasizes the role of certain "archetypes"; and evolutionary theory, which emphasizes the role of "imprinting." In this chapter, I present these theories with an eye to how each contributes to our understanding of the influence of childhood experiences on the internal romantic image and, through it, on the experience of falling in love.

HOW WE CHOOSE WITH WHOM TO FALL IN LOVE: OBJECT RELATIONS THEORY

The word *object* conjures an image of something inanimate, but the meaning of the word in object relations theory is very different. *Object* is an internal representation of a person, a thing, a relationship, or an event that has become part of an individual's psyche. The hungry baby has no internal picture of his mother, and so it cries. Once the mother is "internalized," the baby can handle her temporary absence. In adults, the internalized mother object includes both a concrete representation of their own mothers, the way she was in different stages of their lives, and an abstract image that is influenced by cultural stereotypes and mythologies of motherhood.

A screen, determined by age, genetics, and past experiences, influences our perception of people and events. A baby perceives the mother differently than a person of 50 does. All internalized images remain stored in the psyche. This is why people are surprised when they notice how old and feeble their mothers or fathers look in old age. The new images contradict their childhood images of the parent as young and powerful.

Object relations theorists assume that our inner world consists of objects and *object relations*—our internal perception of the relationships between different objects. The relationships between romantic partners, as well as all other intimate relationships, are always object relations.

One of the most prominent among object relations theorists is Margaret Mahler.[4] As noted in the detailed discussion of her work in chapter 8, Mahler believed that a newborn infant has no personality. Rather, the personality results from a developmental process she termed *psychological birth*.[5] The experience of oneness with mother during the first symbiotic stage of the baby's development is the building block for the ability to form romantic love relationships. Psychological birth happens in stages between the ages of 6 months and 3 years. When the child passes these stages successfully, the result is "the first level of self-identity." The process of *separation–individuation* continues throughout life and is notable especially in adolescence, marriage, and parenthood. A person who passes through this process successfully is a person with a *differentiated* personality capable of stable love relationships.

In other words, to be able to truly love and be intimate with another person, rather than some reflection of ourselves in that person, we need to be individuated. We all struggle to achieve a balance between the need to be one with the person with whom we are in love and the need to be separate, a struggle between togetherness and individuation.[6] The level of "differentiation" that partners can achieve from their families of origin has a critical influence on the quality of their intimate relationship. Actually, it can even be said that if the early bond with the mother is loving and warm, "the first, and perhaps essential step toward a good marriage will have been taken (p. 37)."[7]

The Roots of Obsessive Love

What happens when the initial bond with the mother is not warm and loving? When the behavior of a parent is perceived by a child as rejection, abandonment, or persecution, the child cannot give up or change the "frustrating object" that is the parent. The child deals with the frustration by internalizing parts of the loved/hated parent in an attempt to control the parent in his or her inner world. The frustrating object undergoes various "splits" that are repressed and remain as unconscious *introjects* that become part of the individual's personality structure.[8]

The introjects include both the remainders of infantile needs and the parent's response to these needs. The ego develops and becomes organized around these introjects in different ways. The ego may develop a sense of inferiority and worthlessness, which reflects the baby's helplessness, or a sense of grandiosity and omnipotence that reflect the baby's perception of the parent's omnipotence. The self develops around these unconscious introjects, and both their extremes can be found in it. When we see in the arrogant and snobbish behavior of a person evidence for the presence of an introject of a grandiose self, we can safely assume that we are also going to find an introject of an insecure and inferior self that was repressed. When we see a person who always feels victimized, taken advantage of, and abused, we can be sure that in addition to the introject of a victim, we are going to find a hostile, aggressive, and destructive introject that has been repressed.

In most cases, the individual is only aware of one part of this duality; in the last case, the individual is likely to be aware of the victimized self and unaware of the hostile aggressive self. In the familiar example of the paranoid, the introject of the persecuted victim controls the internal organization of the self, whereas the denied and repressed introject of the aggressive persecutor is projected onto other people. People with whom the individual has a relationship are perceived as fitting those unconscious introjects, as aggressive, abandoning, or persecuting. All this means that the people a person comes in contact with are perceived and understood in the light of that person's internal world of objects and object relations.

Falling in love is an unconscious choice of a partner who fits a repressed, "split-off part" of the self.[7] Once the partner expresses, or is perceived as expressing, that repressed part in the self, there is no need to admit its existence in the self. A woman who feels unlovable because she felt unlovable as a child is likely to choose a man who does not show love. This way, she can blame him for her bad feelings about herself. A man who feels inferior because he felt that way as a child is likely to choose a critical and judgmental wife. This way, he can blame her for his feelings of inferiority. Although the woman will continue to complain that her husband does not show her love and the man will continue to complain about his wife's constant criticism, both are likely to remain with their partners because it is far easier to be with a partner who provides an external justification for your bad feelings about yourself than to confront those feelings directly in yourself.

People always look in their intimate partners for repressed parts in themselves. However, when they are undifferentiated, as a result of traumatic experiences of rejection, abandonment, or persecution in their childhood, their feelings toward these suppressed and denied parts in themselves are especially negative or ambivalent. Because the need to deny the existence of these repressed parts is especially strong, so is the need to find a partner who will express them.

When they discover that repressed part in a potential partner, they fall "madly in love." Their love may appear to others excessive, destructive, or even crazy, but it makes perfect sense given their unconscious needs. After having fallen in love, they unconsciously encourage their partners to express this repressed and denied part. This enables them to criticize and try to control this split-off part in their partners, not in themselves.

On the other hand, when a couple is differentiated and both partners are reasonably integrated people, their personality differences are perceived as complementary, valuable, and enjoyable. The slightly compulsive husband in such a couple may enjoy the spontaneity and impulsiveness of his wife, whereas the wife enjoys her husband's attention to detail and careful planning.

Among the interviewees whose quotes appeared at the opening to this chapter, there was a listless and sad-faced man who said that he fell in love with his girlfriend because "*she is full of joy, sure of herself, attractive. She is one of those people who always makes me happy when I see her. She is one of those optimistic people who always smiles.*" A slow-speaking and slow-moving woman said she fell in love with her boyfriend because he was "*energetic and dynamic.*"

Contrary to the familiar dictum that to be able to love others we first need to love ourselves, psychoanalyst Theodore Reik observed that the more negative our self-perception, the more likely we are to fall in love. People sense something lacking in themselves and seek the missing quality or qualities in a mate. When they fall in love, they project onto the beloved their unfulfilled fantasies.[9]

The projection of split-off parts of the self, *split-off projection*, happens in both partners, with each partner trying to express denied and repressed parts through the partner. For example, a woman who has internalized traumatic childhood experiences of violent conflict between a victim (her mother) and an abuser (her father) views herself as a victim. She has split the two parts of the conflict, repressed the violent abuser part, and projected it onto her partner. The internalized conflict, in this case between abuse and victimization, becomes an ongoing conflict between the partners. The split self becomes a split couple. The woman needs a hostile and aggressive man to project onto him the unconscious and primitive, violent, repressed, split-off part of herself. The internalized conflict pushes her to find a partner who can fill that need, to the shock and dismay of her family and friends, who cannot understand what a sweet and gentle woman like her finds in an aggressive and hostile brute like him. The answer is simple. She finds in him her split-off part.

Her partner has also internalized a violent conflict from childhood between an abuser and a victim. However, in his case the part that was split-off and repressed is the part of the victim. In his relationship with her, he can experience this part and deal with it. In this way, undifferentiated couples import troubled early object relations into their romantic relationship.[7]

Because projection represents a primitive unconscious need, the individual who is projecting often "does not see" behaviors that do not fit the projection. Consequently, the woman is likely to see the man's behavior as hostile and aggressive even when it is not. Similarly, the man is likely to see the woman as a victim even when she is not. As this example demonstrates, partners tend to have the same internalized conflicts, and they project onto each other the complementary, unconscious, and suppressed split-off parts of themselves. Furthermore, each partner identifies with the parts the other partner projects onto him or her. The result is a fascinating dynamic called *projective identification.*[10]

Projective identification is probably object relations theory's most important contribution to the understanding of falling in love. It means, in a word, not only that couples project onto each other repressed parts of themselves, but also that they internalize each other's projection and identify with it. The man, whose wife projects onto him her aggressive, powerful, parental, authoritative split-off part, internalizes this projection, identifies with it, and sees himself as his wife sees him. Similarly, the woman identifies with, and sees herself as her husband's projection of, his victimized split-off part, as weak, infantile, and powerless. In this way, internal, unconscious conflicts in each partner become externalized as patterns of conflict in the couple. Stated differently, a couple's conflicts are a reenactment of internal conflicts in each of the partners. The less-integrated couples are, the more infantile their needs, and the more intense their conflicts.

When two people fall in love, they project onto each other their split-off and repressed parts. A woman who learned to deny her urge for autonomy and independence projects it onto her husband. This causes him to appear even more independent and autonomous than he really is. A man who learned to deny his dependency needs, projects them onto his wife, who then seems even more dependent and needy than she really is. Projective identification makes both of them identify with the respective projections. In most cases, all we see is a traditional marriage in which the man and the woman are playing their so-called natural gender roles comfortably. At times, however, these stereotyped roles can be rather costly for one or both of the partners. An example is a dependent woman who as a result of projective identification loses completely her ability to make judgments and act independently, especially when it involves her domineering husband, who acts as if his wishes and needs ought to be the single most important basis for what she does.[11]

A similar process explains why certain women fall in love and stay with men who abuse them. Many of these women, says psychoanalyst and family therapist Virginia Goldner, grew up with the message that being loved and lovable is contingent on feminine self-abnegation, so they split-off and disavow their "masculine" power and their rage. Such women tend to fall in love with boy-men whose mix of vulnerability and masculine posturing is enormously gratifying to them. Being needed and adored by this "wounded soldier" creates the illusion of a new beginning that can completely overshadow the abuse that eventually explodes. The abusive man splits off and disavows his "feminine" vulnerable victimized self. Together, such couples tie a Gordian knot around each other's hearts in a closed and destructive system of *object addiction.*[12]

Family therapist Murray Bowen believed that people tend to fall in love with romantic partners at similar levels of differentiation but with opposing defensive, or character, styles.[13] Defensive styles are patterns of behavior that protect the self from awareness of unconscious anxiety. Couples tend to compliment each other's defensive styles. Let us take, for example, a man who copes with the anxiety of being flooded with emotions by suppressing his feelings. Bowen predicted that this man would be attracted to women at a similar level of differentiation but whose defense mechanisms are the opposite of his—that is, women with hysterical tendencies, who tend to dramatize and excessively express and exaggerate their emotions. A woman who deals with her anxieties by becoming phobic is likely to be attracted to men who defend against their anxieties by denying them and engaging in daredevil sports and adventures. Similarly, one partner (most often the wife) may appear emotional, and the other partner (most often the husband) rational; one partner may appear dependent and the other quite independent, one active and the other passive. In all these cases, the different defensive or character styles mask the underlying similarity in level of differentiation and emotional maturity.

The most common patterns of couples' complementary defensive styles are as follows[14]:

- One partner is dominant and aggressive; the other is submissive and masochistic.
- One partner is emotionally distant; the other needs affection.
- One partner is helpless and needs to be taken care of; the other is omnipotent.
- Both partners are in a continuous and hostile struggle for control.

Despite the ubiquity of certain patterns, every couple relationship has a unique emotional pattern that is based on the interplay among conscious and unconscious, internalized, repressed, and projected parts of both partners.

When romantic partners are differentiated, the intimacy between them happens without the loss of individuality. These couples feel close to each other and encourage each other's personal growth. This is almost impossible when partners are undifferentiated. When a couple's level of differentiation is low, every effort to develop an independent identity is perceived as a threat to the relationship. The other partner responds with hurt and either attack or withdrawal; emotional flooding is frequent and communication poor. Lack of differentiation prevents the couple from taking responsibility for feeling insecure and inadequate. Instead, they blame each other in the utter conviction that if only the partner was different the feelings of insecurity, inadequacy, and pain would be relieved.[15]

Because undifferentiated partners try to gratify unconscious infantile needs and frustrations through a partner who cannot possibly gratify them, the inevitable result is hurt, despair, disappointment, frustration, hostility, and endless conflicts. A pattern of angry, frustrated, hurt love develops when neither of the partners is willing to give in. A hostile life-and-death dependence develops. Every conflict, even the most trivial, is escalated and imbued with great significance. These couples say that they love each other desperately, that they cannot live without each other, but they also cannot live with the pain they cause each other.

A failure to differentiate can also result in an inability to disconnect from the family of origin and has serious consequences for romantic love relationships. Because the sense of a separate and independent self is missing, all the emotional energy is focused on the family. This can be expressed in an invisible loyalty to the family; a "ledger of unpaid debts" binds the individual to the parents, so that a full investment in the partner is perceived as a disloyalty to the family.[16] An example is a man who feels compelled to visit his mother every day, call her several times a day, and eat at her house, despite the protests of his wife. The fact that the wife complains but stays with him suggests that her level of differentiation is similar to his, but probably manifests itself by severing contact with her family. In other words, she has a good reason, even if unconscious, to stay with him.

Another example is a woman who felt like the "deprived child" in her family of origin. She expects romantic partners to compensate for all her childhood injuries and deprivations and provide the love that she was not given as a child. It is clear that this woman is in fact "collecting from the wrong source," trying to settle a childhood debt within the romantic relationship.[16] Such a deprived child is likely to fall in love with a man who sees himself as a "a kind and nurturing parent."

Both these examples reflect a low level of differentiation. The level of differentiation in a couple reflects, of course, the level of differentiation in both partners. When this level of differentiation is low, both partners bring with them to the relationship problematic object relations that carry over from their childhood. An undifferentiated man is likely to attract and be attracted to similarly undifferentiated women. He creates with these women relationships that have the same conflicts and stresses that he had with his mother as a child.

Problematic internalized objects, *pathogenic introjects*, can result from problematic relationships with either of the parents or from observing the relationship between them. A woman who as a child witnessed her father's infidelity and her mother's pain and helpless rage internalized both the "betrayed victim" and the "unfaithful villain." As an adult, both these introjects play an active role in her romantic relationships. She can play one role in one relationship, the other role in another, or play both in one relationship and never notice the paradox between being unfaithful to her husband and having jealous tantrums at his suspected infidelities.

Pathogenic introjects and unconscious motivations help explain behaviors that are otherwise difficult to understand, such as why people fall in love with romantic partners who seem so inappropriate for them. The reason is that the partner represents a repressed part of the self. It is also difficult to understand why people stay with partners who make their lives a living nightmare. The reason is that it is easier to blame their suffering on the partner than to look inside and touch the pain. Pathogenic introjects and unconscious motivations also help explain obsessive loves in which the lover becomes a drug for an addiction. Such obsessive loves generate intense feelings and a seeming irrationality in romantic choices. Despite tremendous pain, rage, disappointment, and never-ending conflicts, the lovers insist that they are madly in love and seem unable to let go of each other.

In summary, according to object relations theory:

- People actively, albeit unconsciously, create their romantic relationships.
- Childhood experiences, especially those of deprivation, rejection, and abandonment, exert the greatest influence on romantic choices. The explanation is linear: Childhood experiences are reenacted in adult love relationships.
- Couple relationships are object relations that are most powerfully influenced by the childhood relationships both partners had with their parents.
- Falling in love does not happen by chance. People choose wisely, even if it does not always look that way, a person who fits their internalized objects and object relations, because with such a person they can reenact their childhood experiences and hope to gratify needs that were not gratified in their childhood.
- When they find such a person, they feel tremendous excitement, joy, and hope that they experience as falling in love.
- The unconscious needs of couples tend to be complementary, and couples collude in gratifying them. They create such unwritten contracts as: "I will express your anxiety if you will calm me" or "I will think for you if you will feel for me."
- The ability to love and function successfully in love relationships reflects an individual's level of differentiation, which depends on childhood experiences. When the childhood relationship with the parents was warm and loving, the person becomes differentiated and capable of mature and satisfying love relationships. When the childhood relationship with the parents was frustrating or injurious, the person grows up undifferentiated, capable only of immature love relationships.
- Relationships of undifferentiated couples tend to arouse powerful emotions, both positive and negative, and be experienced as obsessive love.
- People tend to fall in love with partners who have a similar level of differentiation, but whose defensive style is opposite: abuser and victim, sadist and masochist. When a certain conflict or pathology is found in one partner, it can be assumed that it can also be found in the other.

Criticism of Object Relations Theory and the Contribution of Heinz Kohut

A number of theorists have criticized object relations theory for positing an ideal of autonomy, differentiation, and individuation and suggested instead the importance of affiliation and connectedness for healthy development and the ability to love.[17] Self-psychologist Heinz Kohut, for example, believes that our self-esteem and well-being are derived from and embedded in relationships. The need for the affirming echo of the mother's approval is never outgrown but transferred to a lover.[18]

Kohut views falling in love as a state in which the beloved is a perfect, primal *self-object* and gratifies completely the lover's narcissistic needs. At the beginning of life, parents are experienced as parts of the self, or self-objects. Once the child's empathy and identification needs are satisfied, the child gradually can accept the parents, and later others, as separate. If these basic needs are not satisfied, other people always remain self-objects, viewed as parts of the self.

For this type of person, someone new triggers no curiosity about who that person is, but anxiety about the effect that this person may have on one's self-image. The idealization of the beloved fills the desperate need for experiencing oneself as part of an admired self-object. All the traits of power, wisdom, and beauty that the person feels lacking in him- or herself are attributed to the beloved. Merging with the beloved provides security and peace. The merging that couples in love experience results from their being self-objects for each other.[19]

HOW WE CHOOSE WITH WHOM TO FALL IN LOVE: JUNGIAN THEORY

> I seem to have loved you in numberless forms, numberless times,
> In life after life, in age after age forever …
> Today it is heaped at your feet, it has found its end in you,
> The love of all man's days both past and forever:
> Universal joy, universal sorrow, universal life,
> The memories of all loves merging with this one love of ours—
> And songs of every poet past and forever.
> —Rabindranath Tagore, *Unending Love*

> If you went to the sky
> I'd become a star
> And catch you
> If you went to the ocean
> I'd become a bullhead
> And catch you.
> —T. F. McIlwraith, The Bella Coola Indians,
> *Man's Love Song*

Carl Gustav Jung was a brilliant Swiss psychiatrist who Freud considered for many years his successor. Their relationship cooled and eventually terminated when Jung rejected key concepts in Freud's theory. Whereas Freud believed that human behavior is conditioned by biological drives and personal history, Jung believed that it is conditioned by goals and aspirations and by individual and racial history. In the human psyche, Jung saw not a drive to satisfy biological needs but a constant search for wholeness. And, unlike Freud, Jung saw in the individual's personality the product and container of all ancestral history, shaped and molded into its present form by the cumulative experiences of all past generations.[20] Based on his vast knowledge of mysticism, religion, mythology, anthropology, and the classics, Jung formulated his notion of a *collective unconscious* that is deeper and more powerful than the personal unconscious. Although the personal unconscious houses the impulses and experiences of the individual, the collective unconscious houses the memories and experiences of the entire human race extending far into its dim and unknown origins. These memories and experiences have been transferred from one generation to the next from the dawn of history. It is possible to learn about them from the appearance of similar images or symbols in different cultures that Jung called *archetypes*.

Archetypes are universal "thought forms" common to all human beings. The archetypes are based on the collective experience of all of humankind and are expressed as the universal symbols of myths, rituals, visions, works of art, and dreams. Archetypes can be human, such as the "earth mother" or "the old wise man"; they can be places, such as the perfect place in which we would have liked to have lived or the perfect place, such as the Garden of Eden, in which humans lived in the past; or states of being, such as the archetype of "perfection," the image of the perfect life. All of us are share innate archetypes of birth, rebirth, death, God, the demon, unity, energy, the hero, the child, as well as an archetype of a mother and an archetype of a father. These last two archetypes are universal symbols. Jung believed that our relationships with our actual mother and father are formed on the basis of these innate archetypes.

Jung emphasized some archetypes more than others because, among other reasons, he saw evidence for their existence in his clinical work. He believed that these archetypes evolve into separate systems within the personality. One of these is "the shadow," the most powerful and dangerous archetype, which includes the most primitive and bestial instincts. This is the "dark side" in ourselves, which we do not like or were taught to hide. The shadow is also the source of creativity, vitality, and spontaneity.

Among the most important archetypes in Jung's theory are the *anima* and the *animus*. Jung believed that the human psyche is androgynous and includes complementary masculine and feminine elements. This duality is represented by the Hermaphrodite, a creature that is half man and half woman. In the psyche of every man there exists an inner woman, the anima, and in the psyche of every woman there exists an inner man, the animus. The combination and integration of the masculine and the feminine elements serve the adaptation and survival needs of the human race, both because of the roles they play in the development of the individual and because they enable romantic love, communication, and understanding between the sexes.

The *animus*, Latin for the male psyche, is the personification of the masculine archetype, "the masculine principle" in the female unconscious. Jung believed that all women hide a latent masculine personality beneath their conscious feminine personality. The animus is the product of the universal experience of women with men. By living with men throughout the ages, women have developed an internal "masculine voice" that is expressed through such masculine qualities as power, ambition, initiative, courage, objectivity, and wisdom; it propels the woman toward a dedication to a "sacred mission." The internal voice of the animus is forceful, persistent, and, at times, cold and distant. It is a voice that emphasizes the ability to be assertive and to control people and situations.

The positive animus helps a woman build "a bridge to the self" through creative work and activities in the outside world. The positive animus is represented in legends and folk tales by Prince Charming, who comes riding on a white horse covered in a shining armor and rescues the beautiful maiden from a terrible danger or imprisonment. In different stages of women's psychological development, it can appear as a "muscle man" such as Tarzan, as "a romantic hero" such as the British poet Shelley, as "a man of action" such as Ernest Hemingway, or "a spiritual guide" such as Mahatma Gandhi.

The negative animus, represented by death, pushes a woman to abandon her human ties, especially those with men. A famous negative animus figure is the murderous and seductive Bluebeard (see Box below).

The animus causes women to manifest masculine traits and behaviors. It also acts as a collective image that motivates women to understand men and respond to them. A woman can truly comprehend the nature of a man by virtue of her animus. But, she can also misunderstand him if she projects her animus onto him without regard for his real personality. Well-adjusted women are able to make a

THE STORY OF BLUEBEARD

The rich and mysterious Count Bluebeard courted and married a young innocent woman and brought her to his castle. The castle was full of treasures, and Bluebeard assured his young bride that they were all hers. One day he told her that he had to leave for a few days. He brought a giant key ring that held the many keys to all the rooms in the castle and told her that she could use all the keys except for one little key, which she was not to use under any circumstance. After he took his leave, his wife could not withstand the temptation. Her curiosity drove her to try to find the door opened by the forbidden key. After a long search, she found the lock that fit the little key in a door to a room hidden in the castle's dark basement. Her heart pounding, she opened the secret door and discovered to her great horror the murdered bodies of Bluebeard's former wives.

distinction and compromise between the demands of their collective unconscious as represented in their animus and the reality as represented by the real men in romantic relationships with them.

The *anima*, Latin for the female psyche, is the personification of the feminine archetype, "the feminine principle," the feminine psychological tendencies in the male unconscious. It is the latent feminine personality hidden underneath the conscious masculine personality and different from it. The anima is the product of all the universal experience of men with women. By living with women throughout the ages, men have developed an internal "feminine voice." It is expressed through feelings and moods, intuitions about future occurrences, sensitivity to nature and to the irrational, and through the ability to love. The anima propels men to connect with people, especially with women.

The positive anima is represented in folktales and fairy tales by the beautiful princess who needs a brave hero to rescue her. At other times, in legends, the anima is a spiritual, glowing, female figure that helps the hero on his dangerous journey by lighting the road ahead. The negative anima is represented by witches and dark sorceresses—the dangerous all-knowing priestesses—who connect with the "spirit world" and the "forces of darkness" that represent the dark side of the unconscious. The negative anima is also represented by dangerous and evil beauties who tempt men to their death, such as the Sirens of Greek mythology or the Lorelei of ancient German mythology, beautiful female water creatures whose enchanting voices seduced and drew sailors into the deadly waves. (See an artist's portrayal of the Lorelei in Figure 15.)

The anima causes men to manifest feminine traits, and it acts as a collective image that motivates men to understand women and respond to them. A man can truly comprehend the nature of a woman by virtue of his anima. It is possible to get to know a man's anima by the type of women with whom he falls in love. But, a man can also misunderstand women if he projects his anima onto them without regard for their true personalities. Well-adjusted men, just like well-adjusted women, are

FIGURE 15. The beautiful Lorelei seduced men to their death with their sweet singing (Jung, 1964).

capable of compromising the demands of their collective unconscious, represented by their anima, with the reality of the women in romantic relationships with them.

The anima and the animus can be positive or negative, destructive or wonderful. The feminine side can correct a one-sided masculinity in a man and make him softer, more sensitive, and more communicative. Similarly, the masculine side can correct a one-sided femininity in a woman and make her more assertive, self-expressive, and active. When a man disregards his anima, she can become demanding, obsessive, and moody. When a woman disregards her animus, he can fold his arms and stubbornly refuse to let her express her creativity. Cruel jailors and sadistic Nazi guards in women's dreams are examples of negative animus figures that can be testimony to women's neglect of their animus. Cruel witches and dangerous sexual women in the dreams of men are examples of negative anima figures that can be testimony to men's neglect of their anima.

Jung's notion that the anima and the animus are archetypes and part of the collective unconscious helps explain a curious phenomenon for which neither object relations theory nor evolutionary theory can account: the fact that there are some men and women with whom many people fall madly in love. These are people who represent archetypal masculinity and femininity. Two famous examples of such anima figures are Madonna, the sexy woman, and Greta Garbo, the mystery woman. James Dean and Humphrey Bogart are famous animus figures.

Femme fatales, women who are introverted, mysterious, and like fairies, who do not surrender to love, tend to attract anima projections more than other types of women do. The reason is that men can project almost anything, weave endless fantasies around creatures so fascinating in their vagueness and mystery.

Because the anima and the animus are archetypes, they can be similar in different people, but because they are also part of the unconscious of an individual, they appear in dreams in the symbolic expression that is appropriate for that individual. Jung believed that a man's anima is shaped by his mother, and a woman's animus is shaped by her father. The anima and the animus play central roles in the life of the individual and the survival of the human race because of their influence on falling in love. Every man carries in him the eternal image of a woman, not a particular woman, but a defined feminine image; the same is true for the woman and her inner image of a man. Because the image is fundamentally unconscious, it is projected onto the beloved and is a primary reason for romantic attraction.

When a man meets a woman who reminds him in some significant way of his anima, his response is immediate and powerful. He projects onto her his unconscious image, and then he no longer sees the real woman, the way she is, but only his projection. If, as is often the case, this man reminds the woman of her animus, she also projects onto him her unconscious image. This mutual projection is experienced by both of them as falling in love.

If the anima helps men find an appropriate romantic partner, what about homosexual men? It has been suggested that the anima figure for homosexual men can be a male rather than a female figure.[21] It can similarly be argued that the animus figure for lesbian women can be a female rather than a male figure.

When a man's anima is projected onto a certain woman (or man), this person is perceived as possessing the traits of his anima. The perceived presence of these anima traits in a woman causes the man to fall in love with her, sure that "she is the one," the ideal woman for whom he has been looking and longing. A similar process happens when women fall in love.

Because the anima is part of a man's psyche, even if an unconscious part, finding a woman who resembles his anima makes him feel as if he has known her, intimately, all his life. And, in a sense he *has* known her all his life through the image that is engraved in his psyche. He falls in love with her so totally and so helplessly that it appears sheer madness to the people around him. In men who are lacking psychological awareness, projection onto a woman is the only way they ever come to know their anima.

HOW WE CHOOSE WITH WHOM TO FALL IN LOVE: EVOLUTIONARY THEORY

Just like Jungian theory and object relations theory, evolutionary theory assumes that early childhood experiences of love play a critical role in adult romantic relationships. The key concept that explains the reenactment of childhood's love bonds in adult romantic relationships is not archetypes or object relations but imprinting.

According to evolutionary theory, humans develop according to a set evolutionary program constantly exposed to environmental influences. There are "critical periods" in which environmental influences shape and mold us with special force. This molding process is termed *imprinting*. Imprinting happens fast during a critical period in the life of the young of every species, causes neural changes in the brain, and is probably irreversible; thus, it has significant long-term effects on behavior.

Concepts such as love are created in the brain in a network of neural wiring. Once a concept is imprinted in the brain, we continue to use it to make sense of the world around us. Evolutionary psychologist Ada Lumpert gives a most appropriate example of the effect of the childhood experience of maternal love on adult romantic attraction.[22] The first love is imprinted on the brain of a child, writes Lumpert, and is engraved on it for better or for worse for the rest of life. A boy who grew up with a cold and hostile mother has such a pattern of love relationships imprinted on his brain. When he grows up and becomes a gifted and good-looking young man, he enjoys the attention of many young women and can choose the most attractive and sweetest among them. Instead, he chooses the meanest and coldest. When his best friend asks him why he has done such a stupid thing, our young man has an interesting answer: "I know she's cold and mean-spirited, but only with her I feel a romantic spark." And he knows what he says. The mean-hearted woman is the one to whom his brain responds. The response of brain cells is electric; this is why they generate a sort of spark. A kind-hearted, sweet woman cannot spark any of his "romantic love wiring"; this is why he does not find such a woman romantically attractive. When our young man marries his mean and cold-hearted sweetheart, other imprintings are sparked in his brain. His hostile and cold mother hurt, humiliated, and angered him as a child. As a result, brain wiring of love, humiliation, pain, and anger are combined, and all of them come to life when sparked in his adult relationships. Later the couple's relationship, these old imprintings are likely to reappear and be enforced on the realities of the couple's life. She may say something as insignificant as, "Do you mind taking out the garbage?" and he will respond with rage, pain, and humiliation: "You are always sending me out with the garbage. This is all I am worth for you." He was first attracted to the landscape of his childhood, but later that same landscape brings up his childhood pain.

Childhood experiences are imprinted on our brains and become the familiar worlds that we seek to recapture for the rest our lives. These are the positive imprints that childhood landscapes, smells, tastes, and people we grew up with leave engraved on our minds. Such positive imprints also direct romantic attraction. Every element of physical shape, color, personality, behavior, and attitude can become imprinted and, in adulthood, desired. This, claimed Lumpert, is the reason for the high frequency of romantic partners who resemble our parents in their appearance, personality attitudes, or abilities.[22]

A mechanism similar to a positive imprint is the love map about which sex researcher John Money wrote.[23] *Love map* is a mental map, a template, replete with brain circuitry that determines the people with whom we fall in love and what arouses us sexually. Children develop these love maps between ages 5 and 8, or even earlier, in response to their parents, family, friends, and life experiences. As they grow up, their love maps create subliminal templates of the image of the ideal lover, including details about physiognomy, build, and color, not to mention temperament and manners. Love maps also include the types of places they will find sexually arousing as well as the types of interactions and erotic activities that will be most exciting to them. Because most of us are surrounded during our childhood by members of our family, it is only natural that, as adults, we will be attracted to people who are similar to our family members and consequently similar to us.[23]

If the greater the similarity, the greater the romantic attraction, why are we not attracted to our family members? The answer evolutionary theorists offer is the same as the answer provided by Freud to the same question, namely, the incest taboo. Incestual mating would have decreased the genetic variability that is necessary to ensure new solutions for problems and challenges the human race might face in the future. The universality of the incest taboo, which exists in some form in all human societies, suggests to evolutionary scientists that it must be the result of natural selection and is well encoded in our genetic makeup. Although the attraction to the similar is aided by positive imprinting, the avoidance, and repulsion, of the too similar is guaranteed by negative imprinting. Negative imprinting ensures that we will not be sexually attracted to people with whom we grew up. Such people are negatively imprinted in our brain and do not arouse our passion. This negative imprinting cancels the effect of the attraction to the similar and prevents sexual attraction toward parents and siblings.

An example of the operation of such a negative imprinting was described in the doctoral dissertation of Joseph Shefer.[24] In his research, Shafer examined marriage records of 2,679 Israeli kibbutz members. Of all these married couples, only 14 had grown up together in the same kibbutz. Of those 14, only 5 couples had lived together in the "children's home" before they were 6 years old. Even among those 5 couples, not even 1 couple had spent all first 6 years of life together. Shefer explained this phenomenon as the extension of the incest taboo. Kibbutz children who spend their early years together develop toward their "potty siblings" a negative imprinting of the kind children develop toward biological siblings.[24]

As a result of the combined effect of these two mechanisms—positive imprinting and negative imprinting—we fall in love with someone who is similar to us but is not a member of our immediate family.

THE PHYSIOLOGY OF FALLING IN LOVE

> The love that is purest and sweetest
> Has a kiss of desire on the lips.
>   —John Boyle O'Reilly

> All trembling in my arms Aminta lay ...
> Her rising breasts with nimbler motions pant ...
> We sigh, and kiss: I waked, and all was done.
>   —Aphra Behn, *The Dream*

Once we fall in love, a certain chemical process is activated that evolutionists believe has evolved to propel us to reproduce. It involves various hormones and other substances, termed *the love brigade* by Theresa Crenshaw, a physician who described "the alchemy of love and lust."[25] When we are in love, it is enough for us to see, think, or even dream about the beloved for the process to be triggered. It starts in a tiny molecule with a long name, phenylethylamine (PEA), and it includes pheromones and the sex hormone DHEA (dehydroepiandrosterone).

The *PEA molecule*, also known as the molecule of love, is contained in high levels in chocolate. This is perhaps why the giving of chocolate has become a traditional part of courtship rituals around the world.[25] PEA is a natural amphetamine produced in our brain and is responsible for the feelings of euphoria, excitement, joy, and ecstasy that are associated with falling in love. When the amount of PEA in the brain goes up, it produces a feeling of sexual excitement and emotional uplift. This is the chemical reason why couples in love can spend whole nights making love and having deep, heart-to-heart talks; why they tend to be absentminded; and why they feel so sexually aroused and so optimistic, full of life and vitality.[26] PEA also serves as an appetite suppressant, which is probably why couples in love often report a loss of appetite for everything but each other. High levels of PEA have been used to explain love at first sight and love addiction. Some people become addicted to the rush of PEA and turn into "love junkies." In addition to eating chocolate, PEA levels can be raised by drinking soft drinks, taking diet pills, reading romance novels (especially if you are a woman), and watching pornographic movies (especially if you are a man).[25]

A *pheromone* is a chemical substance that can serve as a sexual signal transmitted through scent. In the animal world, sexual pheromones dictate courting and mating. In humans, they influence sexual attraction by subliminally effecting our sexual scents. During adolescence, glands located under the arms, around the nipples, and in the sex organs start exuding a smell that attracts the opposite sex. Every person's smell is a little different, said anthropologist Helen Fisher, and each of us has a "personal smell signature." Smells can arouse powerful emotions, including erotic feelings. When we meet someone whose smell we enjoy, the smell arouses in us a passion that enhances our romantic attraction.[26]

DHEA is a versatile sex hormone from which most other sex hormones are derived. It increases sexual desire, serving in a sense as a natural aphrodisiac. DHEA is concentrated in the breasts and pubic region and can activate these two erogenous zones by transmitting erotic fragrances and receiving erotic sensations.

The chemistry of our sexual attraction and arousal also involves the female sex hormone estrogen; the male sex hormone testosterone; dopamine, a neurotransmitter that increases the sex drive; and oxytocin, the touch hormone that promotes touching and bonding between lovers.[25] These chemicals send messages from the brain to the body, causing a chain reaction of escalating arousal that results in the state of heightened sexual arousal and dizzy excitation we associate with falling in love.

Where in the brain does falling in love occur? The well-known work of brain researcher Paul MacLean[27] enabled the identification of the physical location of the experience of falling in love in the human brain. MacLean distinguished among "three brains" or, more accurately, among three layers in the human brain:

The brain stem. The most primitive part of the brain that humans share with reptiles. It is responsible for instinctive behaviors such as aggression; territoriality; self-defense; rituals, including mating rituals; and reproduction. This brain layer is also responsible for physical activity, including breathing, sleep, and blood flow.

The limbic system. The layer that surrounds the brain stem and is shared by humans and primates. This brain layer is responsible for strong emotions, including rage, fear, happiness, sadness, disgust, hatred, and passionate love.

The cortex. The newest brain layer to evolve, covers the limbic system, and is unique to humans. This brain is responsible for cognitive functioning. It is conscious, awake, rational, and in contact with the environment and with reality. It enables us to make decisions, think, plan, respond, and create. It is the brain layer that helps us find logic, order, and causality in things, the part of us we call "I."[27]

According to this analysis it is clear that the emotional ecstasy of falling in love happens in the limbic system.

In summary, I would like to suggest that whether we are talking about a love object in object relations theory, an archetype in Jungian theory, an imprinting or a love map in evolutionary theory, it seems clear that we are talking about the same thing—an internal romantic image that plays a key role in the choice of the person with whom we fall in love.

THE INTERNAL ROMANTIC IMAGE AND FALLING IN LOVE

> Lovers: the one whom you seek
> is with you
> Search within and without,
> He is with you.
> —Shah Nimattuffah,
>   *The One Whom You Seek Is With You*

> My beautiful love as yet unknown
> you are living and breathing
> somewhere far away or perhaps quite close to me,
> but still I know nothing
> of the threads that form the fabric of your life
> or the pattern which makes your face distinctive.
> My beautiful love as yet unknown,
> I would like you to think of me tonight
> as I am thinking of you—
> not in a golden dream that is far from the real self,
> but as I really am, a living person
> that cannot be invented without distorting the truth.
> —Michel Quoist, *My Beautiful Love as Yet Unknown*

We all have an internal romantic image, a romantic code that determines to a large extent our romantic choices. Although most clinical theories emphasize the role of the negative and unconscious elements in this model, when people talk about their love relationships, they tend to emphasize the positive aspects of the romantic image. These positive aspects direct us to find a romantic partner with whom we can replicate the positive aspects of our childhood relationships with our parents.

> *The similarity is in the safety. The fact that the person is always there for you with open arms.*
> *I try to make him fatherly toward me. I made him spoil me like my dad did. But he can also be like my mom in opening up to people and in being warm and loving.*
> *He's very similar to my mother, caring, intelligent, that's probably the reason why we got along so well. I'm closer to my mother than to my father and he's more like her.*

Many of the words I would use to describe our relationship are also words I would use to describe my relationship with my mother: full of laughter, fun, mutually respectful, honest, secure. I see the way my mother treated me as an ideal. Honesty, trust, independence, my mother gave me those things, and in all my good relationships these things are present.

Although the positive aspects of our romantic model help us reenact the good parts of our childhood relationships with our parents, the negative aspects direct us to find a partner who can compensate us for negative childhood experiences and things we wanted but did not get:

He is similar to my father in his love and concern for me, but he is not stingy like my father, he spoils me more. And he listens to everything I have to say without screening like my father does. He is similar to my mother in his concern for me, but he doesn't tell me what to do like she does. He only suggests things.

I felt totally comfortable with her. I never felt totally open with my parents. I was more open with her.

We understand each other much more, and he's more interested in understanding me. He doesn't disapprove or approve whereas they do.

He's the same odd mix of emotion and rational thinking, but I think he's more sensitive and tuned to people than my father ever was, very attuned. When he listens you're the most important person.

At times, the relationship with the parent was rejecting or abusive. This, of course, has a major effect on the choice of a romantic partner.

He was physically scary. There was a great deal of aggression in him, which is similar to the way my father was when I was a girl.

One negative pattern that I've got is trying to provoke him to get really angry, because he is really calm and diplomatic and doesn't fly off the handle. But I can make him crazy, and I find that I do it. It's also a pattern that I had with my dad. A sense of relief that I get from seeing him get so angry.

She would tell me to do stuff in a similar way to the way my mother told me to do things. I wanted someone to dominate me. I wanted someone who will unconditionally love me. For some reason I thought that my mother didn't.

Although our romantic images are influenced by the positive and the negative traits of our parents and other important people in our childhood, there is a significant difference between the impact of the positive and the impact of the negative traits. Sadly, or luckily, which is the way I choose to view it, negative traits have a greater influence on our romantic image. The reason is not, as some psychologists believe, that we choose to marry our worst nightmares, but that with these traits we are far more likely to have unresolved issues. The person who fits our romantic image is the person who can best help us resolve these unresolved issues. This is why we fall in love with people who share the negative traits of our parents.[28]

In the example of a woman whose father was unfaithful to her mother, although reason will direct her to find a man whose fidelity she can trust, in most cases she is far more likely to choose a Don Juan like her father, not because she wants to repeat her childhood trauma, but because only a man like her father can give her what she did not get from her father—the fidelity of a Don Juan. The paradox is that she chooses to fall in love and marry a Don Juan because he is similar to her father, but what she wants more than anything is for him to treat her, and only her, differently from her father. She wants her husband, a sexy and attractive man who loves women and is always surrounded by adoring women, to be a faithful and loving husband. Only a faithful Don Juan can give her the security that her mother did not get as a wife, and that she, because of her identification with her mother, did not get as a child. Even if she cannot satisfy this unconscious need because her Don Juan husband is unfaithful, the adult repetition of her childhood trauma with the added measure of control of herself and her life can have a healing effect.

At other times, a romantic image can dictate the choice of a romantic partner who is the exact opposite of a parent with whom the person has an unresolved issue. A man who as a child witnessed the unfaithfulness of his mother can choose to fall in love with a woman whose most notable trait is her fidelity. He can then either enjoy her fidelity and the security it provides or be pathologically jealous and, without any basis, accuse her of being unfaithful. Her repeated declarations and proofs of fidelity can help heal his childhood wound. They prove to him again and again that, contrary to his cuckolded father, his wife is faithful.[29]

We are attracted to people who fit our romantic image in some significant way. The fit can be in personality, appearance, or behavior. When we meet such a person, we project onto him or her our romantic image. If our beloved projects onto us his or her romantic image and both of us identify with the projection, then the mutual projection and identification is experienced as falling in love. This is why when couples fall in love they feel that they have known each other their entire lives. Because the person with whom we fall in love plays such an important role in the dynamics of our psychological lives, the discovery of such a person is a powerful experience. When we are in love and our love is reciprocated, we are completely and totally happy. We are convinced that we found our true love, that our love will last forever, and that we will never again feel loneliness, pain, or sorrow. Love paints everything pink and gives our entire life a sense of meaning.[30]

SUGGESTIONS FOR PEOPLE SEEKING LOVE

Our romantic image is the internal romantic code that directs us with whom to fall in love. How can this largely unconscious romantic image be made conscious? One pleasant way is to visualize your ideal love relationship. What are, for you, the most important characteristics of such a relationship and of a perfect lover? You can get hints from your relationships with past lovers, or with close friends.

The other, more recommended, way is to look at the projection of your romantic image onto the people with whom you were in love in the past. These people represent your love objects, your anima or animus, your positive imprints, your love map. Take unhurried time for the exciting task of remembering—with as much detail and clarity as possible—each and every one of the people with whom you have been passionately in love. At times, this means recalling one person or two; other times, it may mean recalling many. In every case, it is important to recall and record their most endearing traits—physical, emotional, behavioral—the traits that made you fall in love with them. Are there traits that several of your lovers share? Are there traits that your lovers share with one or both of your parents? These shared traits represent your romantic image; they are the elements constituting your romantic attraction code.

If you have had hundreds of brief falling-in-love experiences and none of the people with whom you were in love showed any similarity to each other or the people who were significant in your childhood, it may mean that you are a love junkie, falling in love with falling in love rather than with a particular person.

If your past love experiences have been frustrating or painful and you have decided that you do not like the prescription of your romantic image, you have two main options. One is to avoid people to whom you have a powerful physical and emotional attraction and choose instead people with whom you are free and comfortable, people who are close and trusted friends and good company. As romantic partners, they will not lift you to the height of passion, but they also will not drop you to the depth of despair. The other option, rather than assume that your problematic past relationships were bad accidents, is to take responsibility for your romantic choices, analyze your romantic image, decipher your romantic attraction code, and try to turn it from a script for disaster into an opportunity for growth. Readers who choose this option will find suggestions for how to undertake this difficult yet exciting and rewarding task in chapter 12.

Chapter 11

FOUR STORIES

By night on my bed I sought
him whom my soul loveth;
…When I found him
whom my soul loveth:
I held him, and would not let him go,
Until I had brought him into my mother's house,
And into the chamber of her that
  conceived me.
      —Old Testament, *Song of Songs*

Seas have their source, and so have shallow springs;
And love is love, in beggars as in Kings.
      —Sir Edward Dyer, *Love Is Love*

WHILE READING THE VARIOUS QUOTES THROUGHOUT THE BOOK, THE READER may have felt a certain curiosity about the man or woman speaking or the particular relationships they describe. In this chapter, I hope to satisfy a portion of this curiosity. The previous 10 chapters of the book used quotations from different interviews to demonstrate a certain aspect of falling in love. In this chapter, I present the family backgrounds and romantic relationships of four of the people interviewed.

Of all the participants in the three qualitative studies on which the book is based, I chose four people for an in-depth analysis. Two, a man and a woman, were chosen because they received the highest score possible for the levels of intimacy they described in their romantic relationships. At age 23, they were either married or about to get married to someone with whom they were very much in love; someone they described as their best friend; someone with whom they had had a long-term, deep, intimate, and highly satisfying relationship. The other two, also a man and a woman, were chosen because they received the lowest possible score in the same category. At age 23, neither had ever been in an intimate relationship. The beginnings of relationships they had were not reciprocal and lacked closeness and intimacy.

Each story begins with a description of the childhood relationship the person had with his or her mother and father and then describes the person's most significant intimate relationship. At the end of each story a table displays a numerical analysis of the romantic relationship.[1] Let me emphasize that, before analyzing their romantic relationships, I did not know anything about their childhood experiences; I learned about them only after I had chosen the four young people based on their different descriptions of their experiences in intimate relationships. It is amazing to see in all four cases just how powerful the influence of childhood experiences is on our romantic choices and how unaware of it we are.

JILL

Jill was an only and very loved child. As long as she can remember, she felt close to her mother. "*Mother used to take me with her everywhere she went,*" and Jill had a hard time separating from her "*even for a short time.*" She was a little less close to her father, who was "*very busy with his work,*" but her relationship with him was also loving and physically expressive. Father was "*very interested in what I thought and gave me a feeling that my opinion was important to him.*"

Jill's father was better in his parental role than in his role as a breadwinner. He used to hug Jill a lot and tell her often that he loved her. She used to sit on his lap when he watched television and loved it when he would tell funny, amusing stories. But, her father had a hard time keeping a steady job, and her mother, who carried the major burden of the household finances on her shoulders, often lost her temper. She "*almost always had a good reason,*" but still felt terrible afterward and would talk about it at great length with Jill. Because of their financial difficulties, Jill and her parents lived in a one-bedroom apartment, enclosed in their own little world.

The most traumatic experience of Jill's childhood was a terrible fear of abandonment she felt when she was about 4 years old. Jill and her parents drove to visit relatives many miles away. After the long and exhausting drive, Jill's father carried his fast-asleep daughter from the car to the guestroom in the relatives' house. Convinced that Jill would never wake up in her state of exhaustion, her parents went out with their relatives to a nearby café. When they returned after about an hour, they found Jill in the middle of the living room screaming, almost paralyzed with fear and exhaustion.

Other experiences that could have been traumatic, such as falling off a swing and breaking her arm, cutting her forehead, or having one of her many severe ear infections, were not that traumatic for Jill because her mother was always there, nurturing, assuring, and comforting. When she was sick, her parents let her stay home; her mother would make soup and let her watch television. One time, when Jill was humiliated in school and was certain she would never be able to show her face there again, her mother assured her that by the next day no one would remember. "*And she was right! It was amazing—how did she know?*" recounted Jill with wonderment.

Although Jill was aware of the many benefits she had as an only child, in terms of the respect she received from her parents as well as the love and attention showered on her, she was also aware of the price she paid. The price was being alone a lot and having to grow up too fast. Jill thinks it would have been wonderful if she had had a brother or a sister. "*As an only child I had to deal with adults and adult issues when I was still supposed to be a child and behave like a child.*"

What type of romantic relationship is a young woman who was the apple of her parents' eyes likely to choose and develop? Well, Jill is married and describes herself as close to her husband. *"He's definitely my best friend. I've never been that close to someone. It sounds so corny, but it's true. I never have a feeling with him that I can't say something. He always knows how I mean something, and I know exactly what he means. We argue sometimes, but we are really in sync. We know what the other person thinks before he even says it."* [This last comment is a sign of a symbiotic relationship.]

When they first met, Jill thought her husband was "a jerk." The second time they actually talked, she thought she would like to go out with him but did not think it was going to last because he came from a small town and she thought he wanted to play around and be wild. She discovered that she was wrong. When asked what attracted her most, she said, *"He had sort of a carefree attitude. He was fresh, not jaded."* When they first started spending time together, they would apologize: "Is it okay if I come over?" Then, *"it avalanched into spending every moment together."*

Jill describes her marriage as "close, secure, loving, inspirational, and constantly growing." *"This aspect of my life is totally taken care of, so I can take care of other aspects of my life without worrying about it. We love each other very much, and we show it often. Through being together, being able to have this support system, we can be more creative and explore other aspects. It gives more options. I can try new things, and to change, and to grow spiritually, sexually, mentally."*

Despite the obvious similarity between the close, secure, and loving relationship Jill has with her husband and the close, secure and loving childhood relationship she had with her parents, when asked about it, she does not see the similarity. *"I don't know ... . We understand each other much more, and he is more interested in understanding me ... being close and being incredibly honest with each other."*

What are likely to be the areas of conflict in the marriage of a woman who thought that her father was *"useless as a breadwinner"*? The answer, *"He's not as ambitious as I am, and I don't understand this. So we made this deal, I go to school full-time and he works, and after I graduate, he goes to school and I support him. We argue about that a lot. We have an argument and then go into a pep talk. I hate it. I hate arguing. But I think it's healthy."* It is clear that not only the content of the fights Jill has with her husband (why aren't you ambitious?) but also their pattern (first fight, then reconcile through talking and analyzing) is similar to the fights between Jill's parents and her own fights with her mother.

What is the approach to separation of a woman who was *"very close"* to her mother, who had a difficult time being away from her even for a short time, and for whom a 1-hour "abandonment" was the most traumatic childhood experience? It turns out that Jill and her husband have never been apart for longer than a day since they got married. *"If we were, we'd be on the phone all the time."*

Jill is an example of a secure attachment style. In her highly intimate, somewhat symbiotic relationship with her husband, Jill reenacts her childhood highly intimate, somewhat symbiotic relationship with her mother. In addition to replicating in her marriage the emotional tone of her close, loving, secure, respectful, and open relationship with her parents, Jill also replicates their unresolved issue—a dominant, explosive, woman and a loving, nonambitious man.

AN ANALYSIS OF JILL'S ROMANTIC RELATIONSHIP

Dating frequency: 4 (average number of dates)

Number of significant intimate relationships: 1 (the relationship with the husband)

Length of this relationship: 30 months

Number of children: 0

Arousal played a role in the initial attraction: No

Propinquity played a role in the initial attraction: No

Similarity played a role in the initial attraction: Yes

Partner's attraction played a role in the initial attraction: No

Physical appearance played a role in the initial attraction: Yes

Personality traits of the partner played a role in the initial attraction: Yes

Status of partner played a role in the initial attraction: No

Was it love at first sight? No

Is the partner described as the "best friend"? Yes

Commitment to the relationship: 7 (happily married)

Sense of security in the relationship: 7 (very high, feels totally secure)

Ability to be oneself in the relationship: 7 (can be totally herself)

Intimacy in the relationship: 7 (very high, symbiosis, "know what other thinks")

Power in the relationship: 4 (both partners have equal power)

Pursuer/distancer: 4 (both partners are equally involved in the relationship)

Physical attraction to partner: 5 (physical attraction mentioned)

Friendship before romance: 3 (knew each other a little beforehand)

Stereotyped sex roles: 2 (sex role stereotypes are not mentioned, are not an issue)

Frequency of conflicts: 4 (fighting sometimes)

Ability to deal with conflicts: 6 (talking about everything and trying to resolve)

How are conflicts resolved: Talking

Abuse: Definitely not

Ability to stand separation: 3 (suffers withdrawal symptoms)

Jealousy is a problem in the relationship: 2 (jealousy was not mentioned at all)

Jealousy is a personal problem: 2 (jealousy was not mentioned at all)

Is/was partner satisfying an important need? Yes

Is partner similar to father? Yes

Is partner different from father? Yes

Is partner similar to mother? Yes

Is partner different from mother? Yes

Are the relationships with partner and parents similar? Yes (close and honest)

STEVE

Steve was also an only child. His parents divorced when he was a baby, and he hardly ever saw his father. His mother had different boyfriends throughout his childhood; some of them lived with her. But neither she nor they were adequate as parents, so Steve spent most of his time at his grandparents' house. As a child, he actually thought his mother was his sister. She would come for visits, stay for a while, and then leave. It was only when he started going to school that Steve moved in with her. He discovered that she could be "*demanding, moody, and cruel*" and had "*a very unconventional*" lifestyle and circle of friends, some of them drug dealers, who were involved in "*crazy and scary things.*" His mother taught him how to answer the door so that if someone came to kill them he would not be shot at the door. Steve thought that his mother "*never did things the way other people did them. She always tried to get around the system, even if it meant cheating and lying. She didn't like working and preferred to stay at home and do nothing.*" Often, she was out of the house, leaving Steve alone, miserable, and terrified. Knowing how cruel and vindictive she could be, he was terrified of being caught in the crossfire between some of the shady characters she knew.

In comparison to the difficult and complex relationship Steve had with his mother, his relationship with his grandparents was wonderful. In their house, he had a taste of normal life. His grandfather took him fishing and bowling and went with him to amusement parks. After he moved to his mother's place, Steve would often wake himself before sunrise, get dressed, and sneak out of the house. He wanted to get to his grandparents' house, have breakfast with them, and watch his grandfather work.

Although Steve's father abandoned him and his mother's boyfriends terrified him, his grandfather was a positive and significant masculine figure in Steve's life. He was wise and knowledgeable, caring, and strong. "*No one ever told him what to do, except grandmother.*" He once got a loud obnoxious person to shut up just by going over and asking him calmly to please be quiet because he did not want his grandson to hear such a language. His size had a lot to do with it. Steve's grandfather was "*a very big man, big hands, big arms.*" Even people who were eager to get into a fight calmed down quickly when they saw him approach.

Steve's grandfather was "*always doing something, always busy with some project. He loved repairing things, building things with his hands.*" And, he was a caring person. He took care of his own mother even though she was never much of a mother to him. Probably identifying with Steve's plight, his grandfather was loving and took good care of him as a child. He gave Steve anything he wanted: an electric train, bicycles, trips. Christmas was wonderful because Steve would get *"a ton of gifts."* Steve loved sitting and watching sports on television with his grandfather and crawling into his grandparents' bed at night.

Steve's grandmother took care of "*everything.*" She cooked, cleaned, took him to the doctor, and was always asking what he was doing, what was troubling him, how he was managing. He loved her dearly but still felt closer to his grandfather.

Even as a young adult, he described himself as feeling close to his grandparents. *"Everything they ask of me I do, if I only can."*

What type of intimate relationships is a man such as Steve, a man who had such a complex and nonnurturing relationship with his mother, likely to have? He is a man who hardly knew his father and whose most stable, deep, and significant male bonding was with his grandfather and whose most significant nurturing figure was his grandmother. When asked if he was currently in an intimate relationship, Steve said, "No." Had he ever been in a romantic relationship? *"No, not really." "It's tough, 'cause I can be guessing wrong. When you finally meet someone you want to go out with, they don't always want to go out with you."*

Steve was in love once. *"One of the only women I really fell in love with is this girl I was going out with a year ago. I knew her a lot of years. She hung around the group that I hung around. I'd always see her around, and one night we were at the same club and started looking at each other. Then we talked and stuff. She had just broken up with a boyfriend. We [I?] liked each other but we [I?] were waiting to make a move."*

He could explain easily what attracted him. *"She's a big girl, about 6 foot. From the moment I saw her, I liked her, red hair, good family, and she's interesting, very independent. I liked everything about her. She was at the center, everybody knew her. Many of the women in our group found themselves a boyfriend and adjusted themselves to his pattern. She didn't do it."*

Steve tried desperately to make the woman he loved respond to him. *"I sent her flowers every Friday. I would arrive at her door with wine and cheese, the whole routine. She was special, and I wanted to make it special. I gave her a lot of space. I didn't call her every night. I didn't tell her 'I love you the way boys love girls.' That's one of the problems. I'm one of these guys who don't say what they feel, and it's hard. Because maybe I'm guessing wrong."*

But, despite all his efforts, things did not work out. The woman he loved rejected him. *"Once, on her birthday, she had a date with me. Then she changed it to breakfast, and then to a lunch, and then she gave me a talk on how she's not ready for a relationship. So I moved back. I don't think I'm ready for the kind of relationship she wanted. I have a bad problem with the physical aspect of the relationship, the whole boy-girl thing. She was comfortable with the physical part in her relationship with other men. But with me she could see that it was more than that. I saw her regularly and tried to spend time with her for 4 months. She was very busy, all the time."*

Nevertheless, when asked how he felt about the relationship, Steve described it as *"exciting, enjoyable, and fascinating, but scary. I liked to talk to her about stuff. I was amazed at the things that she was doing. Just being around her was pleasurable. I liked giving her things, just thinking about places that I could take her to. I was awfully happy but also scared, not knowing the game of relationships. I didn't know what she wants. It scared the hell out of me, a lot of feelings I wasn't used to feeling. It's tough to deal with someone when you feel like that. There was nothing that she could do wrong. I put her on a pedestal."*

In response to the question about possible similarity to his mother, Steve said: *"I'm trying not to see a similarity, but I could see similarities. I can easily do it, but it would spoil the picture in my brain of what I wanted her to be. She was very sure of herself. She ran her life, knew how to be on top. She would tell me to do stuff in a similar way to the way my mother told me to do things. I wanted someone to dominate over me."* It is noteworthy that the woman Steve fell in love with was similar to his rejecting mother and not to his loving grandparents.

Steve is an example of an anxious-ambivalent attachment style. After the relationship ended, Steve went out with only two other women. One seemed interested in him, but he was not sure he was interested in her. Actually, Steve is not sure what he wants. It seems that what he wants, consciously or unconsciously, is yet another strong and dominant woman with whom he can reenact his frustrating, painful childhood experience with his mother.

AN ANALYSIS OF STEVE'S ROMANTIC RELATIONSHIP

Dating frequency: 3 (very few dates)
Number of significant intimate relationships: 1
Length of this relationship: 4 months
Number of children: 0
Sexual preference: Heterosexual
Arousal played a role in the initial attraction: Yes
Propinquity played a role in the initial attraction: Yes
Similarity played a role in the initial attraction: No
Partner's attraction played a role in the initial attraction: No
Physical attraction played a role in the initial attraction: Yes
Personality traits of the partner played a role in the initial attraction: Yes
Status of partner played a role in the initial attraction: Yes
Is/was partner satisfying an important need? Yes
Was it love at first sight? Yes
Is the partner described as the "best friend"? No
Commitment to the relationship: 2 ("actually, nothing really happened")
Sense of security in the relationship: 2 (very low, "I felt scared")
Ability to be oneself in the relationship: 2 (not really)
Intimacy in the relationship: 2 (very low, "I don't know the dating game")
Power in the relationship: 2 (partner had most power, "I wanted to be controlled")
Pursuer/distancer: 2 (interviewee was the pursuer in the relationship)
Physical attraction to partner: 6 (strong physical attraction mentioned)
Friendship before romance: 3 (knew each other a little before)
Stereotyped sex roles: 5 (reversal of traditional sex roles mentioned)
Frequency of conflicts: 3 (low frequency, did not dare to object)
Ability to deal with conflicts: 2 (very low, issues not discussed and not resolved)
How are conflicts resolved? Escaping
Abuse in the relationship: Possibly (emotional abuse in the form of rejection)

Ability to stand separation: 3 (suffers)
Jealousy is a problem in the relationship: 2 (jealousy was not mentioned)
Jealousy is a personal problem: 2 (jealousy was not mentioned at all)
Is partner similar to father? Not clear
Is partner different from father: Not clear
Is partner similar to mother: Yes
Is partner different from mother: Yes (career woman)
Are the relationships with partner and the parent similar? Yes

MARY

Mary's parents separated when she was a young girl. Her father remarried, but her mother did not. Her father was a successful businessman; her mother was a housewife. Mary hardly saw her father even before her parents broke up. He would leave for work early in the morning and come back late at night. He was often away on business, at times for months. After the divorce, there was a period in which he took his children out for dinner often, and they thought it was *"weird";* when he lived with them, they never saw him eat.

Mary was the second of four children. She spent more time with her siblings than with her mother. The mother's way of teaching them to cope was to let them take care of things on their own. Mary felt that other children were much closer to their mothers than she was. When she would have a fight with one of her siblings, her mother refused to hear about it and told them to *"figure it out"* on their own. Knowing that this was going to be her answer, the children avoided approaching her. Mary remembers her mother's favorite saying: *"Take care of number one."* She also remembers not understanding what it meant. Mary described her mother as *"nonjudgmental of other people but very critical of her own children."* For example, she criticized Mary's older sister because she got a B in a class and unjustly assumed that she had not worked hard enough. She was also critical of Mary's appearance. Even when Mary was a young girl sitting on her mother's lap, her mother would tell her she *"could lose some weight,"* which made her feel bad.

As an adult recounting this event, Mary noted that she *"should not have been bothered by weight at that age."* Her mother also used to look critically at Mary's hair and tell her she *"needed a haircut"* or that her hair was *"too thin and needed a perm."* They often argued about how much Mary weighed and how she looked. But, the most painful incident happened when Mary sat on her mother's lap one day: *"I told her that I loved her. Her response was to say that I don't love her but I need her, and, as a child, I am dependent on her. I remember feeling very rejected when she said that I don't love her. It was very hurtful."*

Mary's father was a *"very closed"* and emotionally distant man, and his children never understood him. Before the divorce, he bought himself a car. The family had a family car that was *"quite adequate, and all of a sudden there was another car parked next to the house.*" At first, the children assumed that it belonged to a neighbor. Then, one day they saw their father drive it and thought it was strange. When they asked him about it, he said, *"I decided that we needed another car."* Saying that he needed a place to work *"because his desk stood in a corner in the living room,"* he showed them an apartment that he had rented. All this seemed reasonable, but of course it was the way he chose to gradually introduce the children to the idea that he was leaving the house, and they did not get it. It was Mary's mother who told them about the divorce. Long before that, Mary had felt that *"something bad was happening"* but did not know what.

Mary *"never felt close"* to her father. She described her relationship with him as *"distant and heavy."* A big part of her father's relationship with his children involved his bringing them gifts when he came back from long business trips. The children liked the gifts, but it did not seem to them like *"the normal relationship most children had with their fathers."*

Her father would do *"nice things,"* such as take them to amusement parks, something their mother refused to do, but would never go on rides with them. Instead, he would *"stand on the side taking pictures."* When the children came off the rides, they often could not find him anywhere. They would run around looking for him. *"It didn't seem normal. He would do nice things, but he himself wasn't there. His heart wasn't in it."*

Mary sensed that her father *"didn't like children in general and was uncomfortable around them."* He was *"patient"* with his own children and always seemed happy to help them with their schoolwork. He hated pets and found it difficult that his kids had pets. He had little in common with his children, *"but he made an effort."* Mary felt closer to her mother *"only because she was around more."* When Mary was hurt or sick, her mother was the one who took care of her. *"She made me soup and checked my temperature. She showed care and concern. It was nice."* Father simply *"wasn't there."*

What effect does a father have if he does not like children and maintains a relationship with his own children that is *"distant"* and *"heavy"*? What effect does a mother have if her children experience her as uninvolved, critical, and on occasion rejecting? When asked about romantic relationships, Mary said, *"Well, I'm single, and I don't have a boyfriend, and I haven't had a boyfriend. I would say I have never had a boyfriend. I never dated in high school. When I went to college I dated some. In 5 years I probably went out with about 10 people. That's not very much. And most of those people I didn't see ever again. Since I've been in college, here's my terrible bias, I have even more of a distrust for guys at that age. I feel like it's heartache for a lot of people. Other people are more excited about just being with someone than being with someone in particular. I had a few good male friends, well, two, but as far as a romantic relationship goes, I just was not ready emotionally for it. I was just not used to it. Most people were moving faster than I was, and I just wasn't very comfortable, so I would get out of the romantic relationship. For a while that really bothered me, especially in the first and second years. I thought, what's wrong with me? Then I decided that if it takes me longer, it takes me longer, and that's ok."*

Even with the two men she dated several times, Mary kept her distance. *"There was always a sense that the relationship wasn't my idea. I have no problem being friends with men, but it's sort of a struggle getting into a romantic thing. Something about it just didn't feel right to me. Often I didn't even feel like I had a chance to become attracted to someone. At least with two, two I liked, I could see that I could become romantically attracted to them, but they just moved so fast that I suddenly felt like I was uncomfortable. The whole idea just scared me, and so it ended for me, and so it ended that way."* *"I kind of felt bad about it though. I don't know why I should have. I guess there were just a lot of unsaid assumed things. I assumed that it was going to be a friendship longer, and I was amazed that it wasn't, that was the problem I had. A lot of my female friends had boyfriends or had a steady boyfriend, or they just dated a lot. And so, in comparison, I felt like I was doing something wrong, but it didn't outweigh how uncomfortable I felt. So I decided, well, I guess I'm just different."*

Mary disrespects men she views as taking advantage of women. *"I remember with one person, I knew he had a girlfriend, so I just thought we were friends, and I was kind of attracted to him, but we were just friends. When he made a move to be more than that, I kind of lost respect for him. The next day I saw him. He was kind of mad, but I don't think he was mad because of anything that didn't happen. I think his pride was hurt. I have a hard time seeing men mistreat their girlfriends. Another guy was in one of my classes, and he said 'Do you want to meet after class and talk?' I thought that was weird, but I said okay. I guess I knew him as a friend for about a week, and then he showed this romantic interest that I didn't think was there. I didn't even feel like I knew him well enough to be attracted to him yet. I just said look, things are going too fast. I'm not used to this. He didn't like me after that."*

When analyzing her experiences with men, Mary said: *"I think it may have been partly my fault. I don't trust a guy until I really know him, and if he shows too much interest and just gets physical, then I'm not the right person for him to be with. I have a lot of friends who like to go to parties, and when a guy would show interest it would just be a one-night thing, and they would never see him again. I didn't want to deal with that at all, so I just kind of said no. I'm sure that I could have made it work, if I really wanted to work at the relationship. But I know I get scared real fast."*

Despite never having had an intimate relationship, Mary sees herself getting married and having a family. *"I think that someday I would like to get married and have kids, but I really would like it to start with a friendship first. There are several men that I got to know as friends, and I think it is nice, and that is how it should start, not in getting drunk at a party."* When asked what kind of a person she imagines getting involved with in the future, Mary says: *"Someone who, I was just going to say someone who likes kids. I don't know why. I don't have this great need to have children, but for some reason, a man who likes children and animals appeals to me, someone who cares about living things, aside from any sexual relationship."* Why do these particular characteristics leap into Mary's mind? Mary does not know, but we know because we remember her pain when she described her father as disliking children and hating pets. Mary longs for someone who will be different from her father, *"someone who can show love."* Mary has other requirements: *"and someone who is smart. I also don't think I could live with anyone who was terribly clingy. I'm probably too standoffish right now, so I know I would have to work at being less so. But I still think that I'm going to need someone who doesn't have to do everything together."* But even describing this ideal partner raises anxiety in Mary. *"For some reason I just keep thinking it is going to be scary, but it shouldn't be. It should be just friends, so what does it matter if it's tomorrow or 10 years from now? I don't think it would be in the immediate future. I have to take everything slow, and I can't work fast. I just feel that the slower the better."*

The anxiety aroused in Mary at the mere thought of an intimate relationship suggests an avoidant attachment style. Mary was pushed to be independent too early, before she achieved a sense of security in her early love relationship with her parents, especially her mother. Mary has no internal model of a secure, warm, and loving intimate relationship, and she has no faith in her own lovability because she did not feel loved and cherished as a child.

AN ANALYSIS OF MARY'S ROMANTIC RELATIONSHIP

Dating frequency: 1 (very few dates)
Number of significant intimate relationships: 0
Sexual preference: Heterosexual
Commitment to a relationship: 1 (has never been in an intimate relationship)
All questions about the intimate relationship: Not relevant
All questions about the initial attraction: Not relevant
All questions about partner's similarity/dissimilarity to parents: Not relevant

JACK

Like Jill, Jack was a beloved only child. He grew up in a small college town. His father taught at the college, and his mother was a housewife. Jack's relationship with his parents was always *"very warm,"* and he cannot remember ever having bad feelings toward them. He was often hugged and held in his parents' arms as a child. The three of them often did things together, such as eat in restaurants or go on trips related to his father's work. His parents treated him as an equal from a young age. They raised him the way they wished they had been raised. Jack had no brothers or sisters, and aunts and uncles lived far away. Yet, his father and mother were *"always there"* for him. When Jack wanted to do some *"father-son thing"* with his father, such as play baseball, his father always found the time, despite being a busy man.

But Jack's father was *"strict and demanding,"* and his mother was *"sweet and understanding."* She was the one who said *"it's okay."* She was *"always around the house,"* doing *"all the motherly"* things, such as putting on a Band-Aid when Jack cut himself, cooking, and taking care of the family, the house, and the dog. She was *"always busy doing things"* and seemed happy and content.

Jack's father was the disciplinarian. He would punish Jack by withholding his pocket money, which "*worked very well.*" His mother removed herself from it. Father would get "*very angry*" when Jack's grades were not what he expected or when Jack did things he was not supposed to do, such as "*taking a shortcut through the yard and stepping on his plants.*" He was "*very strict about things like that.*" Jack's father was an "*imposing man with a strong personality,*" who expressed his opinion in a forceful way. But, Jack always knew that his father really loved him and was concerned about him. He also knew that when his father got angry and punished him, "*it was for a good reason.*"

Jack's father "*seemed scary, but was not really.*" He was the type of teacher students are scared to go to, but after they do, say to themselves, "Why didn't I do this earlier?" Jack always tried to please his father. His father was his role model, and Jack wanted to be like him. Jack's father was busy with his work but found time to do things with Jack, his mother, and the dog, and on weekends he worked on projects in the yard.

Despite his admiration for his father, Jack felt closer to his mother because they spent much more time together. As a young child, Jack was with his mother rather than in child care. When his father came home, they were "*a family.*" On weekends, they often did things together as a family.

Jack never felt rejected by his parents; if anything, he said, it was the opposite. Their love and their concern for him were "*almost too much at times.*" His parents were protective and always wanted to know where he was. They were also strict and did not allow Jack to do some of the things he loved doing, which sometimes he did anyway.

What type of a romantic relationship is a man likely to have if he was so close to his mother and his father during his childhood? The answer, according to Jack, is "*a wonderful relationship.*"

"*We've been going out, officially, just us, for 4 years, but we went out for a year before that, so it's 5 years. It's pretty serious. We'll probably get married in a couple of years. It depends on our jobs and such things. If we knew everything, we'd get married tomorrow.*"

"*We met in my sophomore year when she was a freshman. We met at the beginning of school. I used to hang out with a friend that lived right next to her, and we started to hang out together. It's really funny because I had the wrong idea about her. First it was this blond who is living next to my friend Bob. I had the image that she was a party girl, which is totally wrong. When I got to know her I realized that that's not her. I helped her with her Italian, and I found out later that she didn't need any help with her Italian at all! The relationship kind of happened. We started going out, going to movies and hanging out.*"

When asked what most attracted him, he answered: "*She's really cute. That's the first thing. And she's fun to be with. She's funny. She has this naïve streak that is amusing. We got along really well together. We asked each other advice on writing papers and things like that. We used to correct each other's papers. When we had problems with friends we talked about it with each other. We are at the point now that we'd rather be together than with anybody else. Both of us know that we are there for each other.*"

Jack describes the relationship as *"warm, supportive, enjoyable, loving and exciting."* *"She knows how I work, and I know how she works, so we can always tell how the other one is feeling. And there's always warmth there. When I'm with her, I'm always happy. Stuff that I'm doing with her, even if just watching TV, is more fun with her than with other friends or when I'm alone. Even doing stupid things, like washing dishes with her, is so much better. Things are never boring. We never do the same old thing. There's always something that is different. Little things that change it from being a lull."*

When asked about similarity between his romantic relationship and his relationship with his parents, Jack noted a few things: *"I know she loves me, and I know that my parents love me. They all care for me, and that's that. And I care for all of them, so there's that kind of similarity. She's kind of similar to my dad in that she's stubborn as hell. But she's a genuinely nice person, and in that she's like my Mom. I'm really stubborn, too. We both make compromises, but we both want it our way, and we're both stubborn."*

As for differences, he says there are *"certain things that she hasn't experienced that I've experienced and that then we've experienced together, like experimenting with things such as cooking, which we did a lot when I was growing up. She didn't grow up that way. It's neat to see her try new things that are not her way. My parents, who are older, have experienced everything that I've experienced. So it's neat to be close to someone who hasn't experienced everything and being able to re-experience things with them."*

Separations are difficult for Jack. *"I get really sad. I try to immerse myself in doing things. I miss her a lot. We talk a lot on the phone, at least half an hour every day, sometimes more than once a day. Something is missing. I can't explain it."*

Conflicts in the relationship are few. *"We don't have fights. We've had some discussions, but not blatant screaming and yelling type of thing. Both of us are stubborn. But there is nothing we fight over. Recently both of us have been stressed out, so both of us felt a little left out. I felt that she wasn't giving me much attention, and she felt that I wasn't giving her much attention, so there was that kind of tension. But both of us realized what was going on. We talked about it. We sit down and talk everything out. We're close so we bring everything out right away."*

Jack's description of his relationship suggests a secure attachment style. In his close, loving, and egalitarian relationship with his fiancée, Jack reenacts his childhood's close, loving, and democratic relationship with his parents. The closeness, security, mutual respect, and at times insistence on having things his way are also similar to his childhood relationships with his parents.

AN ANALYSIS OF JACK'S ROMANTIC RELATIONSHIP

Dating frequency: 4 (average number of dates)
Number of significant intimate relationships: 2 (another one in high school)
Length of this relationship: 60 months
Number of children: 0
Sexual preference: Heterosexual
Arousal played a role in the initial attraction: No

Propinquity played a role in the initial attraction: Yes
Similarity played a role in the initial attraction: Yes
Partner's attraction played a role in the initial attraction: No
Physical attraction played a role in the initial attraction: Yes
Personality traits of the partner played a role in the initial attraction: Yes
Status of partner played a role in the initial attraction: No
Is/was partner satisfying an important need? Yes
Was it love at first sight? No
Is the partner described as the "best friend"? Yes
Commitment to the relationship: 6 (very good relationship with marriage plans)
Sense of security in the relationship: 7 (very high, feels totally secure)
Ability to be oneself in the relationship: 7 (definitely yes, can be totally himself)
Intimacy in the relationship: 7 (very high, feels very close and intimate)
Power in the relationship: 4 (both partners have equal power)
Pursuer/distancer: 4 (both partners have equal involvement in the relationship)
Physical attraction to partner: 5 (physical attraction mentioned)
Friendship before romance: 4 (were friends before the romance started)
Stereotyped sex roles: 2 (sex role stereotypes are not mentioned and not an issue)
Frequency of conflicts: 3 (low frequency)
Ability to deal with conflicts: 6 (talking about everything, trying to resolve things)
How are conflicts resolved? Talking
Are there signs of abuse in the relationship? No
Ability to stand separation? 3 (feels very sad)
Jealousy is a problem in the relationship: 2 (jealousy not mentioned at all)
Jealousy is a personal problem: 2 (jealousy was not mentioned at all)
Is partner similar to father? Yes
Is partner similar to mother? Yes
Is partner different from father? Yes
Is partner different from mother? Yes
Are the relationships with partner and parents similar? Yes

JACK AND JILL AND MARY AND STEVE

We see that, at age 23, both Jack and Jill, who were loved and respected as children, are in long-term, intimate, loving, and egalitarian relationships, whereas Mary and Steve, whose parents were separated and who felt rejected by their parents, have never been in intimate relationships. Is this a coincidence? Maybe, but a more likely explanation is that the childhood experiences of love, both experienced and observed, affected the internal romantic images of all four.

Jack and Jill reenact in their intimate relationships the loving childhood relationships they had with their parents. Mary and Steve reenact in their relationships with the opposite sex the rejecting and hurtful connections in childhood that they had with their parents.

The fact that family relationships in childhood predict the romantic intimacy of young adults was demonstrated in other studies as well.[2] It was also true for every one of the hundreds of people with whom I have worked in individual and couple therapy. This is not a simple reenactment, a type of "repetition compulsion" of childhood experiences, but an occasion to repeat the positive and overcome the negative. And, as the next chapter will show, there are few human relationships that are more appropriate for healing childhood wounds than an intimate romantic relationship.

SUGGESTIONS FOR PEOPLE SEEKING LOVE

Like the four young people described in this chapter, most of us are not aware of the powerful effect our childhood experiences with our parents have on our love relationships. Tragically, people who were unloved or even rejected as children continue to suffer in unsatisfying love relationships as adults. People with a history of such unsatisfying relationships who are willing to abandon the comfort of blaming their inappropriate partners can try to break free of their familial scripts. How this complex and challenging task can be undertaken and carried out is the subject of the next chapter (12).

Breaking free of unsatisfying love scripts requires, in addition to recognizing the invisible strings of childhood experiences and unconscious forces, conscious investment in goals, hopes, and aspirations. What that means concretely is envisioning in detail the type of relationship of your dreams. Imagine waking up in the morning: What would your beloved sleeping next to you look and feel like? What would you do, alone and together? How would you spend your breakfast? Would you keep in contact during the day? Would you meet for lunch? What would you do when you finish work? How would you spend your evening, your night, and the weekend? The more clear the image is, the more likely you are to make it real.

Part Three
ROMANTIC LOVE IN LONG-TERM RELATIONSHIPS

> People use each other
> as a healing for their pain. They put each other
> on their existential wounds,
> on eye, on cunt, on mouth and open hand.
> They hold each other hard and won't let go.
> —Yehuda Amichai, "People Use Each Other,"
> *Love Poems*

> Let me under your wing
> and be for me mother and sister
> and let your bosom be a shelter for my head
> a nest for my banished prayers.
> I will confess a secret to you:
> My soul has burned in a flame;
> They say there is love in the world—
> What is love?
> —Chaim Nachman Bialik,
> "Let Me Under Your Wing," *Songs*

*K*ITTY AND OWEN, AN ATTRACTIVE COUPLE IN THEIR EARLY FORTIES, are sitting in my office as far away from each other as the furniture will allow. After 22 years of marriage, they feel hopeless, ready to give up, and are contemplating a divorce. They are unprepared for the question I ask them: "What made you fall in love with each other?" But, because I am supposed to be the expert, they decide to oblige me. It turns out that when they met, Kitty was 20 and desperate to leave home. Owen was "big, fatherly, and wise." She loved his broad shoulders, his calm, his gentleness, the attention he showered on her, his ability to listen. Owen was 27 when they met and felt fatherly toward Kitty. "I raised a girl," he explains smiling. He loved Kitty's temperament and "Gypsy-like sex appeal." "It was impossible not to notice her," he recounts. As a shy and reserved man, he enjoyed her wild, sensual energy. With years of marriage and with Owen's support and encouragement, Kitty grew and developed. She now had her own interests in music and movement and was spreading her wings professionally. This proved difficult for

Owen, who became "jealous and suffocating." His gentleness and calm became a bore. Her restlessness in the marriage and growing disinterest in him sexually combined with her obvious appeal to other men became a tremendous stress for Owen.

So, we see that Kitty fell in love with Owen because of his fatherly calm, and now she wants to divorce him because he is a suffocating bore. Owen, for his part, fell in love with Kitty because of her Gypsy-like temperament, sex appeal, and ability be the center of attention. Now, these qualities are his greatest source of stress in the marriage.

THE ROLE OF FALLING IN LOVE IN COUPLES' LONG-TERM ROMANTIC RELATIONSHIPS

While the previous two parts of the book are based on studies, theories, and analyses of qualitative interviews, this third and last part is based primarily on my experience as a couples' therapist. Chapter 12 shifts the perspective from the individual to the couple and addresses the relationship between falling in love and the issues a couple is likely to struggle with later. It is based on my conviction that an intimate relationship provides us with one of the best opportunities for mastering unresolved childhood issues and finding significance in our lives.

Most people choose a therapist because they heard about the therapist from a person they trust, they read a book the therapist wrote, or they heard the therapist speak and liked the things he or she said. This is to say that the choice is based on logical considerations. The unconscious, however, more than anything else, dictates with whom we fall in love. Falling in love is an intense emotional and physical experience that can seem quite illogical, and for a good reason: It is not our faculties of reason that dictate it. As noted in chapter 10, the electrical activity in the brain of a person in love is not occurring in the cortex, the seat of logical thinking, but in the limbic system, the seat of powerful emotions and long-term memories.

Although not logical, in most cases the unconscious romantic choice is wise because it directs us to choose a person who can help us master an unresolved childhood issue. This is why finding such a person ignites the romantic spark and why it causes such elation and excitement. Even when the choice is dangerous, as it is when the unresolved issue involves physical abuse, in principle it still is a wise choice because it is aimed at healing the trauma, not merely repeating it.

When a couple is in love, the unconscious of both partners dictates their mutual selection. The interweaving of their individual core issues creates their core issue as a couple. When, after many years together, a couple comes for therapy and disentangles what seems like an endless morass of problems, conflicts, hurts, and disappointments, that core issue emerges at the center of most of their problems.

As we see next, understanding the connection between unresolved childhood issues and the problems experienced in intimate relationships is only the first step. Both partners need to take responsibility for their own contribution to their problems as a couple, express empathy for their partner's core issue, and—the hardest part—attempt to change the behaviors that are most stressful for the partner. This effort, even more than individual therapy, enables couples to change their problems into opportunities for personal and couple growth. Such an opportunity for growth is imbued with significance for people who expect to derive existential significance from their intimate relationships.[1] Chapter 13 expands this perspective by addressing the relationship between the unconscious choices of love and work as two spheres that people imbue with existential significance.

Chapter 12

TURNING LOVE PROBLEMS INTO OPPORTUNITIES FOR GROWTH

"A wrestling match." He laughs. "Yes, you could describe life
that way."
"So which side wins?" I ask.
"Which side wins?"
He smiles at me, the crinkled eyes, the crooked teeth.
"Love wins. Love always wins."
　　　　—Mitch Albom, *Tuesdays with Morrie*

Nothing in the world is single;
All things by law divine
In one another's being mingle:—
Why not I with thine?
　　　　—Percy Bysshe Shelley

*A*T THE BEGINNING OF THEIR RELATIONSHIP, SHE WAS ATTRACTED TO "*his
sense of humor. He's really funny, always had a joke.*" Later, his humor
came to annoy her. "*I can't talk to him seriously about what's going on in my life.*"

At first, he was attracted to her nuttiness: "*She was very, very active, and funny
and quick. She always seemed to be thinking up something nutty to do.*" Later, her nuttiness terminated the relationship. "*She had serious emotional problems.*"

At first, he was attracted to her shyness and sensitivity: "*She's a really neat person, really shy and reserved, really sensitive to people.*" Later, he said: "*It bothers me just
how sensitive she is to others in the sense that she is hyperaware of what others are thinking about her. It bothered me that she is so shy and reserved.*"

At first, she was attracted to his calm, impressed by his reserve. "*I had a crush
on him. He was very quiet and didn't open up at all.*" Now, she resents his reserve and
sees in it evidence of his lack of interest in her. "*He doesn't ask me about myself and
about my life, he isn't interested. I don't feel it's a two-way thing.*"

"*He comes off as being very confident, almost cocky. That's what attracted me to
him, but that's also what upsets me.*"

What is missing in these quotations is the partner's perspective on both the attraction and the stress. As we now know, for couples in love the causes of attraction are most often complementary. If she was attracted to his carefree attitude, he was probably attracted to her intensity. And, if she later complained about his lack of ambition, it is likely that he complained about her pushiness. The poles of carefree versus intensity and ambition exist in both of them and reflect the core issue in them and in the relationship. Susan and Robert are an example.

SUSAN AND ROBERT

One of Susan's most painful childhood memories was of being sent out of the house when her mother's friends would come for a visit. Susan enjoyed participating in their conversation, which drove her mother crazy. Deaf to Susan's tears and pleas, her mother would send her out and slam the door in her face. Susan can remember herself standing on the wooden balcony, banging on the locked door, sobbing and begging to be let in. One of Robert's most painful memories is escaping from the endless demands of his beautiful, elegant mother. Robert used to hide in his room and imagine that the little carpet he was sitting on was a raft in the middle of the ocean. His mother's angry, demanding voice sounded like a faraway thunderstorm. It no longer intimidated him.

Robert and Susan met when they were both in their early forties, the veterans of many destructive and unsatisfying relationships. It was the holiday season, a time for new resolutions and new beginnings. Robert had just completed a year-long journey around the world on a small boat, and Susan had gone back to college, determined this time to graduate no matter what. They met at a mutual friend's dinner party. There was something about Robert's quiet masculinity, his independence, and his adventurous spirit that sparked Susan's imagination. His obvious admiration flattered her. He was calm and reassuring, and he made her feel safe. Susan's beauty and poise left Robert breathless. The strength of her personality and the sophistication of her language and her interests dazzled him. He could not believe that a woman like her would pay attention to a primitive brute like himself. Her warm response excited him and made him happier than he ever believed possible.

Robert and Susan fell madly in love with each other. Both felt that this time they had chosen the right person, someone with whom they could spend the rest of their lives. Several months later, Robert bought a house, and shortly thereafter, Susan moved in with him. A year after they first met, Susan and Robert got married.

Despite the wonderful beginning, Susan and Robert's relationship was full of frustrating confrontations. The hardest thing for Susan was Robert's tendency to "disappear" when she was in an emotional turmoil and needed him. When she sensed his distancing, she would create "scenes" to engage him, but nothing she said, nothing she did helped. Robert would distance even further, hiding "like a turtle." The hardest for Robert were Susan's angry, unprovoked "attacks." He would distance himself from her, hoping that the angry storm would pass, but nothing he did seemed to help; his distancing only made things worse. When they came for couple therapy, both Susan and Robert felt deeply hurt by each other and disappointed in their marriage.

In the course of their therapy Robert and Susan came to understand their individual core issues and how they combined to create their core issue as a couple. Susan understood that, like the hurt, rejected girl she had been, she was banging on Robert's "door," feeling left out and begging to be let in. But on the other side of the door was not a rejecting mother but a scared boy who was terrified by the banging and anxious that he would not be able to satisfy her demands. Robert, for his part, understood that, like the anxious little boy that he had been, he was escaping Susan's demands, hiding in his room. But on the other side of the door was not a demanding mother who was insensitive to his feelings, but a hurt girl who needed his love. The image of the scared boy hiding and the hurt girl begging to be let in helped Robert and Susan see what they each needed to do. Susan understood that when she needs Robert's love and support she cannot demand it from him in a loud voice or by attack because the louder the demand, the less Robert will be able to respond to it as a mature adult. If she can express her need for him calmly, he will be there for her. Robert understood that his distancing from Susan is not a way to prevent the storm, but a sure way to make it increase in force. If he can respond to Susan's feelings and express his own, her anger will evaporate.

The magic of a couple's relationship is that, when two people fall in love, whatever they need to do for themselves to grow emotionally is most often the very thing that the partner needs from them. What Susan needed most from Robert to heal her childhood wound was the thing that Robert needed to give to grow emotionally. Instead of turning into a scared little boy, running away and hiding, he needed to learn to stay an adult and face whatever was demanded of him as a man. In the same way, what Robert needed most from Susan to heal his childhood wound was the thing that Susan needed to give to grow emotionally. Instead of turning into a rejected little girl that needed to pound on doors to be heard, she needed to learn to stay an adult and ask for what she wanted in a way that would increase her likelihood of getting it.

This seemingly simple change—in fact, a very difficult change for both of them to implement—enabled Susan and Robert to master a painful childhood experience they were both still struggling with as adults. After all, it was not by accident that Susan fell in love with a man whose primary strategy for coping with demands was withdrawal, a strategy that helped him survive as a child and thus became imbued with existential significance. And, it was not by accident that Robert fell in love with a strong woman who learned to demand forcefully what she needed, a strategy that helped her survive as a child and thus had existential significance for her.

Susan's heroic struggle to control the impulse to demand loudly and Robert's response to her distress when she expressed it quietly helped heal her childhood wound. Robert's heroic struggle with the impulse to escape and Susan's gratitude and love when he was able to stay connected to her helped heal his childhood wound. These changes, difficult at first but easier with time and practice, helped turn their marriage into a warm, loving, and rewarding relationship.

FATAL ATTRACTION OR WISE UNCONSCIOUS CHOICES?

> Love looks not with the eyes, but with the mind,
> And therefore is winged Cupid painted blind
> —William Shakespeare,
> *A Midsummer Night's Dream*

Few studies have dealt with the connection between what makes couples fall in love with each other and what causes their later problems, sometimes even their breakup. One of the few, which included 60 married couples, showed that the most annoying trait was often an exaggeration, implication, or the exact opposite of the trait that was first described as the main reason for attraction.[1]

In another study, Diane Felmlee showed that the traits that cause dissatisfaction in the partner are a negative translation of the traits that caused the original attraction.[2] Felmlee termed this phenomenon *fatal attraction*, fatal "in the sense that it foretells a sequence that ends in future disillusionment" (p. 296). She assumed that "the characteristic responsible for the initial attraction to a romantic partner and a characteristic that is later disliked, are often dimensions of the same overall attribute" (p. 297) and described three primary conditions under which such fatal attraction may occur. First is a state of infatuation or intense passionate love, when people are blinded by love and thus likely to underestimate the importance of negative traits. Second, it is likely to occur when an initial attracting quality stands out and is readily noticed. Such a quality is likely to be possessed to an extreme, and extreme positive attributes are especially likely to have negative dimensions. For example, a partner who is attractive because he is successful may soon be viewed as workaholic because it is usually difficult to attain success without a great deal of work. Third, some qualities that may be attractive and rewarding in the short term, such as spontaneity, may prove problematic in an extended committed relationship.

To investigate the extent of fatal attraction, Felmlee asked students to describe their most recent romantic relationships that had ended and asked specific questions about the relationships and the breakups. Among the questions about the relationship, students were asked to describe the features that attracted them. Among the questions about the breakup, they were asked what they found least attractive. Key words, such as *nice*, and phrases, such as *treated me well*, were put into categories. Results showed that, in 29.2% of the cases, the reason for the breakup was the same quality that originally attracted.[2]

My work with couples leads me to believe that the phenomenon is far more common than Felmlee's data suggest. In virtually every case of the hundreds with whom I have worked in couple therapy and in couple groups, if the relationship was based on romantic love, it was possible to find a connection between the traits that attracted the couple to each other and the traits that later became the focus of their problems.[3]

When a couple comes to therapy for the first time, one of the questions I always ask is, "What attracted you to each other when you first met?" I then show the couple the connection between their original attraction and the problem that has brought them to therapy. Similarly, one exercise I do in every couple group is to ask participants what attracted them to each other initially and then ask what they find most stressful about each other. There is almost always some connection between the two.[4] Contrary to Felmlee, who viewed this as fatal attraction, the dark side of every human virtue, I view it as a "wise unconscious choice."[3]

Like other psychodynamic therapists,[5] I believe that unconscious forces operate in both romantic attraction and relationship problems. The unconscious dictates the choice of a partner who can help us master a "core issue" that is the manifestation of an unresolved childhood problem. If one's core issue is fear of abandonment, one's unconscious will dictate the choice of a partner who can help master this fear. Who is more appropriate for the task than a person whose core issue is a fear of engulfment? This is why couples fall in love with each other. Because their choice is complementary, they jointly create their core issue as a couple. Ann and Ed are an example. They would not have been included in Felmlee's fatal attraction category, yet there is an obvious connection between the traits that made them fall in love with each other and the traits that turned their relationship into a living hell.

ANN AND ED

A professional couple in their late thirties, Ann and Ed came to couple therapy as the last resort before applying for divorce. Ann's main complaint was Ed's "*total lack of sensitivity and consideration*" toward her and toward other people. Ed's main complaint was Ann's angry outbursts, which always came as a big surprise to him and were "*incomprehensible and totally unjustified.*" When they first met, however, in addition to Ann's "*obvious good looks and sharp intelligence,*" Ed said he was attracted to her powerful and dynamic personality. "*She was direct and cynical and funny,*" he explained with a smile. For her part, Ann liked "*Ed's mind and the way he thinks,*" as well as his "*laid-back personality. He knew how to enjoy life, and was pleasant and easygoing, no complexes or complications.*"

Both Ann and Ed came from homes in which there was no love between the parents. Ann's parents divorced when she was a young girl, and Ed's parents fought frequently. Ed's father, who was a religious man, forced Ed to attend services with him and demanded a show of respect. Hardest for Ed as a child were his father's angry outbursts, which included screaming and, at times, even beatings. Ed's mother did not love or respect his father but was warm, loving, and nurturing toward Ed. Ann's hardest experience as a child was the loss of her beloved father, who, disregarding her love and need for him, moved away after the divorce. Her mother, who was "*very conscientious about her duties as a mother,*" was insensitive to Ann's feelings and unresponsive to her needs.

Ed's core issue was a fear of his father's angry outbursts and a bitter resentment of being forced to attend religious services and show respect, which Ed felt his father did not deserve. Ann's core issue was the painful feeling that people close to her were not responsive to her needs and wishes. Her eagerness to read her father's feeling and wishes and her longing for him developed into a great sensitivity to people. These core issues combined to create the core issue of Ann and Ed's problems as a couple. Ed cannot stand it when people "*force him*" to behave in a way they consider proper, which does not suit him. He responds by being "*dense and inconsiderate*." Ann responds to his insensitivity with anger and rage. Ed "*doesn't understand*" her "*uncalled-for angry attacks.*" Ann sees his lack of understanding as yet another demonstration of his total lack of sensitivity. This way, both of them reenact their childhood trauma in the relationship.

By analyzing what they found most attractive about each other when they first met and fell in love, it is possible to identify early signs that, at some level, Ann and Ed were well aware of the opportunity they presented to each other to master their unresolved childhood issues. At that time, Ed was attracted to Ann's "*powerful personality*," "*directness*," "*cynicism*," and "*sharp intelligence*." He found those traits exciting and enjoyable. Now, the sharp intelligence and cynicism have turned into "*unfair criticism*," and the powerful direct personality has turned into threatening "*outbursts*." At first, Ann was attracted to Ed's easygoing, uncomplicated way of being and to his ability to enjoy life. Now, she views him as "*insensitive and dense*" and "*totally focused on himself*." Despite the clear connection between Ann and Ed's original attraction and their distress, they would not have been included in the "fatal attraction" category because they used different words and phrases to describe their attraction and distress.

Ed and Ann are an example of the wisdom of unconscious romantic choices in directing us to choose partners with whom we have an opportunity to master psychological issues. When a man such as Ed learns to show sensitivity to his partner's needs, it will enable him to grow tremendously as a person; he can get out of the dense armor he has constructed around himself as a defense against the outbursts and demands of his father. This type of change in Ed will, of course, be a healing experience for Ann. When a woman such as Ann learns to respond without exploding in anger, it will enable her to grow tremendously as a person; she can learn to express herself in a way that keeps others connected rather than pushing them away as a defense against her fear of abandonment.[6] This type of change in Ann will, of course, be a healing experience for Ed.

According to Felmlee, fatal attraction is more likely to happen during infatuation, which can lead to a situation in which "love is blind." Clinical experience with couples such as Ed and Ann suggests that, like the "blind" in Greek mythology who see better than sighted people, and like "winged Cupid painted blind" in Shakespeare's *Midsummer Night's Dream*, love is wise in its choice (see Figure 16).

Because one example is hardly enough, see the Initial Attraction and Subsequent Stress box for 10 brief examples of couples chosen randomly from about 100 couples with whom I have worked in recent years. In each case, I describe the main attraction that made the couple fall in love with each other and what later became their major source of stress.[7] In every case presented, there is an obvious connection

FIGURE 16. "Winged Cupid painted blind" in Shakespeare's *Midsummer Night's Dream.*

between the cause of the couple's attraction to each other and the cause of their later stress. In addition, there is an obvious complementarity between the things mentioned by the husband and those mentioned by the wife.

Despite the obvious connection between the causes of the husbands' and the wives' attraction and the causes of their stress, there are possible criticisms of the conclusion of complementarity between them. It is possible to argue that couples who come to therapy are a select group; they are more likely to experience this type of disillusionment and have more unconscious, unresolved issues. The experiences of people who participate in workshops as part of their professional training or as part of employees' enrichment programs seem to suggest that this is not the case. Unlike couples in therapy, these people do not choose to learn about themselves and their relationships. Yet, to their amazement, they also find the connection between what made them fall in love and what later became the focus of their distress, disappointment, and annoyance.

In my studies on couple burnout, studies that involved hundreds of couples, I also found that the qualities that initially attract couples to each other eventually cause their burnout.[4] A woman who fell in love with her husband because he was "*the strong silent type,*" which she saw as "*very romantic,*" later burned out in her marriage because "*he doesn't communicate.*" A man who fell in love with his wife because of her "*strong personality,*" later burned out in his marriage because she "*argues*" with him about "*everything.*"

Another possible criticism of the "wise unconscious choices" finding is that the things that couples said about their attraction and about their stresses were not subjected to objective coding criteria. It is possible that I looked for evidence to fit my theory and influenced people to see a pattern that was not there. I have two

INITIAL ATTRACTION AND SUBSEQUENT STRESS

Attraction

Wife: He was a very persistent pursuer, made me feel desirable and adored.
Husband: She seemed like a dream come true, unapproachable.

Stress

Wife: He doesn't let me breathe; he is always in my face.
Husband: She never lets me feel that she wants me.

Attraction

Wife: He gave me a sense of security, was always there, always reliable.
Husband: There was something mysterious about her.

Stress

Wife: He is boring.
Husband: She is never completely there; there's no true intimacy.

Attraction

Wife: He seemed like the kind of a man who would reach high, be a success.
Husband: She seemed like someone who could build a home for me.

Stress

Wife: He travels a lot, meets all kinds of people, is never home.
Husband: She is too homely, not exciting.

Attraction

Wife: He seemed very smart, very capable.
Husband: She respected me. I felt accepted and appreciated.

Stress

Wife: He makes me feel stupid and incompetent.
Husband: She feels bad about herself and blames me.

Attraction

Wife: He was like a rock, strong, someone you can lean on.
Husband: She was warm and sensitive, very gentle.

Stress

Wife: He is like a block; you can't change his mind about anything.
Husband: She is too sensitive, too gentle.

Attraction

Wife: He seemed fatherly and wise, someone who would take care of me.

Husband: She was like a little girl who needs protection, vulnerable, sensitive.

Stress

Wife: His fatherly attitude and calm can drive me nuts; I try to shake him.

Husband: Her childish tantrums are very hard to take.

Attraction

Wife: He seemed very wise, mature, and knowledgeable about life.

Husband: She seemed full of life, loved nature, was open to the world.

Stress

Wife: He tries to teach me all the time and wants to tie me to the house.

Husband: She doesn't take care of the house, is not a housewife.

Attraction

Wife: He seemed very easygoing.

Husband: I liked her energy. She was very active, things were always happening around her.

Stress

Wife: He doesn't stand up for his own rights, is not assertive.

Husband: She explodes at the slightest provocation, has tantrums, is pushy about things she wants.

Attraction

Wife: He put me on a pedestal and tried to impress me. It made me feel special.

Husband: I was impressed by her. She seemed very able and very sure of herself.

Stress

Wife: He behaves like an irresponsible child and forces me to be the bad mother.

Husband: I feel put down by her. She doesn't respect my wishes, is withholding.

Attraction

Wife: He adored me. I was the center of his world.

Husband: She was beautiful and smart; all my friends envied me.

Stress

Wife: He is jealous and possessive. His insecurity drives me nuts.

Husband: She criticizes me and puts me down. It hurts my feelings.

responses to this criticism. First, when people identify the connection between the qualities that attracted them and the qualities that have become stresses in their relationships (with or without my help), they are quick to agree with it and do so with excitement and delight. Second, as we see next, seeing the connection has a positive effect on couples.

VARIATIONS ON THE THEME

Some people fall in love, marry the person with whom they fell in love, and remain happily married ever after. Some people repeat over and over the same pattern of frustrating love relationships. They leave one partner because he or she is too suffocating or too withdrawn and withholding only to fall in love with another, similar to the first. Other people, aware of their childhood deprivations and frustrations and determined to avoid them at all costs, choose a partner who is the exact opposite of the parent with whom they had an unresolved issue. However, choosing the opposite still means engagement with the issue, but in its opposite version. As we can see in the following examples of Gary and Joan, even in such cases things that were at first attractive later turn into frustrations.

Gary was born to a large, close-knit Italian family on the East Coast. He felt suffocated by the family's constant pressures and intrusions into every aspect of his life and hated the endless crowded, noisy family events. He moved to the West Coast to escape the family, especially his *"suffocating"* mother. He started dating women who were the exact opposite of his mother. His mother was short, fat, dark, and loud as well as warm and nurturing; the women he fell in love with were all tall, skinny blonds with long straight hair and reserved demeanors. They also did not like cooking, the exact opposite of his mother, whose kitchen was her kingdom. Again and again, Gary would fall in love with one of these *"cool blonds,"* but after a while his enthusiasm would stall. The reason, in every case, was that the tall, skinny blond was not warm enough, was not loving and nurturing enough.

Joan met her husband after the painful termination of a stormy love affair in which she felt like she was *"swinging wildly tied to a dragon's tail."* Her husband was *"a wonderful person,"* the exact opposite of her father. He promised her a life of calm security, and he kept his promise. He was a doting husband and a loving father to their three children. Joan, whose primitive, violent father used to beat her and her brother, appreciated her husband and his warm family, who accepted her with open arms; she loved the home that she and her husband created for their children. Her husband believed in her, and his faith helped build her self-confidence. Her new self-confidence helped her succeed in the world of business, and her business success helped enhance her self-confidence even further. But, with the increase in her self-confidence came a decrease in her need for her husband's support and love. The calm security he provided, so appealing and so significant to her at the beginning of their relationship, turned to boredom. The lack of drama and excitement that she craved after the excessive drama of her abusive childhood had helped build her self-confidence, but now became an intolerable deprivation.

When people are able to resolve a childhood issue through a romantic relationship, therapy, or a significant life change, they are ready for a truly different relationship. These are often cases in which the unresolved childhood issue was not traumatic and did not involve abuse, neglect, or rejection. George is an example.

George was the middle child in a large and poor family. He had six brothers and sisters. His father, who was a hard-working farmer, was a gentle and kind man. His mother was a powerful, dominant woman who constantly criticized the father for his incompetence as a breadwinner. Although the atmosphere in the home was warm and loving, the economic hardship was oppressive. George remembers with great pain the times he was unable to attend friends' birthday parties because his parents could not afford to buy a birthday gift. When he grew up, George fell in love with a woman who came from a wealthy middle-class family. He admired her "*class*" and superior manners and felt grateful when she agreed to be his wife. His wife's supercilious attitude toward him and his family, which she expressed in such "*gentle*" ways as constantly correcting his language, helped reenact George's parents' marriage.

The significant life change that prepared George for a different type of relationship was his huge economic success as a businessman. The respect and prominence that he achieved as a result of this success built George's self-confidence. Although his wife continued her efforts to keep the status difference between them, George felt that her superior attitude toward him was no longer appropriate. Indeed, his next romantic relationship started as a friendship based on deep professional respect. It was with a successful careerwoman with whom he had a business relationship. The woman adored George and saw him as a brilliant businessman and an exciting man. Her perception, and the relationship with her, felt much more "right" for the new George, the George who had freed himself from the feelings of inferiority and vulnerability that were a legacy from his impoverished childhood.

The assumption that unconscious romantic choices are inherently wise is most easily challenged in the cases of people, most often women, who suffered serious abuse in their childhood and who are attracted to partners whose behavior resembles that of their abusive parents. Such a romantic choice seems, for obvious reasons, extremely unwise. It is possible to argue, however, that even in these difficult, and at times even tragic, cases, the attraction is based on an unconscious drive to overcome the early trauma and in that sense is wise. Often, in such cases unless the abusive partner is willing to work on the issues at the root of his abusive behavior, the only way to avoid abusive relationships for a woman who was abused as a child is to avoid men to whom she is strongly attracted.[8]

At times, people who are aware of the destructive and frustrating patterns they have internalized, especially if they have had painful intimate relationships that repeated these patterns, decide to ignore them and choose a person who is a soul mate and a kindred spirit. Such a person tends to be a close friend and has similar attitudes and interests, someone who is kind and considerate and can be trusted. Unfortunately, such a person is often also not exciting sexually. Such friendship relationships tend to be warm, pleasant, comfortable and easy, but lack "insane" boundless passion.

Every choice has advantages and disadvantages. A romantic choice directed by unconscious forces, in an attempt to overcome a childhood trauma, is characterized by powerful, electrifying, physical attraction, intense emotional excitement, and obsessive love—the more serious the early trauma, the more obsessive and passionate the love. A conscious romantic choice, in an attempt to ignore the past and build a relationship with a close, kind, and understanding friend, ensures an easy, comfortable, pleasant relationship that is less exciting, with fewer exhilarating highs and fewer devastating lows.

RELATIONSHIP PROBLEMS AS OPPORTUNITIES FOR GROWTH

The existence of a relationship between the original attraction and the cause of couple distress has an important and practical implication. It suggests that an intimate relationship provides one of the best opportunities to work on unresolved family-of-origin issues. When a couple realizes how the things that made them fall in love with each other later become the core issue in their relationship, feelings of guilt and blame are reduced. Breaking the "blame frame" makes people much more willing to take responsibility for their parts in their relationship problems. This is important because issues related to the family of origin are almost always at the heart of couples' issues.[9]

A couple's problems are often repeated attempts to correct, overcome, cope, re-enact, or erase old conflicts that originated in infantile relationships and were transferred to the adult relationship. Couples try to resolve internal conflicts through conflicts with each other. They cope with old anxieties and frustrations that originated in frustrating or threatening experiences in their childhood by shaping their intimate relationships to fit patterns similar to the ones they experienced in their families of origin. They typically do it in one of three ways: They fall in love with a person who resembles in a significant way the parent with whom they have an unresolved issue. They unconsciously push their partner to act the way that parent acted. Or, they project their internal romantic image on their partner and perceive the partner as similar to the parent even when no real similarity exists.[10]

The feelings generated in such intimate relationships, and in intimate relationships in general, have the type of powerful intensity that is not usually found in other human relationships, such as friendship, work, or neighborhood. A romantic partner who is capable of generating intense positive emotions at the beginning of the relationship is capable later in the relationship of generating equally intense negative emotions. A couple's conflicts, even when they are supposedly centered on trivial issues, are perceived as having existential significance. Indeed, a couple's conflict is in the deepest sense an existential struggle. Couple therapists describe it jokingly when they say that marriage is the battleground to which two families of origin send their representatives to fight a war that will determine which family will direct the couple's lives.

In the course of couple therapy, couples learn to identify the errors they make in their perceptions of each other. A woman, after checking repeatedly with her husband, realizes that when she thinks he is angry, he is actually hurt. They learn to recognize feelings they did not admit to in themselves but instead projected on each other. In the case of this woman, she recognized her own anger that she had denied. This recognition helps develop a more complete, integrated, and secure sense of self in both partners and a perception of the other as different, independent, and nonthreatening.

Working on couple conflicts enables the resolution of individual issues. This does not necessarily mean that couples get over their infantile feelings and needs. In a mature and healthy intimate relationship, they do not have to. In such relationships, partners can tolerate each other's infantile needs and are willing to make an effort to satisfy them.

Couples who learn to accept each other also learn to accept themselves, including those denied and suppressed parts of themselves that they had worked so hard to ignore. Total acceptance of the other, especially of infantile and needy parts, requires empathy. Empathy implies feeling what the other feels. This can be scary for undifferentiated individuals who do not have firm ego boundaries. Such a person does not have a secure sense of self, so feeling what the partner feels means denying or giving up one's own feelings. Here, again, the ability to listen to an intimate partner and express empathy not only testifies to the existence of a separated and individuated self but also helps develop it.

HOW TO TURN COUPLE PROBLEMS INTO OPPORTUNITIES FOR GROWTH

The first step in turning couple problems into opportunities for growth is developing awareness. It starts with an exploration of the things that made you fall in love with each other, the things that are most problematic for you in each other, and the connection between the two. Both families of origin need to be examined, with an emphasis on the relationship each of you had with each parent, the relationship between the parents, the connections among these three relationships for each of you, and your core issue as a couple. At the end of this step, both of you should understand why you chose to be in the relationship and be willing to take responsibility for your part in your couple problems. Taking responsibility for your romantic choice helps to control its outcome. This taking of responsibility, or *self-focus*, requires changing the direction of the flashlight of awareness to point away from the partner and toward oneself; thus, it forgoes the far easier solution of blaming the partner for problems and disappointments in the relationship.

The second step, and the harder step for many, is expressing empathy. Couples can be taught to listen to each other and to express empathy, although the lower the level of differentiation of a couple, the harder this is. *Mirroring*—one of the most basic and most important techniques in behavioral marital therapy—is a good way to start. Here is how it is done. With clear instruction to talk about oneself without judging, criticizing, or attacking the other, each partner is asked, in turn, to talk about an important problem or issue. The other partner is instructed to listen, ask clarification questions, but make no other response and then "mirror" or reflect back in his or her own words what was heard and understood. If it seems to the speaking partner that the listening partner "didn't get it," the speaker can explain again and again until the listener understands.

Harville Hendrix added to this classic exercise the crucial component of empathy. In his version of the exercise, after it is clear that the listener understood fully what the speaker tried to say, all other aspects of the problem are raised and discussed by using such questions as, "Is that all?" or "Is there anything else?" Then, the listener is encouraged to express empathy by explaining how the personality, history, and experiences of the speaker make the speaker's feelings perfectly understandable. The expression of empathy is wonderful for the person receiving it and is a powerful impetus for personal growth in the person expressing it.[11]

The third step is change in behavior. After couples understand the dynamic of their relationship and are able to express empathy for each other's feelings and needs, it is easier for them to give each other the gift of the thing each most desires.[12] Given the special dynamic of couple relationships, the effort to grant the partner's wish is the most effective way to bring about personal growth. After all, the partner is asking for the expression of parts in the self that have been repressed or projected onto the partner. So, when a woman behaves in a more rational manner as a gift to her husband and when a man expresses his deep emotions as a gift to his wife, both the husband and the wife as well as their marriage grow.

SUMMARY AND CONCLUSIONS

From everything said so far in this chapter and throughout the book, it is possible to draw a number of conclusions:

- An intimate relationship provides one of the best opportunities for mastering unresolved childhood issues.
- Unconscious forces more than logical considerations dictate with whom we fall in love.
- The unconscious choice is of a person with whom we can reenact childhood experiences; thus, the person combines the most significant traits of both parents.
- Negative traits of both parents have more of an impact on romantic choices, especially in obsessive loves, than do positive traits because the injury or deprivation caused by them needs healing.
- The more traumatic the childhood injury, and the greater the similarity between the lover and the injuring parent, the more intense the experience of falling in love is.
- In falling in love, there is a return to the primal symbiosis with the mother, a perfect union with no ego boundaries. This is why we only fall in love with one person at a time. The return to the lost paradise recreates the expectation that the lover will fill all our infantile needs.

- Because falling in love is dictated by an internal romantic image, lovers feel as if they have known each other forever. And because it involves a re-enactment of specific and powerful childhood experiences, lovers feel that the beloved is "the one and only," and that the loss of the beloved will be unbearable.
- When a couple falls in love, their unconscious choice is mutual and complementary, enabling both partners to express their own core issues. Together, they create their core issue as a couple, the issue around which most of their later conflicts center.
- Understanding the connection between unresolved childhood issues and later problems reduces feelings of guilt and blame and helps both partners take responsibility for their parts in the relationship problems.
- Couples who listen to each other's feelings, express empathy, and give each other the things they ask for, can keep the romantic spark alive indefinitely.
- Expressing empathy and granting the partner's wishes is the best way to grow. As partners grow, their relationship grows. And growth is the antithesis of burnout.[13]

FINALLY, AGAIN ON THE MANY PERSPECTIVES ON LOVE

As there are as many
minds as there are heads,
so there are as many kinds
of love as there are hearts.
—Leo Tolstoy, *Anna Karenina*

As I noted in the introductory chapter, this book addresses only one of the many forms of love—romantic love. It addresses only the romantic love between two people who actually have a relationship and excludes those cases in which love is one-sided or unrequited. It only addresses one stage of romantic love—falling in love. Only this last chapter refers to problems that couples have later in the relationships, but even this discussion ties the problems to the falling-in-love stage. From the many perspectives on falling in love, this book focuses on the psychological perspective, with only brief mentions of the biological, historical, social, and cultural perspectives. It argues that every experience of falling in love has a unique emotional and psychological dynamic based on an interaction between the conscious and unconscious, repressed and projected, parts of both partners. In a combination unique to each partner, those parts are influenced by two parents and the relationship between them. Because falling in love is a unique experience, a definition of falling in love is never offered. Readers are invited to contemplate their own personal and unique definition.

The emphasis on the unconscious influences on falling in love may leave the impression that the past, especially early childhood, has complete influence on our romantic choices. This is definitely not the case. As we saw in the first part of the book, environmental, situational, dispositional, social, cultural, physiological, and even genetic factors also play a role in falling in love, even more so in mate selection. In addition, logical considerations, social and familial pressures, plans for the future, spiritual quests, and romantic ideals affect romantic choices.

Studies show that people's expectations of love relationships and their romantic ideals affect their experiences in romantic relationships.[14] People who believe in romantic destiny, that potential romantic partners are either meant for each other or they are not, have a stronger connection between their initial satisfaction with a romantic relationship and that relationship's longevity than people who do not. They also tend to use avoidance strategies in dealing with relationship problems and take more responsibility for ending the relationship by describing it as wrong from the beginning. On the other hand, people who believe that successful relationships are cultivated and developed have more long-term approaches to dating, use more relationship-maintaining coping strategies, and even if a relationship has ended, disagree that it was wrong from the start.[15]

So, romantic ideals and expectations about romantic relationships have an impact. But do they tell us the specific person with whom we are going to fall in love or why? The answer is no. The best answer to this most fascinating of questions about romantic love, in my opinion, is offered by the psychodynamic theories that describe, each using its own terminology, the internal romantic image. These theories suggest that people fall in love with a person who reminds them in some significant way of their parents, especially a parent with whom they have an unresolved issue. The more intense the unresolved issue, the more intense the experience of falling in love, with incredible highs when the infantile needs are satisfied and incredible lows when the infantile needs are frustrated the way they were in childhood.

Because parents are complex people whose traits are both positive and negative and with whom our relationships are multilayered and complex because our childhood includes a huge number of people and experiences, some positive and some negative, and because our romantic images continue evolving throughout life, our romantic images are complex and applicable to more than one person. This is why we create with every romantic partner a unique pattern of interaction. A person may fall in love with one lover who satisfies a core issue such as a need for security but, once that need is satisfied, fall in love with another lover who satisfies the opposite need for drama and excitement. At times, people do not see the beloved at all, but fall in love with the projection of their romantic image.

Despite the unique emotional pattern of every romantic relationship, all romantic relationships share one dynamic: a constant battle between forces pulling for symbiosis and forces pulling for individuation. The forces pulling for symbiosis are fueled by the longing to get back to the safety of the primal symbiosis with the mother. The forces pulling for individuation are fueled by the desire to do something unique and significant that will give meaning to life (for most people, these forces are expressed in the sphere of work, the subject of the next chapter). When people fall in love, the forces pulling for merging and symbiosis win. In most relationships, after a period of time that can be days, months, or years, the forces pulling for individuation become stronger. When a relationship remains stuck in the symbiotic stage, the result is a suffocating relationship in which people have little sense of their individual selves as separate from the other.[16]

Intimate relationships that keep the romantic spark alive are characterized by a balance between the need for intimacy and security and the need for individuation and self-actualization. In these relationships, both partners feel secure enough in their individuality and ego boundaries that intimacy and closeness are not perceived as threatening and dangerous. Experiences of fusion when they happen, for example, during orgasm, are experienced as pleasurable rather than scary. This type of relationship can be described by the metaphor of "roots and wings."[4]

In roots-and-wings relationships, the *roots* symbolize intimacy, togetherness, security, and commitment. The *wings* symbolize individuation, self-actualization, and self-expression. The togetherness supports self-actualization, and self-actualization strengthens the togetherness. What is more important, in the context of a book about falling in love, is that in roots-and-wings relationships, couples keep, indefinitely, the romantic spark of the falling-in-love stage.

Falling in love and having a romantic involvement have a positive effect on people's psychological well-being. People in romantic relationships feel closer to their ideal selves and feel better about themselves.[17] In other words, falling in love not only is a positive experience in and of itself, but also is an important experience within the context of people's emotional life and the life of their romantic relationship.

In *Ethics of the Fathers*, it is said that "All is foreseen, yet freedom of choice is granted; and by grace is the universe judged, yet all is according to the amount of work" (Mishna 15). This Mishna (Oral Law) is usually interpreted as meaning that everything is predetermined by God, yet a person still has free will. As a psychologist, I choose to interpret it differently: Although our genetic makeup and childhood experiences are engraved in us, influencing the way we look, our personalities, and our basic attitudes toward ourselves, toward others, and toward love, we can still choose whether, or how, to follow these scripts in our love choices. A positive outlook on ourselves and of others connects us to the grace by which the universe is judged; but ultimately, everything in our life, including our love relationship, is according to the amount of work we invest in it.

Chapter 13

LOVE AND WORK: THE RELATIONSHIP BETWEEN THEIR UNCONSCIOUS CHOICES

One can live magnificently in this world if one knows how to work and how to love
— Leo Tolstoy, a letter to Valerya Aresenyev, November 9, 1856

*L*YNN GREW UP IN A LITTLE FARMING TOWN AND WAS ONE OF FOUR children. Her father was a teacher of religion in a community college, and her mother was a nurse. Lynn was always close to her mother and felt loved and cherished by her, but she felt "unseen" by her father, a closed man with depressive tendencies who often withdrew from his family into his own world. Lynn worked hard to impress her father, getting high grades at school, and developed great sensitivity to his moods, but all to no avail. As an adult, this childhood dynamic influenced not only Lynn's romantic choices, but also her career choice. As an attractive, vivacious, accomplished young woman, she had many men pursuing her, but the ones she found herself repeatedly falling in love with, and in three cases even marrying, were men who had depressive tendencies just like her father. Men who, while adoring her and her vivaciousness, were so involved with themselves and their depression that they did not really see her. Lynn would fall in love with them because they seemed so "deep" and so adoring of her. She would later burn out in her relationships with them because they were draining her energy with their depressions and because they "didn't see her" for who she really was as a person. Lynn's career choice was to become a therapist. She thought she could help people in need with her energy and sensitivity and would be "really seen" by her patients. Here, too, "for some reason," she found herself working primarily with depressed men. She really understood these men, and they felt it and always found their way to her office. The problem that caused her burnout as a therapist was that, just like her father, they "didn't really see her."

It seems that both Lynn's romantic choices and her career choice were motivated by an unconscious desire to heal her childhood wound. The burnout, in both her career and marriages, was related to Lynn's painful realization that she was repeating in both cases her childhood trauma rather than healing it.

People's choices of both a career and an intimate partner provide a wealth of information about who they are. If I want to know something significant about you, finding what you are doing professionally and whom you married would probably provide me with the richest and most significant information. At a deeper level, both choices represent an outside reflection of the inner workings of our psyche. In addition, because work and love are the two most important spheres of our life, their choices have a major impact on the quality of our lives.

Freud believed that the ability to love and to work is evidence of psychological maturity. The importance of both work and love for healthy functioning has been well documented empirically.[1] Yet, studies of love generally ignore its relationship to work, and studies of work most often ignore its relationship to love,[2] adhering to what has been termed the "myth of separate worlds."[3]

This chapter extends the notion of unconscious choices from the sphere of love to the sphere of work and addresses the fascinating question of the relationship between them in the context of the relationship between career and couple burnout.

BURNOUT

Burnout, experienced as a state of physical, emotional, and mental exhaustion,[4] is the end result of a process of attrition in which highly motivated and committed individuals lose their spirit.[5] You cannot burn out unless you were first "on fire." The person who reaches the burnout stage says in one way or another, "I've had it. I can't take it anymore." Burnout has become a frequent topic of research since the mid-1970s, with close to 2,000 studies published in the last decade alone. Studies have documented the existence of burnout in a wide range of occupations; its varied physical, emotional, cognitive, and behavioral symptoms; and its high cost for individuals and society at large.[6] The majority of these studies have focused on career burnout in the human services. Few studies have addressed burnout in marriage.[7] Different conceptual formulations have been offered in attempt to explain burnout,[8] most recently a psychoanalytic existential perspective.[9]

According to the existential perspective, the root cause of burnout lies in people's need to believe that their lives are meaningful, that the things they do are useful and important. Victor Frankl believed that "the striving to find meaning in one's life is the primary motivational force in man."[10] Ernest Becker added that people's need to believe that the things they do are meaningful is their way of coping with the angst caused by facing their own mortality. To be able to deny death, we need to feel heroic, to know that our lives are meaningful, that we matter in the larger "cosmic" scheme of things. People choose to become "heroes" according to their culture-prescribed "hero system." One of the most frequently chosen answers to the existential quest is work. The other is love.[11]

According to existential psychologists,[12] if self-actualization in the sphere of work helps us fend against our fear of death, then an intimate relationship, the merging with another person, helps us fend against our fear of life. Romantic love enables us to bond with someone we adore and see as larger than ourselves.[11] People who expect to derive a sense of existential significance from their work (or their love relationships) enter their professions (or their love relationships) with high hopes, committed and motivated. When they feel that they have failed, that their work (or intimate relationship) is insignificant, that they make no difference, they start feeling helpless and hopeless and eventually burn out.

CAREER CHOICE

If we accept the premise that people try to derive a sense of existential significance from either their work or their intimate relationships, the next question we need to address is why they choose to do it via the particular occupation or person that they have chosen. Why does one person choose to achieve existential significance by being a nurse, another by being a teacher, and a third by being a manager? (Why we choose a particular person, of course, has been the subject of this entire book.) Many attempts were made to answer this question. Most of these attempts included such factors as aptitudes, abilities, interests, resources, limitations, requirements of success, as well as opportunities in different lines of work. Psychoanalytic theory makes a significant contribution to this body of research and practice by adding the dimension of unconscious career choices.[13]

The unconscious determinants of any vocational choice reflect the individual's personal and familial history. People choose an occupation that enables them to replicate significant childhood experiences, gratify needs that were ungratified in their childhood, and actualize occupational dreams and professional expectations passed on to them by their familial heritage.[14] When the choice of a career involves such significant issues, people enter it with high hopes and expectations, with ego involvement and passion. The greatest passion typically involves some unresolved childhood issue or "metaphorical wound," fueled by the hope of resolving and healing it. Success helps heal childhood wounds. When people feel that they have failed, when the work repeats the childhood trauma rather than heals it, the result is burnout. Here for example is how this dynamic operates in the case of nurses.

When nurses are asked why they chose a career in nursing, their answer invariably includes a reference to helping the sick and the dying.[15] The idealized image of nursing implied by these answers—a Florence Nightingale who holds in her arms a sick or dying patient—implies tremendous control. After all, what other human relationship involves as much control as that exercised by a nurse over her incapacitated patient? In support of this notion, research also shows that the need for control, consciously or unconsciously, plays a major role in the decision to become a nurse.[16] And my work with nurses often revealed a traumatic experience related to lack of control.[15] In one case, a nurse's realization of how little control she had over her fate was caused by a traumatic experience at age 12 of being hit by a cab while walking on a sidewalk, an accident that resulted in her being hospitalized for many months. In a second case, it was the trauma of moving away from her childhood home in the country, where she felt like "a flower in a greenhouse" surrounded by open fields and many close friends, to the city, where there were walls instead of trees and she was "all alone." She cried for days and begged her parents not to move, and the inability to change their minds made her feel "helpless and powerless." In a third case, it was the powerlessness against a domineering father who forced her to go to a religious school she hated. "I cried and cried but nothing helped. I was powerless. It was awful," she recalled. Similar relationships between a certain type of traumatic childhood experience and adult career choices was found in teachers,[17] managers,[18] and entrepreneurs.[19]

Different psychodynamic reasons seem to propel people to choose a career in nursing, management, and teaching. The finding that nurses often reveal a traumatic experience related to lack of control may explain, at least in small part, the professional choice of a career that is characterized by immense control over patients who are anesthetized, paralyzed, or otherwise incapacitated. Teachers often reveal a traumatic experience related to being the center of negative attention and feeling humiliated, anxious, and isolated. This may account, at least in small part, for the choice of a career in which one expects to stand in front of a class of adoring students who can be educated, inspired, shaped, and molded. Managers often reveal a traumatic experience related to the absence of a father, real or psychological absence. The desire to be a manager expresses an unconscious desire for power and influence (become a father) and for the recognition of the organization (a metaphoric father). As a result, the causes of burnout also tend to be occupation specific. For nurses, the most frequent cause of burnout involves witnessing human suffering without being able to help. For teachers, it is discipline problems and unmotivated, inattentive, indifferent, impertinent, and disparaging students. For managers, it is not having power and resources to have a real impact and to do things "right."[20]

Unconscious Career and Love Choices

It seems that not only a love relationship, but also a career provides an opportunity for mastering unresolved childhood issues. Both unconscious love and career choices reflect the individual's personal and familial history. We choose a career and a romantic partner that enable us to replicate significant childhood experiences and gratify ungratified childhood needs. Unconscious forces and internal images influence not only with whom we fall in love,[21] but also which career we choose.[14] Just like the unconscious choice of a romantic partner, the unconscious choice of a career directs us to find an opportunity to reenact, and hopefully master, childhood experiences. Negative experiences have more of an impact on both love and career choices because the injury or deprivation caused by them need healing. As in the case of obsessive love, the more traumatic the childhood injury, the more intense and obsessive the involvement with the career will be.

If both romantic choices and career choices are influenced by unconscious forces and are motivated by a desire for mastering unresolved childhood issues, then it would make sense that there will be a relationship between them. The relationship between work and love was indeed noted in studies documenting the spillover of work stress to the family[22] and in studies documenting the spillover of career burnout to marriage.[23] A curious phenomenon, noted in counseling people who ask for help because of either career or couple burnout, is their tendency to confuse between them. A person may come complaining about career burnout, only to realize after a brief exploration that the real problem is the marriage or, alternatively, to come for counseling because of a supposed problem of marriage burnout only to discover that the real problem is the work. It seems that satisfaction in one sphere of life is associated with satisfaction in the other, and stress in one sphere is associated with stress in the other.[2]

A cross-cultural study that I headed also documented a relationship between career and couple burnout.[24] The study involved social science graduate students to ensure similar samples with similar education and socioeconomic status who were old enough to have both a family and a career. These individuals were from the United States, Great Britain, Israel, Finland, Portugal, and Spain. The findings showed similar significant, yet moderate, correlations between career and couple burnout in all six samples (see Table 5 in Appendix 3).

The finding that, in six samples from six different countries, a similar correlation was found between career and couple burnout seems to suggest that the correlation has more to do with an inherent relationship between these two life experiences than with cultural influences. It is possible, of course, that the correlations between career and couple burnout are not the result of a true relationship between the two but an artifact, the result of using a similar measure for studying both. Clinical evidence of a relationship between people's love and career choices (such as Lynn's case in the beginning of this chapter) suggests that this is probably not the case.

The alternative to the artifact explanation is that the correlation between career and couple burnout is caused by people's attempt to derive a sense of existential significance through both love and work, and their sense that they have failed in this request in both spheres. The results of a study that showed a modest correlation between work commitment and family commitment[25] seem to support this interpretation. They suggest that people bring a similar drive and sense of commitment to their work and their family life.

Based on the psychoanalytic-existential perspective, the reason for this correlation is the similarity in the underlying causes of both career and couple burnout. If people's choices of both their career and love relationships are motivated by the need to replicate and thus heal the same childhood trauma, it can be expected that there will be a relationship between the two. Ample clinical evidence supports this notion. Lynn's story is one example; here are two more.

A nurse, who was sexually abused by her father and felt totally helpless as a child, tried unconsciously to heal this childhood wound by choosing an occupation characterized by the professional's control and the patient's helplessness and by marrying a drug-dependent partner. Her career and marriage burnout were caused by a feeling of helplessness and a sense that she was repeating her childhood trauma rather than healing it by her inability to heal her patients and her husband.

An accountant whose father was "very temperamental" with frequent angry out-bursts and a mother who was very "flat emotionally" felt criticized by his mother for being "just like father." The choice to become an accountant and the choice of a romantic partner with whom his relationship was a dispassionate "brother/sister" re-lationship were both motivated by a desire not to be "like father." His career and mar-riage burnout were both related to the painful realization that work and love without passion were not worth living for.

It is possible to expand the focus on the individual in the current chapter to a focus on the couple by addressing the relationship between couples' career and love choices. Do, for example, people choose romantic partners who enable them to actualize (or not actualize) occupational dreams? Do they choose partners who actualize their occupational dreams for them? (If I can't be a doctor, at least I can be a doctor's wife.)

The most important implication of the relationship between career and couple burnout is the importance of addressing this relationship, whether one's problem is one or the other. Addressing this relationship helps shift the focus to the underlying cause, which in most cases is related to an unresolved childhood issue responsible for the original choice of both.

PRACTICAL IMPLICATION

The relationship between career and couple burnout and, on the one hand, peo-ple's failure to derive existential significance from both their work and marriage and, on the other hand, similar unresolved childhood experiences, can be trans-lated to a treatment approach with the following three general steps:

- Identifying the conscious and unconscious reasons for one's love and work choices and how the chosen career and intimate relationship were expected to provide a sense of existential significance.
- Identifying the reasons for one's failure to derive a sense of existential sig-nificance from the work or the intimate relationship and how this sense of failure is related to burnout in that sphere of life.
- Identifying the concrete changes that will enable one to derive a sense of existential significance from both the work and the intimate relationship.

ROMANTIC CHOICES WORKSHOPS: HOW TO DECIPHER YOUR ROMANTIC ATTRACTION CODE

*I*N A ROMANTIC CHOICES WORKSHOP, THE MATERIAL PRESENTED throughout the book is brought together and applied. This material is most effective when presented in the context of experiential learning. Workshop participants not only learn about internal romantic images and the role they play in our romantic choices, but also are given an opportunity to become more aware of the role they play in their failed romantic relationships, to understand the origin of their relationship problems, and to learn new and positive ways to overcome these problems in a highly personal and individualized manner. The presence of other people has a great advantage in helping participants break their fallacy of uniqueness: the discovery that their problems are not unique but are shared by other perfectly normal, well-adjusted people.

Another of the great benefits of a workshop is that it enables people to take time out from their busy schedules and usual activities to concentrate on the relationship problems they are experiencing in a supportive environment, and do so with other people who have similar problems, or have had similar problems in the past. The emphasis on problems in romantic relationships as opportunities for growth, the individualized guidance, and the social support, are the hallmarks of a romantic choices workshop.

There is nothing magical about the actual activities in a romantic choices workshop. These workshops are effective because they represent a focused and concrete attempt to deal with people's problems in intimate relationships in a growth-enhancing way. The activities presented can be used in a workshop context or in the context of either individual or couple therapy. The Romantic Choices box is an example of the way such a workshop was advertised.

A workshop can range in size from a minimum of 8 to a maximum of over 100 participants, but the ideal number is between 12 and 20. It can be homogeneous, with people of a similar age, background, or issues attending, or it can be heterogeneous, with people of different ages, backgrounds, and presenting problems. The length of a workshop can vary from half a day to a week. It can be structured as an intensive weekend or week-long residential program, as several consecutive 2- or 3-hour meetings, or as a semester-long experiential course.

ROMANTIC CHOICES: HOW WE CHOOSE WHOM TO FALL IN LOVE WITH

When we fall in love, we are sure that our beloved is not only perfect, but also perfect for us. In time, we often realize that neither is true. Disappointed and disillusioned, we wonder how we choose whom to fall in love with, and why are we so often wrong?

In this workshop, participants will explore theories and research findings that apply to their own romantic choices, right or wrong. More important, the workshop will help them examine what to do about these choices, both to enhance current romantic relationships and to avoid making the same mistakes in the future. Through group discussions and experiential exercises, the workshop is designed to increase understanding of the causes, conscious and unconscious, of our romantic choices. In addition, it will present tools to improve the quality of intimate relationships. This workshop is for anyone who seeks better understanding of his or her romantic choices, especially those who seem unable to make the "right choice," and for counselors who work with individuals who have a problem in their romantic choices.

A WORKSHOP DESCRIPTION

When the participants in the workshop first get together, whether it is the first hour of a 1-day workshop or the first session of a 5-day workshop, it is important to take as long as necessary to have all participants introduce themselves to the group. In turn, they tell (briefly if time requires and at length if time allows) about their relationship status (how many, if any, significant relationships have they had, what particular problem brought them to the workshop) and what their expectations are for the workshop.

Another version of the self-introductions is to have participants describe what their most significant, most recent, or typical romantic partners would have said about them or about being in a relationship with them. This method has the advantage of having participants focus on their partners' perceptions of them and of the problem in having a relationship with them instead of focusing on their own perspective.

The self-introductions can be put forth as serving two purposes: First, they give an idea of the particular needs of the group so the group leader can direct the workshop as much as possible to fulfill those needs. Second, they give participants an idea of the human resources available to them in the workshop in addition to the group leader. The interaction among group members is an important part of the workshop, and the deepest work is most often done in foursomes. Listening carefully to everyone's introductions enables participants to choose at least one, and preferably all three, of the people most appropriate for them to work with in the foursomes. In addition, the group leader's responses to the introductions provide an opportunity, without explicitly saying so, to establish the group norms: For example, honesty and openness are respected and welcome, but criticisms, judgments, and attacks are not.

Soon after the first few participants tell their romantic relationships' story, it usually becomes abundantly clear that the workshop is a place in which fallacies of uniqueness will be challenged. The statement, "I have a story/problem similar to the one described by ..." is repeated in different versions over and over. Often, it is voiced by people who tend to find themselves in similar types of relationships. Other times, it is echoed by people who are at a different stage of life or in a different relationship who have experienced that same problem in the past. In all cases, it becomes obvious to the participants that they are not alone, that there are other people struggling with similar problems.

After all participants have introduced themselves and told their romantic relationships stories, if it is a weekend or a week-long workshop it is possible to engage them in a nonverbal activity that will remind them of how nurturing a couple's relationship can be. If the participants are evenly divided between (heterosexual) men and women and the room is covered with thick carpets, participants can pair up and give each other a foot massage, a head massage, or a head lift (it is best to avoid activities that may have a sexual connotation). When the room has only chairs, participants can give each other a head-and-shoulder massage, with the receiver sitting on a chair and the provider facing the chair's back.

If it seems that the group will be uncomfortable with any type of physical contact, another nonverbal activity may be appropriate. One example is to give participants colored crayons and large drawing paper (which it is always a good idea to have) and ask them to draw a symbol of their love life. These drawings can then be posted on the walls for the remainder of the workshop. The drawings can be, but do not have to be, analyzed. However, participants should have an opportunity to explain the personal meaning of their symbols. Other group members can give feedback as long as it is personal and is not pathologizing or judgmental.

The second day (in a half-day workshop, this is the first part) starts with a brief presentation of the variables that increase the likelihood of falling in love (chapters 1 through 5) and the internal romantic image (chapters 8 through 10). Clearly, the theoretical material covered in a workshop corresponds to the material covered in this book. The difference between reading the book and receiving the information in a workshop is that, in a workshop, participants are not simply exposed to the material, but rather have an opportunity to experience its relevance to their own lives. The remainder of this appendix describes some ways in which this experiential learning occurs. The exercise I describe next has a number of parts. Some take place in the large groups, most take place in foursomes, and some are done alone. In a half-day workshop, it is only possible to do the first three parts.

To avoid the anxiety and awkwardness associated with choosing and being chosen, participants are reminded of the introductory session in which they identified people who seemed to share their particular issue in intimate relationships (either in the same way or in its opposite). They are asked to choose one of these people to be a member of their support group. Next, each pair is instructed to choose another pair who shares their issue and to form a foursome. Foursomes should not include close friends or people who know each other well, and they should include at least one member of each sex. The reason for this last suggestion is that (as noted in chapter 7) often people's love issues are gender related. It is extremely valuable for a man to hear a woman talk about a problem she has with men that his intimate partner complains about him.

Once the foursomes have formed (they can be two foursomes in an workshop of 8 participants or 25 foursomes in a 100-participant workshop), they are told that they are going to start a multistage exercise. They have 10 minutes each (5 if time is a problem) for the first stage of the exercise and should consider designating one of the group members as the timekeeper. The first stage focuses on falling in love, so references to later stages of the relationship and its demise should be avoided.

In this first stage, participants are asked to describe, in turn, how they met their (most significant or most recent) romantic partners, what were their lives like when they met (in terms of work, relationship history, and so on), and most important, what was it that most attracted them. Participants should be encouraged to avoid such generalities as "good looks" and try to be more specific in describing what it was about the good looks that they found most attractive. Was he rough and masculine or gentle and intelligent looking? Was she poised and ladylike or sexy and sensual? I should add that this part of the exercise is my favorite. I always join one of the foursomes and listen with great delight to their moving and at times magical stories about falling in love.

It is often difficult to stop the foursomes after the allotted time because they are having so much fun. After this stage, participants are more likely to feel free to talk about the problems in their relationships and the aspects of their partners' personality and behavior that were most stressful for them, which is the task in the second stage of the exercise. They are again given 5 to 10 minutes each for this stage. Once participants have permission to complain about their partners, they do it with great enthusiasm.

In the third and most important stage so far, the task is to find the relationship between whatever it was that attracted the participants to their partners and what ended up being the most stressful aspect of the relationship or the partner for them. Examples (many are offered in chapter 12) are most useful in clarifying this point: A man who was attracted to a woman because she seemed "strong and independent" was later stressed by the fact that she always had to have her own way; a woman who was attracted to a man because he was "the strong silent type" that she found "very romantic" ended up divorcing him because he did not communicate.

Some people, especially if not accustomed to psychological thinking, may find this task difficult. This is when the support group (the other members of the foursome) can be helpful. Recognizing the connection between what attracted a couple to each other and what later became the major cause of their distress is as important for couples in therapy or in a couple burnout workshop[1] as it is for individuals trying to figure out what is wrong with their romantic choices.

Once the connection has been identified by all the workshop participants (with the help of the group leader when necessary), they need to do some individual work that will serve them in the next stages of the exercise. The work requires paper and pen and about 10 to 15 minutes. The task involves summarizing in two lists, on one piece of paper, the most attractive and the most stressful traits of the lover. This is, in fact, a written summary of the information that was brought up in the first two parts of the exercise.

The next parts of the exercise have to do with romantic images (discussed in chapters 8 through 10). After a relaxation exercise (such as focusing on breathing or gradually relaxing all parts of the body from forehead to toes), the participants are asked to recall with as much detail as possible a difficult event that happened in their childhood that involved their parents. Next, they are asked to tell their support group (for about 10 minutes each) both about the event (what happened, what did they feel, think, and do) and about what the event taught them about themselves and about life.

Next, participants are asked to take paper and pen and again make two lists. One list includes the positive traits of their mother and father (or step-parent or grandparent if they were significant parental figures in their childhood). The second list includes their negative traits. These two lists represent the building blocks of their romantic image. They are shared with the support group as participants talk (for about 10 minutes each) about their parents and about the type of life they had as children.

The next connection group members are asked to make involves deciphering the romantic attraction code. It is the connection between the two lists they have made: the list of the traits (positive and negative) of their romantic partner and the list of the traits (positive and negative) of both their parents. They are instructed to mark with a star each of the traits of their romantic partner that was either the same or the exact opposite of their parents. The result, in most cases, is a page full of stars.

The reason for putting a star next to traits of the partner that are either the same or the exact opposite of the parents' traits is a well-known psychological phenomenon: Whether we choose a romantic partner who is exactly like the parent with whom we have an unresolved childhood issue (cold and rejecting or intrusive and suffocating) or whether we choose a romantic partner who is the exact opposite of the parent, we are still dealing with the same unresolved issue. The proof (which can be checked by a show of hands) is that most group members have at least three stars. Such is the power of the internal romantic image on our romantic choices.

The next part of the exercise involves deducing from the insights gained in the previous stages one's core issue in intimate relationships. Again, the first part is done alone. Participants are asked to reexamine the list of the most stressful aspects of their romantic partner or relationship and compare it to the list of the negative traits of their parents to see if they can deduce from the comparison between the two lists a notion of what is most important for them in intimate relationships— their *core need*. This core need is likely to be something that they did not get from their parents and did not get from their romantic partner and that manifested in the stress they experienced in their romantic relationship. Core needs tend to be such "simple" things as the need to be loved, to feel safe, to feel special, to feel respected, to be the one and only. Not getting that need met is almost always related to the major stresses in the relationship: "The fact that he's always late shows that he doesn't respect me and my time." "The fact that she can spend hours on the phone with her girlfriends means that I'm not special to her." Identifying one's core need is likely to make the search for a successful intimate relationship simpler. When a potential romantic partner is obviously unwilling or incapable of fulfilling one's core need, such a partner is better avoided, even if otherwise extremely attractive.

The last stage of the exercise is done in the large group. It is inspired by the work of Kurt Lewin, the father of American social psychology, who discovered that people are most likely to change their behavior if they commit themselves to the change in front of a group. Thus, participants describe in turn what they are committed to do differently in future relationships to address their core need and thus provide a better chance for their intimate relationships. This process is similar in structure to the one that took place in the introductory session but is different in content. Rather than describe relationship problems, participants talk about what they can do to change their patterns.

Taking responsibility for one's pattern in romantic relationships is a reflection of an important concept: *self focus*. It is hard for many people to accept that they choose, carefully, even if unconsciously, whom to fall in love with and that they are equally responsible for what happens in their relationships. With self-focus comes a sense of power.

Although the advantage of an experiential workshop is the presence of other people (both in the large group and in the foursomes), this entire process can be done in the context of individual counseling. For an inexperienced counselor, the multistep process presented here provides a structure that is sure to bring about a highly therapeutic process.

The complete process can take anywhere from 2 to 5 days. If the multistep exercise is finished and there is still time left, *role play* can be used. Role play takes advantage of the presence of other people in the group and can be used whenever a participant asks or volunteers to work on a particular relationship issue or when it becomes apparent during the cycle of introductions that there is a relationship issue that is shared by several of the workshop participants. The person who volunteered to work on his or her issue is asked to describe the problem with as much detail as possible. Then, the group is asked whether there is anyone who identifies with the presenter or with the person with whom the presented had a problematic relationship. When two such people have raised their hands, they are asked to sit in the center of the room and have a discussion about the problem. In most cases, the people doing the role play identify with the issues involved and develop a heated and emotional argument. This process can be repeated until there are three or four people on each side of the argument (at times, the whole group takes a position on one or the other side of it). This exercise helps people break their fallacy of uniqueness by making it clear that others share their problem. In addition, it enables people to listen to discussion of their issue by other people and thus obtain a more objective perspective on it. The rest of the group can also see how universal relationship issues are, which encourages them to bring up their own issue for group discussion. In a week-long workshop, it is possible to go through this process with most of the group participants. In a weekend workshop, there is usually time to do it with only a few. Because most of the group members take part in these role plays, they benefit from the process vicariously.

Another exercise that can be used is a *sociodrama*. It is especially useful when a normative issue comes up in the group, such as an issue that tends to be divided by gender (for example, is monogamy better for intimate relationships or is an open relationship better). I start by drawing an imaginary line across the room. On each end of the line is one extreme position (only a monogamous relationship can offer true intimacy and allow the development of deep and committed love versus only by allowing your partner in an intimate relationship to be completely free can you be truly loving and respectful of your partner and the relationship). I ask for two volunteers to present convincingly and with conviction these two extreme views, even if they are more extreme than their own views. Once the two extreme positions have been expounded, I ask for other volunteers who can add information that can reinforce either of these extreme positions. Then, I ask all participants to place themselves on the part of the imaginary line that reflects their position and encourage them to move along the line if they change their position during the lively discussion that invariably ensues.

The final segment of the workshop should be devoted to plans for the future. One way to start is by using *guided imagery*, which directs the participants to imagine, in great detail, a typical day in their lives 3 years into the future (a similar exercise was suggested at the end of chapter 11). It is best to do this activity after a relaxation exercise, with participants lying comfortably on the floor. The guided imagery starts on Friday morning, 3 years ahead, from the minute they wake up and continues in great detail until they fall asleep. Special emphasis is put on feelings, thoughts, and activities having to do with an intimate relationship. For example, when they wake up in the morning, is someone next to them in bed? Do they have a sense of who that person is? What do they feel about him or her? What do they do (cuddle or pretend to be still asleep)? After they get up, do they have breakfast alone or with their partner? Do they keep in touch during the day? How do they spend the evening? The advantage of starting the guided imagery on Friday is that it enables exploring plans for weekend activities.

The use of imagery in projecting the future provides participants with the opportunity to use what they have learned in the workshop to reconstruct their romantic image and reprioritize their lives so that an intimate relationship will be a part of what they now believe is best for them. Later, based on their projections, they can be asked to make a concrete plan that will make the future more likely to unfold in the way that they envision and commit themselves to the group to this plan of action.

The workshop ends with time for feedback and leave-taking. By the end of the workshop, participants who started out as strangers part with hugs (a group hug is a nice parting gesture) and deeply felt and expressed emotions. Participants often exchange phone numbers and e-mail addresses and plan to continue keeping in touch and checking on each other's progress on their way to the ideal intimate relationship they envisioned.

ANALYZING A ROMANTIC RELATIONSHIP

Sex: Male/female
Age: _____
Dating frequency: _____ (from 1 = never dated, to 7 = nonstop dating)
Sexual preference: Heterosexual/homosexual/bisexual
Number of significant intimate relationships: _____
Length of this relationship: _____years and _____months
State of the relationship: _____ (1 = never was in one, to 7 = happily married)
Number of children: _____

Arousal played a role in the initial attraction: Yes/no
Propinquity played a role in the initial attraction: Yes/no
Similarity played a role in the initial attraction: Yes/no
Partner's attraction played a role in the initial attraction: Yes/no
Physical attraction played a role in the initial attraction: Yes/no
Personality of the partner played a role in the initial attraction: Yes/no
Status of partner played a role in the initial attraction: Yes/no
Is/was partner satisfying an important need? Yes/no
Was it love at first sight? Yes/no
Is the partner described as the "best friend"? Yes/no

Commitment to the relationship: _____ (from 1 = very low, to 7 = very high)
Sense of security in the relationship: ___ (from 1 = very low, to 7 = very high)
Able to be oneself in the relationship: ___ (from 1 = definitely no, to 7 = definitely yes)
Intimacy in the relationship: ___ (from 1 = very low, to 7 = very high)
Power in the relationship: ___ (from 1 = very low, to 7 = very high)
Pursuer/distancer: ___ (1 = you are very much the pursuer, 4 = both partners have equal involvement in the relationship, 7 = you are very much the distancer)
Physical attraction to partner: ___ (from 1 = very low, to 7 = very high)
Friendship before romance: ___ (1 = did not know each other, to 7 = were very close friends before the romance started)
Stereotyped sex roles: ___ (from 1 = very low, to 7 = very high)
Frequency of conflicts: ___ (from 1 = very low, to 7 = very high)

Able to deal with conflicts: ___ (from 1 = very low, to 7 = very high)
How are conflicts resolved: Talking/fighting/withdrawal
Signs of abuse in the relationship? ___ (from 1 = very low, to 7 = very high)
Ability to stand separation: ___ (from 1 = very low, to 7 = very high)
Jealousy is a problem in the relationship: ___ (from 1 = very low, to 7 = very high)
Jealousy is a personal problem: ___ (from 1 = very low, to 7 = very high)

Is partner similar to father? Yes/no
Is partner similar to mother? Yes/no
Is partner different from father? Yes/no
Is partner different from mother? Yes/no
Are the relationships with partner and parents similar? Yes/no

The categories presented here are the categories used for analyzing the interviews described throughout the book.

RESEARCH FINDINGS

These research findings were obtained using the coding categories presented in Appendix 2.

HOW WE CHOOSE THE LOVERS WE CHOOSE

- Conscious variables
  Personality 92% (88% men, 96% women)
  Appearance 62% (81% men, 44% women)

- Situational variables
  Proximity 62% (58% men, 67% women)
  Arousal 22% (19% men, 24% women)

- Lover variables
  Lover finds us attractive 41% (35% men, 47% women)
  Lover fills important need 54% (53% men, 54% women)
  Similarity 30% (28% men, 31% women)
  Lover is best friend 25% (21% men, 28% women)

- Unconscious variables: The building blocks of our romantic image
  Similarity to relationship with parents 69% (55% men, 82% women)
  Similarity of lover to father 56% (31% men, 78% women)
  Similarity of lover to mother 47% (50% men, 43% women)
  Love at first sight 11% (9% men, 13% women)

TABLE 1

Attraction Variables by Sex and Country: Percentages
(Pearson Chi Square; df = 1)

	SEX		COUNTRY	
	MEN	WOMEN	UNITED STATES	ISRAEL
Arousal	16%	30%	22%	25%
Chi square		4.6*		(NS)
Propinquity	52%	57%	63%	46%
Chi square		(NS)		4.8*
Similarity	19%	20%	29.50%	8%
Chi square		(NS)		12.2**
Need fulfillment	56%	58%	54%	60%
Chi square		(NS)		(NS)
Best friends	21%	34%	25%	31%
Chi square		3.6*		(NS)
Mate's attraction	35%	46%	41%	40%
Chi square		(NS)		(NS)
Appearance	80%	53%	63%	70%
Chi square		13.8***		(NS)
Personality	89%	97%	92%	94%
Chi square		4.0*		(NS)
Love at first sight	7%	12%	11%	8%
Chi square		(NS)		(NS)
Status	4%	4%	8%	0%
Chi square		(NS)		6.9 (p = 0.14)

NS: not significant
* p < .05
** p < .001
*** p < .0001

TABLE 2

Analysis of Variance (ANOVA)
Attraction Variables by Sex and Country: Means

	UNITED STATES		ISRAEL				
	MEANS				ANOVA		
	MEN	WOMEN	MEN	WOMEN	COUNTRY	SEX	INTER.
					F p	F p	F p
Physical attraction	4.2	2.8	4.5	3.4	3.8*	26***	
Status or dominance	2.6	2.5	2.1	2.3		5.6*	
Friendship preceded	3.2	3.5	2.9	2.8			
Significant relationships	1.2	1.5	1.5	1.8	4.5*	4.1*	
Dating frequency	3.5	3.4	3.7	3.1		8.3**	5.2*

* p < .05
** p < .001
*** p < .0001

TABLE 3

Analysis of Variance (ANOVA)
Relationship Variables by Sex and Country

| | UNITED STATES | | ISRAEL | | | | |
| | MEANS | | | | ANOVA | | |
	MEN	WOMEN	MEN	WOMEN	COUNTRY	SEX	INTER.
					F p	F p	F p
Relationship length	17	25	24	24			
Being oneself	4.3	4.9	5.0	4.9			
Handling separation	4.2	3.9	4.0	3.7		3.2*	
Pursuer/distancer	4.2	4.1	4.1	3.9			
Security	4.1	4.7	4.9	4.8	4.8*		
Power in relationship	4.0	4.0	4.1	3.9			
Frequency of conflicts	4.0	4.2	4.0	3.9			
Intimacy	3.9	4.9	4.8	4.8	3.0*	10.0**	6.0*
Commitment	3.5	4.4	3.9	4.2		9.4**	
Self-understanding	3.5	3.8	3.5	3.5			
Handling of conflicts	3.4	3.9	4.3	4.4	10.9**		
Sex role stereotyping	3.3	2.6	2.3	2.6	5.8*		
Understanding mate	3.0	3.4	3.3	3.4		bn 4.8*	
Relationship jealousy	3.0	3.2	2.8	2.7			
Personal jealousy	2.4	2.8	2.6	2.3			4.3*

$* < .05$
$** < .001$
$*** < .0001$

TABLE 4

Pearson Correlation Coefficients with Relationship Values
(Only Significant Correlations Noted)

	MEN & WOMEN		MEN		WOMEN	
WITH RELATIONSHIP LENGTH	r	p	r	p	r	p
Commitment	.46	.0001	.74	.0001		
Security	.42	.0001	.57	.0001		
Intimacy	.39	.0002	.37	.015	.32	.03
Being oneself	.39	.0002	.38	.01	.34	.02
Understanding mate	.37	.0004	.36	.02	.30	.04
Self-understanding	.33	.002	.36	.02		
Jealousy in the relationship	.29	.006	.37	.01		
Frequency of conflicts	.25	.02				
WITH COMMITMENT		p	r	p	r	p
Security	.65	.0001	.71	.0001	.56	.0001
Understanding mate	.6	.0001	.51	.0004	.65	.0001
Intimacy	.57	.0001	.51	.0004	.54	.0001
Being oneself	.57	.0001	.53	.0003	.54	.0001
Handling conflicts	.53	.0001	.36	.02	.64	.0001
Relationship length	.46	.0001	.74	.0001		
Self-understanding	.43	.0001	.38	.01	.41	.004

TABLE 4

Pearson Correlation Coefficients with Relationship Values

(Only Significant Correlations Noted)

	MEN & WOMEN		MEN		WOMEN	
Dating frequency	.27	.009			.34	.02
Significant relationships	.24	.03				
Frequency of conflicts	-.23	.03			-.48	.0001
Friendship before romance	.22	.03				
Power	.22	.04				
Attraction to dominance	-.22	.04				
Physical attraction	-.21	.04				
WITH POWER	r	p	r	p	r	p
Being the distancer	.8	.0001	.86	.0001	.71	.0001
Security	.54	.0001	.59	.0001	.49	.0005
Handling separation	.51	.0001	.43	.004	.66	.0001
Attraction to dominance	-.22	.04	-.46	.002		
Commitment	.22	.04				
Number of relationships	.22	.04				
Sex role stereotyping			.44	.004	-.39	.007
Dating frequency			.33	.03		
WITH BEING THE DISTANCER	r	p	r	p	r	p
Power in the relationship	.8	.0001	.86	.0001	.71	.0001
Handling separation	.68	.0001	.66	.0001	.71	.0001
Security	.48	.0001	.57	.0001		
Attraction to dominance	-.27	.01	-.48	.001		
Sex role stereotyping			.4	.01	-.37	.01
Dating frequency					-.42	.003
WITH INTIMACY	r	p	r	p	r	p
Being oneself	.82	.0001	.87	.0001	.73	.0001
Understanding mate	.71	.0001	.78	.0001	.51	.0003
Handling conflicts	.65	.0001	.70	.0001	.60	.0001
Security	.62	.0001	.56	.0001	.70	.0001
Commitment	.57	.0001	.51	.0004	.54	.0001
Self-understanding	.44	.0001	.56	.0001		
Friendship before romance	.41	.0001	.49	.0008		
Relationship length	.39	.0002	.37	.015	.32	.03
Sex role stereotyping	-.38	.0002	-.31	.04	-.37	.01
WITH SEX ROLE STEREOTYPING	r	p	r	p	r	p
Understanding mate	-.43	.0001	-.32	.04	-.51	.0003
Intimacy	-.38	.0002	-.31	.04	-.37	.01
Handling conflicts	-.35	.0009	-.3	.05	-.35	.02
Physical attraction	.34	.001	.34	.03		
Friendship before romance	-.31	.004	-.42	.005		
Being oneself	-.28	.008			-.54	.0001
Self-understanding	-.25	.02			-.34	.02
Significant relationships			.5	.002		
Power			.44	.004	-.39	.007
Being the distancer			.4	.01	-.37	.01

TABLE 4

Pearson Correlation Coefficients with Relationship Values

(Only Significant Correlations Noted)

	MEN & WOMEN	MEN	WOMEN	
Security			-.49	.0005
Handling separation			-.45	.002
Attraction to dominance			.44	.003
Commitment			-.33	.03
Jealousy as personal problem			.29	.05

TABLE 5

Career Burnout and Couple Burnout

Pearson Correlations

SAMPLE	n	r	p
Israelis	109	.34	.01
Portuguese	838	.33	.01
Spanish	317	.30	.01
British	144	.31	.01
Finn	110	.35	.01
American	54	.34	.01

Notes

INTRODUCTION: ABOUT FALLING IN LOVE AND ABOUT THIS BOOK

1. Watts, 1985.
2. My research suggests that love at first sight occurs in only 11% of the cases.
3. Lykken and Tellegen, 1993.
4. The research and published books include such topics as couple burnout, romantic jealousy, the psychology of gender, and the juggler: the role-conflict of working women.
5. Pines, 1999.
6. The first study was part of a longitudinal research project carried out at the University of California, Berkeley, by the developmental psychologists Jeanne and Jack Block. The study was initiated a quarter of a century ago by Jeanne Block, who, besides being a pioneer and a leading scholar on the influence of differential socialization on the personality development of boys and girls, was a remarkable human being, a real mensch, and a lady. Jeanne died an untimely death of cancer. Like almost everyone who knew her, I loved and admired Jeanne. I hope I can make in this book a small contribution toward keeping her memory alive. Jeanne and Jack Block followed 103 children from age 3 to age 23. In one of the parts of the follow-up study that took place at 23 years of age, 93 of the young men and women were interviewed extensively about their romantic relationships. (During the 20 years of the research, some of the original 103 subjects dropped out of the study, and others, for one reason or another, were not interviewed in this final stage.) Some of the 93 interviewees had never been in a romantic relationship; others were already married and had a child. Some even managed to get divorced by age 23. After watching these interviews, I transcribed them and created a coding scheme that enabled their quantitative analysis (see Analyzing a Romantic Relationship in appendix 2). Using this coding scheme, the interviews were analyzed by me and by two additional experienced clinical psychologists. The data obtained are discussed throughout the book (and are presented in the form of tables in the appendix). The data gathered in the study were supported by National Institute of Mental Health grant M11 16080. I wish to thank Adam Kreman for his computer implementations and Jack Block for his help and permission to use these data. Some of the results of the study were presented in an article, "A Prospective Study of Personality and Gender Differences in Romantic Attraction" (Pines, 1998b).
7. The Israeli part of the second, cross-cultural, study was carried out at Tel Aviv University and the Institute of Technology Arts and Sciences with the help of my psychology students Liat Bernstein, Keren Adir, Dana Talmor, Shalhevet Cohen,

Michal Katz, Irit Noiberg, Rachel Radsevski, Sarit Reisman, Ruti Sharf, and Dalit Shoshan. Each interviewed about 5 men and 5 women about 23 years old. Results of the study were published in an article, "The Role of Gender and Culture in Romantic Attraction" (Pines, 2001).

8. The third study is described in the third part of the book as well as in the article, "Fatal Attraction or Wise Unconscious Choices: The Relationship Between Causes for Entering and Breaking Intimate Relationships" (Pines, 1997).

9. While analyzing the interviews, I focused on various components of the process of falling in love and the variables that helped turn some of the love relationships into deep and significant bonds. I examined such questions as the following: Who has more power in the relationship? Who is the "pursuer" and who is the "distancer"? How rigidly defined are the sex roles in the relationship? Does the relationship provide a sense of security? What is the level of intimacy and commitment in the relationship? Can one be oneself in it? What is the frequency of conflicts? What are conflicts about? How, and how successfully, are conflicts handled? Is jealousy a problem either for the person or in the relationship? How difficult are temporary separations? Is there any evidence of physical or emotional abuse or of drug use? Is the relationship heterosexual, bisexual, or homosexual? What are the plans for the future? People who were not currently in a relationship were asked with what type of a person would they like to be involved in the future. Appendix 2 presents the analysis schedule, and Appendix 3 presents some of the data based on these analyses.

10. The research on which the chapter is based is described in the article, "Love and Work: Unconscious Choices and Their Relationship to Burnout" (Pines & Nunes, 2003).

11. See for example, Lindholm, 1998, for an elaboration of the argument that romantic love exists within a particular cultural context.

12. This point is elaborated in my book, *Couple Burnout* (Pines, 1996).

13. See for example, Lasswell and Lobsenz, 1980; J. A. Lee, 1998. The Greek names for the six styles of love were *storge* (best friends), *agape* (unselfish), *mania* (possessive), *pragma* (practical), *lodus* (playful), and *eros* (romantic). The six styles of love are described in the box.

14. Robert Sternberg's "triangular model of love" describes what he considers the three "basic components of love": intimacy, passion, and commitment. When none of the components is present, the result is "non-love." A relationship with intimacy only is "liking." A relationship with passion only is "infatuation." A relationship with commitment only is "empty love." A relationship with passion and commitment is "Hollywood style" fatuous love. A relationship with intimacy and commitment but no passion is "companionate love." "Romantic love" has passion and intimacy but not commitment, whereas the "perfect love," the love that includes intimacy, commitment, and passion is "consummate love" (Sternberg, 1986).

15. Fromm, 1956.

16. Reik, 1957, p. 9.

17. May, 1969, pp. 72–73.

18. Regan, 1996.

19. Alberoni, 1983.

20. Peck, 1978, pp. 81–84.

THE SIX STYLES OF LOVE

Passionate love. You are in love with love and willing to tolerate anything for love.

Game-playing love. You view a relationship as a challenge without a need for commitment.

Friendship love. You enjoy a comfortable, nonromantic intimacy in which sex is secondary.

Logical love. You are concerned with a mutual compatibility in which reason rules.

Possessive love. You are consumed by the need to possess and be possessed.

Selfless love. You subordinate yourself to others and are devoted and sacrificing.

21. My book *Couple Burnout* (Pines, 1996) is devoted to a discussion of what happens to intimate relationships after the falling-in-love stage.
22. Lindholm, 1998.
23. Beall and Sternberg, 1995.
24. Becker, 1973, p. 160.
25. Rank, 1945.
26. de Rougemont, 1940/1983, pp. 291–292.

CHAPTER 1
PROXIMITY: THE HIDDEN MATCHMAKER

1. In 63% of the interviews, proximity was mentioned as a cause of attraction. It may also be worth noting that, despite the somewhat larger effect that acquaintance had on women, the gender difference in this case was small and insignificant (67% of the women compared to 58% of the men).
2. Bossard, 1932.
3. Clarke, 1952.
4. Festinger, 1951.
5. Newcomb, 1961.
6. Segal, 1974.
7. Bescheid and Hartfield-Walster, 1978.
8. Zajonc, 1968.
9. Moreland and Beach, 1992.
10. Kellerman et al., 1989.
11. White and Shapiro, 1989.
12. Bornstein et al., 1987.
13. Thelen, 1988.
14. Pierce et al., 1996.
15. Mita et al., 1977.

16. Darley and Berscheid, 1967.
17. Pines, 1996.
18. Rindfuss and Stephen, 1990.
19. Brickman et al., 1972.

CHAPTER 2
AROUSAL: THE ELIXIR OF LOVE

1. In 22% of the interviews, the romantic relationship started in a period of great emotional turmoil. Although women were more likely than men to describe a state of arousal at the start of the relationship (24% of the women versus 19% of the men), the sex difference was not significant. In several cases, the woman was not attracted to the man at first, but he was there for her in her hour of need, and with time her feelings of gratitude and appreciation turned to love.
2. Walster and Berscheid, 1971.
3. Schachter, 1964.
4. The first studies of Arthur Aron are described in a charming book he wrote with his wife Elaine called *The Heart of Social Psychology* (1989).
5. Dutton and Aron, 1974.
6. The Thematic Apperception Test (TAT) was developed by Murray (1943).
7. Stephan et al., 1971.
8. Cohen et al., 1989.
9. Barclay and Haber, 1965.
10. Valins, 1966.
11. White et al., 1981.
12. A study showed that, even in a laboratory setting, misattribution can generate in subjects feelings of love and excitement within 2 minutes of acquaintance (Kellerman et al., 1989). Also, a meta-analysis that summarized the results of 33 studies on the effect of arousal on romantic attraction suggested that arousal exerts a stronger influence on attraction when it is ambiguous. (*Ambiguity* refers to an inability to perceive the arousal as caused by its true source; see Foster et al., 1998.)
13. Allen et al., 1989.
14. Walster-Hartfield and Walster, 1981.
15. Pennebaker et al., 1979.
16. The psychology of reactance suggests that when our freedom is threatened or denied, we are motivated to do something to get it back (Brehm and Brehm, 1981).
17. Driscoll et al., 1971.
18. Aronson and Mills, 1972.
19. Walster et al., 1973.
20. Wright and Contrada, 1986.
21. Clark and Watson, 1988.
22. Kaplan, 1981.
23. May and Hamilton, 1980.
24. Veitch and Griffit, 1976.
25. Gouaux, 1971, p. 94.
26. Shapiro, 1988.

27. Cunningham, 1986.
28. Clore and Byrne, 1974.
29. Rozin et al., 1986.
30. The survey was conducted in Israel and included 240 men and 253 women, of whom 56% said they believed in love at first sight, 37% said they did not, and 7% said they did not know. In addition, 60% said they believed that love can last forever, and 40% said they believed that everyone has a twin romantic soul.
31. This point is elaborated in my book *Couple Burnout* (Pines, 1996).
32. Hartfield and Rapson, 1993.

CHAPTER 3
BEAUTY AND CHARACTER

1. In 92% of the American interviews and 94% of the Israeli interviews, interviewees mentioned some aspect of the partner's character when trying to explain why they fell in love. Women mentioned personality traits more often than men: in the American interviews, 96% of the women and 88% of the men. However, the sex difference was small and insignificant.
2. A smaller percentage, 63% of the Americans and 70% of the Israelis, mentioned appearance. Here, however, the sex difference was large and statistically significant. Specifically, 81% of the American men, as compared to 44% of the women, mentioned being attracted to the physical appearance of the partner. This finding was replicated in many other studies. See, for example, Feingold, 1990.
3. Hadjistavropoulos and Genest, 1994.
4. The research on the "split-second evaluations that shape our moods and action" was done (among others) by John Bargh and Shelly Chaiken and was described in the September 1998 issue the *APA Monitor* (p. 13).
5. Hartfield and Sprecher, 1986.
6. Hartz, 1996.
7. Walster et al., 1966.
8. Dion et al., 1972.
9. Gillen, 1981.
10. Calvert, 1988.
11. Karraker et al., 1987.
12. Johnson and Pittenger, 1984.
13. Feingold, 1990.
14. Sprecher and Duck, 1994.
15. Sigall and Aronson, 1969.
16. Banner, 1983.
17. Silverstein et al., 1990.
18. Cunningham et al., 1986.
19. Jones, 1995.
20. Cunnigham et al., 1995.
21. Etcoff, 2000.
22. Gangestad and Thornhill, 1997.
23. Alicke et al., 1986.

24. D. Singh, 1994.

25. Kleinke and Staneski, 1980.

26. Singh, 1993.

27. Diamond, 1996.

28. Lavrakas, 1975.

29. Pierce, 1996.

30. Lynn and Shurgot, 1984.

31. Hensley, 1994.

32. Sheppard and Strathman, 1989.

33. These three explanations and the studies supporting them are discussed by Sharon Brehm in her book *Intimate Relationships* (1992).

34. Geiselman et al., 1984.

35. Dion and Dion, 1987.

36. Buss, 1994.

37. Reis et al., 1980.

38. Curran and Lippold, 1975.

39. Archer and Cash, 1985.

40. Umberson and Houghs, 1987.

41. Frieze et al., 1991.

42. Cash and Duncan, 1984.

43. Major et al., 1984.

44. Kalick and Hamilton, 1986.

45. Pines, 1998a.

46. Lot et al., 1960.

47. Krueger and Caspi, 1993.

48. Anderson, 1981.

49. Aronson, 1998, p. 356.

50. Goodwin, 1990.

51. Smith et al., 1990.

52. Desrochers, 1995.

53. Hoyt and Hudson, 1981.

54. Aron et al., 1989.

55. Guthrie, 1938.

56. M. Snyder, 1993.

57. Murray et al., 1996.

58. Freud, 1914/1957.

59. Erikson, 1959.

60. Kacerguis and Adams, 1980.

61. Sperling, 1987.

62. Dion and Dion, 1975.

63. Maslow, 1970.

64. Dietch, 1978.

65. Dion and Dion, 1985.

66. Greek philosophers distinguished among six styles of love: *storge* (best friends' love), *agape* (unselfish and sacrificing love), *mania* (possessive love), *pragma* (practical

love), *lodus* (playful and game-playing love), and *eros* (romantic, erotic love.) They were mentioned and discussed briefly in the Introduction.
67. Levy and Davis, 1988.

CHAPTER 4
BIRDS OF A FEATHER OR OPPOSITES ATTRACT?

1. Analysis of the romantic attraction interviews suggests that 28% of the men and 31% of the women mentioned similarity as playing a role in the initial attraction. For some reason, possibly greater social homogeneity, similarity was mentioned significantly less frequently in the Israeli sample than it was in the American sample.
2. Literature reviews on the effect of similarity on mate selection can be found in Pines (1996); Brehm (1992); Berscheid and Hartfield-Walster (1978).
3. Galton, 1884.
4. One study, involving 1,499 American couples, showed that the couples were similar in a wide range of cognitive and personality traits (Phillips et al., 1988). Another study, using British couples, showed that the couples were similar in such diverse traits as intelligence, introversion, extroversion, and inconsistency (Taylor and Vandenberg, 1988). A third study done in Hawaii showed that the couples were similar in level of education, verbal ability, and professional success (Nagoshi et al., 1987). The participants in the study were couples and their siblings. The researchers compared the siblings, the couples, and the couples to the siblings. They concluded that the similarities of the couples were caused by both attraction to the similar and a similar social environment. The authors concluded that the similarity resulted from both physical proximity and personal preference, which is to say that, among those who live in their neighborhoods, study in their schools, or work in their offices, people choose those who are similar to them in levels of intelligence and personality. Introverts choose introverts, and extroverts prefer extroverts.
5. Mehrabian, 1989.
6. Hartfield and Rapson, 1992.
7. Burleson et al., 1997; Neimeyer, 1984.
8. When the weights of 330 married couples were examined during four stages of their life cycle, it was discovered that, even among young couples, there was a similarity in the partners' weights. This correlation probably reflects people's original attraction to potential partners who are similar to themselves in physical appearance. It is less surprising that similarity was found in the couples' weights at the age of retirement—the probable result of similar eating habits and similar lifestyles (Schafer & Keith, 1990).
9. The similarity in the likelihood of a mental problem was limited to cases in which the woman's schizophrenia was discovered at a young age. It should also be noted that, in those cases in which both partners suffered from a mental problem, there was a much greater likelihood for a mental problem to appear in their offspring (Parnas, 1988).
10. Merikangas et al., 1988.
11. Lock and Horowitz, 1990.
12. Buss, 1985.

13. Rushton, 1988.
14. Caspi and Harbener, 1990.
15. Folkes, 1982.
16. The study that was done by Greg White (1980) involved following up couples with different levels of commitment. The findings that the more similar couples were in attractiveness the more they were likely to stay together and express love for each other was true for couples at the beginning of their relationship, but was not true for engaged couples or for couples living together. This suggests that similarity in attractiveness is part of the screening process at the start of a romantic relationship. Once a couple has committed to each other, the similarity in the attractiveness between them is a given and thus stops playing a part in their relationship.
17. See for example, Brehm, 1992; Feingold, 1988.
18. Margolin and White, 1987.
19. Berscheid and Hartfield-Walster, 1978.
20. Hinsz, 1989.
21. Zajonc et al., 1987.
22. Byrne, 1997.
23. Byrne et al., 1970. Don Byrne and his colleagues have repeatedly validated their findings on the effect of attitude similarity on attraction (Byrne, 1971, 1997). Their studies took the following procedure: Subjects received a questionnaire in which they were asked about their attitudes on various topics—for example, "Do you believe in God? "What are your political views?" and so on. Later, while participating in what they supposed was a separate study, the subjects were asked their impressions of another person and given a copy of that person's completed questionnaire. In fact, the questionnaire had been completed by the experimenter in referral to the opinions expressed earlier by the subject. In some cases, this questionnaire portrayed the other person as possessing similar attitudes; in the remaining cases, the other person possessed different attitudes. Byrne and his colleagues discovered that the *ratio* of similar to different attitudes determined the level of attraction. The higher the ratio of similar to different attitudes, the greater the attraction. Neither the number of similar attitudes nor the type of different attitudes had an effect. This finding was replicated with the very young and very old and with both men and women who came from different backgrounds and lived in different situations.
24. Darwin, 1910. Darwin also mentioned expertise or excellence in some area, returned affection, and traits that are pleasant or admirable, such as loyalty, honesty, and goodness.
25. Carnegie, 1982.
26. Aronson, 1998.
27. Berscheid and Hartfield-Walster, 1978.
28. Marks and Miller, 1982.
29. Orive, 1988.
30. Singh and Tan, 1992; Drigotas, 1993.
31. See for example, Byrne and Blaylock (1963) and Levinger and Breedlove (1966), as well as Berscheid and Hartfield-Walster (1978).
32. Levinger and Breedlove, 1966.
33. Grush and Yahl, 1979.

34. Smith et al., 1993.
35. Burleson and Denton, 1992. Similarities in social and communication skills (which include the ability to talk about sex) predict attraction and marital satisfaction. These similarities promote couples' attraction by fostering enjoyable interactions. Indeed, married couples were found to be more similar in their social and communication skills than were random, computer-generated couples.
36. See for example, Richard et al., 1990; Marioles et al., 1996.
37. See for example, Caspi and Harbener, 1990; Richard et al., 1990.
38. Caspi and Harbener, 1990. In a longitudinal study at the University of California, Berkeley, an analysis of the criteria for mate selection showed that "homogeneity," which is to say, similarity, is a basic norm in marriage.
39. Reader and English, 1947.
40. Izard, 1960.
41. Bowen, 1978.
42. Hendrix, 1992.
43. Rushton, 1988.
44. Lumpert, 1997.
45. Dryer and Horowitz, 1997. Their study was based on the assumption that dyadic relationships can be described on two dimensions: attachment (which ranges from hostility to friendship) and control (which ranges from dominance to submissiveness). Results of the study showed that complementary couples (in which one of the partners was dominant and the other was submissive) reported greater satisfaction from the relationship than couples in which both partners were either dominant or submissive. Complementary couples are similar on the dimension of attachment and complementary on the dimension of control; this is why they report great satisfaction from their relationships.
46. Jones et al., 1971.
47. Kruglanski and Mayseless, 1987,
48. Snyder and Fromkin, 1980.
49. Rytting et al., 1992.
50. Shaikh and Suresh, 1994.
51. Krueger and Caspi, 1993.
52. Larson, 1992.
53. Nowicki and Menheim, 1991.
54. Wilson, 1989.
55. Solomon, 1986.

CHAPTER 5
SATISFYING NEEDS AND RECIPROCATING LOVE: WE LOVE THOSE WHO LOVE US

1. Shaver et al., 1978.
2. Analysis of the romantic attraction interviews showed that, in 54% of the American interviews and 60% of the Israeli interviews, the subject mentioned that the beloved satisfied an important need.
3. Reik, 1964.

4. Murstein, 1976.
5. See for example, the classic works of Homans (1961) and Thibaut and Kelley (1959).
6. Lee, 1998.
7. Goffman, 1952.
8. Foa and Foa, 1980.
9. Brinberg and Castel, 1982.
10. Davis, 1990.
11. Carnegie, 1982.
12. See for example, the study by Aronson and Linder (1965) as well as the series of studies by Jones (1964).
13. Jones, 1964
14. Amabille, 1983.
15. Dittes, 1959.
16. Pines, 1998c.
17. Barnett, 1993.
18. Rabin, 1995.
19. Winch, 1958.
20. Analysis of the romantic attraction interviews showed that, in 40% of the American interviews and 41% of the Israeli interviews, an indication of attraction by the beloved played an important role in the initial attraction. For women, the rate was 47%, a bit higher than the 35% rate for men.
21. Aronson, 1998.
22. Curtis and Miller, 1986.
23. Aron et al. (1989) examined three types of falling-in-love accounts. The first type was a lengthy and detailed account obtained from students who had fallen in love during the previous 8 months. Content analysis of the variables in the stories revealed that reciprocal liking was mentioned in practically all the stories. Desirable characteristics were mentioned in most of the stories, and satisfying needs appeared in less than a quarter of the stories. The second type of accounts was obtained from participants in weekend seminars on "love and consciousness." Participants, whose average age was 31, were asked to take part in a 10-minute exercise describing an experience of "developing a strong attraction to someone," of "falling in love," or of "falling in friendship." They were given 11 × 14 cm index cards on which they were told to describe briefly how it happened, what they felt, and what resulted. Of the accounts of falling in love, 100 were then compared to 100 accounts of falling in friendship. Content analysis revealed that two thirds of these stories mentioned reciprocal liking and desirable traits of beauty and character in the beloved. Similarity and propinquity appeared in one quarter to one third of the stories. Satisfying needs was mentioned in only one tenth of the stories. Based on the results of both the long and the short love stories, a questionnaire was built, responses to which constituted the third type of falling-in-love account. The respondents were asked to recall their most recent experiences of falling in love and then to rank their feelings on different scales. In the analysis of their responses, again, reciprocal affection and desirable characteristics appeared most frequently as the reasons for falling in love. Filling needs was mentioned in only about one third of the cases. Falling-in-friendship accounts gave relatively

more emphasis to similarity and propinquity and somewhat less emphasis to reciprocal liking, desirable characteristics, and filling needs.

24. Robinson and Price, 1980.

CHAPTER 6
THE COURSE OF ROMANTIC LOVE: FALLING IN LOVE AS A PROCESS

1. In 33% of the cases, falling in love was gradual. In 11%, love was at first sight.
2. For example, Berscheid and Reis, 1998.
3. de Munck, 1998.
4. Fisher, 1998.
5. Rodin, 1987.
6. Winch, 1958.
7. Kerckoff, 1974.
8. A study that inspired this theory looked at predictors for the continuance of relationships. Agreement about values served as the best predictor for couples who had been together less than a year and a half, whereas the best predictor for couples who had been together more than a year and a half was complementarity.
9. Murstein, 1976. Even though all three components—stimulus, value, and role—influence the development of a romantic relationship, each component becomes central only during one developmental stage. For example, in the second stage the attraction is based primarily on similarity in values and less on physical appearance or satisfying role requirements.
10. Backman, 1981.
11. Lewis, 1973.
12. Ziv, 1993.
13. Stephen, 1987.
14. Surra and Hyston, 1987.
15. Burgess and Huston, 1979.
16. Kelley et al., 1983.
17. Keller and Young, 1996.
18. Pines, 1996.
19. Alberoni, 1983.
20. Aron et al., 1995.
21. Aron and Aron, 1986.
22. In 30% of the men's stories and 35% of the women's stories, there was a description of falling in love as a process.
23. Basow, 1992.
24. Moore, 1985.
25. Green and Sandos, 1983.
26. Rose and Frieze, 1989.
27. Rubin et al., 1981.
28. Muehlenhard and Hollabaugh, 1988.
29. Buss, 1994.
30. Hyde, 1990.
31. Perper, 1989.

CHAPTER 7
ON MEN, WOMEN, AND LOVE: THE ROLE OF STATUS AND BEAUTY

1. There was no gender difference in the effect of geographic proximity; 58% of the men compared to 67% of the women were influenced by it. There was no gender difference in the effect of arousal; 19% of the men compared to 24% of the women were influenced. There was no gender difference in the effect of attractive personality traits; 88% of the men compared to 96% of the women were influenced. There was no gender difference in the effect of similarity; 28% of the men compared to 31% of the women were influenced. And, there was no gender difference in either the effect of reciprocity in attraction (35% of the men and 47% of the women were influenced) or the effect of satisfying needs (53% of the men and 54% of the women were influenced).

2. The only variable in which there was a significant gender difference (in both the Israeli and the American samples) was physical attraction: 81% of the American men as compared to 44% of the women mentioned it as a significant cause of attraction (χ^2 = 12.8, df = 1, p = .000). In addition, when describing the things that made them fall in love with their mates, men described physical attraction as having played a more significant role. On a 7-point scale, the average for men was 4.2, and for women it was 2.8 (t = 4.0, p = .0001). The emphasis on physical appearance was especially pronounced in men who defined sex roles rigidly and stereotypically. The correlation between mentioning physical attraction as an important variable at the beginning of the relationship and the tendency to define sex roles in a rigid and stereotypic way was r = .34 (p = .001).

3. The study by Alan Feingold (1990) was a "meta-analysis." For those interested, I would like to add a few words about what a meta-analysis is. As the quantity of information in different areas of science exploded, an accompanying need arose to develop statistical techniques that would enable a significant summary of large volumes of research data. Meta analysis is just such a summary. It is a statistical summation of research findings, akin to a literature review. It provides *in a single number* a summary of many studies that were done on a certain subject. Meta-analysis takes into account the size of the samples when evaluating the significance of their findings. Thus, one general finding, based on a large number of studies, can include a huge number of subjects.

4. Sprecher et al., 1994.

5. Weiderman and Allgeier, 1992. In the study, young men and women and middle-aged men and women, were asked to estimate their own earning potential and rate the importance of various criteria for choosing a mate. Results showed that men gave a higher rating to "a nice-looking appearance," and women gave a higher rating to "good economic potential," nothing new so far. However, there was a correlation between the income young women expected to earn and the income they wanted a potential partner to earn. The higher their own income, the more important the income of their partners was. The fact that this correlation did not exist among older women suggests that what influences romantic attraction can change during different stages of life.

6. Townsend and Wasserman, 1998. The study used photographs of models and models in bathing suits to demonstrate gender differences in (a) the ability to determine romantic attraction by means of visual scan and (b) which types of information men and women need in addition to a visual scan. Results showed that for men a visual scan of a potential partner's "physical attributes" was enough. For women, a partner's "nonphysical attributes," such as ambition, status, and dominance, were needed to establish a pool of acceptable potential partners.

7. Greenlees and McGrew, 1994. In addition, men, favoring casual relationships, were more promiscuously inclined than women, who favor long-term, monogamous relationships.

8. Cunningham, 1986.

9. Sprecher and Duck, 1994.

10. Townsend and Levy, 1990.

11. Yarab et al., 1998. Studies also showed that, more frequently than women, men engage in sexual fantasies about someone other than a partner.

12. Kenrick and Keefe, 1992. According to evolutionary theory, these choices maximize the potential for successful breeding for both genders by combining a young woman with an established man.

13. Patterson and Pettijohn, 1982. The examination was of marriage licenses granted during the 50-year period between 1928 and 1978.

14. Pierce et al., 1996.

15. Jackson and Ervin, 1992.

16. Sadalla et al., 1987.

17. Ellis, 1992. Presumably, such men are more likely to invest in their offspring, hence their attractiveness to women.

18. Jensen-Campbell et al., 1995. The attraction of women to dominant yet helpful men was demonstrated in three studies in which young women watched a video showing (a) a man being dominant or not and (b) helpful and cooperative or not.

19. Darwin, 1871.

20. See for example, Buss and Schmitt (1993), Trievers (1972), Trost and Alberts (1998).

21. Lumpert, 1997.

22. Buss, 1994.

23. Buss et al., 1990.

24. Mulder, 1990.

25. Suman, 1992.

26. Trost and Alberts, 1998.

27. Kirkpatrick, 1998.

28. Schmitt and Buss, 1996.

29. Cashdan, 1993.

30. Tooke and Camire, 1991.

31. In recent years, a huge number of studies were done on the psychology of gender differences. Meta-analyses involving hundreds of studies and thousands of subjects were done on such topics as gender differences in mathematical ability, verbal ability, spatial orientation, and aggression, most of them showing small gender differences. For example, a meta-analysis of 143 studies that investigated gender differences in

aggression revealed that gender accounts for only 5% of the explained variance in aggression (Hyde, 1984). Similarly, a meta-analysis of 165 studies (and 1,418,899 subjects) that investigated gender differences in verbal ability showed that over 99% of a given score is influenced by things other than gender (Hyde and Linn, 1988). A meta-analysis of 100 studies (involving 3,985,682 subjects) revealed an even smaller gender difference—close to zero—in mathematical ability (Hyde and Linn, 1986). And, a meta-analysis of 172 studies that examined gender differences in spatial orientation revealed that less than 5% of the variance is explained by gender (Hyde, 1981). Given these consistent findings that showed no gender difference in various areas, the results of a meta-analysis showing a large and significant gender difference in attitudes toward sexual intimacy are especially notable. The study showed that the differences between men and women regarding sex and intimacy are among the largest gender differences found. They are far greater than the gender differences in verbal ability, mathematical ability, and spatial orientation and similar in size to the difference in the ability to throw to a distance (Hyde, 1993).

32. Kenrick et al., 1993.

33. Regan, 1998.

34. Clark and Hatfield, 1989.

35. Townsend, 1995.

36. Hubbard, 1990.

37. Hrdy, 1988.

38. de Munck, 1998.

39. Nevid (1984) work is an example of a study that achieved results similar to those of evolutionary theorists but was explained by a social theory. In terms of determining the choice of a romantic partner for both short-term sexual and long-term meaningful relationships, 500 young men and women rated the importance of physical features, demographic variables, and personal qualities. Findings showed, again, that men placed greater emphasis on the physical appearance of their prospective romantic partners, and women placed greater emphasis on the personal qualities. In the context of a meaningful, long-term relationship, however, both men and women weighed various personal qualities more heavily than physical characteristics. Contrary to the evolutionary explanation of the effect of innate genetic programming, these findings were explained by the effect of sex role stereotypes and traditional sex roles on the romantic preferences of men and women. Because all of us are influenced by the masculine and feminine stereotypes dominant in our culture, we tend to choose partners who fit those stereotypes.

40. Benton et al., 1983.

41. Basow, 1992.

42. A *schema* is a cognitive framework, acquired through experience, that directs the way we process new information. After a schema is created, it influences the way new information is absorbed, explained, processed, and remembered. We categorize people according to social schemas. To some of those schemas we belong; to others, we do not belong. There are many social groups to which we can belong, groups that are defined by such things as race, religion, nationality, profession, political views, and, of course, gender. A gender schema is a cognitive framework that reflects social beliefs about men and women. Sexual schemas influence people's responses to

sexual-romantic cues, sexual desire, and romantic attachment (Cyranowski and Andersen, 1998).

43. Park and Rothbart, 1982.
44. Skrypneck and Snyder, 1982.
45. Zana and Pack, 1975.
46. Tavris, 1992.
47. Ickees, 1993.
48. Martin, 1987.
49. Unger, 1975.
50. Steinman and Fox, 1970.
51. Gillen, 1981.
52. Green and Kenrick, 1994.
53. Cramer et al., 1993.
54. Desrochers, 1995.
55. Maybach and Gold, 1994.
56. Grube et al., 1982.
57. Dion and Dion, 1973.
58. Aron and Aron, 1986.
59. Low, 1990.
60. Chafetz, 1975.
61. Hyde, 1993. Furthermore, the famous study that demonstrated a gender difference in the approach to casual sex also showed that men are as choosy as women when it comes to selecting a marriage partner (Kenrick et al., 1993).
62. Small, 1992.
63. Cohen and Shotland, 1996.
64. Leigh and Aramburu, 1996.
65. Davis, 1990. Even studies that were presented as supporting the evolutionary perspective can be explained by gender stereotypes. In the study of personal ads, it can be said that women emphasize traits such as economic status because it fits the masculine stereotype, and men emphasize the attractive appearance of women because it fits the feminine stereotype.
66. Pines, 1998b. In a study of personality and gender differences in romantic attraction, I found that the closer to one of the gender role stereotypes young people's personalities were at age 18, the more this predicted their intimate relationships at age 23.
67. De-Raad and Boddema-Winesemius, 1992. This Dutch/German study demonstrated that although young single people follow the stereotypical male preference for good looks and female preference for financial prospects, older people value a steady relationship and exhibit a stronger desire for home and children, chastity, and ambition.
68. See, for example, Nancy Chodorow, 1978; Dorothy Dinnerstein, 1976; Lillian B. Rubin, 1983; and Jean Baker Miller, 1976.
69. Rich, 1976.
70. Rubin, 1983.
71. Blatt and Blass, 1996.
72. Pleck, 1977.

73. Miller, 1976.
74. Results of the study showed that, significantly more so than men, women were likely to describe a partner as a best friend and to describe higher levels of intimacy, commitment, and security in their intimate relationships. More than men, women were "themselves" in their relationships and expressed greater understanding of their partner than men did. Men's relationships tended to be shorter in duration and more sex role stereotyped: Women were also more likely to describe a partner as a best friend (21% of the men and 34% of the women described a partner as a best friend; $\chi^2 = 9.2$; $p = .01$), and their descriptions of their relationships indicated higher levels of intimacy (men's mean [Mm] = 3.9, women's mean [Wm] = 4.9; $t = 3.5$; $p = .001$), commitment (Mm = 3.5, Wm = 4.4; $t = 3.1$; $p = .02$), and security (Mm = 4.1, Wm = 4.7). Women felt more themselves in their relationships (Mm = 4.3, Wm = 4.9; $t = 3.1$; $p = .002$), and women showed greater understanding of a partner than men did (Mm = 2.9, Wm = 3.4; $t = 3.1$; $p = .002$). On the other hand, men described relationships that were more sex role stereotyped (Mm = 3.3, Wm = 2.6; $t = 2.3$; $p = .02$). Women's intimate relationships tended to last longer than men's. The average length of a relationship for men was 18 months; for women, it was 26 months ($t = 2.1$; $p = .03$).

    In most cases, when men described an intimate relationship, they were describing a relationship with a woman. By the same token, when women described an intimate relationship, they were describing a relationship with a man. How, then, can these descriptions be so different? It is as if there are two relationships: "his relationship," marked by physical attraction and sex role stereotyping, and "her relationship," marked by intimacy, commitment, security, and a sense that intimate partners are each other's best friends. One explanation for this puzzling finding is that it is an artifact, a result of the difference in emotional maturity between men and women at the tender age of 23. Another possible interpretation is that the men and women are describing the same relationships, but their perceptions of these relationships are different, the result of different socialization or different evolutionary programming. Because of these differences, deep friendship, intimacy, commitment, and security are more important to women, causing them to notice these factors more in their love relationships. On the other hand, because physical attraction is more important to men, it causes them to notice it more.
75. See Beall and Sternberg, 1995; Benjamin, 1998; deLamater and Hyde, 1998; Eagly, 1987; Goldner, 1998; Hyde, 1990; Tavris, 1992.
76. DeLamater and Hyde, 1998.
77. Gergen and Gergen, 1992.
78. Beall and Sternberg, 1995.
79. Jacobson and Christensen, 1996.
80. Goodwin, 1990; Smith et al., 1990.
81. Buss and Barnes, 1986.
82. Goodwin, 1990.
83. Smith et al., 1990.
84. Cochran and Peplau, 1985.
85. Small, 1992.
86. In addition, women have the capacity to be multiorgasmic.
87. Goldner, 1998.

88. Benjamin, 1998.

89. Tavris, 1992.

90. Peng and Nisbett, 1999.

91. Pines, 2001. In this study, I analyzed the romantic attraction interviews and compared the responses of the 93 young American men and women to the responses of the 89 young Israeli men and women.

92. Here are the results of the gender-by-culture comparison: 80% of the men and 53% of the women mentioned the physical appearance of their partner when describing why they fell in love, whereas 4% of the men and 4% of the women mentioned status. Culture did have an effect on the importance of status. Although 8% of the Americans interviewed were attracted to the status of their partner, almost none of the Israelis (0%) were. Americans were also more influenced by propinquity, 63%, as compared to 46% of the Israelis, and by similarity, 30%, as compared to 8% of the Israelis. Women attributed arousal to romantic attraction significantly more than men did: 30% of the women vs. 16% of men. And, men were as likely as women to be attracted to someone who satisfied their needs: 56% of the men vs. 58% of the women.

CHAPTER 8
OPENNESS TO LOVE

1. There were 12% of the American interviewees and 5% of the Israeli interviewees who said that at age 23 they still had never had a romantic relationship. Of the men, 2% had four or more significant relationships.

2. Tennov, 1979.

3. Bowlby, 1982.

4. Ainsworth et al., 1978.

5. Bartholomew and Horowitz, 1991; Shaver and Clark, 1994.

6. Hazan and Shaver, 1987; Shaver and Hazan, 1993.

7. Mickelson et al., 1997.

8. Bartholomew, 1990.

9. Brennan and Shaver, 1995.

10. Stein et al., 1998.

11. Simpson et al., 1992.

12. Ainsworth, 1989.

13. Dion and Dion, 1975.

14. Mickelson et al., 1997; Shaver and Brennan, 1992.

15. Erikson, 1959.

16. Macerguis and Adams, 1980.

17. Sperling, 1987.

18. Walster, 1965.

19. Kiesler and Baral, 1970.

20. Rubin, 1973.

21. The relationship between self-confidence and different love styles was first noted at the end of chapter 3 (pp. 44–45).

22. Levy and Davis, 1988.

23. Kernberg, 1974, p. 79.

24. It is important to note that Kernberg's view of personality development and organization varies somewhat from traditional object relations theory. It is also somewhat idiosyncratic diagnostically. For example, there is no diagnosis of narcissistic schizophrenic personality in the *Diagnostic and Statistical Manual of Mental Disorders, Fourth Edition* (*DSM-IV*; American Psychiatric Association, 1994). One is Axis I; the other is Axis II.

25. Mahler et al., 1975.

26. Winnicott, 1976.

27. The dual needs for closeness and for independence exist in each of us and in all romantic love relationships. Neither is preferred, and neither exists all the time. Rather, there is an ongoing interplay between the two. Couples in romantic love relationships need to consciously allow, and move back and forth between, close intimacy and independence.

28. Another theoretician who talks about difficulties with intimacy that arise from different types of personality disorders is Masterson (1981). With the borderline personality disorder comes the need to merge, rage, and withdraw, with the narcissistic personality disorder comes the self-absorption that only connects in the mirror of the other person by seeing the self reflected in a positive way. Masterson noted how often the borderline woman marries a narcissistic man and how these relationships erupt in major drama, or how two narcissists essentially exist for each other in the mirror each holds up for the other's reflection.

29. When the mother cannot stand the baby's withdrawal, when the baby's move away from the symbiosis with her causes her anxiety, the baby internalizes symbiotic remnants such as narcissistic needs, infantile dependence, and ambivalence about them. The self develops around these pathological internalizations (called *introjects*), and both their extremes can be found in the adult: feelings of inadequacy and inferiority together with grandiosity, submission, and aggression. When we see in a person evidence of a grandiose self, we can be sure to also find evidence for an inferior self. When we find the submissive self of a victim, we also can be sure to find evidence of aggression, hostility, and destructiveness.

30. See for example, Benjamin (1998); Goldner (1998); Tavris (1992).

31. See for example, Chodorow (1978) and Dinnerstein (1976).

32. Fairbairn (1952/1992) believes that the study of the schizoid personality is most fascinating and productive in the area of psychopathology. Although the schizoid condition is among the most difficult psychopathological conditions, because of his introversion, the schizoid still has an ability for self-examination that far exceeds that of the average person. Fairbairn also believed that everyone has schizoid episodes. Examples of such episodes that are familiar to all of us are the strange feeling we sometimes have in the presence of a familiar person or environment or the feeling of déjà vu, of having experienced an event before.

CHAPTER 9
THE SON FALLS IN LOVE WITH "MOTHER,"
THE DAUGHTER WITH "FATHER"

1. Freud, 1905/1962.
2. A significantly higher percentage of women than men described their partners as similar to their fathers, 78% of the women in the American sample compared to 31% of the men, and in the Israeli sample, 27% of the women compared to 3% of the men. A significantly higher percentage of men than women described their partners as similar to their mothers, 50% of the American men as compared to 43% of the women, and in the Israeli sample, 21% of the men as compared to 11% of the women. The cross-cultural differences between the Israelis and the Americans can be attributed to the greater psychological sophistication of the American sample and their greater familiarity with Freud's ideas in their popular version.
3. Freud, 1917/1963.
4. Horney, 1922/1973, 1967.
5. It should be noted that most people, both men and women, view sexuality and motherhood as mutually exclusive. If a woman is described as sexual, they do not see her as a mother, and if they are told she is a mother, they assume she is a bad mother. See Friedman et al., 1998.
6. Anna Freud lived with a woman called Dorothy Burlington for over 30 years, and there has been ample speculation as to the nature of that relationship, but without doubt, sexual or not, it was a primary attachment.
7. Freud, 1910/1957a.
8. Freud, 1914/1957b.
9. Romantic love as an expansion of the self is the subject of a book by Arthur and Elaine Aron (1986).
10. Drigotas et al., 1997.
11. Nathan, 1981.
12. Horney, 1922/1973, 1967.
13. Goldner, 1998.

CHAPTER 10
THE INTERNAL ROMANTIC IMAGE

1. When asked if there was a similarity between their relationship with their parents and their most significant romantic relationship, 70% of the interviewees (83% of the women and 55% of the men) answered yes. Because we can assume that the gender difference does not mean that women's relationships are more similar to their relationships with their parents than are those of the men, then another explanation is needed. One possible explanation is that women are more familiar with psychological thinking than men are, in part because they read more psychological books, and thus see the similarity between a childhood and adult relationship more clearly than men do. Support for this interpretation is provided by the cross-cultural comparison between the Americans and the Israelis. Only 30% of the Israeli interviewees, 38% of the women and 21% of the men, noticed a similarity between their

childhood relationship with their parents and their current romantic relationship. Again, it is far easier to explain both these cultural and gender differences as a result of differences in psychological sophistication than it is to explain them in terms of the different dynamics of intimate relationships in the two cultures.

2. People who described their childhood relationship with their parents as more similar to the relationship they had with their romantic partner also described their partner as more similar to their mother ($r = .31$; $p = .004$) and their father ($r = .41$; $p = .000$). They described themselves as feeling more secure in the relationship ($r = .24$; $p = .03$), as more able to be themselves in the relationship ($r = 22$; $p = .047$), and as more able to handle conflicts in the relationship ($r = .29$; $p = .009$). The romantic relationships they described had fewer conflicts than relationships described by people who did not notice a similarity between their partner and their parents ($r = .23$; $p = .036$).

3. Weinberg, 1997.

4. Other notable theoreticians of object relations theory, in addition to Margaret Mahler (1974), are Melanie Klein (1959), Ronald Fairbairn (1952), and Donald Winnicott (1965).

5. Mahler, 1974.

6. Blatt and Blass, 1996.

7. Dicks, 1967.

8. Givelber, 1990.

9. Reik, 1964.

10. See for example: Dicks (1967), Framo (1990), Meissner (1978), and Ogden (1979).

11. Low, 1990.

12. Goldner, 1998a.

13. Bowen, 1978.

14. Mittelman, 1944.

15. Meissner, 1978.

16. Boszormeny-Nagy and Ulrich, 1980.

17. Josselson, 1992; Klein, 1976.

18. Kohut, 1977.

19. Kohut, 1971.

20. Jung, 1964.

21. Hopcke, 1992.

22. Lumpert, 1997.

23. Money, 1986.

24. Shefer, 1971.

25. Crenshaw, 1996.

26. Fisher, 1992. In a later article, Helen Fisher distinguished three primary emotion categories for mating and reproduction that can be found in humans as well as other mammals: the sex drive, attraction, and attachment. Each emotion category is associated with a discrete constellation of neural correlates, and each has evolved to direct a specific aspect of reproduction. The sex drive is associated primarily with the sex hormones estrogen (female) and androgen (male). It evolved to motivate individuals to seek sexual union. The attraction system is associated primarily with

the catecholamines, neurotransmitters that activate various systems in the brain. This system evolved to facilitate mate choice and enable individuals to focus their mating efforts on preferred partners. The attachment system is associated primarily with peptides, amino acids that regulate various systems in the brain, including the reproductive system. The attachment system evolved to motivate individuals to engage in positive social behaviors and assume parental duties (Fisher, 1998).

27. MacLean, 1973.
28. Hendrix, 1992.
29. Pines, 1998a.
30. Pines, 1996.

CHAPTER 11
FOUR STORIES

1. The four tables demonstrate how the romantic interviews presented throughout the book have been analyzed. They serve to help interested readers understand the research appendix and how the numbers presented in it were obtained. They can also help interested readers to analyze their own relationships. It is recommended that couples do this type of analysis separately by using copies of the form presented in appendix 2 and then compare their scores.
2. For example, Feldman et al., 1998.

PART THREE: ROMANTIC LOVE IN LONG-TERM RELATIONSHIPS

1. Yalom, 1980; Pines, 1996.

CHAPTER 12
TURNING LOVE PROBLEMS INTO OPPORTUNITIES FOR GROWTH

1. Whitehouse, 1981.
2. Felmlee, 1995.
3. Pines, 1997.
4. Pines, 1996.
5. See for example, Bowen (1978), Dicks (1967), Freud (1921), Hendrix (1992), Kernberg (1974), and Meissner (1978). The psychodynamic perspective was presented in chapter 10 as part of the discussion on object relations theory.
6. A woman like Ann is likely to push intimate partners away with her angry outbursts because in this way, rather than be as helpless as she felt as a child when her father abandoned her and her mother, she can have some control on their leaving.
7. See Pines (1997) for details.
8. When the abusive partner is willing to work on the issues at the root of the abusive behavior, feminist psychoanalytic theory has some profound insights about the early childhood determinants of this behavior. Some of these were described in chapter 10 of this book. For an especially deep and profound article, see Virginia Goldner's

article, "Violence and Victimization in Intimate Relationship: A Feminist Intersubjective Perspective" (1998a).

9. This point was made by many leading couple therapists, among them Bowen (1978), Dicks (1967), Framo (1980), Givelber (1990), and Meissner (1978).

10. As noted in chapter 10, when these dynamics were first mentioned, most people did not see their partners the way they really were because old family ghosts obscured their views.

11. Hendrix, 1992.

12. Hendrix, 1988.

13. Pines and Aronson, 1988.

14. Morrow and O'Sullivan, 1998.

15. Knee, 1998.

16. Bader and Pearson, 1988.

17. Campbell et al., 1994.

CHAPTER 13
LOVE AND WORK: THE RELATIONSHIP BETWEEN THEIR UNCONSCIOUS CHOICES

1. See for example, Barnett, 1993; Baruch, Barnett and Rivers, 1983; Hazan and Shaver, 1990; Lee and Kanungo, 1984.

2. Hazan and Shaver, 1990.

3. Kanter, 1977.

4. Pines and Aronson, 1988.

5. See for example, Freudenberger, 1980, p. 13; Maslach, 1982, p. 3; Pines, 1993, p. 386; and Pines and Aronson, 1988, p.9.

6. See for example, Maslach and Leiter, 1997; Schaufeli et al., 1993.

7. See for example, Leaman, 1983; Pines, 1996.

8. See for example, psychoanalytic theory (Fischer, 1983; Freudenberger, 1980); Jungian theory (Garden, 1989, 1995); social comparison theory (Buunk et al., 1994); social exchange theory (Schaufeli et al., 1996; Van Yperen et al., 1992); and equity theory (Van Dierendonck et al., 1994).

9. See for example, Pines, 2002b.

10. Frankl, 1976, p. 154.

11. Becker, 1973.

12. See for example, Yalom, 1980.

13. See for example, Obholzer and Roberts, 1997.

14. Pines and Yanai, 2001.

15. Pines, 2000a.

16. See for example, Ellis and Miller, 1993.

17. Pines, 2002c.

18. Pines, 2000b.

19. Pines, 2002a.

20. Pines, 2002b.

21. For writers in the psychoanalytic tradition who address romantic choices, see Bowen, 1978; Dicks, 1967; Freud, 1917/1963; Mittelman, 1944.

22. See for example, Boles et al., 1997; Eckenrode and Gore, 1990; Golembiewski, 2000; Hochschild, 1999; Kinnunen and Mauno, 1998; Pensa, 1999; Valtinson, 1998; Zedeck, 1992.
23. See for example Bulka, 1984; Jackson and Maslach, 1982; Jayaratne et al., 1986; Westman, 2001; Westman and Etzion, 1995.
24. The study is described in Pines and Nunes, 2003. It included 109 Israelis (38% men and 62% women, mean age 31.8, 7 years of marriage), 838 Portuguese (51.6% men and 48.4% women, mean age 35.4, 10.0 years of marriage), 317 Spaniards (51.1% women and 48.9% men, mean age 34, 6.7 years of marriage), 144 British (86% men and 14% women; mean age 38.9, 6.7 years married), 54 Americans (mean age 41.8, 7.4 years of marriage), and 110 Finns (64% men and 36% women, mean age 33, 5.8 years of marriage). The Finn data were collected by Timo and Tuula Laes. The Portuguese, Spanish, and British data were collected by Renato Nunes. The American data were collected by Dale Larson. The findings showed similar significant moderate correlations (around $r = .30$) between career and couple burnout in all six samples.
25. Marks and MacDermid, 1996.

APPENDIX 1
ROMANTIC CHOICES WORKSHOPS: HOW TO DECIPHER
YOUR ROMANTIC ATTRACTION CODE

1. For a description of a couple burnout workshop, see chapter 9 in Pines, 1996.

References

Ainsworth, M. D. S. (1989). Attachment beyond infancy. *American Psychologist, 44,* 709–716.

Ainsworth, M. D. S., Blehar, M., Waters, E., & Wall, S. (1978). *Patterns of attachment.* Hillsdale, NJ: Erlbaum.

Alberoni, F. (1983). *Falling in love.* New York: Random House.

Alicke, M. D., Smith, R. H., & Klotz, M. L. (1986). Judgments of physical attractiveness: The roles of faces and bodies. *Personality and Social Psychology Bulletin, 12,* 381–389.

Allen, J.B., Kenrick, D.T., Linder, D.E., & McCall, M.A. (1985). Arousal and attribution: A response facilitation alternative to misattribution and negative reinforcement model. *Journal of Personality and Social Psychology, 57,* 261–270.

Amabille, T. (1983). Brilliant but cruel: Perceptions of negative evaluators, *Journal of Experimental Social Psychology, 19,* 146–156.

American Psychiatric Association. (1994). *Diagnostic and statistical manual of mental disorders* (4th ed.). Washington, DC: Author.

Anderson, N. H. (1981). *Foundations of information integration theory.* New York: Academic Press.

Archer, R. P. & Cash, T. F. (1985). Physical attractiveness and maladjustment among psychiatric inpatients. *Journal of Social and Clinical Psychology, 3,* 170–180.

Aron, A. & Aron, E. N. (1986). *Love and the expansion of self.* New York: Hemisphere.

Aron, A. & Aron, E. N. (1989). *The heart of social psychology.* Lexington, MA: Lexington Books.

Aron, A., Dutton, D. G., Aron, E. A., & Iverson, A. (1989). Experiences of falling in love. *Journal of Social and Personal Relationships, 6,* 243–257.

Aron, A., Paris, M., & Aron, E. N. (1995). Falling in love: Prospective studies of self-concept change. *Journal of Personality and Social Psychology, 69,* 1102–1112.

Aronson, E. (1998). *The Social Animal* (7th ed.). San Francisco: Freeman.

Aronson, E. & Linder, D.E. (1965). Gain and loss of esteem as determinants of interpersonal attractiveness. *Journal of Experimental Social Psychology, 1,* 156–171.

Aronson, E. & Mills, J. (1972). The effect of severity of initiation on liking for a group. *Journal of Personality and Social Psychology, 59,* 177–181.

Backman, C. W. (1981). Attraction in interpersonal relationships. In R. Turner and M. Rosenberg (Eds.), *Sociological perspective in social psychology* (pp. 235–268). New York: Basic Books.

Bader, E. & Pearson, P.T. (1988). *In quest of the mystical mate.* New York: Brunner/Mazel.

Banner, L. W. (1983). *American beauty.* New York: Knopf.

Barclay, A. M. & Haber, R. N. (1965). The relation of aggressive to sexual motivation. *Journal of Personality, 33,* 462–475.

Barnett, R. (1993). Multiple roles, gender, and psychological distress. In L. Goldberger and S. Breznitz (Eds.), *Handbook of stress* (2nd ed.). New York: Free Press.

Bartholomew, K. (1990). Avoidance of intimacy: An attachment perspective. *Journal of Social and Personal Relationships, 7,* 147–178.

Bartholomew, K. & Horowitz, L. M. (1991). Attachment styles among young adults: A test of a four-category model. *Journal of Personality and Social Psychology, 61,* 226–244.

Baruch, G., Barnett, R. C., & Rivers, C. (1983). *Lifeprints: New patterns of life and work for today's women.* New York: McGraw-Hill.

Basow, S. (1992). *Gender stereotypes and roles.* Pacific Grove, CA: Brooks/Cole.

Beall, A. E. & Sternberg, R. J. (1995). The social construction of love. *Journal of Social and Personal Relationships, 12,* 417–438.

Becker, E. (1973). *The denial of death.* New York: Free Press.

Benjamin, J. (1998, August). How was it for you? How intersubjective is sex? Keynote address presented at the annual convention of the American Psychological Association, Boston, MA.

Benton, C., Hernandez, A., Schmidt, A., Schmitz, M., Stone, A., & Weiner, B. (1983). Is hostility linked with affiliation among males and with achievement among females? A critique of Pollak and Gilligan. *Journal of Personality and Social Psychology, 45,* 1167–1171.

Berscheid, E. & Hartfield-Walster, E. (1978). *Interpersonal attraction* (2nd ed.). New York: Random House.

Berscheid, E. & Reis, H. T. (1998). Attraction and close relationships. In D. T. Gilbert et al. (Eds.), *The handbook of social psychology* (Vol. 2, pp. 193–281). Boston: McGraw-Hill.

Blatt, S. J. & Blass, R. B. (1996). Relatedness and self definition: A dialectic model of personality development. In G. G. Noam & K. W. Fischer (Eds.) *Development and vulnerabilities in close relationships.* Hillsdale, NJ: Elbaum.

Boles, J., Johnston, M. W., & Hair, J. F. (1997). Role stress, work–family conflict and emotional exhaustion: Inter-relationships and effects on some role related consequences. *Journal of Personal Selling and Sales Management, 17,* 17–28.

Bornstein, R. F., Leone, D. R., & Galley, D. J. (1987). The generalizability of subliminal mere exposure effects: Influence of stimuli perceived without awareness on social behavior. *Journal of Personality and Social Psychology, 53,* 1070–1079.

Bossard, J. H. S. (1932). Residential propinquity as a factor in mate selection. *American Journal of Sociology, 38,* 219–224.

Boszormeny-Nagy, I. & Ulrich, D. (1980). Contextual family therapy. In A. S. Gurman and D. P. Kniskern (Eds.), *Handbook of family therapy* (pp. 159–186). New York: Brunner/Mazel.

Bowen, M. (1978). *Family therapy in clinical practice.* New York: Jason Aronson.

Bowlby, J. (1982). *Attachment and loss. Vol. 1. Attachment* (2nd ed.). New York: Basic Books.

Brehm, S. (1992). *Intimate relationships.* New York: McGraw-Hill.

Brehm, S. S. & Brehm, J. W. (1981*). Psychological reactance: A theory of freedom and control.* New York: Academic Press.

Brennan, K. A. & Shaver, P. R. (1995). Dimensions of adult attachment, affect regulation, and romantic relationship functioning. *Personality and Social Psychology Bulletin, 21,* 267–283.

Brickman, P., Redfield, J., Harrison, A. A., & Crandall, R. (1972). Drive and predisposition in the attitudinal effects of mere exposure. *Experimental Social Psychology, 8*, 31–44.

Brinberg, D.M. & Castel, P. A. (1982). A resource theory approach to interpersonal interactions: A test of Foa's theory. *Journal of Experimental Social Psychology, 43*, 260–269.

Bulka, R. P. (1984). Logotherapy as an answer to burnout, *International Forum for Logotherapy, 7*, 8–17.

Burgess, R. L. & Huston, T. L. (1979). *Social exchange in developing relationships.* New York: Academic Press.

Burleson, B. R. & Denton, W. H. (1992). A new look at similarity and attraction in marriage: Similarities in social-cognitive and communication skills as predictors of attraction and satisfaction. *Communication Monographs, 59*, 268–287.

Burleson B. R., Kunkel, A. W., & Szolwinski, J. B. (1997). Similarity in cognitive complexity and attraction to friends and lovers. *Journal of Constructivist Psychology, 10*, 221–248.

Buss, D. M. (1985). Human mate selection. *American Scientist, 73*, 47–51.

Buss, D. M. (1994). *The evolution of desire: Strategies of human mating.* New York: Basic Books.

Buss, D. M., Abbott, M., Angleitner, A., & Asherian, A., et al. (1990). International preferences in mate selection: Evolutionary hypothesis tested in 37 cultures. *Behavioral and Brain Sciences, 12*, 1–49.

Buss, D.M. & Barnes, M. (1986). Preference in human mate selection. *Journal of Personality and Social Psychology, 50*, 559–570.

Buss, D. M. & Schmitt, D. P. (1993). Sexual strategies theory: An evolutionary perspective on human mating. *Psychological Review, 100*, 204–232.

Buunk, B. P., Schaufeli, W. B., & Ybema, J. F. (1994). Burnout, uncertainty, and the desire for social comparison among nurses. *Journal of Applied Social Psychology, 24*, 1701–1718.

Byrne, D. (1971). *The Attraction Paradigm.* New York: Academic Press.

Byrne, D. (1997). An overview (and underview) of research and theory within the attraction paradigm. *Journal of Social and Personal Relationships, 14*, 417–431.

Byrne, D. & Blaylock, B. (1963). Similarity and assumed similarity of attitudes between husbands and wives. *Journal of Abnormal and Social Psychology, 67*, 636–640.

Byrne, D., Ervin, C. E., & Lamberth, J. (1970). Continuity between the experimental study of attraction and real life computer dating. *Journal of Personality and Social Psychology, 16*, 157–165.

Calvert, J. D. (1988). Physical attractiveness: A review and reevaluation of its role in social skill research. *Behavioral Assessment, 10*, 29–42.

Campbell, W., Sedikides, C., & Bosson, J. (1994). Romantic involvement, self discrepancy and psychological well-being. *Personal Relationships, 1*, 399–404.

Carnegie, D. (1982). *How to win friends and influence people.* New York: Pocket Books.

Cash, T. F. & Duncan, N. C. (1984). Physical attractiveness stereotyping among black American college students. *Journal of Social Psychology, 122*, 71–77.

Cashdan, E. (1993). Attracting mates: Effects of parental investment on mate attraction strategies. *Ethology and Sociobiology, 14*, 1–23.

Caspi, A. & Harbener, E. S. (1990). Continuity and change: Assortive marriage and the consistency of personality in adulthood. *Journal of Personality and Social Psychology, 58*, 250–258.

Chafetz, J. S. (1975). *Masculine/feminine or human?* Itasca, IL: Peacock.

Chodorow, N. (1978). *The reproduction of mothering.* Berkeley, CA: University of California Press.

Clarke, A. C. (1952). An examination of the operation of propinquity as a factor in mate selection. *American Sociological Review, 27,* 17–22.

Clark, L. A. & Watson, D. (1988). Mood and the mundane: Relations between daily life events and self reported mood. *Journal of Personality and Social Psychology, 54,* 296–308.

Clark, R. D. & Hatfield, E. (1989). Gender differences in receptivity to sexual offers. *Journal of Psychology and Human Sexuality, 2,* 39–55.

Clore, G. L. & Byrne, D. (1974). A reinforcement–affect model of attraction. In T. L. Houston (Ed.), *Foundations of interpersonal attraction* (pp. 143–170). New York: Academic Press.

Cochran, S. D. & Peplau, L. A. (1985). Value orientation in heterosexual relationships. *Psychology of Women Quarterly, 9,* 477–488.

Cohen, B., Waugh, G., & Place, K. (1989). At the movies: An unobtrusive study of arousal attraction. *Journal of Social Psychology, 129,* 691–693.

Cohen, L. L. & Shotland, R. L. (1996). Timing of the first sexual intercourse in a relationship: Expectations, experiences and perceptions of others. *Journal of Sex Research, 33,* 291–299.

Collins, N. L. & Read, S. J. (1990). Adult attachment: Working models and relationship quality in dating couples. *Journal of Personality and Social Psychology, 58,* 644–663.

Cramer, R. E., Cupp, R. G., & Kuhn, J. A. (1993). Male attractiveness: Masculinity with a feminine touch. *Current Psychology Development, Learning, Personality, Social, 12,* 142–150.

Crenshaw, T. L. (1996). *The alchemy of love and lust.* New York: Putnam.

Cunningham, M. R. (1986). Measuring the physical in physical attractiveness: Quasi-experiments in sociobiology of female facial beauty. *Journal of Personality and Social Psychology, 50,* 925–935.

Cunningham, M. R, Roberts, A. R., Barbee, A. P., Druen, P. B., & Wu, C. H. (1995). Their ideas of beauty are, on the whole, the same as ours: Consistency and variability in cross-cultural perception of female physical attractiveness. *Journal of Personality and Social Psychology, 68,* 261–279.

Curran, J. P. & Lippold, S. (1975). The effects of physical attraction and attitude similarity on attraction in dating dyads. *Journal of Personality, 43,* 528–539.

Curtis, R. C. & Miller, K. (1986). Believing another likes or dislikes you: Behaviors making the beliefs come true. *Journal of Personality and Social Psychology, 51,* 284–290.

Cyranowski, J. M. & Andersen, B. (1998). Schemas, sexuality and romantic attachment. *Journal of Personality and Social Psychology, 74,* 1364–1379.

Darley, J. M. & Berscheid, E. (1967). Increased liking as a result of the anticipation of personal contact. *Human Relations, 20,* 29–40.

Darwin, C. (1871). *The descent of man and selection in relation to sex.* New York: Appleton.

Darwin, C. (1910). *The expression of emotion in man and animals.* New York: Appleton.

Davis, S. (1990). Men as success objects and women as sex objects: A study of personal advertisements. *Sex Roles, 23,* 43–50.

de Munck, V. C. (1998). Lust, love, and arranged marriages in Sri-Lanka. In V. C. de Munck (Ed.), *Romantic love and sexual behavior: Perspective from the social sciences* (pp. 285–300). Westport, CT: Praeger.

de-Raad, B. & Boddema-Winesemius, M. (1992). Factors in the assortment of human mates: Differential preferences in Germany and the Netherlands. *Personality and Individual Differences, 13,* 103–114.

de Rougemont, D. (1983). *Love in the Western world.* New York: Pantheon. (Original work published in 1940.)

Desrochers, S. (1995). What types of men are most attractive and most repulsive to women? *Sex Roles, 32,* 375–391.

Diamond, J. (1996). The best ways to sell sex. *Discover, 17,* 78–86.

Dicks, H. V. (1967). *Marital tensions.* New York: Basic Books.

Dietch, J. (1978). Love, sex-roles and psychological health. *Journal of Personality Assessment, 42,* 626–634.

Dinnerstein, D. (1976). *The mermaid and the minotaur: Sexual arrangements and human malaise.* New York: Harper and Row.

Dion, K. (1972). Physical attractiveness and evaluations of children's transgressions. *Journal of Personality and Social Psychology, 24,* 207–213.

Dion, K. K., Berscheid, E., & Walster, E. (1972). What is beautiful is good. *Journal of Personality and Social Psychology, 24,* 285–290.

Dion, K. K. & Dion, K. L. (1975). Self-esteem and romantic love. *Journal of Personality, 43,* 39–57.

Dion, K. K. & Dion, K. L. (1985). Personality, gender and the phenomenology of romantic love. In P. Shaver (Ed.), *Self, situation and social behavior: Review of personality and social psychology* (Vol. 6, pp. 209–238). Beverly Hills, CA: Sage.

Dion, K. L. & Dion, K. K. (1973). Correlates of romantic love. *Journal of Consulting and Clinical Psychology, 41,* 51–56.

Dion, K. L. & Dion, K. K. (1987). Belief in a just world and physical attractiveness stereotyping. *Journal of Personality and Social Psychology, 52,* 775–780.

Dittes, J. E. (1959). Attractiveness of groups as function of self-esteem and acceptance by group. *Journal of Abnormal and Social Psychology, 59,* 114–140.

Drigotas, S. M., Rusbult, C. E., Wieselquist, J., & Whitton, S. W. (1997, August). *Close partner as sculptor of the ideal self: Behavioral affirmation and the Michelangelo phenomenon.* Paper presented at the annual convention of the American Psychological Association, Chicago, IL.

Drigotas, S. M. (1993). Similarity revisited: A comparison of similarity-attraction versus dissimilarity-repulsion. *British Journal of Social Psychology, 32,* 365–377.

Driscoll, R., Davis, K. W., & Lipetz, M. E. (1971). Parental interference and romantic love. *Journal of Personality and Social Psychology, 24,* 1–10.

Dryer, D. C. & Horowitz, L. M. (1997). When do opposites attract? Interpersonal complementarity versus similarity. *Journal of Personality and Social Psychology, 72,* 592–603.

Dutton, D. G. & Aron, A. P. (1974). Some evidence for heightened sexual attraction under conditions of high anxiety *Journal of Personality and Social Psychology, 30,* 510–517.

Eagly, A. H. (1987). *Sex differences in social behavior: A social role interpretation.* Hillsdale, NJ: Erlbaum.

Eckenrode, J. & Gore, S. (Eds.) (1990). *Stress between work and family.* New York: Plenum.

Ellis, B. H. & Miller, K. I. (1993). The role of assertiveness, personal control, and participation in the prediction of nurse burnout. *Journal of Applied Communication Research, 21,* 327–342.

Ellis, B. J. (1992). The evolution of sexual attraction: Evaluative mechanisms in women. In J. H. Barkow, L. Cosmedes, & Tooby (Eds.), *The adapted mind: Evolutionary psychology and the generation of culture* (pp. 267–288). New York: Oxford University Press.

Erikson, E. H. (1959). Identity and the life cycle. *Psychological Issues, 1,* 1–171.

Etcoff, N. (2000). *Survival of the prettiest.* New York: Ancorbooks.

Fairbairn, W. R. D. (1952). *An object-relations theory of personality.* New York: Basic Books.

Fairbairn, W. R. D. (1992). Schizoid factors in the personality. In *Psychoanalytic studies of personality* (pp. 3–27). New York: Routledge. (Original work published in 1952.)

Feingold, A. (1988). Matching for attractiveness in romantic partners and same sex friends: A meta-analysis and theoretical critique. *Psychological Bulletin, 104,* 226–235.

Feingold, A. (1990). Gender differences in effects of physical attractiveness on romantic attraction: A comparison across five research paradigms. *Journal of Personality and Social Psychology, 59,* 981–993.

Feingold, A. (1992). Gender differences in mate selection preferences: A test of the parental investment model. *Psychological Bulletin, 112,* 125–139.

Feldman, S. S., Gowen, L. K., & Fisher, L. (1998). Family relationships and gender as predictors of romantic intimacy in young adults. *Journal of Research on Adolescence, 8,* 263–286.

Felmlee, D. H. (1995). Fatal attractions: Affection and Disaffection in intimate relationships. *Journal of Social and Personal Relationships, 12,* 295–311.

Festinger, L. (1951). Architecture and group membership. *Journal of Social Issues, 7,* 152–163.

Fisher, H. E. (1992). *Anatomy of love.* New York: Norton.

Fisher, H. E. (1998). Lust, attraction and attachment in mammalian reproduction. *Human Nature, 9,* 23–52.

Foa, E. B. & Foa, U. G. (1980). Resource theory: Interpersonal behavior as exchange. In K. J. Gergen, M. S. Greenberg, & R. H. Willis (Eds.), *Social exchange: Advances in theory and research* (pp. 77–94). New York: Plenum.

Folkes, V. S. (1982). Forming relationships and the matching hypothesis. *Personality and Social Psychology Bulletin, 8,* 631–636.

Foster, C. A., Witcher, B. S., Campbell, W. K., & Green, J. D. (1998). Arousal and attraction: Evidence for automatic and controlled processes. *Journal of Personality and Social Psychology, 74*, 86–101.

Framo, J. (1990). Integrating families of origin into couple therapy. In R. Chasin, H. Grunebaum, & Herzig, M. (Eds.), *One couple four realities: Multiple perspectives on couple therapy* (pp. 49–82). New York: Guilford Press.

Frankl, V. E. (1976). *Man's search for meaning.* New York: Pocket Books.

Freud, A. (1946). *The ego and the mechanisms of defense.* New York: International Universities Press.

Freud, S. (1955). *Group psychology and the analysis of the ego* (Standard ed., Vol. 18, pp. 65–143). London: Hogarth Press. (Original work published in 1921.)

Freud, S. (1957a). *Leonardo da Vinci: A study in psychosexuality* (Standard ed., Vol. 11). London: Hogarth Press. (Original work published in 1910.)

Freud, S. (1957). *On narcissism: An introduction* (Standard ed., part 14, pp. 73–102). London: Hogarth Press. (Original work published in 1914.)

Freud, S. (1962). *Three essays on the theory of sexuality.* New York: Basic. (Original work published in 1905.)

Freud, S. (1963). *Introduction lectures on Psychoanalysis* (Part 3). London: Hogarth Press. (Original work published in 1917.)

Freudenberger, H. J. (1980). *Burn-out: The high cost of high achievement.* Garden City, NY: Doubleday.

Friedman, A., Weinberg, H., & Pines, A. M. (1998). Sexuality and motherhood: Mutually exclusive in perception of women. *Sex Roles, 38*, 781–800.

Fischer, H. (1983). A Psychoanalytic view of burnout. In B. Farber (Ed.), *Stress and burnout in the human service professions* (pp. 40–45). New York: Pergammon.

Frieze, I. H, Olson, J. E., & Russell, J. (1991). Attractiveness and income for men and women in management. *Journal of Applied Social Psychology, 21*, 1039–1057.

Fromm, E. (1956). *The art of loving.* New York: Harper and Row.

Galton, F. (1884). The measurement of character. *Fortnightly Review, 36*, 179–185.

Gangestad, S. W. & Thornhill, R. (1997). Human sexual selection and developmental stability. In J. A. Simpson & D. T. Kenrick (Eds.), *Evolutionary social psychology.* Mahwah, NJ: Erlbaum.

Garden, A. M. (1989). Burnout: The effect of psychological type on research. *Journal of Occupational Psychology, 62*, 223–234.

Garden, A. M. (1995). The purpose of burnout: A Jungian interpretation. In R. Crandall & P. L. Perrewe (Eds.), *Occupational stress: A handbook. series in health psychology and behavioral medicine* (pp. 207–222). Philadelphia: Taylor & Francis.

Geiselman, R. E., Haight, N. A., & Kimata, L. G. (1984). Context effects in the perceived physical attractiveness of faces. *Journal of Experimental Social Psychology, 20*, 409–424.

Gergen, M. M., & Gergen, K. J. (1992). Attributions, accounts and close relationships: Close calls and relational resolutions. In J. H. Harvey, T. L. Orbuch, & A. L. Weber (Eds.), *Attributions, accounts and close relationships.* New York: Springer.

Gillen, B. (1981). Physical attractiveness. A determinant of two types of goodness. *Personality and Social Psychology Bulletin, 7*, 277–281.

Givelber, F. (1990). Object relations and the couple. In R. Chasin, H. Grunebaum, & M. Herzig (Eds.), *One couple four realities: Multiple perspectives on couple therapy* (pp. 171–190). New York: Guilford Press.

Goffman, E. (1952). On cooling the mark out: Some aspects of adaptation to failure. *Psychiatry, 15,* 451–463.

Goldner, V. (1998, November). Theorizing gender and sexual subjectivity: Modern and post-modern perspectives. Paper presented at the Israeli Association of Psychotherapy, Israel.

Goldner, V. (1998a, November). Violence and victimization in intimate relationships: A feminist intersubjective perspective. Paper presented at the Israeli Association of Psychotherapy, Israel.

Golembiewski, R. T. (2000). Family and work: An integrating design. In R. Golembiewski (Ed.), *Handbook of organizational consultation* (2nd ed). New York: Dekker.

Goodwin, R. (1990). Sex differences among partner preferences. Are the sexes really very similar? *Sex Roles, 23,* 501–513.

Gouaux, C. (1971). Induced affective states and interpersonal attraction. *Journal of Personality and Social Psychology, 20,* 37–43.

Green, B. L. & Kenrick, D. T. (1994). The attractiveness of gender-typed traits at different relationship levels: Androgynous characteristics may be desirable after all. *Personality and Social Psychology Bulletin, 20,* 244–253.

Green, S. K. & Sandos, P. (1983). Perceptions of male and female initiators of relationships. *Sex Roles, 9,* 849–852.

Greenlees, I. A. & McGrew, W. C. (1994). Sex and age differences in preferences and tactics of mate attraction: Analysis of published advertisements. *Ethology and Sociobiology, 15,* 59–72.

Grube, J., Kleinhesselink, R., & Kearney, K. (1982). Male self-acceptance and attraction toward women. *Personality and Social Psychology Bulletin, 8,* 107–112.

Grush, J. E. & Yehl, J. G. (1979). Marital roles, sex differences and interpersonal attraction. *Journal of Personality and Social Psychology, 37,* 116–123.

Guthrie, E. R. (1938). *The psychology of human conflict.* New York: Harper.

Hadjistavropoulos, T. & Genest, M. (1994). The underestimation of the role of physical attractiveness in dating preferences: Ignorance or taboo? *Canadian Journal of Behavioral Science, 26,* 298–318.

Hartfield, E. & Rapson, R. L. (1992). Similarity and attraction in intimate relationships. *Communication Monographs, 59,* 209–212.

Hartfield, E. & Rapson,, R. L. (1993). *Love sex and intimacy: Their biology, psychology and history.* New York: Harper Collins.

Hartfield, E. & Sprecher, S. (1986). *Mirror, mirror … the importance of looks in everyday life.* Albany: State University of New York Press.

Hartz, A. J. (1996). Psycho-socionomics: Attractiveness research from a societal perspective. *Journal of Social Behavior and Personality, 11,* 683–694.

Hazan, C. & Shaver, P. R. (1987). Romantic love conceptualized as an attachment process. *Journal of Personality and Social Psychology, 52,* 511–524.

Hazan, C. & Shaver, P. R. (1990). Love and work: An attachment-theoretical perspective. *Journal of Personality and Social Psychology, 59,* 270–280.

Hendrick, S. S. (1981). Self disclosure and marital satisfaction. *Journal of Personality and Social Psychology, 40,* 1150–1159.

Hendrix, H. (1992). *Keeping the love you find.* New York: Pocket Books.

Hensley, W. E. (1994). Height as a basis for interpersonal attraction. *Adolescence, 29,* 469–474.

Hinsz, V. B. (1989). Facial resemblance in engaged and married couples. *Journal of Social and Personal Relationships, 6,* 223–229.

Hochschild, A. R. (1999). *The time bind: When work becomes home and home becomes work.* New York: Henry Holt.

Homans, G. (1961). *Social behavior: Its elementary forms.* New York: Harcourt Brace.

Hopcke, R. H. (1992). *The male soul figure.* Talk presented at the Men's Center Forum, The Men's Center Foundation, Berkeley, CA.

Horney, K. (1973). On the genesis of the castration complex in women. In J. P. Miller (Ed.), *Psychoanalysis and women.* New York: Brunner/Mazel. (Original work published in 1922, pp. 49–64.)

Horney, K. (1967). *Feminine psychology.* New York: Norton.

Hoyt, L. L. & Hudson, J. W. (1981). Personal characteristics important in mate preference among college students. *Social Behavior and Personality, 9,* 93–96.

Hrdy, S. B. (1988). Empathy, polyandry, and the myth of the coy female. In R. Bleier (Ed.), *Feminist approaches to science.* New York: Pergammon, 119–146.

Hubbard, R. (1990). *The politics of women's biology.* New Brunswick, NJ: Rutgers University Press.

Hyde, J. S. (1981). How large are the cognitive gender differences? A meta analysis. *American Psychologist, 36,* 892–901.

Hyde, J. S. (1984). How large are gender differences in aggression? A developmental meta analysis. *Developmental Psychology, 20,* 722–736.

Hyde, J. S. (1990). Meta-analysis and the psychology of gender differences. *Signs: Journal of Women in Culture and Society, 16,* 55–73.

Hyde, J. S. (1993, August). *Sex, love and psychology.* Paper presented at the annual convention of the American Psychological Association, Toronto, Ontario, Canada.

Hyde, J. S. & Linn, M. C. (1986). *The psychology of gender: Advances through meta analysis.* Baltimore, MD: Johns Hopkins University Press.

Hyde, J. S. & Linn, M. C. (1988). Gender differences in verbal ability: A meta analysis. *Psychological Bulletin, 104,* 53–69.

Ickees, W. (1993). Traditional gender roles: Do they make, and then break, our relationships? *Journal of Social Issues, 49,* 71–86.

Izard, C. E. (1960). Personality similarity and friendship. *Journal of Abnormal and Social Psychology, 61,* 47–51.

Jackson, L. A. & Ervin, K. S. (1992). Height stereotypes of women and men: The liability of shortness for both sexes. *Journal of Social Psychology, 132,* 433–445.

Jackson, S. E. & Maslach, C. (1982). After-effects of job-related stress: Families as victims. *Journal of Occupational Behavior, 3,* 63–77.

Jacobson, N. & Christensen, A. (1996). *Integrative couple therapy.* New York: Norton, chap. 10.

Jayaratne, S., Chess, W. A., & Knukel, D. A. (1986). Burnout: Its impact on child welfare workers and their spouses. *Social Work, 31,* 53–59.

Jensen-Campbell, L. A., Grazino, W. G., & West, S. G. (1995). Dominance, prosocial orientation and female preference: Do nice guys really finish last? *Journal of Personality and Social Psychology, 68*, 427–440.

Johnson, D. E. & Pittenger, J. B. (1984). Attribution, the attractiveness stereotype, and the elderly. *Developmental Psychology, 20*, 1168–1172.

Jones, D. (1995). Sexual selection, physical attractiveness and facial neoteny: Cross cultural evidence and implications. *Current Anthropology, 36*, 723–748.

Jones, E. (1964). *Ingratiation.* New York: Appleton Century Crofts.

Jones, E., Bell, L., & Aronson, E. (1971). The reciprocation of attraction from similar and dissimilar others: A study in person perception and evaluation. In C. G. McClintock (Ed.), *Experimental social psychology* (pp. 142–183). New York: Holt, Rinehart, and Winston.

Josselson, R. E. (1992). *The space between us.* San Francisco: Jossey-Bass.

Jung, C. G. (1964). *Man and his symbols.* New York: Dell.

Kacerguis, M. A. & Adams, G. R. (1980). Erikson's stage resolution: The relationship between identity and intimacy. *Journal of Youth and Adolescence, 9*, 117–126.

Kalick, S. M. & Hamilton, T. E. (1986). The matching hypothesis reexamined. *Journal of Personality and Social Psychology, 51*, 673–682.

Kanter, R. (1977). *Work and family in the United States: A critical review and agenda for policy.* New York: Sage.

Kaplan, M. F. (1981). State disposition in social judgment. *Bulletin of the Psychonomic Society, 18*, 27–29.

Karraker, K. H., Vogel, D. A., & Evans, S. (1987, August). *Responses of students and pregnant women to newborn physical attractiveness.* Paper presented at the annual convention of the American Psychological Association, New York.

Keller, M. C. & Young, R. K. (1996). Mate assortment in dating and married couples. *Personality and Individual Differences, 21*, 217–221.

Kellerman, J., Lewis, J., & Lard, J. D. (1989). Looking and loving: The effects of mutual gaze on feelings of romantic love. *Journal of Research in Personality, 23*, 145–161.

Kelley, H. H., Berscheid, E., Christensen, A., Harvey, J. H., & Huston, T. L., et al. (1983). Analyzing close relationships. In H. H. Kelley, E. Berscheid, A. Christensen, & J. H. Harvey, et al. (Eds.), *Close relationships* (pp. 20–67). San Francisco: Freeman.

Kenrick, D. T., Groth, G. E., Trost, M. R., & Sadalla, E. (1993). Integrating evolutionary and social exchange perspectives on relationships: Effects of gender, self-appraisal and involvement level on mate selection criteria. *Journal of Personality and Social Psychology, 64*, 951–969.

Kenrick, D. T. & Keefe, R. C. (1992). Age preferences in mates reflect sex differences in human reproductive strategies. *Behavioral and Brain Sciences, 15*, 75–113.

Kerckoff, A. C. (1974). The social context of interpersonal attraction. In T. L. Huston (Ed.), *Foundations of interpersonal attraction* (pp. 61–78). New York: Academic Press.

Kernberg, O. (1974). Barriers to falling and remaining in love. *Journal of the American Psychoanalytic Association, 22*, 486–511.

Kernberg, O. (1980). Love, the couple, and the group: A psychoanalytic frame. *Psychoanalytic Quarterly, 129*, 78–108.

Kiesler, S. B. & Baral, R. Z. (1970). The search for romantic partner: The effects of self-esteem and physical attractiveness on romantic behavior. In K. Gergen & D. Marlow (Eds.), *Personality and social behavior* (pp. 155–165). Reading, MA: Addison–Wesley.

Kinnunen, U. & Mauno, S. (1998). Antecedents and outcomes of work-family conflict among women and men in Finland. *Human Relations, 51*, 157–177.

Kirkpatrick, L. A. (1998). Evolution, pair-bonding and reproductive strategies: A re-conceptualization of adult attachment. In J. A. Simpson et al. (Eds.), *Attachment theory and close relationships* (pp. 353–393). New York: Guilford Press.

Klein, G. S. (1976). *Psychoanalytic theory.* New York: International University Press.

Klein, M. (1959). *The psychoanalysis of children.* London: Hogarth.

Kleinke, C.L. & Staneski, R. A. (1980). First impressions of female bust size. *Journal of Social Psychology, 110*, 123–134.

Knee, C. R. (1998). Implicit theories of relationships: Assessment and prediction of ro-mantic relationship initiation, coping and longevity. *Journal of Personality and Social Psychology, 74*, 360–370.

Kohut, H. (1971). *The analysis of the self.* New York: International Universities Press.

Kohut, H. (1977). *The restoration of the self.* New York: International Universities Press.

Krueger, R. F. & Caspi, A. (1993). Personality, arousal, and pleasure: A test of competing models of interpersonal attraction. *Personality and Individual Differences, 14*, 105–111.

Kruglanski, A., E. & Mayseless, O. (1987). Motivational effects in the social compari-son of opinions. *Journal of Personality and Social Psychology, 53*, 834–842.

Lahm, H., Weismann, U., & Keller, K. (1998). Subjective determinants of attraction: Self perceived causes of the rise and decline of liking, love and being in love. *Personal Relationships, 5*, 91–104.

Larson, J. H. (1992). "You're my one and only": Premarital counseling for unrealistic beliefs about mate selection. *American Journal of Family Therapy, 20*, 242–253.

Lasswell, M. & Lobsenz, N. (1980). *Styles of loving: Why you love the way you do.* New York: Ballantine.

Lavrakas, P. J. (1975). Female preferences for male physique. *Journal of Research in Personality, 9*, 324–334.

Leaman, D. R. (1983). Needs assessment: A technique to reverse marital burnout. *Journal of Psychology and Christianity, 2*, 47–51.

Lee, J. A. (1998). Ideologies of lovestyle and sexstyle. In V. C. de Munck et al. (Eds.), *Romantic love and sexual behavior: Perspectives from the social sciences* (pp. 33–76). Westport, CT: Praeger.

Lee, M. D. & Kanungo, R. N. (Eds.). (1984). *Management of work and personal life.* New York: Praeger.

Leigh, B. C. & Aramburu, B. (1996). The role of alcohol and gender choices and judge-ments about hypothetical sexual encounters. *Journal of Applied Social Psychology, 26*, 20–30.

Levinger, G. & Breedlove, J. (1966). Interpersonal attraction and agreement: A study of marriage partners. *.Journal of Personality and Social Psychology, 3*, 367–372.

Levy, M. B. & Davis, K. E. (1988). Love styles and attachment styles compared: Their relations to each other and to various relationship characteristics. *Journal of Social and Personal Relationships, 5*, 439–472.

Lewis, R. A. (1973). A longitudinal test of the developmental framework for premarital dyadic formation. *Journal of Marriage and the Family, 35,* 16–25.

Lindholm, C. (1998). The future of love. In V. C. de Munck et al. (Eds.), *Romantic love and sexual behavior: Perspectives from the social sciences* (pp. 17–32). Westport, CT: Praeger.

Lock, K. D. & Horowitz, L. M. (1990). Satisfaction in interpersonal interactions as a function of similarity in level of dysphoria. *Journal of Personality and Social Psychology, 58,* 823–831.

Lot, A. J., Lot, B. E., Reed, T., & Crow, T. (1960). Personality trait description of differently liked persons. *Journal of Personality and Social Psychology, 16,* 284–290.

Low, N. (1990). Women in couples: How their experience of relationships differs from men's. In R. Chasin, H. Grunebaum, & M. Herzig (Eds.), *One couple four realities: Multiple perspectives on couple therapy* (pp. 249–268). New York: Guilford Press.

Lumpert, A. (1997). *The evolution of love.* Westport, CT: Praeger.

Lykken, D. T. & Tellegen, A. (1993). Is human mating adventitious or the result of lawful choice? A twin study of mate selection. *Journal of Personality and Social Psychology, 65,* 56–68.

Lynn, M. & Shurgot, B. A. (1984). Responses to lonely hearts advertisements: Effects of reported physical attractiveness, physique and coloration. *Personality and Social Psychology Bulletin, 10,* 349–357.

Macerguis, M. A. & Adams, G. R. (1980). Erikson's stage resolution: The relationship between identity and intimacy. *Journal of Youth and Adolescence, 9,* 117–126.

MacLean, P. D. (1973). *The triune concept of the brain and behavior.* Toronto: Toronto University Press.

Mahler, M. (1974). Symbiosis and Individuation: The psychological birth of the human infant. *The Psychological Study of the Child, 29,* 98–106.

Mahler, M. S., Pine, F., & Bergman, A. (1975). *The psychological birth of the human infant.* New York: Basic Books.

Major, B. Carrington, P. I., & Carnevale, P. I. D. (1984). Physical attractiveness and self-esteem: Attributions for praise from other-sex evaluator. *Personality and Social Psychology Bulletin, 10,* 43–50.

Margolin, L. & White, G. L. (1987). The continuing role of physical attractiveness in marriage, *Journal of Marriage and the Family, 49,* 21–28.

Marioles, N. S., Strickert, D. P., & Hammer, A. L. (1996). Attraction, satisfaction, and psychological types of couples. *Journal of Psychological Type, 36,* 16–27.

Marks, S. R. & MacDermid, S. M. (1996). Multiple roles and the self: A theory of role balance. *Journal of Marriage and the Family, 61,* 476–490.

Marks, G. & Miller, N. (1982). Target attractiveness as a mediator of assumed attitude similarity. *Personality and Social Psychology Bulletin, 8,* 728–735.

Martin, C. L. (1987). A ratio measure of sex stereotyping. *Journal of Personality and Social Psychology, 52,* 489–499.

Maslach, C. (1982). *Burnout: The cost of caring.* Englewood Cliffs, NJ: Prentice Hall.

Maslach, C. & Leiter, M. P. (1997). *The truth about burnout: How organizations cause personal stress and what to do about it.* San Francisco: Jossey Bass.

Maslow, A. (1970). *Motivation and personality.* New York: Harper and Row.

Masterson, J. F. (1981). *The narcissistic and borderline disorders.* New York: Brunner/Mazel.

May, J. L. & Hamilton, P. A. (1980). Effects of musically evoked affect on women's interpersonal attraction and perceptual judgment of physical attractiveness of men. *Motivation and Emotion, 4,* 217–228.

May, R. (1969). *Love and will.* New York: Dell.

Maybach, K. L. & Gold, S. R. (1994). Hyperfemininity and attraction to macho and non-macho men. *Journal of Sex Research, 31,* 91–98.

Mehrabian, A. (1989). Marital choice and compatibility as a function of their trait similarity-dissimilarity. *Psychological Reports, 65,* 1202.

Meissner, W. W. (1978). The conceptualization of marriage and family dynamic from a psychoanalytic perspective. In T. Paolino & B. McCrady (Eds.), *Marriage and marital therapy: Psychoanalytic, behavioral and systems therapy perspectives* (pp. 25–88). New York: Brunner/Mazel.

Merikangas, K. R., Weissman,, M. M., Prusoff, B. A., & John, K. (1988). Assortative mating and affective disorders: Psychopathology in offspring. *Psychiatry, 51,* 48–57.

Mickelson, K. D., Kessler, R. C., & Shaver, P. R. (1997). Adult attachment in a nationally representative sample, *Journal of Personality and Social Psychology, 73,* 1092–1106.

Miller, J. B. (1976). *Toward a new psychology of women.* Boston: Beacon Press.

Mita, T. H., Dermer, M., & Knight, J. (1977). Reversed facial images and the mere–exposure hypothesis. *Journal of Personality and Social Psychology, 35,* 397–601.

Mittelman, B. (1944). Complementary neurotic reactions in intimate relationships. *Psychoanalytic Quarterly, 13,* 479–491.

Money, J. (1986). *Lovemaps: Clinical concepts of sexual/erotic health and pathology, paraphilia and gender transposition in childhood, adolescence and maturity.* New York: Irvington.

Moore, M. M. (1985). Nonverbal courtship patterns in women: Context and consequences. *Ethology and Sociobiology, 6,* 237–247.

Moreland, R. L. & Beach, S. R. (1992). Exposure effects in the classroom: the development of affinity among students. *Journal of Experimental Social Psychology, 28,* 255–276.

Morrow, G. D. & O'Sullivan, C. (1998). Romantic ideals as comparison levels: Implications for satisfaction and commitment in romantic involvements. In V. C. de Munck (Ed.), In *Romantic love and sexual behavior: Perspectives from the social sciences.* Westport CT: Praeger (pp. 171–199).

Muehlenhard, C. L. & Hollabaugh, I. C. (1988). Do women sometimes say no when they mean yes? The prevalence and correlates of women's token resistance to sex. *Journal of Personality and Social Psychology, 54,* 872–879.

Mulder, M. B. (1990). Kipsigis women's preferences for men: Evidence for female choice in mammals? *Behavioral Ecology and Sociobiology, 27,* 255–264.

Murray, H. A. (1943). *Thematic apperception test (TAT) manual.* Cambridge, MA: Harvard University Press.

Murray, S. L., Holmes, J. G., & Griffin, D. W. (1996). The self-fulfilling nature of positive illusions in romantic relationships: Love is not blind, but prescient. *Journal of Personality & Social Psychology, 71,* 1155–1180.

Murstein, B. I. (1976). *Who will marry whom?* New York: Springer.

Nagoshi, C. T., Johnson, R. C., & Ahern, F. M. (1987). Phenotype assortative mating versus social homogamy among Japanese and Chinese parents. *Behavior Genetics, 17*, 477–485.

Nathan, S. G. (1981). Cross cultural perspective on penis envy. *Psychiatry, 44*, 39–44.

Neimeyer, G. J. (1984). Cognitive complexity and marital satisfaction. *Journal of Social and Clinical Psychology, 2*, 258–263.

Nevid, J. S. (1984). Sex differences in factors of romantic attraction. *Sex Roles, 11*, 401–411.

Newcomb, T. M. (1961). *The acquaintance process.* New York: Holt, Rhinehart, and Winston.

Nowicki, S., Jr. & Menheim, S. (1991). Interpersonal complementarity and time of interaction in female relationships. *Journal of Research in Personality, 25*, 322–333.

Obholzer, A. & Roberts, V. Z. (1997). *The unconscious at work.* London: Routledge.

Ogden, T. H. (1979). On projective identification. *International Journal of Psychoanalysis, 60*, 357–373.

Orive, R. (1988). Social projective and social comparison of opinions. *Journal of Personality and Social Psychology, 54*, 953–964.

Park, B. & Rothbart, M. (1982). Perceptions of outgroup homogeneity and levels of social categorization. *Journal of Personality and Social Psychology, 42*, 1051–1068.

Parnas, J. (1988). Assortative mating in schizophrenia. *Psychiatry, 51*, 58–64.

Patterson, C. E. & Pettijohn, T. F. (1982). Age and human mate selection. *Psychological Reports, 51*, 70.

Peck, S. (1978). *The road less traveled.* New York: Simon & Schuster.

Peng, K. & Nisbett, R. E. (1999). Culture, dialectics, and reasoning about contradiction. *American Psychologist, 54*, 741–754.

Pennebaker, J. W., Dyer, M. A., Caulkins, R. S., Litowitz, D. L., Ackerman, P. L., & Anderson, D. B., et al. (1979). Don't the girls get prettier at closing time: A country and western application to psychology. *Personality and Social Psychology Bulletin, 5*, 122–125.

Pensa, E. (1999). Family and professional choices: Conflict or complicity? In U. Gielen & L. Anna, et al. (Eds.), *International approaches to the family and family therapy. Series on international and cross cultural psychology* (pp. 273–289). Padua, Italy: Unipress.

Perper, T. (1989). Theories and observations on sexual selection and female choice in human beings [Special issue]. *Human Sexuality and Biocultural Perspective.*

Phillips, K., Fulker, D. W., Carey, G., & Nagoshi, C. T. (1988). Direct marital assortment for cognitive and personality variables. *Behavior Genetics, 18*, 347–356.

Pierce, C. A. (1996). Body height and romantic attraction: A meta-analytic test of the male-taller norm. *Social Behavior and Personality, 24*, 143–149.

Pierce, C. A., Byrne, D., & Aguinis, H. (1996). Attraction in organizations: A model of workplace romance. *Journal of Organizational Behavior, 17*, 5–32.

Pines, A. M. (1993). Burnout—An existential perspective. In W. Schaufeli, C. Maslach, & T. Marek (Eds.), *Professional burnout: Developments in theory and research* (pp. 33–52). Washington, DC: Taylor & Francis.

Pines, A. M. (1996). *Couple burnout.* New York: Routledge.

Pines, A. M. (1997). Fatal attraction or wise unconscious choices: The relationship between causes for entering and breaking intimate relationships. *Personal Relationship Issues, 4*, 1–6.

Pines, A. M. (1998a). *Romantic jealousy*. New York: Routledge.

Pines, A. M. (1998b). A prospective study of personality and gender differences in romantic attraction. *Personality and Individual Differences, 25*, 147–157.

Pines, A. M. (1998c). *Psychology of gender* [in Hebrew]. Tel Aviv: Open University Press.

Pines, A. M. (1999). *How people choose whom to fall in love with, and why this question is important for psychotherapists*. Boston, MA: American Psychological Association.

Pines, A. M. (2000a). Nurses' burnout: An existential psychodynamic perspective. *Journal of Psychosocial Nursing, 38*, 2, 1–9.

Pines, A. M. (2000b). Treating career burnout: A psychodynamic existential perspective. *Journal of Clinical Psychology. In Session: Psychotherapy in Practice, 56*, 1–10.

Pines, A. M. (2001). The role of gender and culture in romantic attraction. *European Psychologist, 6*, 96–202.

Pines, A. M. (2002a). The female entrepreneur: Burnout treated using a psychoanalytic existential approach. *Clinical Case Studies, 1*, 171–181.

Pines, A. M. (2002b). A psychoanalytic existential approach to burnout: Demonstrated in the cases of a nurse, a teacher and a manager. *Psychotherapy: Theory/Research/Practice/Training, 39*, 103–113.

Pines, A. M. (2002c). Teacher burnout: A psychodynamic existential perspective. *Teachers and Teaching: Theory and Practice, 8*, 121–140.

Pines, A. M. (2004). Attachment styles and burnout. *Work and Stress, 18*, 66–80.

Pines, A. M. & Aronson, E. (1988). *Career burnout: Causes and cures*. New York: Free Press.

Pines, A. M., & Nunes, R. (2003). The relationship between career and couple burnout: Implication for career and couple counseling. *Journal of Employment Counseling, 40*, 50–64.

Pines, A. M. & Yanai, O. (2001). Unconscious determinants of career choice and burnout: Theoretical model and counseling strategy. *Journal of Employment Counseling, 38*, 170–184.

Plato. (1956). *The symposium* (pp. 315–318) (B. Jowett, Ed.). New York: Tudor.

Pleck, J. (1977). The work–family role system. *Social Problems, 24*, 417–427.

Rabin, C. (1995). *Partners as Friends*. New York: Routledge.

Rank, O. (1945). *Will therapy and truth and reality*. New York: Knopf.

Reader, N. & English, H. B. (1947). Personality factors in adolescent female friendships *Journal of Consulting Psychology, 11*, 212–220.

Regan, P. C. (1996). Of lust and love: believes about the role of sexual desire in romantic relationships. *Personal Relationships, 5*, 139–157.

Regan, P. (1998). Minimum mate selection standards as a function of perceived mate value, relationship context, and gender. *Journal of Psychology and Human Sexuality, 10*, 53–73.

Reik, T. (1957). *Of love and lust*. New York: Grove Press.

Reik, T. (1964). *The need to be loved*. New York: Bantam.

Reis, H. T., Nezlek, J., & Wheeler, L. (1980). Physical attractiveness in social interaction. *Journal of Personality and Social Psychology, 38*, 604–617.

Rich, A. (1976). *Of woman born*. New York: Norton.

Richard, L. S., Wakefield, J. A., & Lewak, R. (1990). Similarity of personality variables as predictor of marital satisfaction: Minnesota Multiple Personality Inventory (MMPI) item analysis. *Personality and Individual Differences, 11,* 39–43.

Rindfuss, R. R. & Stephen, E. H. (1990). Marital noncohabitation: Separation does not make the heart grow fonder. *Journal of Marriage and the Family, 52,* 259–27.

Robinson, E. A. & Price, M. G. (1980). Pleasurable behavior in marital interaction. An observational study. *Journal of Consulting and Clinical Psychology, 48,* 117–118.

Rodin, J. (1987). Who is memorable to whom? A study of cognitive disregard. *Social Cognition, 5,* 144–165.

Rose, S. & Frieze, I. H. (1989). Young singles' scripts for a first date. *Gender and Society, 3,* 258–268.

Rozin, P., Millman, L., & Nemeroff, C. (1986). Operation of the laws of sympathetic magic in disgust and other domains. *Journal of Personality and Social Psychology, 50,* 703–712.

Rubin, L. B. (1983). *Intimate strangers: Men and women together.* New York: Harper and Row.

Rubin, Z. (1973). *Liking and loving.* New York: Holt Reinhart.

Rubin, Z., Peplau, L. A., & Hill, C. T. (1981). Loving and leaving: Sex differences in romantic attachments. *Sex Roles, 7,* 821–835.

Rushton, P. (1988). Genetic similarity, mate choice, and fecundity in humans. *Ethology and Sociobiology, 9,* 329–334.

Rytting, M., Ware, R., & Hopkins, P. (1992). Type and the ideal mate: Romantic attraction or type bias? *Journal of Psychological Types, 24,* 3–12.

Sadalla, E. K., Kenrick, D. T., & Vershure, B. (1987). Dominance and heterosexual attraction. *Journal of Personality and Social Psychology, 52,* 730–738.

Schachter, S. (1964). The interaction of cognitive and physiological determinants of emotional states. In L. Berkowitz (Ed.), *Advances in experimental social psychology* (Vol. 1, pp. 49–80). New York: Academic Press.

Schafer, R. B. & Keith, P. M. (1990). Matching by weight in married couples: A life cycle perspective. *Journal of Social Psychology, 130,* 657–664.

Schaufeli, W. B., Maslach, C., & Marek, T. (Eds.). (1993). *Professional burnout: Recent developments in theory and research.* Washington, DC: Taylor & Francis.

Schaufeli, W. B., Van-Dierendonck, D., & Van Gorp, K. (1996). Burnout and reciprocity: Toward a dual-level social exchange model. *Work and Stress, 10,* 225–237.

Schmitt, D. P. & Buss, D. M. (1996). Strategic self-promotion and competitor derogation: Sex and context effects on the perceived effectiveness of mate attraction tactics. *Journal of Personality and Social Psychology, 70,* 1185–1204.

Segal, M. W. (1974). Alphabet and attraction: Unobtrusive measure of the effect of propinquity in a field setting. *Journal of Personality and Social Psychology, 30,* 654–657.

Shaikh, T. & Suresh, K. (1994). Attitudinal similarity and affiliation need as determinants of interpersonal attraction. *Journal of Social Psychology, 134,* 257–259.

Shapiro, J. P. (1988). Relationships between dimensions of depressive experience and evaluative beliefs about people in general. *Personality and Social Psychology Bulletin, 14,* 388–400.

Shaver, P. R. & Brennan, K. A. (1992). Attachment styles and the "Big Five" personality traits: Their connection with each other and with romantic relationship outcomes. *Personality and Social Psychology Bulletin, 18*, 536–545.

Shaver, P. R. & Clark, C. L. (1994). The psychodynamics of adult romantic attachment. In J. M. Masling & R. F. Bornstein (Eds.), *Empirical perspectives on object relations theories* (pp. 105–156). Washington, DC: American Psychological Association.

Shaver, P. R. & Hazan, C. (1993). Adult romantic attachment: Theory and evidence. In D. Perlman & W. Jones (Eds.), *Advances in personal relationships* (Vol. 4, pp. 29–70). London: Jessica Kingsley.

Shaver, P. R., Hazan, C., & Bradshaw, D. (1988). Love as attachment: The integration of three behavioral systems. In R. J. Sternberg & M. Barnes (Eds.), *The psychology of love* (pp. 68–99). New Haven, CT: Yale University Press.

Shaver, P. R., Schwartz, J., Kirson, D., & O'Connor, C. (1978). Emotion knowledge: Further exploration of the prototype approach. *Journal of Personality and Social Psychology, 52*, 1061–1086.

Shefer, J. (1971). Mate selection among second-generation Kibbutz adolescents and adults: Incest avoidance and negative imprinting. *Archives of Sexual behavior, 1*, 293–307.

Sheppard, J. A. & Strathman, A. J. (1989). Attractiveness and height: The role of status in dating preferences, frequency of dating, and perception of attractiveness. *Personality and Social Psychology Bulletin, 15*, 617–627.

Sigall, H. & Aronson, E. (1969). Liking for an evaluator as a function of her physical attractiveness and nature of the evaluation. *Journal of Experimental Social Psychology, 5*, 93–100.

Silverstein, B., Carpman, S., Perlick, D., & Purdue, L. (1990). Nontraditional sex-role aspirations, gender identity, conflict and disordered eating among college women. *Sex Roles, 23*, 687–695.

Simpson, J. A., Roles, W. S., & Nelligan, J. S. (1992). Support seeking and support giving within couples in an anxiety-provoking situation: The role of attachment styles. *Journal of Personality and Social Psychology, 62*, 434–446.

Singh, D. (1993). Adaptive significance of female physical attractiveness: role of waist to hip ratio. *Journal of Personality and Social Psychology, 65*, 293–307.

Singh, D. (1994). Body fat distribution and perception of desirable female body shape. *International Journal of Eating Disorder, 16*, 289–294.

Singh, R. & Tan, L. S. (1992). Attitudes and attraction: A test of the similarity-attraction and dissimilarity-repulsion hypothesis. *British Journal of Social Psychology, 31*, 227–238.

Skrypneck, B. J. & Snyder, M. (1982). On the self-perpetuating nature of stereotypes about women and men. *Journal of Experimental Social Psychology, 18*, 277–291.

Small, M. F. (1992). The evolution of female sexuality and mate selection in humans. *Human Nature, 3*, 133–156.

Smith, E. R., Becker, M. A., Byrne, D., & Przybyla, D. P. (1993). Sexual attitudes of males and females as predictors of interpersonal attraction and marital compatibility. *Journal of Applied Social Psychology, 23*, 1011–1034.

Smith, J. E., Waldorf, V. A., & Trembath, D. L. (1990). "Single male looking for thin, very attractive ... ." *Sex Roles, 23*, 675–685.

Snyder, C. R. & Fromkin, H. L. (1980). *Uniqueness: The human pursuit of difference.* New York: Plenum.

Snyder, M. (1993). When belief creates reality: The self fulfilling impact of first impressions on social interaction. In A. M. Pines & C. Maslach (Eds.), *Experiencing social psychology* (pp. 24–77). (3rd ed.). New York: McGraw-Hill.

Solomon, Z. (1986). Self acceptance and the selection of a marital partner: An assessment of the SVR model of Murstein. *Social Behavior and Personality, 14,* 1–6.

Sperling, M. (1987). Ego identity and desperate love. *Journal of Personality Assessment, 51,* 600–605.

Sprecher, S., Cate, R., & Levin, L. (1998). Parental divorce and young people's beliefs about love. *Journal of Divorce and Remarriage, 28,* 107–120.

Sprecher, S. & Duck, S. (1994). Sweet talk: The importance of perceived communication for romantic and friendship attraction experienced during a get-acquainted date. *Personality and Social Psychology Bulletin, 20,* 391–400.

Sprecher, S., Sullivan, Q., & Hartfield, E. (1994). Male selection preferences: Gender differences examined in a national sample. *Journal of Personality and Social Psychology, 66,* 1074–1080.

Stein, H., Jacobs, N. J., Ferguson, K. S., Allen, J. G., & Fonagy, P. (1998). What do adult attachment scales measure? *Bulletin of the Menninger Clinic, 62,* 33–82.

Steinman, A. & Fox, D. J. (1970). Attitudes toward women's family role. *Family Coordination, 19,* 363–368.

Stephan, W. A., Berscheid, E., & Walster, E. (1971). Sexual arousal and interpersonal perception. *Journal of Personality and Social Psychology, 20,* 93–101.

Stephen, T. (1987). Taking communication seriously? A reply to Murstein. *Journal of Marriage and the Family, 49,* 937–938.

Sternberg, R. J. (1986). A triangular theory of love. *Psychological Review, 73,* 119–135.

Suman, H. C. (1992). Toward choosing a mate: Perceived dimensions of mate selection. *Journal of Personality and Clinical Studies, 8,* 143–146.

Surra, C. A. & Hyston, T. L. (1987). Mate selection as a social transition. In D. Perlman & S. Duck (Eds.), *Intimate relationships: Development, dynamic and deterioration* (88–120). Newbury Park, CA: Sage.

Tavris, C. (1992). *The mismeasure of women.* New York: Simon & Schuster.

Taylor, M. & Vandenberg, S. G. (1988). Assortative mating for IQ and personality due to propinquity and personal preference. *Behavior Genetics, 18,* 339–345.

Tennov, D. (1979). *Love and limerence: The experience of being in love.* New York: Stein and Day.

Thelen, T. (1988). Effect of late familiarization on human mating preferences. *Social Biology, 35,* 251–601.

Thibaut, J. W. & Kelley, H. H. (1959). *The social psychology of groups.* New York: Wiley.

Tooke, W. & Camire, L. (1991). Patterns of deception in interpersonal and intrasexual mating strategies. *Ethology and Sociobiology, 12,* 345–364.

Townsend, J. M. (1995). Sex without emotional involvement: An evolutionary interpretation of sex differences. *Archives of Sexual Behavior, 24,* 173–206.

Townsend, J. M. & Levy, G. D. (1990). Effects of potential partners' physical attractiveness and socioeconomic status on sexuality and partner selection: Sex differences in reported preferences of university students. *Archives of Sexual Behavior, 19,* 149–164.

Townsend, J. M. & Wasserman, T. (1998). Sexual attractiveness: Sex differences in assessment and criteria. *Evolution and Human Behavior, 19*, 171–191.

Trievers, (1972). Parental investment and sexual selection. In B. Campbell (Ed.), *Sexual selection and the descent of man 1871–1971* (pp. 136–179). Chicago: Adline-Atherton.

Trost, M. & Alberts, J. K. (1998). An evolutionary view on understanding sex effects in communicating attraction. In D. J. Canary et al. (Eds.), *Sex differences and similarities in communication: Critical essays and empirical investigations of sex and gender in interaction. LEA's Communication Series* (pp. 233–255). Mahwah, NJ: Erlbaum.

Umberson, D. & Houghs, M. (1987). The impact of physical attractiveness on achievement and psychological well being. *Social Psychology Quarterly, 50*, 227–236.

Unger, R. K. (1975). Sex stereotypes revisited: *Psychological approaches to women's studies*. New York: Harper and Row.

Valins, S. (1966). Cognitive effects of false heart rate feedback. *Journal of Personality and Social Psychology, 4*, 400–408.

Valtinson, G. R. (1998). A multi-sample confirmatory analysis of work-family conflict. *Dissertation Abstracts International, 59* (3-B), 1401.

Van Dierendonck, D., Schaufeli, W., & Sixma, H.J. (1994). Burnout among general practitioners: A perspective from equity theory. *Journal of Social and Clinical Psychology, 13*, 86–100.

Van Yperen, N. W., Buunk, B. P., & Schaufeli, W. B. (1992). Communal orientation and the burnout syndrome among nurses. *Journal of Applied Social Psychology, 22*, 173–189.

Veitch, R. & Griffitt, W. (1976). Good news bad news: Affective and interpersonal effects. *Journal of Applied Social Psychology, 6*, 69–75.

Walster, E. (1965). The effect of self-esteem on romantic liking. *Journal of Experimental Social Psychology, 1*, 184–197.

Walster, E., Aronson, V., Abrahams, D., & Rottman, L. (1966). The importance of physical attractiveness in dating behavior. *Journal of Personality and Social Psychology, 4*, 508–516.

Walster, E. & Berscheid, E. (1971, June). Adrenaline makes the heart grow fonder. *Psychology Today*, 47–62.

Walster, E., Walster, G. W., Piliavin, J., & Schmidt, L. (1973). Playing hard to get: Understanding an elusive phenomenon. *Journal of Personality and Social Psychology, 26*, 113–121.

Walster-Hartfield, E. & Walster, G. W. (1981). *A new look at love*. Reading, MA: Addison-Wesley.

Watts, A. (1985). Divine madness. In J. Welwood (Ed.), *Challenge of the heart*. Boston: Shambhala.

Weiderman, M. W. & Allgeier, E. R. (1992). Gender differences in mate selection criteria: Sociobiological or socioeconomic explanation? *Ethology and Sociobiology, 13*, 115–124.

Weinberg, H. (1997). On two psychodynamic approaches to love, couple relationships, and marital therapy. *Sihot* [Conversations], *11*, 93–99.

Westman, M. (2001). Stress and strain crossover. *Human Relations, 53*, 557–591

Westman, M. & Etzion, D. (1995). Crossover of stress, strain and resources from one spouse to another. *Journal of Organizational Behavior, 16*, 169–181.

White, G. L. (1980). Physical attractiveness and courtship progress. *Journal of Personality and Social Psychology, 39,* 660–668.

White, G. L., Fishbein, S., & Rutstein, J. (1981). Passionate love: the misattribution of arousal. *Journal of Personality and Social Psychology, 41,* 56–62.

White, G. L. & Shapiro, D. (1989). Don't I know you? Antecedents and social consequences of perceived similarity. *Journal of Experimental Social Psychology, 23,* 75–92.

Whitehouse, J. (1981). The role of the initial attracting quality in marriage: Virtues and vices. *Journal of Marital and Family Therapy, 7,* 61–67.

Wilson, W. (1989). Brief resolution of the issue of similarity versus complementarity in mate selection using height preference as a model. *Psychological Reports, 65,* 387–393.

Winch, R. (1958). *Mate selection: A study of complementary needs.* New York: Harper and Row.

Winnicott, D. W. (1976). Ego distortion in terms of true and false self. In D. W. Winnicott (Ed.), *The maturational process and the facilitating environment* (pp. 140–152). London: Hogarth Press.

Winnicott, D. W. (1965). *The family and individual development.* New York: Basic Books.

Wright, R. A. & Contrada, R. J. (1986). Dating selectivity and interpersonal attractiveness: Toward a better understanding of the "elusive phenomenon." *Social and Personal Relationships, 3,* 131–148.

Yalom, I. D. (1980). *Existential psychotherapy.* New York: Basic Books.

Yarab, P. E., Sensibaugh, C. C., & Algeier, E. R. (1998). More than just sex: Gender differences in the incidence of self-defined unfaithful behavior in heterosexual dating relationships. *Journal of Psychology and Human Sexuality, 10,* 45–57.

Zajonc, R. B. (1968). Attitudinal effects of mere exposure. *Journal of Personality and Social Psychology,* (Monograph Supplement 9), *2,* 1–27.

Zajonc, R. B, Adelman, P. K., Murphy, S. T., & Niedenthal, P. M. (1987). Convergence in physical appearance of spouses. *Motivation and Emotion, 11,* 333–335.

Zana, J. J. & Pack, S. J. (1975). On the self fulfilling nature of apparent sex differences in behavior. *Journal of Experimental Social Psychology, 11,* 583–591.

Zedeck, S. (Ed.) (1992). *Work, families and organizations.* San Francisco: Jossey-Bass.

Ziv, A. (1993). *Psychology: The science of understanding human beings* [in Hebrew]. Tel Aviv: Am Oved.

About the Author

Ayala Malach Pines is a clinical, social, and organizational psychologist and a professor and the head of the Department of Business Administration at the School of Management, Ben-Gurion University, Israel. She is both an American and an Israeli citizen with many years of experience as a couple's therapist in both countries. She has published 10 books, 20 book chapters, and well over 80 research articles. Among her books are the following: *Couple Burnout: Causes and Cures, Romantic Jealousy: The Shadow of Love,* and *Career Burnout: Causes and Cures* (coauthored with Elliot Aronson). Her books have been translated into many languages, including French, German, Spanish, Hungarian, Greek, Turkish, Korean, Japanese, Chinese, and Hebrew.

Photo Permissions

We have made every reasonable effort to identify and locate copyright owners of materials. If any information is found to be incomplete, we will gladly make whatever additional permissions acknowledgements might be necessary.

FIGURE 1. Bouguereau. *The Ravishment of Psyche*, c.1895 (oil on canvas).

FIGURE 3. BAL 179901 *Cupidon*, 1891 (oil on canvas) by William-Adolphe Bouguereau (1825–1905). Roy Miles Esq./Bridgeman Art Library, London/New York.

FIGURE 6. Sustris, Lambert. *Venus Awaits the Return of Mars*. Louvre, Paris, France. Reprinted by permission of Cameraphoto/Art Resource, New York.

FIGURE 8. Giraudon/Art Resource, New York S0031146 34062 B&W Print. Falconet, Etienne. *Pygmalian Admiring his Statue* (*Pygmalion and Galatea*). Musee des Artes Decoratifs, Paris, France.

FIGURE 9. Caravaggio. *Narcissus*, c.1597 (oil on canvas). Palazzo Barberini, Rome, Italy.

FIGURE 16. BEN44372 *Primavera*: Detail of Cupid, by Sandro Boticelli (1444/5–1520). Galleria delgi Uffizi, Florence, Italy/Bridgeman Art Library, London/New York.

Index